COLONIES INTO COMMONWEALTH

BLANDFORD HISTORY SERIES
(General Editor R. W. Harris)

PROBLEMS OF HISTORY

HISTORY OF EUROPE SERIES

THE HISTORY OF ENGLAND SERIES

Colonies into Commonwealth

W · D · McINTYRE

Professor in History
Canterbury University, New Zealand

WALKER AND COMPANY
New York

Printed and Bound in Great Britain

Contents

Acknowledgements

The illustrations have been reproduced by permission of the following:

Radio Times Hulton Picture Library 1, 3, 4, 5, 8, 13, 15, 22, 24, 29

High Commissioner for Canada 6

Canadian Pacific 9

High Commissioner for New Zealand 10, 11, 21, 25

Australian News 14

Government of India Tourist Office 28

High Commissioner for Pakistan 32, 33

High Commissioner for Malawi 44

High Commissioner for Uganda 45

High Commissioner for Zambia 46

High Commissioner for Jamaica 47

Alexander Turnbull Library 12

Camera Press 16, 23, 27, 30, 31, 34-43, 48, 49

Imperial War Museum 19, 20

Associated Press 26, 50

Central Office of Information 52-54

United Press International 51

List of Illustrations

(*between pages* 116 *and* 117)

The artist's impression of No. 14 Downing Street, the Old Colonial Office on page 42 is by Mary Camidge.

List of Maps

Drawn by A. Spark

1

Preface

During the period in which I was writing this book a bewildering succession of events occurred in the Commonwealth. Independence was achieved or decided upon for the last of the West African and West Indian colonies, for Mauritius and for the former High Commission Territories in South Africa. The founding of the Secretariat and the appointment of the first Secretary-General seemed to presage a new age of fruitful Commonwealth co-operation. But in the same period the illegal declaration of independence by Rhodesia threatened the whole fabric of the Commonwealth. Two Asian members went to war with each other. Two African members broke of diplomatic relations with Britain while retaining their Commonwealth membership. Military *coups* occurred in two African states and the constitution was suspended in another.

Some of the tensions which beset the modern Commonwealth were all too evident to me during a series of journeys which took me round the world in the same period. A flight to Singapore was diverted around India and Pakistan because of the war. In Kuala Lumpur, I met a Pakistani diplomat who was packing his bags because his country had broken off relations with Malaysia for the same reason. In Singapore I was halted by police checks at many cross-roads, a security measure because of the Indonesian confrontation, and by Malaysian police at the end of the causeway connecting the island to the peninsula, because of Singapore's recent withdrawal from Malaysia. In Canada, Australia and New Zealand, I had to fill in the detailed questionnaire now required to satisfy the immigration authorities of these former British Dominions. The Commonwealth is certainly in the news, and it is hoped that a simple account of the origins of the modern Commonwealth will be of interest.

I would like to thank most gratefully a number of friends who read early drafts of this book in whole or in part: Professor J. A. S. Grenville, University of Leeds; Dr Ann Massa and Dr G. W. O. Woodward, University of Nottingham; Mr George Halse, Nottingham College of Education; Dr I. J. Catanach, University of Canterbury; and Mr R. W. Harris, the General Editor of the Blandford History Series. Their criticism and advice was a great encouragement, but they share no responsibility for the shortcomings of this book.

W. D. McINTYRE
Christchurch, N.Z., May 1966

Introduction

The Emergence of a Multi-Racial Commonwealth

'GREAT BRITAIN has lost an Empire and has not yet found a role.' These blunt words were spoken in 1962 during the aftermath of the Cuban missiles crisis by a distinguished American statesman, Dean Acheson. They highlight one of the most interesting and significant transformations in recent international affairs. What will be Britain's future role in the world? This is surely one of the most critical questions which face the British people. It is also a question which fascinates people of other nations, whether they are well-wishers or detractors.

For three centuries the peculiar character of Britain's role in international affairs largely stemmed from her position as a colonial power. Her armed forces were developed, not so much for the defence of the British Isles or for expeditions into Europe, as to keep open ocean shipping lanes for her trading and colonizing activities overseas and to overwhelm her rivals in Asia, Africa and America. From the Dutch wars of the seventeenth century, Britain's role as a power became increasingly associated with maritime supremacy and colonial defence, until by the later years of Queen Victoria's reign Lord Salisbury regarded the defence of the empire as the prime aim of British diplomacy.

In the twentieth century, and more particularly since the 1939–45 war, Britain's wealth and power have declined in relation to the United States, Germany, Japan, the Soviet Union and China. Most of the colonies have been granted their independence, usually with little violence. Wars of Independence on the American or Algerian pattern have not marked the end of British imperial hegemony. In spite of many delays, which infuriated Asian and African nationalists, Britain

B

pioneered the way in the dismantling of empire. From the independence of India, Pakistan and Ceylon in 1947–48 and, more rapidly, since the independence of Ghana and Malaya in 1957, the progress towards final self-rule has been remarkably fast. How and why this process took place, and what the legacy we know as the Commonwealth means, is a vital part of the background which needs to be understood by those who venture solutions to the problem of Britain's role in the post-colonial era.

One of the most important points to remember is that colonial self-government had a long pedigree. Assemblies representing, in some manner, the opinion of the people go back to the seventeenth-century plantations in the New World. Parliamentary government, by which the executive in the colonies became responsible to a legislature elected by a proportion of the people, goes back to the constitutions of Nova Scotia and Canada in the 1840s. Although the British empire was always notable for its diversity, the constitutional development of the various nations which succeeded it was fairly consistent. In geography, climate and economy, and in religion, race and culture, the nations of the Commonwealth are often sharply differentiated. Yet in political evolution they were, during their 'British periods', remarkably similar. The various groups of colonies developed at various times, but they all at one stage in their evolution passed through a constitutional phase based on the British parliamentary system.

At home the Crown made laws by the consent of Parliament. In the colonies the governor made local laws with the advice and consent of a council or assembly. Later, as parliamentary democracy gradually evolved in Britain, so two quite different forms of colonial government became merged into a system of parliamentary government in the colonies.

One system was known as 'representative government'. From the first General Assembly of Virginia in 1619, which was permitted by the King to make laws for the colony provided that they were not repugnant to English law, it became customary for the North American and West Indian colonies to have a measure of representative government. Although all the early colonies eventually became royal provinces, assemblies chosen by a proportion of the colonists were still called to represent colonial opinion. As they did this they soon tried to emulate the House of Commons.

The second system of government, based upon experiments in

Bengal, Quebec and the West Indies at the end of the eighteenth century, was known as the 'Crown colony'. Here a representative form of government, with elected assemblies, was deliberately avoided. When the governor convened a legislative council to approve his ordinances, the councillors were all government officers or prominent colonists nominated by the governor himself. This system was first adopted in colonies captured from the French and the Dutch, where the population was not English. It was later widely extended to Asia and Africa. Yet both representative and Crown colony systems were eventually adapted to follow the British parliamentary system.

In Nova Scotia and Canada, between 1846 and 1848, representative government was transformed into 'responsible government'. By making the main officers-of-state in the colonies 'ministers' responsible to the Assembly, by handing over the leadership of the government to a 'prime minister' who chose his own Cabinet, and finally by selecting as premier the leader of the majority party in the Assembly (or someone who could command a majority), the governors in British North America became constitutional figureheads, whose role was to represent the Crown. The parliamentary system of the early Victorian age was thus quickly transplanted into the colonies. During the following thirty years the system was extended to Australia, New Zealand and the Cape of Good Hope.

Responsible government was originally granted to colonies of English settlers. Most of Britain's possessions in Asia, Africa and the Caribbean were, in the Victorian age, ruled autocratically under the Crown colony system or indirectly as protectorates and protected states. But representative government was not completely lacking, particularly in India and Ceylon. By the end of the 1914–18 war it was also beginning in the West African colonies. By the 1940s, a century after responsible government was granted in Canada, it also began to develop from the Crown colony system in Asia and Africa. Legislative councils, which had been created originally as instruments of autocratic rule, proved to be remarkably flexible. By nominating additional non-official members to sit with the government officers who provided most of the early councillors, governors could sound local opinion more effectively. By gradually increasing their numbers until there was a non-official majority, they could claim that government was by consent. By allowing the non-official members (or a proportion of them) to be elected, rather than nominated by himself, a governor could virtually convert Crown colony government into representative government as it had existed in the old American colonies.

Furthermore, the appointment of elected members as departmental spokesmen in the legislature, or later as 'ministers' in place of officials, and the selection of the leader of the majority party among the elected councillors as 'leader of government business', 'chief minister', or finally 'prime minister', became from the 1940s onwards the normal mode of political advance. Finally, when the complete control of the government was handed over to a Cabinet, responsible to a Legislative Assembly, the transition to full responsible government was complete, as it had been in Canada a century before. Thus, although the modern nations of the Commonwealth have gone on, after independence, to produce a fascinating galaxy of new constitutions – which range all the way from monarchies, parliamentary democracies, federal republics, a confederation, to states ruled by presidential, one-party or military government – they have all, at one stage of their development in the past century, gone through a system very like that worked out in North America in the 1840s. The mid-nineteenth century, then, is of crucial significance in the genesis of the Commonwealth. But responsible government, when it began in the 1840s and 1850s, left unanswered the fundamental question which faces all empires: what should be the relationship between the mother country and the colonies?

Throughout the history of the empire the conflicting forces of provincialism and centralization pulled in opposite directions. The inhabitants of the colonies naturally sought to foster their own provincial interests. Policy-makers at home rarely had a conception of the empire as a whole; those who did favoured centralization. How were these two contradictory forces to be reconciled? In the 1770s in North America reconciliation proved impossible and thirteen of the provinces rebelled. Seventy years later the remaining North American colonies were prevented from secession by the grant of responsible government, but still the basic question of the correct colonial relationship remained unanswered. For nearly a century, until the 1930s, there were two schools of thought on this subject. One school demanded that the relationship should be loose and voluntary, based solely on ties of interest, sentiment and convenience. But the opposing school called for imperial consolidation. They toyed with ideas of a great

Britannic Union or an Imperial Federation, and they envisaged the empire as a super-state. Thus, provincial and centralizing forces continued to exercise their opposing pulls.

It is one of the great ironies of modern British history that the name 'Commonwealth of Nations' was first popularized by the centralizers around the time of the 1914–18 war. Yet the Commonwealth of today is a voluntary association based upon ties of history, convenience and sentiment. The Commonwealth is, in fact, the legacy of Britain's three centuries as a colonial power. It is not itself a unified body, a 'Power' in the normal sense, or even a sort of 'third force'. Its members are rarely, particularly after the Suez War of 1956, united on world affairs. Some former British possessions, such as Burma, Eire, Somaliland and South Africa, are not even members.

If the Commonwealth is not a unified body, what, then, is its character? It is a voluntary association of extremely diverse, fully sovereign states, which are internationally equal but which have in common a historical background with a period of British rule and a political evolution which led up to responsible government. This common experience left as its legacy a host of practical and useful ties of commerce and finance, language and education, agricultural and technical co-operation, and in some cases of defence, law and citizenship. These are the continuing ties of 'convenience'. But what are the ties of sentiment?

One significant feature stands out. A common colonial history makes all the Commonwealth members (apart from the United Kingdom) 'new nations'; historically, they fall into two groups. The new nations of the Victorian age were Canada, Australia, New Zealand and South Africa, the last of which left the Commonwealth in 1961. The new nations of the period 1947–65 are all in Africa, Asia and the Caribbean, and they are comprised of a considerable diversity of races. The original popularizers of the concept of a 'Commonwealth of Nations' were undoubtedly thinking of the first group. But about 1909 Lionel Curtis, their leading writer, realized that self-government was, as he said, the 'goal to which all human societies must tend' and he felt that this ought to apply, in the Commonwealth, to 'all races and kindreds and peoples and tongues'.

Thus after the 1914–18 war, as nationalism spread in Asia and Africa, a few visionaries began to evolve an entirely new concept of the Commonwealth. Indeed a notable Indian liberal politician, who visited a number of Commonwealth countries as representative of the Government of India, declared in 1922 that

> the British Commonwealth is the greatest instrument for human freedom the world has ever seen . . . this great political organization stands unique amongst the political institutions of the world for one thing above all others . . . and that is the reconciliation of the East and the West, the bringing together in happy harmony the people of varied races and varied complexions.*

In the bitterness of the Indian nationalist struggle of the inter-war years, and through all the uncertainties about Britain's ultimate goals elsewhere in Asia and Africa during the same period, these idealistic words must have sounded hollow, even foolhardy. But with India's request, on becoming a Republic in 1950, that she should remain in the Commonwealth, and with the accession since 1957 of no fewer than ten African states (most of them republics) to places in the Commonwealth alongside Canada, Australia and New Zealand, the idea of the 'New Commonwealth' as a human 'bridge' between the continents has opened up significant new opportunities for voluntary co-operation.

It is important to realize that since 1960 the periodical meetings of the Commonwealth prime ministers have all had a preponderance of Asian, African and Caribbean members. Indeed, the communiqué issued after the 1960 meetings emphasized that the Commonwealth 'is a multi-racial assocation'. This suggests that the member-nations of the Commonwealth were evolving a new aim: that of creating a genuine multi-racial co-operative body. In the following year, the attitude of the Asian–African–Caribbean premiers on racial policies was largely responsible for South Africa's decision to withdraw from the Commonwealth.

On the positive side, many sceptics were amazed when in the ten years from 1953 to 1963 Kenya, once dubbed a 'pukka sahib's paradise', moved, from a constitution which permitted only six elected African councillors, to sovereign independence with African majority rule. In the lengthy debates since 1959 over the future of Rhodesia, which led to the creation of an illegal, rebel, régime by the

---

* V. S. N. Srinivasa Sastri (1869–1946) quoted in S. R. Mehrotra, *India and the Commonwealth* 1885–1929, London, 1965, p. 158.

settler minority in 1965, the overwhelming insistence of all Common-wealth nations, especially those in Africa, that genuine independence must depend on the condition of eventual majority rule, made it im-possible for the British government to compromise.

Britain moves into the post-colonial era with only the problematical remnants of empire left from her former world-wide domains. In the Commonwealth, she is traditional leader rather than the predominant contemporary influence. Indeed, on the issue of racial discrimination among nations, there is a case for saying that in the 1960s the initiative was taken by the Asian–African–Caribbean members. The question as to Britain's role in world affairs, and indeed in the Commonwealth, remains unanswered. The 'New Commonwealth' itself has, as yet, to enunciate clear goals. But maybe, as a member of this multi-racial association, Britain has lessons to learn from the new nations of the Commonwealth which will better fit her to face the future and to find her role.

1

The Loss of the American Colonies

THE FIRST colonies to free themselves from British rule are not members of the Commonwealth. The United States is the oldest of the 'new nations'. In 1776 thirteen colonies on the Atlantic seaboard of North America seceded from the British empire and founded a nation which has come to have an immense influence, not only on the rest of the colonies and the Commonwealth but upon Britain herself. The loss of the American colonies is obviously of very great significance for the Commonwealth.

Why did thirteen colonies rebel and fight for independence, while other American colonies, like Nova Scotia, moved gradually and peacefully to self-government? The answer may be stated, at this stage, very simply: the opposing pulls of provincialism and centralization were evident from a very early stage in the development of the colonies. When the crisis occurred in the eighteenth century the British governments of the day failed to evolve a formula which could reconcile the two tendencies. Yet it is important not to forget that in the whole era of the American rebellion a number of ideas were born which profoundly affected the shape of Britain's empire in later years.

What, then, was the American empire like? Why did it break up? What lessons did Britain learn from the loss of the thirteen colonies?

Provincialism in the Colonies

The first preoccupations of colonists were always local and provincial. In motives for settlement, type of government, religion, soil and climate, economy and society the early colonies were sharply differentiated. Virginians produced their tobacco on comparatively isolated farms. Barbadians grew their sugar on a compact island, which

was the first great source of colonial wealth. The Puritans in Massachusetts turned from an inhospitable soil to make their living from
the sea – from the cod-fisheries and the Atlantic trade. Explanations
for this early emphasis on the local and the provincial are not hard to
find. They may be found in the very manner in which the early
foundations were made and the way in which they were governed.

The British empire was not 'planned'. It was a by-product of
England's attempts to open up new lands for trade. In a sense, it was a
symbol of her failures. With Spain controlling much of Central and
South America, Portugal well established in parts of Africa and India,
and the Dutch gaining supremacy in the Indonesian archipelago,
England was a late starter in the quest for overseas power. Thus
Elizabethan geographers, like Dr John Dee, seeking lands unclaimed
by a 'Christian Prince', looked to the Pacific: to the ancient civilizations
of China and Japan, to the Spice Islands, to the western coasts of the
Americas, and to the great unknown southern, or 'Austral', continent.

The projects of the Elizabethan adventurers failed. But the
foundations of the later empire were laid. Abortive attempts to find a
north-west passage to China led to interest in North America. The
quest for an 'El Dorado' in South America led to the discovery and
settlement of St Kitts (1623) and Barbados (1626) in the Caribbean.
The East India Company's failure to fulfil its aims in the 'East Indies'
led it to fall back upon trade to India. Far from being the outcome of a
conscious plan, the first successful overseas ventures were the result of
English backwardness and failure. The first colonies and trading bases
were the work of groups of private individuals making the best of a bad
job.

The empire began, then, as a 'private enterprise' empire, and this
was reflected in the first colonial governments. The colonies were
founded by companies of 'adventurers', chartered by the Crown and
loosely supervised by a committee of the Privy Council. Under their
charters the companies were granted a two-tier system of self-government. The Virginia Company, for example, was controlled at home by
a governor, council and general assembly of shareholders, who were
authorized to appoint a governor to reside in Virginia itself. The
governor in the colony called a council of state to advise him and
appointed courts to administer English law. In 1619 a general assembly,
consisting of two representatives from each of eleven settlements, was
elected by all men over the age of seventeen.

At this very early stage the first colonial legislature was born. It was permitted by the King to make laws for the colony, provided they were not repugnant to English law. Thus, by the favour of the Crown, expressed in the early seventeenth-century charters to the Virginia Company, a considerable measure of representative government was allowed. At home, the shareholders elected their governor and council; in the colony, the colonists elected their assembly. With plenty of variations the Virginia precedent was adopted elsewhere.

In some cases, as in Massachusetts, the charter was once again granted to a company. But the Puritans went a stage further. They decided in 1629 to take their charter to America with them, so that the 'home' branch of the Massachusetts Bay Company ceased to exist. In several cases colonial charters were granted to individuals, or 'proprietors'.

The proprietary colony was pioneered in Maryland by the second Lord Baltimore. His father had earlier made some abortive attempts at colonizing in Newfoundland, but in 1632 Baltimore received a charter as 'Lord Proprietor of Maryland'. He became a tenant-in-chief of the King, a feudal lord, with the same position as the medieval Bishops of Durham. The same system was also adopted, at first, in the West Indies, where the Earl of Carlisle became 'Lord Proprietor of the Caribees'. Maine and Pennsylvania were also granted to individuals, while the Carolinas were granted to a group of eight proprietors. And just as medieval monarchs found it necessary to call parliaments, so the proprietors called councils and assemblies to assist in the work of colonial government.

In a third group of the early colonies, the assembly existed before the charter. After the Pilgrim Fathers reached Cape Cod in 1620, a select group (the church members) signed a compact by which they constituted a 'civil body politic' to enact laws for the settlement. They then sought to legalize their position by getting a grant of land from the Council of New England. Rhode Island was founded by a group of radical Puritans, under Roger Williams, who were repelled by the intolerance of the established Congregationalists of Massachusetts. After founding a group of settlements around Narragansett Bay they drew up a compact in 1641, which envisaged 'a democracie of popular government' based upon the principle 'that it is the Power of the Body of Freemen orderley assembled to make just laws'. Williams then went to England to secure a charter for the colony. Another group of

Puritan dissidents moved eastwards from Massachusetts into the Connecticut valley. In 1639 they drew up a constitution called the Fundamental Orders of Connecticut, under which a General Assembly would meet twice a year. The Orders did not mention the English King, although at a later date Connecticut received its charter.

From these examples we can see that the earliest colonies were founded for different motives. They were all preoccupied with their own problems of government and survival, and although they were all, in a sense, 'extensions' of England, subject to the Crown and to English law, they had a considerable measure of local self-government.

The Trend towards Centralization

The 'private enterprise' empire did not survive. The small colonies in North America and the Caribbean could not remain isolated from British politics and European wars. When the Virginia Company became critically divided by rivalries at home, James I revoked the charter in 1624. Virginia then became the first royal colony, although the colonial assembly was not abolished. The New England colonies were small and vulnerable. They feared the French in the St Lawrence, the Dutch in the Hudson, and the Indians inland. In 1643 delegates met in Boston and drew up 'Articles of Confederation' in an attempt to unite the New England colonies for mutual defence. The measure was ineffective. But it was the first of a number of attempts at colonial federation, which all illustrate a tendency towards centralization. As the seventeenth century wore on, successive English governments accelerated this trend.

A significant development occurred during the interregnum (1649–60). As the Crown was abolished, Parliamentary sovereignty over the colonies was proclaimed. But some of the colonies wished to remain neutral during the revolution in England; others were avowedly royalist. A few even proclaimed Charles II after the execution of his father. Thus Parliament had to assert its authority, and the English civil war was extended, in a sense, to the colonies. An armed expedition had to be sent before the royalist colony of Barbados would submit in 1652. Although Virginia made an agreement with commissioners sent by Parliament, its governor did not disguise his royalist leanings. Bermuda and Antigua were both royalist colonies which had to submit to Parliamentary authority. Rhode Island, on the other hand, benefited from the Parliamentary régime by receiving its first charter.

The Parliamentarians also added Jamaica, the first conquered colony, to the empire. After the Restoration in 1660 centralization proceeded rapidly. Jamaica became a royal colony, when it received a civil government. In 1664 New Netherland, in the Hudson Valley, was captured from the Dutch, and the Duke of York became proprietor of all the land lying between Maryland and Connecticut. On his accession to the throne as James II, New York became a royal colony. For the first time England had a king with a direct interest in the colonies. He was also the second Governor of Hudson's Bay Company, founded in 1670, for the purpose of founding a colony in the far north.

James II's most notable contribution to centralization, however, was the creation of the 'Dominion of New England'. First Massachusetts, Maine and New Hampshire were placed under a single governor, then Rhode Island and Connecticut, and finally New York and the Jerseys, were added. For a single year, in 1688, a large, unified, royal province existed in North America. A considerable proportion of colonial provincialism seemed to have been eradicated. But at that very moment James II was swept from the throne. In 1689 a series of minor revolts broke out in Massachusetts, New York, Maryland, Virginia and the Leeward Islands. They indicated that the colonists obviously took the English Revolution of 1688 and William III's accession as a signal for reasserting their provincialism and for demonstrating their dislike of the royal policy of centralization.

The set-back was only temporary. The Dominion of New England was broken up, but centralization continued. Under a new Massachusetts charter, which added Maine and Plymouth to the colony, the governorship became a royal appointment. In subsequent years the same thing happened to most of the colonies. Eventually all became royal provinces except two proprietaries, Maryland and Pennsylvania, and the small company colonies, with elected governorships, of Rhode Island and Connecticut. Of the few new colonies founded in the eighteenth century, Georgia (1732) was controlled by a board of trustees until it became a royal colony, and Nova Scotia (captured from the French in 1710) was regarded as a military outpost. By the end of the seventeenth century, in fact, a colonial system had emerged, the basic features of which endured until Queen Victoria's reign. The 'Old Colonial System', as it was called, was a centralized system. It was designed to supervise the trade of the empire, to encourage British manufacturing, shipping and fisheries, and to foster the growth of British power.

The Old Colonial System

The Old Colonial System was based upon the theory that wealth was, in a sense, static; that a nation could only prosper at the expense of others. The success of the Dutch in gaining a large foothold in the carrying trade of the colonies convinced the merchant interest in England, which was influential in Parliament, that legislation was needed to exclude foreign rivals from the colonial trade. English trade, wealth and power were to be built up by encouraging the growth of a large mercantile marine. This would enable England to prevail over her Spanish, French and Dutch rivals. English-controlled sources of raw materials were sought, to prevent adverse balances of trade. In short, economic theorists demanded a 'self-sufficient' trading economy.

The foundations of the system lay in the trade and navigation laws. Beginning with the Commonwealth Trade Ordinance of 1651 and culminating in William III's Navigation Act of 1696, these laws embodied a threefold monopoly of export, import and transit. All imports from, and exports to, Asia, Africa and America were to be carried in English ships, which included, of course, colonial ships. Major enumerated items of colonial produce had to be sent to England or to the colonies, and the colonies had to purchase their manufactures from England. In other words, a highly centralized system was envisaged. England was to be the manufacturing centre; the colonies the producers of raw materials and a market for manufactured goods. To ensure effective communication between the two and to promote defence through naval power, ships under the English flag, with English crews, were given a monopoly of the carrying trade. So much, then, for the theory. How did it work?

For the southern plantation colonies – Maryland, Virginia, the Carolinas and Georgia – producing their tobacco and indigo and rice, the system worked well. The middle colonies – Pennsylvania and New York – were the granary of the empire, and found a ready market for their wares. The West Indies were regarded as the jewels of the empire. Their sugar and coffee were the most valuable colonial products, and through their wealth the British West Indies became the privileged colonies. Absentee planters, living in state at home, gained seats in Parliament and exercised political influence. The Molasses Act of

1733, which imposed a high duty on sugar imported into British territory from the French or Spanish colonies, was the work of West Indian planters seeking to protect their prices. In 1739 they went on to secure the further privilege of being allowed to export sugar direct to southern Europe.

One important group of colonies, however, did not really fit into the Old Colonial System. From the earliest days of the Puritan migrations, New Englanders had always been the most independent colonists. Later, they were to lead the American rebellion. Economically, they were not, on the whole, suppliers of raw materials. They were commercial rivals of England. They had no staple products of their soil to export, like the plantation and grain colonies. Their wealth was based on cod-fishing, overseas trade and the manufacture of rum – all of which England was capable of doing herself. Thus, New England did not fit into a system by which the colonies produced the raw materials for English manufacturers.

In theory, the West Indies ought to have solved the problem. They could absorb New England fish and shipping products and also supply the molasses used in the making of rum. But by the eighteenth century the British West Indies were too small to bear the system. Barbados, Jamaica and the Leewards were too small a market, so the New Englanders sold illegally to the French, Spanish and Dutch colonies. In the same way, the British islands failed to satisfy the mainland's demand for tropical produce. The wealth of New England came increasingly to be based on illegal trade, in defiance of the navigation acts, with the French islands of Guadeloupe and Martinique, the Spanish island of Cuba and the Dutch ports of St Eustatius and Curaçao. Smuggling became a respectable profession among the descendants of the Puritans, and the trade and navigation acts were enforced with laxity.

The theory of centralization was not only applied to trade. The colonies were gradually brought under a broadly similar constitutional system. As the Crown took over the bulk of the company and proprietary colonies, the colonial governor became a royal representative, governing through English officials. These officials sat on an 'executive council' to advise the governor. With the addition of leading colonists, they also sat on the legislative council, which usually formed the upper house of a colonial legislature. The people of the colonies were represented in the assemblies, which gave consent to new laws – subject to the final approval of the Crown. From 1696 a department of state at home, the Board of Trade, was responsible for scrutinizing colonial laws and corresponding with the governors. Once again, therefore, theory assigned the colonies to a system centralized on the Crown. In practice, a wide measure of local self-government remained. By the middle of the eighteenth century, theory and practice were badly out of line. In theory, the Crown was supreme, subject to Parliament's consent. The trade and navigation acts and the Board of Trade's scrutiny of colonial laws, were the working instruments of a centralized colonial system. In practice, the acts of trade were not really enforced, and Britain's legislative supremacy was lightly and tardily maintained. The colonies became accustomed to virtual self-government. The assemblies acquired a good deal of political maturity and began to claim that they were miniatures of the House of Commons. They won the right to initiate legislation on colonial finance; they sometimes refused their consent to taxes, in order to press their views on a governor. So although the general trend of British colonial policy, such as it was, was one of centralization, the dominant theme was one of provincialism. A vivid example of this was the fate of the Albany Plan of Union.

Representatives from seven colonies met at Albany, New York, in 1754, to try to co-ordinate their policies towards the Indians. But the delegates were persuaded to widen their horizons and they accepted the draft of a plan for an inter-colonial union. A single American government was envisaged, under a sort of 'Viceroy', to be styled President-General, and a Grand Council, in which the colonial assemblies would be represented. The Albany Plan seemed to imply the creation in America of something akin to the later 'Dominions', but the individual colonies rejected it.

In 1754 provincial feeling was too strong. Yet only twenty years later, twelve colonies sent representatives to the first of a series of inter-colonial Congresses which gave birth to the United States, and led to its secession from the empire. What happened in twenty years to sweep provincialism away in this the first great upsurge of colonial nationalism?

The Rebellion of the Thirteen Colonies

The American rebellion should not be viewed as the inevitable result of the opposing pressures of provincialism and centralization. Our knowledge of the Commonwealth in the twentieth century might suggest that full self-government, even complete separation, *was* probably inevitable. But in most cases this could be achieved peacefully. Nova Scotia provides the classic American example. Only in the case of the U.S.A. was a prolonged war of independence, leading indeed to a world war, necessary.

The reasons for the disastrous American crisis may be found in the entirely new predicament in which Britain found herself after defeating the French in the Seven Years War (1756–63). The war was only one phase in the long struggle with France, waged over more than a century in Europe, Asia and America, and ending only with Napoleon's defeat at Waterloo. But, for the colonies in the New World, the Seven Years War was the crucial watershed.

France capitulated in Canada, the West Indies, and West Africa. Thus, not only was a long-standing threat to the colonies removed, but a unique opportunity was presented for making the Old Colonial System work. The possession of the prosperous French sugar islands of Guadeloupe and Martinique and the Spanish island of Cuba, along with the gum-producing areas of Senegambia, in West Africa, could have removed all need for smuggling. Sufficient markets and sources of raw materials for all the empire were now in England's grasp. But the opportunity was thrown away. The West Indian planters, jealous of their sugar prices, prevented the retention of the French islands. Britain was left without rival on the North American mainland, but with the basic anomalies of the colonial system unsolved, and with critical new problems in the offing. Three problems in particular interacted upon each other. They may be termed the continental problem, the revenue problem and the problem of imperial relations. The American rebellion arose because of Britain's failure to find solutions which satisfied the colonists.

The continental problem concerned Britain's newly acquired empire in the west. How should she rule it, dispose of the land, deal with the Indian inhabitants? What were the defence requirements and how would they be paid for? Similar dilemmas were later to appear in South Africa and elsewhere. Settlers demand new lands; the indigenous peoples require protection; clashes between the two lead to costly military expeditions.

To meet the needs of American defence the government decided to station 10,000 troops in seaports and frontier forts in the west. The

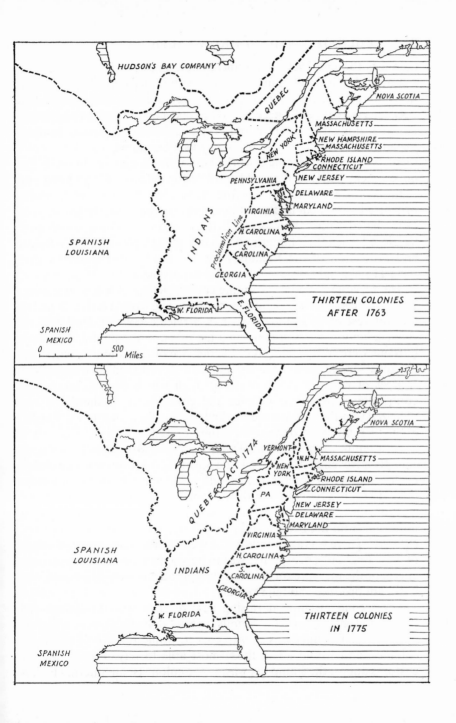

HUDSON'S BAY COMPANY

QUEBEC

NOVA SCOTIA

MASSACHUSETTS
NEW HAMPSHIRE
MASSACHUSETTS
NEW YORK
RHODE ISLAND
CONNECTICUT
NEW JERSEY
PENNSYLVANIA
DELAWARE
MARYLAND
VIRGINIA

Proclamation Line

INDIANS

N. CAROLINA

SPANISH
LOUISIANA

S. CAROLINA

GEORGIA

W. FLORIDA

E. FLORIDA

THIRTEEN COLONIES
AFTER 1763

SPANISH
MEXICO

0   500 Miles

NOVA SCOTIA

VERMONT
N.H.
MASSACHUSETTS
NEW YORK
RHODE ISLAND
CONNECTICUT
PA
NEW JERSEY
DELAWARE
MARYLAND

QUEBEC ACT 1774

VIRGINIA

SPANISH
LOUISIANA

N. CAROLINA

INDIANS

S. CAROLINA

GEORGIA

W. FLORIDA

THIRTEEN COLONIES
IN 1775

SPANISH
MEXICO

colonists thought they were unnecessary, since the French had been removed. But an Indian uprising, led by the chief Pontiac in 1763–64, not only proved the need for western defence but also showed that decisions were urgently needed. To this end a boundary line was drawn in 1763 along the spine of the Appalachians as a bar to colonial expansion. It was intended originally as a temporary check to settlement, while the government worked out new policies for the west. The government believed it should provide for defence, government and relations with the Indians before permitting limited and properly organized settlement in places like the Ohio valley. But the line of 1763 exacerbated, rather than solved, Britain's problem. The colonists were aggrieved when their hinterland was cut off. The plans for government and protection of the Indians were too costly, and therefore they served to highlight Britain's second great problem.

The revenue issue had a simple cause: victory in the Seven Years War had been purchased at immense cost. The British taxpayer had to find interest of £5 million a year to service a debt of £130 million. English landowners were paying a tax of 4s. in the pound. Now new burdens were to be incurred in the defence of the colonies, where the customs service cost more to run than it collected in duties. New sources of revenue were needed through which the colonies might contribute to their own defence and government. It should be emphasized that the colonies were asked to contribute, not to the English exchequer, but only to the costs of the empire.

An attempt was made, first of all, to enforce the trade and navigation acts. By a Revenue Act of 1764 (the Sugar Act) new duties were placed on the import of foreign coffee, silk and wines. A more important provision was a reduction of the duty on foreign sugar from 6d. to 3d. a gallon. On the face of it, the colonists would have to pay less for sugar imported from the French and Spanish islands. But the tax was to be *enforced*. There was an outcry, as the illegal trade, one of the mainstays of New England's prosperity, was to be stopped. As it turned out, the effects of the measure on colonial rum producers were debatable, and it did not produce enough revenue.

The second attempt at raising new revenue was the Stamp Act (1764). Revenue stamps on various types of documents were common in England. The duty was easy to collect, would fall evenly on all the colonies, and would affect those most able to pay. But, unlike the customs duties, the stamp tax was, to the colonists, an 'internal tax'. A furious, sometimes violent, controversy broke out. Delegates from nine colonies met at an inter-colonial 'Congress' in New York, where they decided to boycott British goods. Businessmen in Britain faced the prospect of losing a major market, so the stamp tax was repealed. The same thing happened to a new 'external tax', known as the Townshend duties, proposed in 1767. Duties on paint, lead, paper and tea were designed to raise enough customs revenue to enable the Chancellor of the Exchequer to reduce the English land tax from 20 per cent to 15 per cent. The taxes were to be collected by a new autonomous American customs service centred on Boston. But another colonial outcry followed, and the duties were removed except for 3d. a pound on tea. Even this was lower than the duty paid on tea imported into England.

By the beginning of the 1770s the home government was squarely faced with a crisis of imperial relations. The problems of the western expansion and the revenue were unsolved. The solutions which had been attempted had only stirred up colonial opposition to a point where the constitution itself was challenged. More than a century of virtual self-government had led the colonial politicians to forget that their system was based, theoretically, on the central authority of the Crown and Parliament.

How could the conflict be resolved? This was the daunting challenge presented by the problem of imperial relations. Some very fundamental questions were being posed in an unfortunate atmosphere of crisis. How should an expanding empire of overseas settlements be governed by the consent of its peoples? What was the appropriate relationship between a colony and the mother country? They were not easy questions to answer. They have *never* been answered simply and categorically. The problem was resolved in the nineteenth and twentieth centuries by the evolution of the Commonwealth. But, as later chapters will show, the process was slow, gradual, sometimes painful, and involved practical political compromises rather than theoretical constitutional formulas. What happened in the tense atmosphere of the 1770s?

There were those at home, and in the colonies, who realized that in the circumstances which followed the Seven Years War, the colonial relationship needed re-definition. Governor Francis Bernard of Massachusetts completed a book in 1764 in which he argued that if the Crown in Parliament was to be recognized as sovereign in the empire, Parliament would have to be made to appear as the forum of the whole empire. In theory, of course, Parliament already fulfilled such a role, for the colonies were 'represented' in Parliament just as much (or as little) as most Englishmen. Governor Bernard wanted genuine empire reform. He proposed creating a few large colonial governments in America, admitting colonial members into the Parliament at Westminster, and defining the respective roles of the imperial and colonial governments. More radical ideas still were put forward by the 'new economists', such as Josiah Tucker and Adam Smith, who believed that amicable commercial co-operation was the only valid tie between England and the New World. They hoped that colonies would be permitted to separate voluntarily from the mother country, and that the two parties would sign agreements to ensure mutually profitable trade. Unfortunately for the empire in America, the time was hardly ripe for experiments of this kind.

A series of violent incidents in the colonies, followed by an equally violent reaction on the part of the British government, poisoned the atmosphere. The presence of British troops in the colonies gave rise to the brawling and unpleasantness that so often follows alien garrisons. Sentries were abused, property plundered, and soldiers were mobbed. There was provocation on both sides. Matters finally came to a head in 1773 in the 'Boston Tea Party'.

It may seem odd that the British empire should seem to break up over so wholesome a commodity as tea. But the tea which was dumped into Boston Harbour was regarded as a symbol of Parliamentary sovereignty. Even with the duty of 3*d.* a pound, tea was cheaper in America than in England, but the colonists preferred to evade the duty by drinking smuggled tea bought from the Dutch. In 1772 this system of trade was challenged from an unexpected direction. The East India Company found itself unable to sell a surplus of tea in England, so the government decided to allow the company to import tea direct to America. Thus the East India Company was about to undercut the smuggled tea in the colonies, and also to put a few merchants or smugglers out of business. Hardly a cause for revolution! But the real point was that if the tea was marketed by the East India Company in America, the 3*d.* duty would have to be paid and a Parliamentary decision practically demonstrated. By resisting the landing of the tea the Boston 'Patriots' were protecting their commercial interests and also demonstrating against Parliament's authority to regulate and tax their trade.

The British government reacted sternly: the law was to be upheld! In 1774 the port of Boston was closed until the East India Company was reimbursed for its sodden tea. The constitution of Massachusetts was modified; trial by jury was suspended and, for good measure, Parliament authorized the billeting of troops in colonial homes. To many of the colonists these were 'intolerable' acts, and they coincided with another measure, which convinced them that they were in the hands of tyrants. By the terms of the Quebec Act (1774), which provided a new constitution for the former French colony of Canada, the triangular region bounded by the Ohio, the Mississippi and the Great Lakes, was added to Quebec. 'Canadiens' regarded this as their natural and historic hinterland; but so did the colonists. Now the home government seemed to be favouring the Catholic, French-speaking subjects in the north over their Protestant kinsmen.

As unrest spread in America in 1774 another inter-colonial conference, known as the 'Continental Congress', convened. Many people believed that a major conflict could not be avoided. But it is well to remember that the colonists were divided among themselves. The radicals, or 'Patriots', it is true, wanted a direct challenge to the British government. They sought freedom for their individual colonies. But there was a large body of moderate and conservative opinion, who wanted to avoid a show-down, who believed that what was needed was a plan for reconciling colonial interests and aspirations with Parliamentary sovereignty.

A most interesting series of ideas were presented to the Congress by Joseph Galloway of Pennsylvania, which were known as the 'Plan of Union'. Closely following the Albany Plan, Galloway proposed a colonial federation and the creation of a 'Grand Council' of all the colonies to be elected by the assemblies. This American Parliament would be a branch of the British Parliament and be responsible for American affairs. The Crown would be represented by a President-General. Here, then, was a genuine proposal of 'Home Rule' for America through some sort of union or federation between Britain and America.

There were also conciliatory voices in England, who wanted to find a way of making Parliamentary sovereignty acceptable to the colonies. 'Leave the Americans as they anciently stood', declared Edmund Burke. And in February 1775 a Bill was presented to Parliament by the ailing Lord Chatham, who sought, while upholding Parliament's supremacy in matters of genuine imperial concern, to permit the colonies to tax and govern themselves in local matters. He proposed that the colonial constitutions should be guaranteed, that the Crown should not send troops to America without consent from colonial assemblies, and that the Continental Congress should be recognized as a colonial Parliament and asked to make a contribution to the costs of the empire.

The schemes of the moderates failed. Soon the thirteen colonies would leave the empire. The Congress rejected Galloway's Plan of Union by one vote; Parliament did not even give Chatham's Reconciliation Bill a second reading. It is true that Lord North, the prime minister, succeeded in persuading Parliament to accept a measure which promised to exempt any colony from imperial taxes if it agreed to make a contribution to the defence of the empire and set aside a fixed sum for civil government. But it was too late.

In the early months of 1775 a series of spontaneous revolts occurred in the colonies, which presented the conservative home-rulers with a painful dilemma. Should they remain loyal to the British connection and risk defeat, or should they throw in their lot with the rebels and hope to retain a measure of control? Most of them chose the latter course. A second Continental Congress, meeting in May 1775, decided, in effect, to make the rebellion 'official' and to raise an army of 20,000 men under the command of the Virginian, George Washington.

This was the crucial divide in America. Here, more than a year before the thirteen colonies severed their connection with the British Crown on 2 July 1776 and adopted the Declaration of Independence two days later, the 'United Colonies' defied the British government. Their flag still incorporated the Union Jack along with thirteen stripes, but an expedition was dispatched northwards in the hope of bringing Nova Scotia and Quebec into the rebellion.

So far the colonists have been referred to as 'rebels', but in a literal sense they were also 'revolutionaries'. They had long enjoyed virtual self-government, but only by grace and favour of the English King and subject to the legislative supremacy of Parliament. But they had begun to challenge the doctrine of imperial sovereignty. They believed in government by consent of the governed. This is not to imply that they all subscribed to the idea of democratic representation – some of the colonies had a very wide (virtually democratic) franchise, but most had not. However, they all wanted 'Home Rule'. To have kept the colonies within the empire, as a good many Americans desired, Britain should have adapted her constitutional theory to admit a truly representative empire Parliament, a federal union, or a system of divided sovereignty in which America could have a separate Parliament, or the King be a separate 'King in America'.

Such ideas were completely unacceptable to all but a tiny minority in England. 'The die is now cast,' said George III, after the second Continental Congress, 'the colonies must either submit or triumph.' Eight years of war followed. Not only did Britain have to fight the Americans, but France entered the war in 1778, followed by Spain in 1779, and Britain declared war against the Netherlands in 1780. The colonial revolt became one of the great 'world wars' for the British empire. It spread from America to the West Indies, the English Channel and the Mediterranean, and to India, the Indian Ocean and the Indonesian archipelago. The most remarkable thing about the War of Independence, from the viewpoint of the empire, is that, while thirteen colonies were lost, so much else was saved.

The Lessons of the War of Independence

It is often said that Britain 'learnt her lesson' in the War of Independence and avoided a repetition elsewhere. Her failure to grant American demands led to the secession of a large part of the empire. Similar losses were avoided elsewhere by the grant of satisfactory forms of local autonomy, so that most of the former colonies remain associated in the Commonwealth. If this were true, however, it is difficult to explain why it took so long for the lesson to be learnt. Responsible government was not granted in British North America until the 1840s, and then only after minor revolts had occurred in Canada. Important lessons were indeed learnt from the American war, but few Englishmen at the time drew the conclusions popularly attributed to them. What, then, were the real lessons?

The first lesson was demonstrated by the very outbreak of the rebellion. It meant an admission that all attempts to reconcile the provincial and centralizing tendencies since 1763 had been futile. Thus, two forlorn attempts were made at a final reconciliation. In 1778 peace commissioners were sent to America with Lord North's last desperate bid for a settlement. He was now prepared to suspend all the measures relating to the colonies passed since 1763 and to agree not to station an army in the colonies in peacetime. He would rely on colonial assemblies to provide finance for government, permit the election of governors and admit colonial representatives to Parliament. In other words, to end the war he was prepared to concede nearly everything except the sovereignty of Parliament and the commercial monopoly. In the last resort he was prepared to consider recognizing independence. But, as usual, the offer was too late. It reached America after the French alliance had been signed. Yet North's terms were not the last attempt at reconciliation.

In 1782, after Lord Cornwallis's army had surrendered at Yorktown, North's government resigned and he was succeeded after a short interval by the Earl of Shelburne. Even in the shadow of military catastrophe Shelburne made a remarkable bid to recover the American colonies. He offered nothing short of a federal union, in which England, America and Ireland would be the constituent parts, each with complete autonomy under the Crown. The British Parliament would retain control only of subjects of general imperial concern such as trade, defence and foreign affairs.

Theoretically, Shelburne's peace plan was an extraordinary concept. It has been seen as a presage of the Commonwealth system of the early twentieth century. But after the bitter years of war, the plan was unacceptable to the Americans. Yet even when his scheme was rejected, Shelburne's conciliatory spirit continued. He decided to grant unqualified recognition of American independence, to withdraw from the remaining British-held portions of the thirteen colonies, and to grant to the new U.S.A. boundaries extending inland to the Mississippi and from the Great Lakes to the borders of Florida. 'Entire and cordial reconciliation' was Shelburne's watchword, and in order to retain the trade of the new nation he was prepared to admit it to the privileges of the Old Colonial System. In spite of the fact that they were now 'foreign', he wanted to treat American imports as if they were still British and to allow the Americans to continue their trade in the West Indies. But in 1783 Shelburne himself was swept from power. His successors drew a very different conclusion from the recent war.

The main lesson of the war to them was that the Old Colonial System would have to be maintained with greater stringency. Lax enforcement of the trade and navigation acts and loose control over colonial governments had contributed to the causes of American independence. The government must uphold its authority in the future. In commercial terms, this meant that if the United States wanted to be independent, it must take the economic consequences. It would now have to trade with Britain and her colonies as any other foreign nation, like France and Spain.

In constitutional terms this lesson implied a reduction, or certainly a standardization, of colonial self-government. Let the remaining colonies do as the thirteen colonies had done, it was argued, and they will defy the constitution again! Thus, although in the celebrated legal judgment of *Campbell* v. *Hall* in 1774 it had been declared that the Crown could not revoke legislative powers once granted, and North's 1775 Act had renounced the imperial taxative power, the government was determined – and this was the second lesson of the war – to make colonial constitutions conform to the British constitution as closely as possible. The result may be seen in the Canadian constitution of 1791.

Imperial Authority Revived

The former French colony of Quebec had been promised an assembly, on the normal colonial model, in 1763. But the 'Canadiens' were unused to representative institutions. Thus by the Quebec Act (1774) an autocratic constitution, providing for a governor with a nominated council, combined with safeguards for French language, religion, social usages and land tenures, was devised, which satisfied the inhabitants. Nevertheless, the War of Independence had a profound effect upon Quebec. The territory south of the Great Lakes was lost to the United States, and 20,000 loyalist refugees, who were accustomed to political rights, settled in the province. Thus the government faced the delicate task of extending to Quebec British constitutional rights, without encouraging radicalism or democracy, and also avoiding a clash between the French and English-speaking sections of the community.

The solution was embodied in the constitutional act of 1791. Quebec was partitioned into two colonies: Upper Canada on the Ontario peninsula, where most of the loyalists had settled; and Lower Canada, corresponding with the French-settled part of the St Lawrence valley. Each colony was to have a Lieutenant-Governor and a two-chamber legislature. The upper house, or legislative council, was intended to be a colonial 'House of Lords' consisting of hereditary peers. The Assembly was to be elected by 40s. free-holders and £10 householders. The new legislatures were clearly modelled on the

English Parliament. But in this they were more 'conservative' than several of the pre-War of Independence constitutions, some of which included elected governors and a near-democratic franchise.

The Canadian constitutions were, however, of great significance. They provided for the first major grant of representative government to a non-English population in the empire. The legislative councils never became houses of peers, but cliques of nominated officials and wealthy landowners. Above all, the political experience gained in the assemblies under this system paved the way – indeed, gave rise to the demand – for responsible government in the nineteenth century. But it should not be forgotten that the system became, as we shall see in the next chapter, an instrument of domination by a narrow oligarchy, and it led to rebellions in 1837. It is therefore quite wrong to suggest that Britain gave Canada responsible government because of the War of Independence.

The third lesson of the war was a strategic one. It served to emphasize a 'swing to the East' in Britain's commercial strategy which had begun during the Seven Years War under Chatham's imaginative leadership. The American crisis was so catastrophic, and the subsequent rise of the U.S.A. of such wide significance, that it is easy to forget that while the British government was wrestling with its trans-Atlantic problems in the 1760s and 1770s, it also had to devote a great deal of attention to the East.

Immense labour was expended in trying to inculcate a sense of responsibility into the East India Company, which had ousted the French from India in 1763 and had become the 'paramount power', indeed the revenue-collecting agent, of Bengal. During the same period Captain Cook was exploring the Pacific, charting the coasts of New Zealand and New South Wales and the American north-west. The East India Company was endeavouring to open trading bases in Borneo and the South-East Asian mainland. Finally, there was the lure of a mass market in China. Thus, after French intervention in 1778, the War of Independence had also to be fought in the East. In India, the French sent help to the Company's adversaries in South India and planned to re-establish their empire. When Spain entered the war an expedition was planned to occupy the Philippines, as a stepping-stone in a trans-Pacific attack on South America. To break the Dutch strategic stranglehold on the trade routes to China, expeditions were sent to the Cape of Good Hope, Ceylon and Indonesia. At the Cape

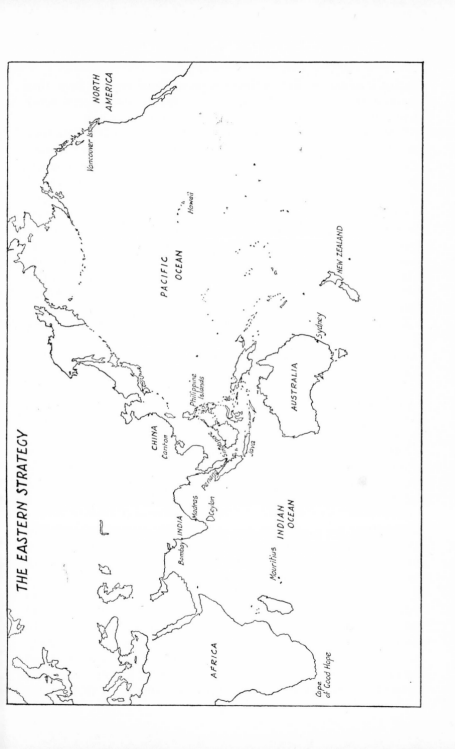

THE EASTERN STRATEGY

the French got in first; in Ceylon, Britain's occupation of Trincomalee was short-lived; and in Indonesia the only success was on the west coast of Sumatra. Outside India itself, then, the eastern strategy failed.

But in the thirty years which followed the loss of the American colonies, the whole shape of the empire changed. When, after the French revolution, Britain again found herself at war with France, the eastern strategy succeeded. At the end of the Napoleonic wars the Cape, Ceylon and Mauritius were retained. Java was occupied for four years and then returned to the Dutch, but the East India Company established a permanent base in South-East Asia known as the Straits Settlements. Not only did the empire change in strategy and shape during the era of the French revolution. In the new possessions which were captured in the French wars, fundamentally new concepts of government were evolved. In particular, an autocratic system of government, known as the Crown colony, was created, which in the nineteenth and twentieth centuries was to be a characteristic form of colonial rule in Africa and Asia.

Aspects of the 'Second Empire'

Two completely new experiments were launched in the peaceful years of the 1780s. A convict colony was started in Australia and a colony for freed slaves was founded in Sierra Leone. They were both the outcome of the rise of humanitarian feeling in Britain.

In 1772, the anti-slavery agitation, which had started many years before among the Quakers of Pennsylvania, bore fruit in the famous Somerset case, when the Lord Chief Justice of England declared slavery illegal in the land. After the American war humanitarians then turned their attention to the trans-Atlantic slave trade from West Africa. But one group of philanthropists took up the plight of the freed Negroes in England and of the loyalist Negroes expelled from the U.S.A. The result was the founding, in 1787, of the colony of Sierra Leone on a small peninsula in West Africa. It was a unique experiment. We shall see that in Victoria's reign it made a remarkable contribution to African development. In its very early years a form of representative system was devised under which every ten families elected 'tithingmen', who then elected 'hundredors', who met with the governor in council.

If Sierra Leone was a by-product of the anti-slavery crusade, Australian settlement was an outgrowth of the prison reform movement. Harsh penalties for petty crimes combined with the loss of convict contracts from the American colonies to cause overcrowding in Britain's deplorably inadequate jails. Land for a prison colony was therefore sought overseas, and in 1779 Sir Joseph Banks suggested that some of Cook's discoveries in the Pacific might be utilized. In 1788, seven hundred men and women convicts, escorted by two hundred marines under Captain Arthur Phillip, landed in the great harbour of Port Jackson, New South Wales, to found the town of Sydney. Ten years later, when the French war severely interrupted the shipping lanes, a population of about 4,000 convicts existed. This was Australia's humble beginning: a small prison colony under military rule.

Sierra Leone and Australia were both exceptional, but the French wars (1793–1815) brought into British hands a medley of new colonial possessions, all of which had certain characteristics in common: they were small; they had been captured for strategic reasons; and, most important of all, they had non-English populations. How were they to be ruled and fitted into the colonial system?

In some of the captured Caribbean islands – Tobago, St Vincent, Grenada and Dominica – normal representative assemblies had been granted. But bitter conflicts followed among the British and French inhabitants, and, as we have seen, the War of Independence raised doubts about this policy. Some new colonial system was needed for small, non-British, conquered colonies. The solution which was adopted bore some affinity to the system in Canada from 1774 to 1791. It was outlined in the instructions given to the military governors of Martinique and Santo Domingo, which were occupied during the years 1794–1815. The basis of the new system was the idea that the rights of the inhabitants would be safeguarded, but *not* by the grant of an assembly. To this end, the colonies were to retain their languages, revenue systems and existing laws. The governor would call small advisory councils of leading citizens. But the governor would *rule*, under direct instructions from home, and with the minimum of reference to local opinion. Here is the basis of the 'Crown colony' system. It was adopted in Trinidad (captured in 1797) which retained its Spanish laws, and Guiana, which retained its Dutch laws. It was also adopted in the Cape, Mauritius and in Ceylon (after a period, 1796–1801, when the island was placed under the East India Company). The same system was extended to Sierra Leone, when the Crown took over the colony in 1808. The first Crown colonies were, therefore, small experiments, but Crown colony rule is a stage through which most of the modern nations of the Commonwealth have passed.

The Concept of Empire

The era of the American revolution was one of gain as well as loss. While Britain lost most of her American colonies, she acquired new possessions in the Caribbean, the Indian Ocean and the Pacific. If the movement towards colonial self-government received something of a set-back, at least some fundamental problems of government had been posed. In some of the rejected ideas about colonial parliaments, imperial federation and divided sovereignty, lay the seeds of a good deal of later constitutional debate.

But of all the questions raised at the time of the American revolution, one stands out: what should be the relationship between the colonies and the mother country? The answer given at the opening of the nineteenth century was clear: the relationship should be one of subservience. The alternative, as it seemed from American experience, was independence. Any middle road appeared to be unacceptable. It is true that a few Englishmen and colonists had toyed with the idea of trying to define the precise roles of the home and colonial governments, as in a federation, but few practical formulas were produced.

Yet this fundamental question about the nature of empire continued to be asked. Some neat, clearly defined colonial relationship remained for many people an ever-elusive goal. As we shall see in subsequent chapters, a rather different solution was worked out in the late Victorian 'Dominions' and in the 'New Commonwealth' of today.

2

The End of the Old Colonial System

THE VICTORIAN age will always be regarded as the great age of the *Pax Britannica*. Many parts of the world came to be dominated by British trade, finance and naval power. The Indian empire spread from the frontiers of Persia to Burma; its commercial tentacles stretched onwards to Singapore and Hong Kong. Large portions of Africa were acquired. By the later years of the nineteenth century, Queen Victoria's diamond jubilee and the South African war seemed to stamp the nation of shopkeepers with the imprint of a mighty imperial power.

Yet the first three decades of Victoria's reign witnessed one of the most significant peaceful revolutions of modern history. The Old Colonial System was abolished. The trade and navigation monopolies gave way to free trade. At the same time a system of self-government was devised in the North American and Australasian colonies, which was to be gradually extended in the twentieth century to all the major portions of the empire.

Possibly because the new system, known as 'responsible government', was, in the main, achieved without violence, it is not often readily called to mind even by those who pride themselves on a knowledge of the past. Yet, without a doubt, it is one of the great achievements of British history. For the subsequent development of the Commonwealth it is the greatest single landmark.

Why was central control over the commerce and government of the colonies relaxed in these years? The answer to each part of this question must be different. Free trade was the achievement of the political economists at home; responsible government was the demand of frustrated politicians in the colonies.

Free Trade

The end of the threefold monopoly of export, import and transit did not come quickly. Even Adam Smith, who wanted to sweep it away, admitted that the navigation acts had boosted British naval power. But he complained that the Old Colonial System was the work of merchants: 'their interest has been more considered than either that of the colonies or that of the mother country.' Therefore he deplored the 'mercantile system' in his great work, *The Wealth of Nations*, published in 1776, the very year when the Americans declared their independence. The coincidence was appropriate. Adam Smith declared that restrictions on colonial industry were 'a manifest violation of the most sacred rights of mankind'. He believed that unless colonists were given a voice in determining the policy of the empire – possibly by representation at Westminster – they would never 'voluntarily submit'. He suggested that if Britain gave up her power, negotiated with the Americans a trade treaty which would 'secure to her a free trade', then the Americans would be transformed from being 'turbulent and factious subjects, to become our most faithful, affectionate and generous ally'.

A more satisfactory relationship with America was not the only advantage Adam Smith proposed. He asserted that the Old Colonial System damaged British prosperity by diverting capital into the colonial trade. Capital ought to be employed, he argued, where it maintained the greatest amount of labour and production. The monopoly system diverted capital away from manufacture, and export to European markets, into the carrying trade to distant colonies. The system was 'a clog' which, for the benefit of a few, embarrassed many others.

As we saw in the previous chapter, Adam Smith's ideas had little immediate effect on colonial policy. But in the nineteenth century the 'Manchester School' of political economists came to exercise a remarkable influence. After the 1840s, ideas of individual liberty, limited government, free trade and international peace became revered as a great system of moral law. David Ricardo reiterated Smith's argument that the colonial monopoly diverted capital which would be distributed more productively 'by a universally free trade'. Richard Cobden believed that artificial props like the trade and navigation acts were unnecessary. Jeremy Bentham ridiculed the Old Colonial System by his famous question: 'What are colonies for? For nursing so vast a navy. What is our navy for? For keeping and conquering colonies.' In face of arguments like these the monopolies were ended by a process of gradual erosion.

To start with, exceptions were made for particular interests or regions. In the Caribbean, for example, a series of 'free ports' was created – colonial ports where the customs duties were not levied. Jamaican and Dominican free ports were designed to 'tap' the trade of the French and Spanish colonies, and after the American War of Independence further ports were 'opened' in Bermuda, the Bahamas and Nova Scotia. After 1795 small American ships were permitted to trade direct to the British West Indies. In the East, foreign traders were admitted to the territories of the East India Company when its trade monopoly in India was abolished in 1813. Singapore was acquired in 1819 as a free port to tap the trade of the Indonesian archipelago and the China Sea.

A further stage in the reduction of the monopolies occurred in the 1820s. After the successful independence movements in South America British traders sought a reduction of restraints on trade. William Huskisson, as President of the Board of Trade (1823–27), lowered customs duties on many items and offered a reciprocal reduction of the shipping regulations to foreign nations. It is true that comparatively high duties remained, but preferences were granted to many of the colonies. Timber from the Baltic paid higher duties than Canadian lumber. West Indian and Mauritian sugar retained an advantage. Canadian wheat paid a low duty in spite of the Corn Laws, which were designed to protect English agriculture, and empire trade was still reserved for British shipping.

By the 1840s the main core of the protection system began to crumble. The single-minded campaign of the Anti-Corn Law League combined with the Irish potato famine in 1845 to convince Sir Robert Peel to abandon his land-owning supporters and repeal the Corn Laws. In 1849 the repeal of the Navigation Acts followed. During the next few years the sugar and coffee duties were equalized and the timber duties abolished. The Australian colonies were permitted to levy their own tariffs; Canadians made a reciprocity agreement with the United States and even put up a tariff against English manufactures. By 1853 Disraeli declared that the Old Colonial System was in 'rags and tatters'. The free trade movement reached its climax in 1860 with Cobden's treaty with France and Gladstone's budget, when customs duties were removed from all but forty-eight articles.

The commercial system which had been erected to foster British wealth and power in the seventeenth century now gave way to a system better fitted to the commerce of the leading industrial nation. Nassau Senior once said that 'the question of free trade is, next to the Reformation, the most momentous that has ever been submitted to human decision'. But it should not be forgotten that the centralized commercial system was abolished by Britain in her own interest. There were colonial leaders who believed that Britain was 'cutting the cable' which bound them to the mother country.

It is true that some of the most passionate free-traders such as Richard Cobden believed, with Adam Smith, that trade came before empire and that the colonies would probably separate from Britain. Cobden was as much a pacifist as a free-trader and he worried about the effects on the British character of military adventures and autocratic rule overseas (especially in India). Some writers, like Goldwin Smith, called frankly for the abandonment of the colonies.

The Colonial Reformers

Another group of reformers emerged during the 1830s who proclaimed a more constructive view of empire. They were not opponents of free trade. Indeed, they wished to go further and to extend freedom from the commercial to the political sphere. From the 1830s to the 1850s a small group of enthusiasts, which included Sir William Molesworth, Lord Durham, Edward Gibbon Wakefield, Charles Buller and Charles Adderley, campaigned steadily for any number of colonial causes. They encouraged certain forms of emigration from Britain, devised a new land settlement system and founded new colonies. But above all they wished to see the widest measure of self-government granted to English communities overseas. Few members of the group were great statesmen or even achieved high office, but we shall see their influence appearing in a number of places.

In one important respect their influence on the later Commonwealth was vital. It was they who first preached effectively the doctrine that colonial freedom and self-government was not incompatible with loyalty to the empire. In the aftermath of the American revolution, British colonial policy had been dominated by a fear that if the reins of empire were loosened the rest of the colonies would go the way of the

U.S.A. It was the colonial reformers of the early Victorian age who demonstrated what Edmund Burke and Charles James Fox had urged in vain, that the only lasting ties between mother country and colonies should be based upon a maximum grant of self-government.

It would, however, be wrong to assume that colonial self-government, when it was achieved, stemmed from the enlightened dreams of a group of idealists at home. The only reason why the reformers were listened to was that the existing colonial constitutions were on the point of breakdown. If the initiative in the free trade movement came from the British political economists, the initiative in the movement for responsible government came from colonial politicians.

Political Unrest in British North America

Political unrest first appeared in the British North American colonies. Here, in the upper St Lawrence basin and the Lakes Peninsula, could be found the greatest growing point of the empire. Indeed, by the middle of the nineteenth century, as new Canadian Parliaments embarked upon the practice of responsible government, the population of British North America reached nearly $2\frac{1}{2}$ million. This was roughly the population of the thirteen colonies on the eve of independence. But the most notable feature in the growth of the North American colonies was the progressive eclipse of the Quebec and Montreal fur-trading economy and of the French-speaking element in the population. While the population of Lower Canada (the former French settlements) roughly doubled between 1822 and 1851, to reach 890,000, the English, Irish, Scots and American population of Upper Canada expanded no less than ten times between the end of the Napoleonic wars and 1851. At that date, with 952,000 inhabitants, Upper Canada was the most populous colony. The Maritime provinces of Nova Scotia and New Brunswick multiplied roughly three times in the same period, to reach 277,000 and 194,000 respectively.

These changes were accompanied by a marked shift in the focus and preoccupations of colonial life in North America. The pattern of life in the older settlements continued. Nova Scotians looked to the Atlantic, to the fisheries, and to trade. Halifax, the capital, remained Britain's naval base in the north Atlantic. Along the St Lawrence in Lower Canada, the ribbon-like farms, running back from narrow river frontages, still supported a hierarchical provincial society of *seigneur*, priest and *habitant*. But the chief basis of the old French colony's wealth had been the fur trade of the west. The *coureurs des bois* had made heroic penetrations into the interior. But when American independence cut off the Mississippi valley, and the colony of Upper Canada opened up the upper St Lawrence to settlement, the great days of the Montreal fur trade were doomed. Following the success of New Brunswick, Lower Canada began to exploit the rich forests. Great pine logs began to flow down the tributaries of the St Lawrence, and the life of the boisterous, migrant lumberman began to be a characteristic Canadian manner of living.

But the most significant developments in British North American life were occurring on the northern shores of the lakes. As trees were cleared by the English-speaking settlers, and colonists began to reap the fruits of their labour in the fertile lowlands, trim farmsteads and proudly laid out townships appeared. Flour mills sprang up beside the lakes. In 1829 the Welland Canal, by-passing the giant Falls of Niagara, was opened, so that the wheat and flour of Upper Canada could flow down the St Lawrence. Now the produce of Canada's soil joined the produce of her rivers and forests.

Yet in spite of their growth, the British North American colonies compared unfavourably with the more prosperous United States. They chafed under a system of government which dated from the previous century. It is true that each colony had an assembly. The oldest, in Nova Scotia, was founded in 1758; Prince Edward Island had followed in 1769, New Brunswick in 1784 and the two Canadas in 1791. But all these colonies were dissatisfied. What, then, was wrong with the Canadian constitutions?

The chief complaint may be summed up in Lord Durham's phrase: 'irresponsible government'. A governor, it is true, was responsible to the Crown for the good government of his province. But he was often an inexperienced administrator, new to the scene, and a short-term incumbent. He had to find his 'government' from the more experienced officials on the spot. At the other end of the constitutional scale, the assemblies were responsible to the electors but, aside from the right to vote taxes, they had little power. But what of the 'middle element' of the constitutional structure – the executive and legislative councils? Each governor's executive council consisted of certain officials and prominent colonists. It performed the function of an advisory 'cabinet'. Usually the executive councillors sat on the legislative council, along with other officials and colonists (usually rich landowners), to form the upper house of the colonial legislature. In the Maritime provinces the two councils were usually identical.

These were the men who, in effect, formed the 'government' of the colonies. They knew their colony better than the governor; they were appointed for life and as residents they had a close interest in affairs. But to whom were they responsible? Not to the assemblies and the electors, because the councillors were appointed. In theory they were responsible to the governor, who in turn was responsible to the Crown. But interposing between governor and Crown lay the Colonial Office* which tended to control affairs closely unless a major crisis occurred.

In effect, therefore, the councillors made up a narrow governing class, responsible largely to themselves. Successive governors complained that men of the right social standing, talent, wealth and education for service on the councils were in short supply. Thus in Lower Canada they tended to select from the English-speaking 'château clique' of Quebec, and in Upper Canada from the closely related, Anglican upper class, which was dubbed the 'family compact', centred on Toronto. The government was always formed from a narrow oligarchy, while the representatives of the people in the assemblies were denied the power to influence their decisions. Lacking real power, therefore, the assemblies attracted grievance-mongers. And as they were frustrated in the attempts to obtain redress, they began to demand basic constitutional reforms. In varying degrees, in all the colonies, the assemblies tried to increase their powers. They demanded full control over revenue and the executive. They sought, in fact, to emulate the English House of Commons.

Each North American colony had its own peculiar political problems and each had a particular contribution to make to the movement for reform. The clearest demand for a new constitution came from Upper Canada. By 1828 an accumulation of grievances over land policy, education, banking monopoly, trade laws, the reservation of land for supporting Anglican clergy and the repeated expulsion of the radical agitator William Lyon Mackenzie from the assembly, had combined to produce organized political parties. Dr William Warren Baldwin wrote to the Duke of Wellington in 1829 requesting that the government of the colony should be made responsible to the provincial assembly and thus be forced to resign from

* See page 42.

An artist's impression of No 14 Downing
Street, the old Colonial Office

From 1798 to 1876 the colonies were supervised from offices in No. 14 Downing
Street, a rather dilapidated house which stood by the steps at the St James's Park end.
In the days of the American empire there was no real 'Colonial Office'. A series of
committees of the Privy Council were appointed and from 1696 to 1783 the 'Board of
Trade and Plantations' scrutinized commercial matters and laws. Matters of wider
policy were handled by one of the two 'secretaries of state'. The experiment of a third
secretary of state for the 'American Department', between 1768 and 1782, was abandoned on the establishment of American independence. Colonial affairs were then
handled by the 'Home Office' which built up a small 'Plantations Bureau'. When a
'secretary of state for war' was created in 1794 after the outbreak of the French
revolutionary war, Henry Dundas, the first incumbent, supervised the Plantations
Bureau, which in 1801 was formally added to the office of 'secretary of state for war
and colonies'. After the end of the Napoleonic wars the major preoccupations of this
office were the colonies, until in 1854 during the Crimean war a separate 'secretary of
state for colonial affairs' was appointed.

The 'Colonial Office' moved into the New Government Buildings in 1876 when the
old house was demolished. In 1925 a separate 'Dominions Office' was created to deal
with the autonomous colonies, but a separate 'secretary of state for dominions affairs'
was not appointed until 1931. This office became the 'Commonwealth Relations
Office' in 1947. By the 1960s the rapid growth of African and Asian independence
caused the whole Whitehall system to be reviewed. Between 1963 and 1964 a single
minister was appointed as 'secretary of state for Commonwealth and colonial affairs'
and between 1962 and 1964 a separate 'Central African Office' was created under the
first secretary of state. From the beginning of 1965 a single Diplomatic Service was
created to represent Britain abroad, but its instructions from London still came from
separate Foreign and Commonwealth Relations Offices. Plans were then made for the
eventual merging of the Colonial Office and the Commonwealth Relations Office as a
new 'Commonwealth Office' in 1966.

office when it lost the 'confidence of the people as expressed by the voice of their representatives in the assembly'. Here was one of the earliest direct requests for 'responsible government'.

After 1830 the British government, prompted largely by Sir James Stephen, the permanent under-secretary of the Colonial Office, conceded that in principle the assemblies should be taken more seriously. In 1835 Governor Francis Bond Head was instructed to reform grievances and give 'the most studious attention and courtesy' to the Upper Canada assembly. He therefore appointed three reformers from the assembly to his executive council. But when the councillors began to argue that the governor should consult them on all issues, Head denied that he was responsible to the people. The executive council was the servant of the governor, not of the people, he argued. Power and responsibility could not be separated. If the assembly gained responsibility, they would next demand power – then to whom could the people look for redress?

Head precipitated a constitutional crisis in Upper Canada. His council resigned. The assembly expressed its lack of confidence in the governor's new appointments and in 1836 they withheld the vote of supplies. Head thereupon dissolved the assembly, called an election, and by appealing to the patriotism and loyalty of the people against his late councillors, he ensured that the reformers suffered a set-back at the polls. Thus Upper Canada's tentative movement towards responsible government was dramatically brought to an end. As the unrest in the colony was largely based upon class conflict, and the assembly was not united behind Baldwin, the governor won a victory over responsible government. But there had been clear indications that gradual change might come about.

In Lower Canada the unrest took a much more serious form. A conflict of nationality was added to a conflict of interest. Here the chief protagonists were the strong French majority party in the assembly. Led by their fiery Speaker, Louis Joseph Papineau, they challenged the rule of the English minority of Montreal and Quebec who constituted the 'château clique' and dominated the executive council.

Until the 1830s there were moments of co-operation between the English and French, between the government and the assembly of Lower Canada. The Roman Catholic Bishop of Quebec was put on the executive council and in 1831 Papineau himself was offered a place. But gestures of this nature made even less headway in Quebec than in

Upper Canada. The assembly's attention focused increasingly on the appropriation and expenditure of revenue, until by the 1830s it would accept nothing short of complete control over the colony's finances. An unfortunate outbreak of violence during a by-election in Montreal in 1832 when three 'Canadiens' were killed, caused the 'Patriots' to close ranks behind Papineau. A long list of grievances was drawn up by the assembly. The chief demands were for an elected legislative council, assembly control over finance and for a reform of the 'irresponsibility of the executive'.

As in Upper Canada, the British government was prepared to make concessions. Commissioners were sent to Lower Canada in 1835 to meet the grievances and to appoint more Frenchmen to the executive and the legislative councils. But on the main issues of an elected upper house and assembly control of finance the British government would not give way. Thus in 1837 a revolutionary ferment broke out in Lower Canada. The 'Patriots' tried to consume home-made or smuggled produce to avoid contributing to the customs revenue. The assembly refused to vote supplies and was dismissed by the Governor. By the autumn of 1837 the 'Canadiens' were ready for rebellion.

In the Maritimes the move for responsible government was taken a stage further. Here the surface of political life was more sedate than in the two Canadas. Nova Scotia, in particular, looked back on a peaceful evolution from the eighteenth century and was adamant in its professions of loyalty to Britain. Nevertheless, the Maritimes had their grievances and aspirations like the Canadas. As Charles Fairbank of Nova Scotia said, 'The principles of the British Constitution ought to be in operation here. . . . The present system cannot continue.' In 1836 Joseph Howe, Editor of the *Novascotian*, persuaded the assembly to pass an Address to the Crown calling for the 'blessings of the British Constitution'. Howe pointed out that in England a ministry could not remain in office without a Parliamentary majority. Sir Robert Peel's experience in 1835 bore him out. Howe implored the British government to separate the Nova Scotian executive from the legislative council and to appoint to it some members of the assembly and so secure its 'responsibility to the Commons'.

It was, in fact, in the Maritimes that this system was first adopted. In 1837 the assembly of New Brunswick agreed to grant a fixed revenue to maintain the government – a civil list – in return for receiving control over Crown lands and territorial revenues. The

Lieutenant-Governor of the colony was instructed by the Colonial Office to change his executive council so that it would command the 'entire confidence' of the assembly. Here, in effect, responsible government was put into practice, without rebellion, fanfares, or even a recognition that a great landmark had been passed.

At the same time the secretary of state for the colonies commended this change to the Lieutenant-Governor of Nova Scotia. Unfortunately before he had a chance to do anything rebellions broke out in the two Canadas. For a further decade Britain's policy was under review in North America. Joseph Howe regarded the 1837 rebellions as the 'maddest rebellions on record'. He was convinced that, in principle, the Colonial Office had already conceded that the executive would soon have to be made responsible to the assembly in Nova Scotia.

In the 1830s, then, the British government was feeling its way towards granting a wider element of self-government in North America. It was recognized that the executive councils should be reorganized and that they might become 'embryo cabinets which would be chosen and dismissed by governors as the political situation in the colony changed'.* The chief reason why reform was delayed was not reluctance by the government, so much as disunity within the colonies and the conservatism of the legislative councils.

The Rebellions of 1837 and the Durham Report

In 1837 the peaceful, if slow, progress towards self-government was dramatically halted. Rebellions broke out in Upper and Lower Canada. They achieved nothing except publicity, but for this reason they were an important landmark.

Both rebellions were short-lived and strictly localized. After the dismissal of the Assembly in Lower Canada in August 1837 'Sons of Liberty' societies formed among the French, who gathered in their own 'Assembly' at St Charles in October 1837 to proclaim a Republic. Violence broke out on 6 November, after a brawl between French agitators and Englishmen outside the Loyalist Doric Club in Montreal. Bloodshed followed two weeks later as British troops advanced on the rebels in the Richelieu Valley. The final skirmishes took place at St Eustache, near Montreal on 14 December, by which time Papineau had fled to the United States.

* H. T. Manning, 'The Colonial Policy of the Whig Ministers 1830–37', *Canadian Historical Review*, 1952, 33(4), p. 355.

Events followed a somewhat similar pattern in Upper Canada but the rebels were not assemblymen. Here William Lyon Mackenzie gathered a few hundred discontented farmers at Montgomery Tavern on 4 December 1837 with the intention of capturing Toronto. Two days of street fighting and riots followed, until the advance of British troops cleared the city on 7 December. After a skirmish north of the city the rebels fled to the U.S.A. There Mackenzie formed a 'provisional government' in exile and continued to press guerrilla raids into Canada in 1838. Both rebellions were ignominious failures, but they did achieve one thing.

They awakened the British government to the seriousness of North American dissatisfaction. Gradual reform, to which the Whigs in Britain were committed after 1830, was shown to be ineffective. The government decided to send a High Commissioner to America to advise it on ways of solving the discontent of the colonies. Their choice of Lord Durham testifies to the seriousness of their concern.

Durham was the first Governor-General to come from the highest ranks of the British ruling class. He was the son-in-law of a former Prime Minister, and an ex-Cabinet member himself, as well as being one of the richest men in England. He was only in North America for about six months in 1838, but it is significant that he took with him as private assistants two of the colonial reformers, Charles Buller and Edward Gibbon Wakefield. The *Durham Report*, published in 1839, is the most famous single document in the history of the Commonwealth.

In spite of its fame, we must not assume that its diagnosis was entirely correct, nor that its prescriptions were successful. In some ways the *Report* was based upon prejudice, and in the long run some of its solutions have simply failed. For all its well-deserved renown a lot of the *Report* is pretty dull reading today – a politician's re-hash of the recent history of Canada. But in his main conclusions Durham expressed himself with devastating clarity and force.

Durham found two great evils in North America. The first was the conflict between the French and the English. 'I expected to find a contest between a government and a people; I found two nations warring in the bosom of a single state.' He called the second great evil 'this system of irresponsible government'. 'It may fairly be said, that the natural state of the government in all these Colonies is that of collision between the executive and the representative branch.' The officers of state were independent of the assemblies, who had no voice in their appointment and no influence on their policies. This relieved the popular leaders in the assemblies of 'the responsibility of opposition', said Durham. Thus, 'the colonial demagogue bids high for popularity without the fear of future exposure.' At the same time there was no strong government, since the governor was a subordinate official of the Crown, relying on instructions from the secretary of state, remote in Britain. The normal experts in government, the civil servants, were 'permanent but utterly irresponsible' office-holders. The governor's real advisers had to be his executive council: 'an instrument more simply calculated for preventing the responsibility of the acts of the government resting on any body, can hardly be imagined.'

What were Durham's remedies? The first was stated simply: to concede what Baldwin, Papineau and Howe had been demanding; to develop, indeed, along the lines of New Brunswick where the government had already, Durham noticed, 'been taken out of the hands of those who could not obtain the assent of the majority of the Assembly, and placed into the hands of those who possessed its confidence'. In other words, no new constitutional system was needed. 'It needs but to follow out consistently the principles of the British Constitution,' wrote Durham. 'But the Crown must submit to the necessary consequences of representative institutions; and if it has to carry on the government in unison with a representative body, it must consent to carry it out by means of those in whom that representative body has confidence.' If the colonists made bad laws, at least they would be the sufferers and soon find new remedies.

Durham's second solution was the anglicization of Canada. Upper and Lower Canada were to be united into a single province. This would be dominated by the English-speaking population, with English law and language, 'hereafter obliterating the nationality of the French Canadians'. Finally he suggested that the Union might eventually include all British North America to form 'a great and powerful people', which 'might in some measure counterbalance the preponderant and increasing influence of the United States on the American continent'. Durham believed in the colonial connection but wanted it to be based on full internal self-government. The only matters he reserved for the Imperial Parliament were the constitution, foreign affairs, trade policy and public lands.

What effect did Durham's *Report* have? His attempt to obliterate

French nationality failed completely. The Quebec 'separatists' of the 1960s are a perpetual reminder of Canada's 'two nations'. Federation or Union of British North America had to wait for nearly thirty years. When it was achieved in the 1870s it provided the foundation of the first 'Dominion'. Responsible government, in the sense that Canadian reformers wanted it, also had to wait for a few years. No formal division of 'colonial' and 'imperial' subjects was ever made. In fact, the only immediate achievement was the Union of the two Canadas in 1841. The question which still remains, therefore, concerns the grant of responsible government: how did the British government hope to avoid this concession, and why did it finally give way?

Responsible Government by Stages

Although responsible government was virtually in practice in New Brunswick, had been conceded morally for Nova Scotia, and now received the endorsement of Durham for Canada, Lord John Russell, the colonial secretary in 1839, tried to resist its full implications. He authorized the Union of Canada and ordered Charles Poulett Thomson (Lord Sydenham), the new Governor-General, to make important reforms. But, like his predecessors at the time of the American revolution, he wished to preserve the sovereignty of the Crown in North America. He refused to accept a Canadian ministry responsible to the assembly. 'Can the colonial council be the adviser of the Crown in England?' he asked:

> Evidently not, for the Crown has other advisers for the same functions, and with superior authority. It may happen, therefore, that the governor receives, at one and the same time, instructions from the Queen and advice from his executive council totally at variance with each other.

Russell simply instructed Sydenham to make a rough division between 'imperial' and 'colonial' business. In the purely local issues he was to obey the wishes of the assembly; where wider empire affairs were at stake the assembly was to modify its measures.

One big change, however, was to be permitted. The main officers of state in Canada (the colonial secretary, treasurer, auditor-general, attorney-general and solicitor-general) were no longer to be permanent. They would be called upon to retire as often as motives of policy demanded it. In practice this meant that the governor could use these offices to appoint Canadian politicians who had the confidence of the assembly. The governor, in a way, became his own 'prime minister' and selected his ministry in such a way as to ensure that he could retain the support of Parliament for his measures. In this Sydenham was notably successful in the short period before his death in 1841. But his successor Sir Charles Bagot ran into difficulties.

Representation in the Parliament of the United Province was equally divided between the former French and English colonies. The governor soon realized that he could not maintain a majority for his government unless he won the support of both French and English reformers. Lord Stanley, the conservative colonial secretary in London, warned the governor to keep out of the hands of radicals, to risk defeat in Parliament if necessary. But in 1842 Bagot made a bold stroke to retain the support of the Canadian Parliament. He appointed a coalition government which included the radical leaders Louis Lafontaine (from Canada East) and Robert Baldwin (from Canada West). Reporting this move to a shocked and furious colonial secretary, Bagot declared: 'whether the doctrine of responsible government is openly acknowledged, or is even tacitly acquiesced in, *virtually it exists.*' It only remained now for the British government itself to concede the principle.

It is perhaps appropriate that responsible government was first officially granted to Nova Scotia – the oldest and most loyal of the North American colonies. As in Canada, Sydenham first persuaded the leading reformers to join a coalition. But by 1843 Joseph Howe realized that this could only be temporary. Resigning from the council, he told the governor that full responsible government would depend upon the appearance of organized political parties, one of which, after securing a majority in the assembly through a general election, should form a cabinet of heads of departments united among themselves on all important issues.

When the third Earl Grey, an associate of the colonial reformers, became colonial secretary in 1846, he instructed the Governor of Nova Scotia on the principles which should guide him in calling a government. The call should come, he said, not as an act of the governor 'but of the wishes of the people themselves'. After a general election in 1847 a reform government, headed by James Boyle Uniacke, became the first fully responsible ministry in the British empire. A great turning-point had been passed as Nova Scotia moved, without violence or bloodshed, from eighteenth-century representative institutions to responsible government.

Canada followed rapidly upon Nova Scotia's heels. After a period of set-back from 1843 to 1847, Lord Elgin was sent as Governor-General to inaugurate the system in Canada. A general election was held at the end of 1847 and the new Parliament opened in March 1848. Elgin called the first fully responsible ministry in the province and stood by its decisions. Even when the government passed an unpopular Bill compensating those who had suffered losses at the hands of the British troops during the 1837 rebellion, he upheld his ministers and suffered personal abuse at the hands of the Montreal mob. Elgin was able to retain the loyalty of the Canadians at a time when Britain's adoption of free trade made many colonists turn to the U.S.A.

Elgin did more than conciliate Canada. He made a notable contribution to the future of the empire. He confronted the British government with the ideal of the colonial reformers; he demonstrated that self-government did not destroy the empire. 'You must renounce the habit of telling the colonies that the colonial is a provisional existence', he insisted.

'Is the Queen of England to be the sovereign of an empire, growing, expanding, strengthening itself from age to age, striking its roots deep into the fresh earth and drawing new supplies of vitality from virgin soils? Or is she to be for all essential purposes of might and power monarch of Great Britain and Ireland merely . . . ?'

The faith which Elgin proclaimed for Canada was very different from the attitude which had been taken to the colonies in the 1780s. Responsible government was the device by which the provincial and centralizing tendencies were reconciled. In Canada, the Crown still ruled – but on the advice of Canadian ministries responsible to the local parliaments.

Different Paths to the Same Goal in Australia

No sooner was responsible government accepted in North America than the system was demanded by the Australian colonies and New Zealand. By the middle of the 1850s, less than a decade after responsible government was adopted in Canada, the new Australasian parliaments represented some of the most democratic societies in the world. In many ways the rapid spread of responsible government to

Australia and New Zealand was a most remarkable event in the history of the empire. Indeed, it took place so rapidly, compared with the long struggle in Canada, that few historians have troubled to highlight the achievement.

In nearly every respect the colonies in Australasia presented a contrast to the North American provinces. When Baldwin first began to talk of responsible government for Upper Canada, New South Wales, the oldest and largest colony, was still governed rather as Canada was under the Quebec Act. By the middle of the nineteenth century New South Wales still had a population smaller than Nova Scotia. In origin, motive, soil and climate, type of settlement and economy, the Australian colonies were all quite different from Canada. The population did not reach the 2½ million mark until the 1880s. Yet, for all these contrasts, they 'caught up' with North America constitutionally, as it were, in the 1850s.

The first question we must ask, therefore, is: how did they do it? How in half a century, did free, politically conscious societies evolve in Australia, from the small, harsh, soldier-ruled settlement of a few thousand convicts of 1800? The answer has to be found in four main elements of Australia's early growth: free immigrants, systematic colonization, wool and gold.

Australia's rough beginnings as a prison colony around Sydney Harbour need not be romanticized. By the end of transportation in 1868, 160,000 convicts had been sent from Britain – mainly, before 1840, to New South Wales. A few were political prisoners, who excite our admiration and sympathy, such as the 'Tolpuddle martyrs'; over seventy Chartists, and several hundred Irish nationalists. Some were transported for very petty crimes. But most of Australia's 'first families' came from the dregs of English society and were poor material for building a new nation in the Antipodes. This, however, was only the beginning.

It had always been hoped that immigrants would be attracted to New South Wales by the prospect of cheap land and abundant convict labour. Emancipated convicts were also expected to become productive settlers. But progress was slow. Free settlers came in a tiny trickle, ex-convicts often made poor farmers, and a good deal of land was collared by the army officers who dominated the colony from 1792 to 1808. Not until 1828 did freemen outnumber convicts. But by this time nearly 5 million acres had been alienated. New settlements had

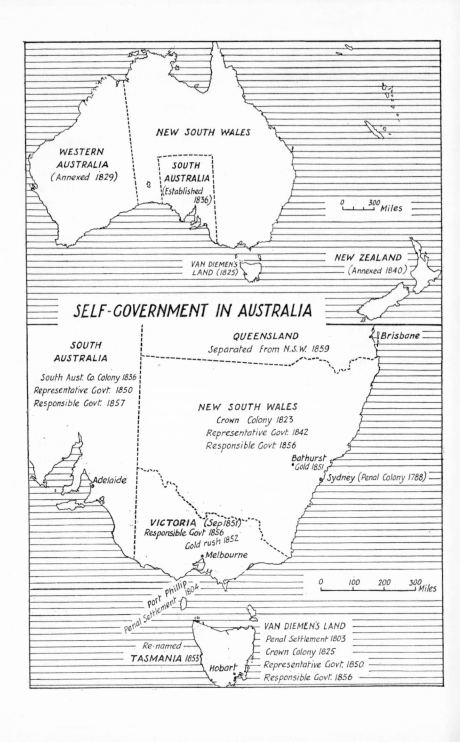

WESTERN
AUSTRALIA
(Annexed 1829)

NEW SOUTH WALES

SOUTH
AUSTRALIA
(Established
1836)

0   300 Miles

VAN DIEMEN'S
LAND (1825)

NEW ZEALAND
(Annexed 1840)

SELF-GOVERNMENT IN AUSTRALIA

SOUTH
AUSTRALIA

South Aust. Co. Colony 1836
Representative Govt. 1850
Responsible Govt. 1857

QUEENSLAND
Separated from N.S.W. 1859

Brisbane

NEW SOUTH WALES
Crown Colony 1823
Representative Govt. 1842
Responsible Govt. 1856

Bathurst
Gold 1851

Adelaide

Sydney (Penal Colony 1788)

VICTORIA (Sep 1851)
Responsible Govt. 1856
Gold rush 1852
Melbourne

0   100   200   300 Miles

Port Phillip
Penal Settlement 1804

Re-named
TASMANIA 1855

Hobart

VAN DIEMEN'S LAND
Penal Settlement 1803
Crown Colony 1825
Representative Govt. 1850
Responsible Govt. 1856

been started at Port Phillip in the south (1804), Van Diemen's Land (1804) and the small isolated colony of Western Australia was founded on the Swan River in 1829.

The greatest landmark in the peopling of the early settlements was a decision of the British government in 1831. The principle of assisting the payment of emigrants' passages was accepted, and officials were appointed to supervise emigration. Australia was now seen, not merely as a solution to prison overcrowding, but as a relief for unemployment and poverty among law-abiding citizens. In the next twenty years 200,000 assisted immigrants entered Australia.

Possibly of even greater significance for Australia was the new publicity which was directed to the Antipodes at this time. New colonies were therefore soon founded in South Australia and New Zealand which were in many ways quite different from any that had gone before. The biggest influence behind the new colonization was probably Edward Gibbon Wakefield. Wakefield, who lies buried in Wellington, New Zealand, was the disreputable son of a minor diplomat, who was placed in jail for abducting an heiress. From prison he published his ideas about colonization in newspapers. Although henceforth he had to exercise his influence from the background because of the stigma of his disgrace, he was nevertheless one of the most interesting empire theorists of the nineteenth century.

In Wakefield's view, colonies should be transplantations of British society. Where land was very cheap, as in New South Wales, colonists took up more than they could efficiently use, they became widely dispersed and labour became expensive as everyone tried to become land-owners. Wakefield advocated *concentration* of settlement. He wanted to adjust the supply of land, labour and capital in such a way that a balanced society would be created. To achieve this he adopted the device known as 'sufficient price'. If land was sold at a price high enough to deter the poor from trying to become farmers but low enough to attract those with capital, the rich need never want for labour and labourers would not go unemployed. Concentrated settlement of a truly mixed sort would result, and the proceeds of land sales and land taxes could be used to provide an immigration fund to pay for a steady supply of new settlers. Jeremy Bentham, its inventor, called it the 'Vicinity-maximizing or Dispersion-prevention principle'. As a theory it seemed foolproof. What success did Wakefield's 'systematic colonization' have in Australia?

E

In practice, Wakefield's theory was never fully tried. His figure of 40*s*. per acre was too high. It is true that various restrictions on land alienation were made in New South Wales. Grants to emancipists were stopped and in 1831 5*s*. per acre was charged, which was raised to 12*s*. seven years later. In 1842 a British Act of Parliament imposed a uniform price of £1 per acre in all the colonies. But this was quite understandably disliked by the Australians, who reduced the price as soon as they received control over land policy in 1850. Wakefield's fine theory of the 'sufficient price' floundered against the self-interest of the colonists.

Yet Wakefield's basic aim of creating a mixed society had some degree of success. As one of the founders of the colony of South Australia in 1836 and of some of the New Zealand settlements of the 1840s, he saw a number of his ideas put to the test. South Australia was supposed to charge 12*s*. per acre for land, and it selected its colonists carefully to ensure a balance between the sexes. Convicts were excluded. Most of the early settlers were middle-class town-dwellers, with a fair number of ministers of religion, who were all dedicated to the pursuit of civil liberty, free trade and social and religious opportunity. Within a few years every one of these ideals of South Australia floundered in a financial crisis. But the colony retained a distinct flavour from its 'dissenting' birth. As a visitor to Australia in 1841 remarked: compared with Sydney, where the scum of the earth had risen to be aristocrats, and Melbourne, which was full of gay young men, Adelaide was a town full of families – less pretentious, but most agreeable. The first colony of the systematic colonizers had produced a society of freemen with a character of its own.

The arrival of numerous freemen and the founding of the new colonies, then, made an important contribution to Australian development. But how did these colonies pay their way? Here the first answer must be wool. Wool was Australia's first great source of wealth; and wool remained dominant until the late nineteenth century. On the vast sheep runs of eastern Australia the life of the 'squatters', who grazed sheep over lonely expanses, became the most distinctive feature of Australian society.

The pastoral economy owed its origin to the persistence of an officer from the early penal settlement. John MacArthur, who came to New South Wales in 1790, imported sheep from India and South Africa. Sent home under arrest in 1801, he took specimens of his wool to England. There he so impressed a committee of merchants with its quality that when he returned to the colony four years later he carried authority from the government to acquire 5,000 acres of land. By the time of his death in 1834 the annual wool clip of New South Wales had reached 4 million pounds.

Wool turned out to be Australia's passport to the world economy. Free immigrants were attracted, capital flowed in, local fortunes were made, and finally a profitable export trade developed. As the Yorkshire woollen industry increased its appetite after the 1820s Australian production expanded to meet its needs. By 1859 40 million pounds from Australia represented half the raw wool imported into Britain. Over 70 million acres of the best grazing land in eastern Australia had been occupied by the pastoralists, who became, in effect, the 'aristocracy' of Australia. Wool provided the first solid foundation for Australia's growth.

But the most dramatic event in Australian development was the discovery of gold. On 15 May 1851 the *Sydney Morning Herald* carried the news of Edward Hargraves's precious finds near Bathurst, New South Wales. Sydney was soon convulsed with the same excitement which had hit San Francisco three years earlier, as the rush to the diggings began. Ironically, however, gold was to raise a rival to New South Wales for dominance in the Antipodes. By the end of 1851 the centre of the gold-fields had shifted to Ballarat and Bendigo in the newly created colony of Victoria. After the news reached England in 1852 the majority of the immigrants to the diggings went through Melbourne.

Most of the diggers were doomed to disappointment. A mere 10 per cent may have gained more than £100 for their effort; the vast majority made no more than they would have in wages. But the effects of the gold rush are not to be measured in individual fortunes among the diggers. Big money was made by store-keepers and gold buyers; but the real effect of the gold rush was the acceleration of economic, social and political development in the infant colony. In Victoria's first decade the population grew from 77,000 in 1850 to over half a million. Melbourne became a city of 125,000. One-third of the world's gold, and a sixth of Britain's wool were produced in the colony.

The new population, mostly unassisted immigrants, had a small percentage of illiteracy and compared very favourably with the other colonies. The gold rush atmosphere induced a democratic frontier spirit, in which the poor could aspire to become middle-class. Thus Victoria kept at the head of social and political progress in Australia. The interval between Victoria's separation from New South Wales in 1850 and the grant of responsible government was only five years. With its amazing population growth and swift political evolution, Victoria could claim to have had the most glorious launching of all the colonies.

Government in the Australian Colonies

Australia's rapid political evolution stemmed partly from her social and economic progress, and partly from Canada's constitutional pioneering. Until 1823 the government of New South Wales was virtually a military autocracy. The penal colony was governed by army and navy commanders, and the officers of the garrison became a self-seeking, ruling oligarchy.

Free immigration in the 1820s led to the appointment of a civil government. In 1823 a legislative council was created, consisting, at first, of five to seven officials, with later some nominated representatives of the colonists. At the same time civil rights were conceded to the free colonists, civilian judges were appointed, and trial by jury begun. Van Diemen's Land became a separate colony, with its own council, in 1825.

The end of convict transportation to New South Wales brought a major political advance. The New South Wales Government Act was passed in 1842, in the period when the British government was trying for the last time to make the Old Colonial System work in Canada. The governor, as in Canada, remained the 'executive' and was granted a civil list to cover official salaries, government expenses and the maintenance of the Church of England. But a single-chamber legislature was authorized, which would consist of a legislative council of thirty-six members. Twelve were to be nominated (half of them being officials) and twenty-four would be elected according to a moderate property franchise. Local government was to be provided by elected district councils. Thus New South Wales received a grant of representative government. But as it was accompanied by an unpopular measure raising the price of land according to Wakefield's theory, the council soon demanded larger powers, and even insisted on responsible government.

Before responsible government became practical in Australia an imaginative project was put forward in Britain. During the 1840s a good deal of unrest became evident in Australia. There was discord about land prices. The Port Phillip district (later Victoria), with only six out of the twenty-four elected members of the New South Wales legislative council, demanded separation. Van Diemen's Land and South Australia wanted representative government like New South Wales. Therefore, in 1847, Earl Grey, the colonial secretary who first granted responsible government in North America, suggested that political advance in Australia should be coupled with a federal constitution and a single Governor-General.

But there were few supporters for the idea in the colonies. The bulk of the Australians were interested in strictly local affairs. The federal project was dropped. Instead, the Australian Colonies Government Act of 1850 provided for the separation of Victoria, and granted representative constitutions to Victoria, South Australia and Van Diemen's Land (renamed Tasmania in 1853); their legislative councils were to be one-third nominated and two-thirds elected. Western Australia received its first legislative council. Thus, the colonies in the east were constitutionally 'standardized', but federation would have to wait for half a century.

The 1850 Act, however, was a great landmark for Australia. Two of its provisions should be noted in particular. First, the colonies were permitted to levy customs duties, even on British goods, provided they did not discriminate. Secondly, the colonies were given the power to alter their constitutions and change the voting qualifications of the electors. These rights were to be the basis of significant changes in the future.

Yet in the short run Australians were disappointed by the 1850 Act. The political leaders of New South Wales, who had been studying the progress of the *Durham Report* in North America, led the way in demanding further political advance. In a 'Declaration, Protest and Remonstrance' in 1851 the legislative council demanded an end to imperial rights of taxation and control over land, customs and other revenues. They insisted that colonists should fill all offices (except that of Governor) and that no bill should be subject to the veto of the Crown unless it affected the royal prerogative or the general interest of the empire at large. Concluding with an offer of a full civil list (to cover the costs of internal government), the Remonstrance demanded a constitution 'similar in its outline to that of Canada'. In other words, the first act of the legislative council under the 1850 constitution was, in effect, a demand for responsible government. Earl Grey looked on this demand with disfavour.

In 1852, however, Grey left office, and the attitude of the Colonial Office changed. Herman Merivale, the permanent under-secretary, recognized the rapid growth which was occurring because of the gold rush. On 15 December 1852 Sir John Pakington, the new colonial secretary, conceded that Britain should 'place full powers of self-government in the hands of a people thus advanced in wealth and prosperity'. He reminded the governors of New South Wales, Victoria and South Australia that the power to alter their constitution had already been granted in the 1850 Act. A suitable way of obtaining a constitution like that of Canada would be for the legislatures to draft new constitutions for the consideration of the British government. Pakington expressed a preference for two-chamber legislatures, with elected assemblies and nominated councils. In 1853 further encouragement came from the Duke of Newcastle, who succeeded Pakington and removed the restriction about a nominated upper house. In a confidential dispatch to the governors of all the colonies except Western Australia (4 August 1853) he 'agreed as to the extraordinary difficulty of . . . keeping our fellow subjects in Australia on a different political footing from those to which these rights have been fully conceded in America'. British North America had successfully pioneered the way. The transition in Australia therefore became almost automatic.

Pakington and Newcastle sparked off an intensive period of constitution-writing in Australia. In 1854 draft constitutions were received by the Colonial Office from New South Wales, Victoria and South Australia, and these were soon followed by Tasmania. In July 1855 the British Parliament authorized the new constitutions. It only remained for the colonial legislative councils to pass their new constitutional acts. By 1856 and 1857 the first Parliaments of New South Wales, Victoria, South Australia and Tasmania had met. When, in 1859, the northern part of New South Wales was detached to form the new colony of Queensland, the new province moved to responsible government in only three years.

What sort of political system did the new Australian constitutions provide? In some ways they appear very democratic. South Australia admitted manhood suffrage for assembly elections; this, along with the secret ballot, triennial parliaments and the separation of church and state, led Merivale, in the Colonial Office, to declare that the colony had 'the only thoroughly Benthamite Constitution in the empire'. Triennial parliaments and the ballot were accepted in the other colonies, where the property qualifications for electors (in elections for the assembly) were such that virtual manhood suffrage was also attained.

But in other respects the new constitutions were the harbingers of conservatism. In New South Wales, indeed, the rich pastoralists were frank opponents of democracy. W. C. Wentworth expressed the hope that the new constitution would be 'a lasting one – a conservative one – a British, not a Yankee constitution'. He recalled Pitt's attempt to transplant an hereditary aristocracy in Canada and he hoped that the New South Wales upper house would eventually achieve this end. His proposal was ridiculed by references to 'Botany Bay magnificos', 'Australian mandarins' and the 'bunyip aristocracy', but New South Wales stuck to a nominated legislative council.

What is striking, and perhaps ironical, is that this general conservatism was not incompatible with democracy. Australia had no real aristocracy, with social and constitutional privileges. The economic privilege of the wealthy was not, as yet, really challenged, since so many either had a stake in Australia's wealth or aspired to one. The tenor of Australian politics was perhaps best summed up by the Melbourne newspaper, *The Age*, in 1855 in these words:

> Where there are no class distinctions, and no aristocratic monopoly
> of property, democracy itself becomes Conservative.

'Over-government' in New Zealand

Twelve hundred miles to the east of Sydney one of the most striking colonial experiments of the early Victorian age was enacted. New Zealand was proclaimed British territory in 1840, and its advance towards responsible government was at the same rapid pace as Victoria's. In 1854, after very few years as a Crown colony, and with a population of only 33,000 settlers, New Zealand elected its first General Assembly.

New Zealand's constitution was unique among the colonies and for good reasons. Partly because of geography, and partly because of the very individual social and religious character of the separate settlements, very little direct inland communication developed between them. Moreover, the large Maori population (estimated at about 100,000, mainly in the North Island) presented formidable problems both for the British and colonial governments. The question of the Maoris' future overshadowed the early years of the colony and led, in fact, to a period of tragic warfare.

Years before Britain annexed the islands, New Zealand had become a sort of adjunct to New South Wales. Trading ships and whalers resorted to New Zealand's shores; missionaries went to evangelize the Maoris; small colonies of settlers made a foothold on the islands. By the 1830s New Zealand began to awaken interest in Europe. Lord Durham, Gibbon Wakefield and the colonial reformers started a New Zealand Company to plant another 'systematic colony'. An ambitious Frenchman managed to interest the French government.

All these activities forced a reluctant British government into action. With Englishmen living in the islands without proper government, and British and French expeditions of settlers in the offing, the missionaries were anxious to protect the Maoris. In 1839 Captain William Hobson was appointed Consul in New Zealand. After securing by the Treaty of Waitangi (6 February 1840) the cession of their lands from most of the Maori chiefs, in return for a promise of protection by the Crown, Hobson proclaimed British sovereignty. Now Britain, as protector of the Maoris, had to face the company and the systematic colonizers.

In many ways the political climate of the times was not suitable for an ideal solution of this problem. The ardent humanitarian and missionary societies in Britain did not look kindly on the Company's demands for land, but the government found it could not deny the settlers' demand for self-government. The Company was persuaded to abandon its charter in 1850, but after only five years of Crown colony rule the Colonial Office drafted a representative constitution for New Zealand. It prepared a partly federal scheme under which separate two-chamber legislatures would exist in North and South Islands, which would become two colonies, New Ulster and New Munster. These would then elect a general assembly with specific powers. But the scheme was rather artificial and never properly put into effect. In 1852 a constitution more adapted to the settlements in New Zealand was enacted.

The new constitution provided for a 'provincial' system of government. The New Zealand Government Act of 1852 created the six

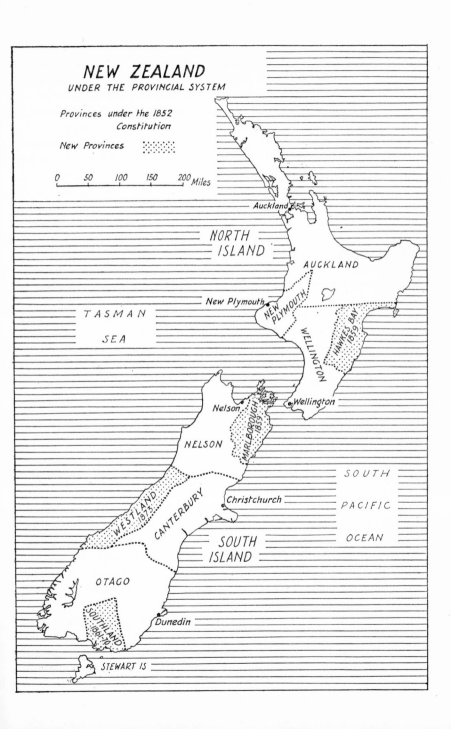

NEW ZEALAND
UNDER THE PROVINCIAL SYSTEM

Provinces under the 1852
        Constitution

New Provinces

0   50   100   150   200 Miles

Auckland

NORTH
ISLAND

AUCKLAND

New Plymouth

NEW
PLYMOUTH

TASMAN

SEA

WELLINGTON

HAWKES BAY
1859

Nelson

MARLBOROUGH
1859

Wellington

NELSON

WESTLAND
1873

CANTERBURY

Christchurch

SOUTH

PACIFIC

OCEAN

SOUTH
ISLAND

OTAGO

SOUTHLAND
1861-70

Dunedin

STEWART IS

provinces of Auckland, New Plymouth, Wellington, Nelson, Canterbury and Otago, each with its own elected superintendent and provincial council. A two-chamber general assembly was to consist of a legislative council (nominated by the governor) and a representative assembly elected by the people. The government was to be carried on by the Governor-in-Chief and three or four officials, and the oversight of the superintendents, the control of Crown land and Maori affairs would come under his jurisdiction. Here, then, was a representative system, basically similar to that in Canada and Australia, but, in its elaboration and 'over-government', adapted to New Zealand's own peculiar pattern of settlement.

Yet, like their fellow countrymen in New South Wales, the New Zealand settlers were not satisfied. When the very first General Assembly met in 1854, Gibbon Wakefield rose immediately to demand responsible government. And now, having conceded this in North America and Australia, the British government did not even hesitate in the face of New Zealand's insistence. As the colonial secretary wrote in December 1854, 'Her Majesty's Government have no objection whatever to offer to the establishment of the system known as responsible government in New Zealand.' No new legislation was needed, he went on:

> In this country the recognized plan of Parliamentary government by which Ministers are responsible to Parliament, and their continuance in office practically depends on the votes of the two Houses, rests on no written law, but on usage only.

It was left for the Governor of New Zealand in 1856 to follow the example of his Canadian prececessors and select his government from those who had the confidence of the colony's House of Representatives. With its small population, represented in provincial and central legislatures, elected according to a modest property qualification which excluded few but the Maoris, New Zealand achieved one of the more democratic political systems of the mid-nineteenth century. 'A most Brobdingnagian Government for a series of Lilliputian States', was the verdict of one of Wakefield's friends.

The problem of the Maoris remained. Until 1863 the British government retained formal control over Maori affairs: it was a dangerous anomaly. New Zealand thus received responsible government without full responsibility. This was only the most dramatic of the many 'loose ends' which the grants of responsible government left untied. The resolution of this and other issues must be left to a later chapter.

Provincial and Centralizing Tendencies in Mid-century

Twenty years separated the Canadian rebellions of 1837 and the opening of the Australian and New Zealand Parliaments in 1856–57. During the same period the basis of the monopoly system was also swept away. By the 1860s an entirely new concept of empire had emerged. When the question was now asked, what the relationship between colonies and the mother country should be, the answers provided for North America and Australasia were very different from those uttered after the American revolution.

We must not assume, however, that the answer was a completely simple one, that the system was for uniform application or that British politicians were all united. The Crown colonies remained; the East India Company still ruled in large parts of India; in the South African colonies of the Cape and Natal, English colonists still lived (for reasons described in Chapter 4) under modest representative institutions. But it is interesting to speculate how far the idea of responsible government had been accepted.

There were still those who expected that the colonies would all go the way of the United States. Sir Frederic Rogers, brilliant fellow of All Souls, leader-writer on *The Times*, friend and associate of Palmerston and Gladstone and legal adviser to the Colonial Office, examined the new Australian constitutions with dismay. He thought that they were nothing less than a 'legislative Declaration of Independence'. 'It is a great pity that, give as much as you will, you cannot please the colonists with anything short of absolute independence.' Rogers was frankly pessimistic.

On the other hand, Mr W. E. Gladstone, who on two occasions during this period served in the Colonial Office and who later, as prime minister, would preside over numerous imperial crises, thoroughly approved of the coming of free trade and responsible government. The colonial reformers regarded Gladstone as an exponent of their views. Gladstone believed that the colonies bore the relation to Britain of children to a parent, and that as they reached manhood Britain should reduce 'not political influence, but power over colonies to a minimum'. He also believed that the colonies should become responsible for their own defence. In part this was to save Britain money, but he was also convinced that without self-defence colonies could never reach the 'full possession and enjoyment of freedom'. Gladstone was not a pessimist like Rogers. But he thought colonies would remain loyal only on the basis of the maximum amount of self-government. The changes of the 1840s and 1850s were the true salvation of empire.

Gladstone's great political rival of the future thought otherwise. As the Australian constitutions were under discussion in Parliament, Benjamin Disraeli became leader of the Conservatives in the House of Commons, and he expressed many misgivings about the coming of free trade and responsible government. He refused to join the colonial reformers' society and expressed a distaste for 'Wakefieldism'. As the Old Colonial System was swept away Disraeli believed the Conservatives should find ways of 'reconstructing' the empire; that empire 'consolidation' might be made a great Conservative principle. He toyed with the idea of a customs union with the colonies, of making them an integral part of the United Kingdom with representation at Westminster.

Although he failed to persuade the Conservative leaders in the 1850s, and eventually accepted free trade and responsible government as irrevocable, it is clear that at the time of their inception he viewed the new system with regret and doubt. At a later date, when the Liberal party caused some heart-searching in the colonies, he returned to his ideas of imperial consolidation.

Two quite different views about the destiny of the colonies emerged, therefore, from the great changes of the early Victorian age. They were new versions of the opposing pulls of provincialism and centralization. On the one hand, there was the liberal view of empire, implying that the only true tie of empire was that based on the greatest concession of local self-government. On the other hand, there were the 'reconstructors', few as yet, who wanted to consolidate the empire, and who still hankered after an empire centred on Great Britain.

3

The New Nations of the Victorian Age: Canada and New Zealand

THE EXTENSION of English parliamentary government to the colonies, through the system of responsible government, was one of the great achievements of the early Victorian age. Colonial governments became 'ministries' which retained power only if they had majorities in elected Parliaments. But the colonies were still unmistakably colonies. In matters of internal security and defence, commercial policy and finance, law and justice, the 'imperial factor' remained. Legally, the Crown was still supreme. In practice, the colonies required a good deal of assistance from the mother country.

The remaining constitutional ties between Britain and the colonies were loosened over a very long period. But the mid-Victorians took the first steps towards converting the colonies into nations. The building of the Dominion of Canada between 1867 and 1872 laid the foundations of a nation which has recently played a notable role in world affairs. It might be called the senior 'new nation' of the Commonwealth.

Two things must, however, be said at the outset about the new nations of the Victorian era. They were built initially by binding together regional groups of colonies into a federation or a union.

> These are not the days for small states [declared James Anthony Froude to a South African audience in 1875]. Small states make small men; the parish makes vestrymen; the town makes aldermen; the county makes politicians; but it is the country which makes statesmen and the greater the country the greater the statesmen.

The Dominion of Canada (1867) the Commonwealth of Australia (1901) and the Union of South Africa (1910) were all, in their different ways, fulfilling this doctrine. New Zealand, it is true, stood aloof from the Australian federation but she abolished her own provincial governments in 1876 and was the first of the colonies to produce a national economic development plan.

Nations, however, cannot be made against the will of their peoples. It is very striking that the only successful 'new states' of the Commonwealth, whether federal or unitary, were created by the consent, indeed the initiative, of colonial leaders. All the early federal schemes in the British empire failed. The American colonies would not agree to union in 1754. Federal schemes put forward for Australia and South Africa by the third Earl Grey in the 1840s were rejected. Lord Durham's proposal of a North American federation gained little support for twenty years.

Federations and unions dreamed-up in Whitehall tended to fail – as they have in recent years in the West Indies and Central Africa. Even where the initiative was local, as in Malaysia, permanence is not guaranteed. What, then, were the reasons which led the colonists to take the initiative themselves in the Victorian age? To find the answer, we must look at each case in some detail.

THE BUILDING OF THE DOMINION OF CANADA

The resentment and rebelliousness of British North America ended with responsible government. But problems of a different kind were very soon revealed. The colonial parliaments represented electorates which were too small to call forth noble statesmanship and the political parties were usually too ill-developed to permit really stable government. Thus colonial politics had a petty character. Governor Arthur Gordon (the son of a former Prime Minister, Lord Aberdeen) found in New Brunswick that 'as a rule, to be a member of the Assembly is proof that a man is uneducated and not a gentleman'. In the Canadian House of Commons the premier once cried to a notable opponent: 'You damned pup, I'll slap your chops for you.'

At the end of the 1850s the British North American empire, in spite of the achievement of responsible government in four colonies, remained an untidy array of unequal possessions. The maritime provinces – Nova Scotia, New Brunswick, Prince Edward Island and Newfoundland – remained small and comparatively static. Their links were still with Britain and New England, rather than with Canada and the hinterland. The largest colony, and centre of energy, was the United Province of Canada. With a population of 2 million and with most of its good land already settled, its ambitious sons began to turn their eyes to the west. Here, for two thousand miles to the Pacific, stretched the territories of Hudson's Bay Company. In contrast to the American west, where new states were steadily admitted to the Union (like Minnesota, 1858, and Oregon, 1859) only three small British settlements existed in the west.

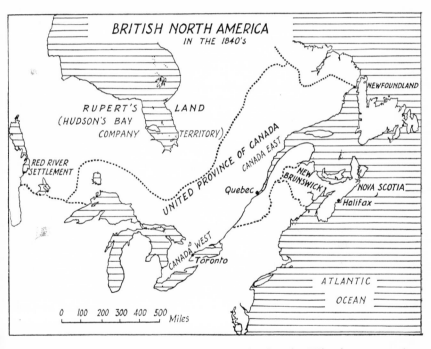

In the Red River valley, running south of Lake Winnipeg, a settlement founded by Lord Selkirk in 1811 now consisted of about a thousand English, Scots and American settlers, along with 8,000 *métis* of mixed French-Indian or English-Indian descent. Since 1836 the settlement had been ruled modestly by the governor and council of a Hudson's Bay Company district. In the Pacific North-west lay the Crown colony of Vancouver Island. Founded in 1849 as an outpost, the tiny settlement had a sudden boost when the news of gold finds in the Thompson and Fraser rivers on the mainland brought 25,000 prospectors from California in 1858. But just as the Australian gold rush raised a rival to New South Wales, so the Fraser River gold rush caused the foundation of the colony of British Columbia, which eventually swallowed Vancouver Island.

Britain had a vast domain in North America awaiting development. But Vancouver Island and Nova Scotia were so separated, both politically and geographically, that they appeared to be in different worlds. In fact, British North America, with its chartered company, Crown colony, representative institutions and responsible government, presented a complete spectrum of colonial history. How were all the pieces ever brought together?

Federation or Union?

The 1850s were, in general, a period of prosperity and expansion in British North America. The population increased by more than a million in ten years. Millions of pounds were invested by British capitalists in colonial railways – notably in the project for a Grand Trunk line to link up the eastern colonies, to tap the western hinterland and eventually to create a land route to the Far East. A union of the colonies had frequently been advocated and in 1851 Sir Edmund Head, governor of New Brunswick, looked forward to 'a powerful independent state' as a counter to the United States. British politicians realized that the new governments were too small. 'I believe the consolidation of the provinces into one Government', wrote the Duke of Newcastle in 1853, 'will eventually be found the surest, if not the only remedy, for . . . evils attaching to these small assemblies.' Railway projects and talk of settling Hudson's Bay Company lands created a favourable climate for union. The railway and the western dreams were, perhaps, the first move in the direction of confederation.

The new Dominion when it came, however, was based on severely practical issues rather than general inclinations. In 1856 Sir Edmund Head (now governor of Canada) informed the Colonial Office that federal union between Canada and the Maritimes was still impracticable. Canada's interests were to the west; only the Maritimes had their interests in common. Head proposed that Nova Scotia, New Brunswick and Prince Edward Island should unite. 'Maritime Union' was soon under discussion, and thus a second step towards eventual confederation was made.

Political Deadlock in the Province of Canada

The most important reason for Canadian confederation lay in the Province of Canada. Although it was the largest, most dynamic colony, the Union of 1841 led to political instability and deadlock. The cause is not hard to find: union did not eradicate English and French rivalry. The former colonies of Upper Canada (Canada West) and Lower Canada (Canada East) had equal representation in the Assembly. Yet by the 1850s the population of English-speaking Canada West had surpassed the French in Canada East. The cry went up from George Brown, editor of the Toronto *Globe* and leader of the radical reformers of the west, for 'Representation by Population'. The future certainly seemed to lie with the English and the west.

For the present, however, any government, in order to retain power, needed a 'double majority' – a majority from both East and West. The only stable element was the moderate *Parti Bleu* of Canada East, which was always the majority party in the French-speaking section and also provided the biggest single group in the provincial Assembly. Until 1854 they allied with a Reform majority from Canada West to form a series of 'Reform' ministries. After 1854 the *Bleus* allied with the Conservatives of Canada West to make a Liberal-Conservative alliance. No united opposition party developed. The radicals of Canada East, the *Parti Rouge*, were too small. The growing body of liberals in Canada West were divided between the moderates, who supported the Liberal-Conservative ministry, and Brown's radical, frontier reformers, known as the *Clear Grits* ('All sand and no dirt – clear grit all the way through'). Thus, ironically, instead of 'Rep. by Pop.', Canada was always governed by consent of the French *Bleus*.

The Liberal-Conservative alliance found its majority precarious. Voting on issues like the choice of Ottawa as a provincial capital cut across party lines and produced a return to national divisions. Yet an alternative government became even more unlikely. In 1858 when the *Grits* and *Rouges* formed a government under George Brown, it was defeated after only two days. This political strait-jacket in the province of Canada was the basic cause of confederation.

The Federation Policy

After the crisis of 1858 and the failure of Brown's two-day government, a Liberal-Conservative ministry under John A. Macdonald and George Étienne Cartier approached Alexander Galt, one of the

F

notable financiers of the colony. Galt had already produced a solution for the colony's political deadlock. He realized that two basic conditions were necessary for union: 'it is impossible to say to Upper Canada that larger population is not to bring larger representation, but it is equally true that Lower Canada has feelings and prejudices which could not be over-ridden.' To satisfy both and to ensure a great future, Galt suggested splitting the United Province into two colonies, forming a federal union with the Maritimes, and acquiring Hudson's Bay Company's territories in order to open up and colonize the Canadian west. In 1858 Galt made this plan a condition for joining the government, and Sir Edmund Head, the governor, undertook to persuade the British government.

Unfortunately the Colonial Office found the scheme 'very startling'. They realized that the Canadian government was using it 'as a way of getting out of a political scrape'. Sir Edward Bulwer-Lytton, a romantic novelist in poor health, was colonial secretary, and Canadian delegates who visited London made no headway. But in 1859 the Duke of Newcastle took over the Colonial Office and was obviously more open-minded towards the scheme. Moreover in 1860 Newcastle visited Canada in attendance with the Prince of Wales, who went to lay the corner-stone of the Parliament House in Ottawa. For a colonial secretary to visit the empire was a rare thing in the Victorian age. Newcastle became uniquely qualified to appreciate Canadian problems. It was he who laid down the procedure which led to confederation.

Privately Newcastle thought that federal union was desirable. He approved of Maritime Union and did not think it would preclude a wider union later. But he was convinced that the initiative had to come from the colonies. In 1860 he informed the North American Governors that the British government did not feel it their duty to 'initiate any movement towards such a union', but they did not want 'to impede any well-considered scheme which may have the concurrence of the people of the provinces'. It was now up to the colonies. As the Canadian government became preoccupied with other matters, the most likely project in the early 1860s appeared to be Maritime Union.

The Role of the United States

Another crisis occurred in 1862, which served to emphasize a further major reason for confederation. British North America was overshadowed by, even fearful of, the United States. Ever since Durham, advocates of union had talked of a 'counterbalance' to American power. Canadians were anxious to gain Hudson's Bay Company's territory for fear that the expanding American frontier would not respect the 49th parallel. In 1861 Canadian fears had more serious point. After the outbreak of the civil war, Canada as neutral territory became the scene of activity by American anti-government 'fifth columnists' from the north and Confederate agents from the south. As British territory, the North American colonies became vulnerable when the Union government engaged in disputes with Britain. The kidnapping of two confederate agents from the s.s. *Trent* in November 1861 produced a diplomatic crisis which might have developed into war between Britain and the Union in North America.

For this reason the question of colonial defence, which was one of the problems left unsolved at the granting of responsible government, contributed to the political instability of Canada. Although the British government sent reinforcements to North America after the *Trent* affair, it was well known that a Select Committee of Parliament had urged the government to reduce her military commitments in the colonies. The Canadian government realized that local defence forces were urgently necessary. But a militia Bill presented to the Canadian Parliament in May 1862 led to the government's downfall. The opposition managed to build a 'reform ministry' under John Sandfield Macdonald, but it lasted less than a year. By 1864, after three ministries in twelve months, and a steady growth of Confederate activity on Canadian soil, the colony began to feel doubly vulnerable. Canada's precarious political balance only intensified her military weakness.

The main rivals in Canada now agreed to sink their differences. On the condition that Galt's confederation project be adopted, George Brown led the Canada West *Grits* into a coalition with John A. Macdonald's Conservatives and Cartier's *Bleus*. A most remarkable group of eager politicians, mostly still in their forties, were welded together, and are revered today as the 'fathers of the confederation'. On 1 September 1864 they descended upon Charlottetown, the charming capital of Prince Edward Island, to confer with the leaders of the Maritime provinces. Here, amid cigar smoke and grandiose after-dinner talk, the idea of Maritime Union was quietly dropped in favour of a wider North American Union. After sessions at Halifax and St John (10 and 14 September) the conference agreed to re-convene in Quebec after a month to draft a federal project which would be put to the British government.

Then, even while the new constitution was taking shape, a further warning of their insecurity was given. Twenty Confederate agents had crossed the border into Vermont and put up in hotels in St Albans as members of a Montreal angling club. On 19 October the leader melodramatically declared, 'In the name of the Confederate States, I take possession of St Albans.' They then raided the banks, stole horses and raced for the border. They were about to be arrested by U.S. sheriffs who had crossed the border in pursuit, when a British officer persuaded the Americans to leave them in his hands. As a result of the incident, the American military commander of the border region ordered that in future raids his troops should 'pursue them into Canada if necessary and destroy them'. The St Albans raid was only the most dramatic of a series of incidents which compromised the British colonies, and convinced their leaders that adequate defence was necessary. Thus, in a moment of excitement the Quebec conference completed its work. The Quebec Resolutions, which were to be the basis for the constitution of a British North American confederation, were sent to the Colonial Office on 7 November 1864, with the hearty approval of Lord Monck, the Governor-General.

Britain's Immediate Approval

The British government's reply was prompt and favourable. Newcastle had already made it clear that projects from the colonies would be seriously considered. The government was anxious to economize on overseas garrisons and to avoid embarrassing entanglements with the United States. The Quebec Resolutions were immediately circulated to the Cabinet. On 2 December 1864 George Brown arrived in England and after he had called on the Colonial Office next day, Edward Cardwell, the colonial secretary, replied to the Governor-General that he approved of the resolutions as the basis for a new constitutional act. Brown went to visit the prime minister, Lord Palmerston, in Hampshire, and the Editor of *The Times* was told to support the new constitution. By the end of 1864 Britain was firmly committed to building a great new state in North America.

Unfortunately all was not plain sailing. In 1865 the colonial parliaments had to consider the project. In grand, lengthy debates in the

Canadian Parliament during February and March 1865, John A. Macdonald argued that not only would confederation break their own political deadlock and contribute to colonial defence, but that 'a great nationality' would be born. Canada voted 91—33 in favour. But in the Maritimes there was a great deal of opposition. Prince Edward Island and Newfoundland stood aloof; Nova Scotia was disunited; in New Brunswick the pro-confederation government was swept from power. Indeed, to bring the Maritimes into line a good deal of pressure from London and Ottawa was employed.

Canadian delegates in London in 1865 persuaded Cardwell to order the Governor-General to use 'every proper means' to persuade the Maritimes. He informed the governor of New Brunswick that in a small colony which relied on Britain for its defence he had a duty to urge the colonists to adopt policies which would contribute to their security. The governor had to convey to his Parliament 'the strong and deliberate opinion of Her Majesty's government in favour of Confederation'. In the end thousands of dollars were forthcoming from Canada to ensure the election of a Unionist government in New Brunswick in 1866.

The British North America Act

The final step was reached when Lord Carnarvon presented the British North America Act to the House of Lords on 19 February 1867. All parties supported the measure. The new constitution united the four provinces of Ontario, Quebec, Nova Scotia and New Brunswick, and made provision for the later admission of Newfoundland, Prince Edward Island, British Columbia and new provinces in the west. Government was to be conducted in the name of the Crown, on the advice of a Privy Council for Canada. Parliament would consist of the Senate (comprising originally 72 senators appointed by the Governor-General for life) and the House of Commons, elected, for the time being, according to existing electoral qualifications. In the Provinces, Lieutenant-Governors appointed by the Governor-General-in-Council would be officers of the Dominion. In the distribution of powers between central and provincial governments certain exclusive powers were granted to the central government, some specific matters were delegated to the provincial governments, but any matters not exclusively reserved to the provinces were reserved to the confederation. Thus, in intention, Canada, in contrast to the

U.S.A., was to be a 'strong centre' not a 'states rights' federation.

Although the words 'cabinet' and 'prime minister' do not appear in the act, Canada was to follow the British constitution, by which the acts of the Crown were decided by the Cabinet. The name 'Kingdom of Canada' was, indeed, briefly mooted as a possible title for the confederation. But to avoid offending the United States the new nation was styled the 'Dominion of Canada'.

'We are laying the foundations of a great state,' said Carnarvon in the House of Lords, 'perhaps one which at a future day may even overshadow this country.' Sir Charles Adderley emphasized, in the House of Commons, that the confederation adhered strictly to the constitutional forms of the mother country. Cardwell declared that the main justification was 'the development of the U.S.A.' Gladstone, supporting a loan for the building of an inter-colonial railway from Halifax and the St Lawrence (a condition of the act), extolled the moral virtues of self-government and self-defence. He declared his faith in the new colonial system which Canada, through responsible government, and now confederation, had pioneered. 'The connection between this country and her colonies is not a selfish and sordid connection, and ought not to be so on either side. No; it is at once a connection of interest, of honour, feeling, and duty.'

Dominion from the Atlantic to the Pacific?

The Dominion of Canada was heralded by a salute of guns before the Parliament House in Ottawa on 1 July 1867. Canadians celebrate this annually as 'Dominion Day'. In the next few years, the Dominion faced numerous challenges. Canada still relied for her wealth on agriculture, fisheries and lumbering. Her folk heroes were 'lumberjacks'. Montreal, the biggest town, only numbered about 100,000 citizens. The inter-colonial railway was not completed until 1876. Some Nova Scotians tried to separate from the Dominion in 1868; Prince Edward Island did not join until 1873; Newfoundland kept out for nearly a century.

The Dominion's most immediate problem concerned the west. In 1868 the British Parliament passed the Rupert's Land Act permitting the territories of Hudson's Bay Company to be transferred to the Dominion, and in the following year (after more than a decade of wrangling) agreement was reached on the terms of the transfer. Canada would pay £300,000 to the company, which would also retain its

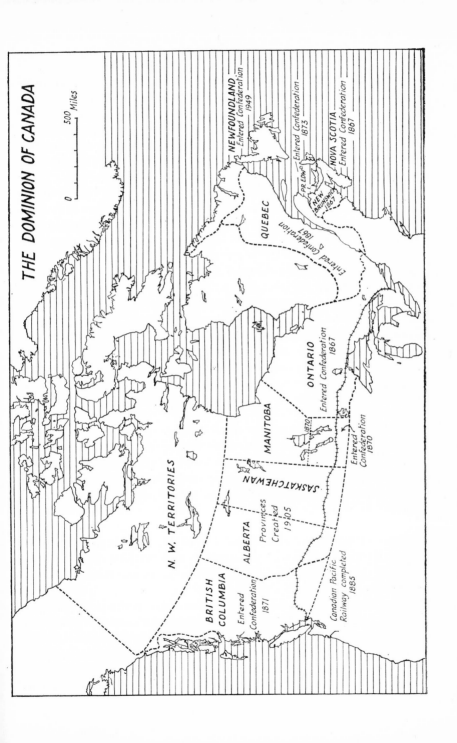

THE DOMINION OF CANADA

500 Miles

0

NEWFOUNDLAND
Entered Confederation
1949

PR. EDW'D
Entered Confederation
1873

NEW
BRUNSWICK
1867

NOVA SCOTIA
Entered Confederation
1867

QUEBEC
Entered Confederation
1867

ONTARIO
Entered Confederation
1867

MANITOBA
1870

SASKATCHEWAN

Entered
Confederation
1870

N. W. TERRITORIES

ALBERTA
Provinces
Created
1905

BRITISH
COLUMBIA
Entered
Confederation
1871

Canadian Pacific
Railway completed
1885

trading posts and a proportion of fertile land. The date of transfer for the new Canadian empire was fixed for 1 December 1869.

Riel's Rebellion and Manitoba

Unfortunately both the British and Canadian governments had reckoned without the inhabitants of the Red River valley. If there were many who welcomed the end of the company's moribund régime, there were several thousand French-speaking *métis* – men of mixed Indian-French descent – who resented being 'sold' to the Canadians. As the Dominion government instructed William McDougall, the new governor, to take over the territory, the passions of the *métis* were inflamed by the presence of a survey party preparing a road to link up the settlement with the Great Lakes. A 'National Committee' was hastily formed in October 1869 to resist the Canadian 'invasion', led by Louis Riel, an eloquent, bilingual, well-educated young man of French-Indian blood. Fort Garry was occupied by the insurgents. Their grievances were legitimate; Riel agreed to negotiate. But a number of unfortunate incidents occurred.

Although the prime minister carefully warned McDougall that 'you cannot force your way in', the new governor (after being turned away) crossed the border on the night of 30 November 1869 and proclaimed Canadian sovereignty to the moonlit prairies. A week later Riel promulgated a 'Declaration of the People of Rupert's Land' and announced the formation of a provisional government. The Dominion government was so alarmed that it tried to wriggle out of the crisis by 'postponing' the transfer and leaving the responsibility for a settlement to the British government. Most serious of all was the shooting in March 1870 of one of the road survey party, a drunken Ulsterman named Scott, as an example to unruly Canadians. Thus, although an amnesty had been proclaimed and negotiations were already beginning through the mediation of the Roman Catholic bishop, Riel's 'execution' or 'murder' of Scott cast a shadow over the whole affair.

In one sense Riel succeeded. The Dominion government agreed to create the first new province in the Red River region. The Manitoba Act of 1870 provided safeguards for the French language and Roman Catholic worship and education. In some ways Manitoba became a second French province. No opposition was offered when a military expedition under Colonel Garnet Wolseley marched to the Red River to symbolize Dominion authority in the summer of 1870. Riel ordered the Union Jack to be hoisted over Fort Garry and he disbanded the *métis* army. Manitoba became a province without further bloodshed.

But many Canadians – especially Ontario Ulstermen – wanted to avenge the death of Scott. The British government refused to grant an amnesty to Riel and insisted this was now a Dominion decision. But the prime minister of Canada dared not offend a large group of the electorate. He offered $1,000 to Riel to keep outside Dominion jurisdiction, and although Riel was twice elected a Member of the federal Parliament for Manitoba, he was never allowed to take his seat. The addition of the first new province, therefore, was an ominous reminder to the new Dominion that Anglo-French passions still lay beneath the surface.

British Columbia

British Columbia was the final link in the unbroken dominion from the Atlantic to the Pacific about which so many had dreamed. But, as in the Maritimes, pressure from Britain was necessary before British Columbia would join the confederation. The first stage was passed in 1866 when Vancouver Island, under threat of abandonment, agreed to merge with the mainland to form a single colony of British Columbia. To this day the provincial capital remains in the pleasant English town of Victoria on Vancouver Island. But the inhabitants of British Columbia were not eager to enter confederation. As the governor reported in 1867, 'merely to join the Confederation on the condition of sending delegates to Ottawa, and receiving a Governor from the Canadian Ministry, would not satisfy the popular desire.' Moreover the colony had fallen on hard times; it had debts amounting to $1½ million and wished to put its terms high.

Thus, after the transfer of Rupert's Land, it was left to the Colonial Office to apply some pressure. In 1869 a new governor was sent to British Columbia with instructions to take such steps as he 'properly and constitutionally' could to promote support for confederation. In 1870 a delegation went to Ottawa and secured agreement to the colony's terms. British Columbia would receive responsible government, her debts would be taken over and federal subsidies granted, and above all a railway to the Pacific was promised in ten years. In July 1871 British Columbia entered the Dominion.

Canada and the Mother Country

The first 'new nation' of the Commonwealth was built by a combination of colonial initiative and imperial pressure. It was designed
primarily to solve problems which responsible government did not
solve. Its chief aim was to create a state in place of a congeries of
colonies, to widen the scope of Canadian politics, to improve self-
defence, and to relieve Britain of expensive, ambiguous and constitutionally tricky commitments. What did Englishmen and
Canadians think of the result?

British statesmen, whatever their party, were conscious that they
were laying the foundations of a great nation. The respect which
Canada has earned in the United Nations has amply fulfilled their
hopes. In their attitude to Britain's relations with the new Dominion
British leaders were eager to relax irksome ties. Lord Granville, the
colonial secretary, made a most significant statement of the government's view in 1869:

> It has been more and more felt on both sides that Canada is part of the
> British Empire because she desires to be so, and that under the influence
> of this conviction the attachment of the Colonies to Great Britain had
> grown with the growth of their independence. Her Majesty's Govern-
> ment value the existing relation as the symbol and support of that
> attachment. They value it while it is valued by the Canadians and
> while it is useful to the Canadians. They have no desire to maintain it
> for a single year after it had become injurious or distasteful to them.

Granville may not have intended the Governor-General to announce,
as he did, that Canada was 'in reality independent'. But, when in
subsequent years disputes arose over technical problems of British
jurisdiction in Canada, the Colonial Office usually supported the
Canadian case. In 1876 Carnarvon agreed that in theory the powers of
Parliament in Westminster were not superseded by the grant of local
self-government. But 'whether and in what way the responsibility of
using this power should at any time be exercised is', he suggested, 'a
separate question'. Political expediency dictated that Britain should
not interfere in the affairs of the Dominion.

Canadians, for their part, evolved their own brand of nationalism
combined with imperial attachment. For all but seven of the twenty-
five years which followed Confederation, Canada was led by Sir John
A. Macdonald, the first Dominion premier and greatest of the 'fathers

of confederation'. In building Canada's first great political party Macdonald achieved the remarkable feat of uniting Protestant Orangemen of Canada West and Catholic *Bleus* of Canada East. Thus Macdonald was the great reconciler of the passions of the old colony, and his Liberal-Conservative Party, the party of businessmen and industrialists, came to stand for a 'National Policy'. Government combined with business to build a viable Canadian economy. Tariffs were raised to protect native industry. The last spike was driven into the track of the Canadian Pacific Railway in 1885, after massive government land grants, subsidies and loans had kept the company from disaster. A revolt by the Indians and *métis* of the Saskatchewan River region in 1885, led once more by Louis Riel, was suppressed by force and ended in Riel's execution. Free homesteads were then granted to settlers to open up the prairies.

The Dominion overcame its growing pains. The 1880s were a decade of depression; the North-West rebellion and the cost of the Canadian Pacific Railway nearly broke the government; many Canadians emigrated to the U.S.A., and the provinces began to assert a 'states rights' interpretation of the constitution. But when the Liberal opposition party produced an alternative policy of 'Commercial Union' with the United States, Macdonald fought and won an election in 1891 with the slogan 'The old man, the old flag, the old policy!' 'A British subject I was born, a British subject I will die!' The 'National Policy' was vindicated.

By the end of the nineteenth century, as the population approached 5½ million, Canada's main characteristics as a nation had emerged. She was a North American state, where the 'businessman' was fast becoming the typical figure, but where prairie farmers contributed greatly to the national wealth, and where a 'frontier' still existed in the forests of the west. In all this she followed the United States.

But Canada was also a British state, with a Parliamentary government, allegiance to the Crown, and many attachments to Great Britain. Scarlet-coated Royal Canadian Mounted Police rode through London at Queen Victoria's diamond jubilee in 1897, when Sir Wilfrid Laurier (recently elected Liberal prime minister) received his knighthood from the Queen. A great test to the British connection came during the South African war when, after bitter controversy and much soul-searching, Canada agreed that volunteer detachments might support the British army. But the decision was definitely a Canadian one. Laurier announced:

> I claim for Canada this, that in future she shall be at liberty to act, or not to act, to interfere or not to interfere, to do just as she pleases.

With these words the Canadian Prime Minister set the tone for Canada's attitude to relations with Britain and the wider affairs of the empire.

SELF-GOVERNMENT IN NEW ZEALAND

After the Dominion of Canada, New Zealand was the first colony to assert its nationhood. This could be seen by the 1870s in Sir Julius Vogel's development programme which involved borrowing £10 million over ten years for building roads and railways and for attracting population. Although he was much criticized at the time, Vogel was only doing what has become normal for developing nations today. He produced the Commonwealth's first 'Ten Year Plan'.

By the 1880s New Zealand's government had become, in practice if not in theory, independent of Whitehall. When Sir Arthur Gordon arrived as governor in 1880 he found that he was reduced to being the rubber stamp of the government in power. 'Here,' he wrote, 'the jealousy of the legislature and the arrogance of successive ministries have deprived the Governor not only of all influence in public affairs but to a great extent even the means of obtaining any knowledge of them.' His first news of many government acts came from the newspapers. With a population only one-tenth the size of Canada, New Zealand achieved a similar status in relation to Britain.

Yet, for all her early 'independence' of government, New Zealand became the most loyal of the new nations. To this day she remains the most 'British' portion of the Commonwealth. How do we account for her early grasp of autonomy, and her continuing affection for the mother country?

Responsible Government in Difficulties

Responsible government was always a transitory phase. We have seen that when it was granted in the 1840s and 1850s many questions remained open. No clear demarcation between 'imperial' and 'colonial' responsibilities was drawn. Thus, responsibility for internal security, defence, commercial policy, and relations with non-European inhabitants led to subsequent disputes. In New Zealand, with its scattered settlements and large Maori population, responsible government led to confusion and bitterness.

Although the original grant of responsible government had been generously made almost immediately after the calling of a General Assembly, it was qualified in two ways. First, the governor insisted that Maori affairs should be conducted subject to the Secretary of State's approval. As Britain would have to provide for defence, he felt she should have a voice in Maori policy. Secondly, the provinces became the really effective centres of political power. The Provincial Councils developed parliamentary procedures and the superintendents became virtually elected Lieutenant-Governors. Waste lands, land revenue and immigration were controlled by the provinces, which also received three-eighths of the customs revenue and all surplus general revenue not allocated to general purposes. Thus New Zealand had, until 1876, a *de facto* federal system. As one writer has put it, 'Responsible government was curtailed at both ends.' New Zealand emerged as a nation, only after the problems of the Maoris and the provinces had been solved.

The Causes of the Maori Wars

The Maori wars were the main reason for tension between Britain and New Zealand. Conflict between the races was probably inevitable, because when Britain annexed New Zealand she adopted two contradictory policies. She undertook to protect the Maoris by the treaty of Waitangi (1840) and she also permitted colonization. Two entirely different cultures, the one expanding and the other contracting, competed for the same soil. It would have taken incredible enlightenment on the part of the colonists and great forbearance and adaptability on the part of the Maoris to avoid conflict. As it was, settlers clamoured for more and more land, and for forty years the Maoris resisted in various ways.

Part of the trouble arose because contact with European traders, missionaries and settlers caused a decline of Maori institutions. As a chief complained in 1848, 'Now this land is mixed up with the customs of the Europeans. New thoughts or habits have been imbibed and darkness has ensued in consequence.' The greatest single problem was the land. All land was owned tribally and at first its *use* alone was allowed to Europeans. But the colonists wanted to buy land. A Land Department was created to purchase land from the tribes to sell to the settlers. Great efforts were made, at first, to ensure consent to the purchases, but government agents became increasingly slack, and the settlers clamoured for direct purchases and sales by individual Maoris.

The government's chief fault was its failure to decide upon a way of regulating the contact between English and Maori cultures. Most colonists assumed that the Maoris were doomed to extinction. Others thought that they should have their own exclusive districts. A few like Governor George Grey believed that by adapting European ideas of government for the Maoris for a time, while providing education, mixing settlement, and tying the Maori to the colonial economy, they would be gradually integrated into New Zealand settler society. Unfortunately the colonial government failed to acquire the loyalty of the Maoris, and therefore was an inadequate substitute for the old Maori form of government.

Thus, the Maoris resisted colonial encroachments. At first they merely interrupted surveyors, burnt a few houses or pulled down the

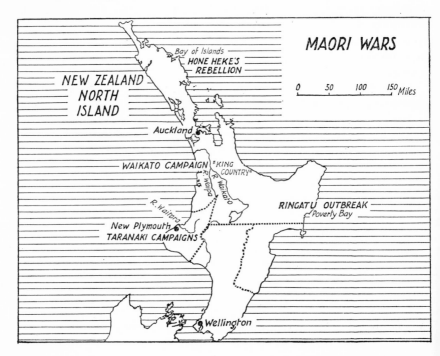

Union Jack. Later they turned to killing. Hone Heke's 'rebellion' in the Bay of Islands in 1844 led to two years of fighting. In the 1850s the government found itself faced with a formidable movement, as many of the Maoris in North Island began to think of national unity.

A chief, Tamihana Te Rauparaha, who in 1851 had visited Britain and been presented to Queen Victoria, began to preach a form of Maori nationalism. In 1854, as the colonists clamoured for responsible government, the first of a series of great Maori meetings took place which led to the election of a Maori king. In 1858, a great Waikato chief Te Whero Whero (one of those who had not signed the treaty of Waitangi) became King Potatau I, and received a loose allegiance from most of the tribes of the central portion of North Island. The 'Kingites' did not want war. But when in 1859 the governor upheld an individual land sale by a minor chief which was strongly opposed on behalf of the tribe by a senior chief, a series of tragic conflicts began.

In 1860–61 there was war in Taranaki. After an uneasy truce, and another attempt to provide for a local government for the Maoris by Governor Grey, war flared up in the Waikato River in July 1863. Gallantly defending their fortified villages, or *pas*, against over-whelming odds, the Maoris held off government troops until the spring of 1864. After this the second Maori king, Matutaera, retired into the hills of central North Island, where he refused to submit for seventeen years.

In Taranaki, meanwhile, a still more dangerous Maori resistance appeared. In 1862 Te Ua, a Maori well versed in the Bible, claimed a vision in which the Angel Gabriel assured him that the Europeans would be driven from New Zealand. This became the basis of a new religion, a compound of Old Testament myth, Christian teaching and primitive Maori belief. The *Hau Hau* fanatics, as they were called, reverted to cannibalism, fearlessly attacked the settlers and caused constant alarm in New Plymouth for five years.

In 1868 a new threat appeared on the east coast. Te Kooti, a Maori imprisoned in the Chatham Islands, escaped to found another pseudo-Christian sect, called *Ringatu*. Striking first at Poverty Bay, he killed thirty-three settlers. For three years he terrorized the area and eluded capture, until in 1872 he was allowed to slip away to the 'King' country. He was finally pardoned in 1883.

During the decade of the 1860s, therefore, North Island was racked by the Maori wars. First in the 'King' movement, then in the religious fanaticism, thousands of Maoris defied the settlers. Probably 2,000 resisters were killed, along with 500 Europeans and nearly as many friendly Maoris. Although 7 million acres of their lands were confiscated as punishment, the Maoris were not completely subdued. The central part of North Island, the 'King' country, was given a wide berth until the 1880s. Maori prowess in arms excited admiration, and colonial militia served under friendly Maori officers. In 1867, a start was made at atoning for the conflict by the starting of a Maori school system and the election of four Maoris to the House of Representatives. The Maori wars had painfully taught New Zealand to respect the original inhabitants. What effect did they have on the colony's relations with Britain?

The Effects of the Maori Wars

Responsibility for Maori affairs and defence had both been reserved to the home government. In practice, the governor and secretary of state usually upheld the land purchases of the New Zealand government in the 1850s. But during the 1860s, as many New Zealanders seemed over-anxious to fight the Maoris and to confiscate large tracts of land to punish their resistance, the Colonial Office became increasingly uneasy. British taxpayers objected to providing troops to enforce Maori policies which they disapproved of. Thus, in 1863 the New Zealand government was persuaded to take responsibility for Maori affairs and over the next few years the imperial troops were withdrawn. Britain's attitude during the Maori wars, in fact, led to a major crisis in relations with the mother country.

In 1864 there were 10,000 British troops in New Zealand. The editor of *The Times* declared:

> We have lost all Imperial control in this portion of the Empire, and are reduced to the humble but useful function of finding men and money for a Colonial Assembly to dispose of in exterminating natives with whom we have no quarrel.

Already, because of the lesson of the American civil war, Parliament had called upon the government to withdraw the overseas garrisons and to urge the self-governing colonies to defend themselves. As Gladstone asserted, 'the burdens of war are the providential preventatives of war.' In 1863 the Colonial Office had warned the New Zealand government that the war was 'not chargeable to the Imperial

Government', that the imperial troops would be reduced and any remaining would require a local subsidy of £40 a man. In 1865 Cardwell, the colonial secretary, notified the New Zealand government that the garrison would be reduced to three battalions, for which the £40 charge would have to be paid. Thus, in spite of the *Hau Hau* atrocities, the British government continued to reduce its commitments to New Zealand. It was determined to force the colonial government to face the consequences of its Maori policy.

Frantic appeals from New Zealand were rebuffed by a succession of secretaries of state. There was, of course, no question that if a massacre of the colonists had been imminent Britain would have aided them. But when, as the last battalion prepared to leave in 1869, final appeals were cabled from the governor, Lord Granville decided: 'I think we must harden our hearts.' In fact, through dispatches which were published in New Zealand in 1869 and 1870, he roundly blamed the New Zealanders for the Maori troubles. It was no service to the colony to provide a false sense of security, he said; real safety lay in a 'deliberate measuring of their resources . . . and adjusting their policy to them'.

Britain's recall of her troops during the Maori wars embittered many of the colonists. Like the Canadians immediately after confederation, New Zealanders felt that the mother country was seeking to 'drive the colony out of the Empire'. A leading New Zealand politician on a visit to London in 1896 wrote accusingly to Lord Granville, 'You have, in fact, resolved upon abandoning the colony.' William Fox, the premier, even approached the U.S. consul in New Zealand and expressed a hope that closer relations might develop between New Zealand and the United States as a result of a steamship line across the Pacific which was about to be inaugurated.

There was no real substance in the New Zealand accusations, and Granville categorically denied any intention of abandoning the colony. He explained (what might have been made clear rather earlier) that the troops were withdrawn from 'a conviction that employment of British troops . . . in a colony possessing responsible government was objectionable in principle except in the case of foreign war'. One of the anomalies of responsible government was, in fact, being removed.

The New Zealanders' resentment soon gave way to protestations of imperial loyalty. But the lesson of the defence controversy was learnt. In the 1870s the colonial government disposed of the other unsolved

G

questions of responsible government by steadily excluding the discretion of the governor from all aspects of its government. By the 1880s full ministerial responsibility had become accepted in New Zealand. Sir Arthur Gordon, who became governor in 1880, found the duties of governor 'altogether formal and mechanical'. Lord Kimberley, the secretary of state, confirmed, in 1882: 'It is for his ministers to judge what advice they give . . .' New Zealand had, therefore, in a matter of thirty years achieved full internal autonomy. But this did not mean that she did not require British assistance or that she wished to be really 'independent' of Britain. The policy of Vogel in the 1870s well illustrates New Zealand's imperial ties.

Vogel's Ten-Year Plan

As the Maori wars drew to a close a figure rose to prominence who managed to combine the roles of New Zealand's first 'nation builder' and her first great 'imperialist'. Julius Vogel was a small, London-born Jew, who had trained at the School of Mines before trying his fortune in the Australian and Otago gold rushes. After making a name for himself as a journalist in Otago, he was elected to the Provincial Council, and in 1863 to the General Assembly. By 1869, at the age of thirty-four, he became treasurer in a ministry headed by William Fox, and he prepared to launch the first colonial development project.

He rose in the Assembly in 1870 to announce his Public Works and Immigration Programme. New Zealand needed artificial stimulus. 'I contend that during the next ten years the Colony will run no risk if it commits itself to an expenditure of ten millions for railway and other purposes.' The money would be borrowed from abroad on the security of the public lands. In 1871 Vogel successfully negotiated the first loan in London and signed the first railway contracts.

For the next decade Vogel's policy dominated the scene. Although he filled the office of premier for only a few years, his mark on New Zealand was great. A colony which, in 1870, still had a population of only 250,000 embarked on a career of national development. Eventually £20 million were borrowed, over 1,000 miles of railway were built, along with 2,000 miles of roads. A network of telegraphs was created, including a link to Australia, and thus to Britain. A government Life Insurance Department and Public Trustee Office were founded. Over 100,000 immigrants were attracted. When the provincial governments threatened to frustrate his schemes, Vogel led the movement to abolish the provinces in 1876. In addition, New Zealand subsidized a short-lived American shipping line between San Francisco and Auckland, and dreamed of expansion into the Pacific Islands. Vogel revealed himself as an ardent imperialist as well as a national visionary and pictured New Zealand as the 'Great Britain of the South Seas'.

In spite of all the stimulus in the 1870s, Vogel's development programme was not an unqualified success. He was a gambler. Lavish borrowing lowered standards of public probity and saddled New Zealand with a crippling burden of debt. In the depression years of the 1880s money was tight and expenditure had to be cut. There was a good deal of poverty and an 'exodus' of population from the colony. New Zealand had, in fact, to find new ways of earning a living if its national development was to be fulfilled. Thus the opening of the government-supported Edendale cheese factory in 1882, and the arrival in London of the first load of frozen lamb in the refrigerator ship *Dunedin* in the same year, were landmarks as significant to the new nation's growth as Vogel's loans.

Seddon and the Founding of the 'Welfare State'

If the events of the 1860s and 1870s set New Zealand firmly on her course as a small, autonomous, unitary state, the peculiar character of New Zealand's nationhood became more formed by the social reforms of the Liberals at the turn of the century. By 1900 the population reached ¾ million, the majority of whom were in North Island. Half of them now were native-born. After the election of a Liberal government in 1890 New Zealand experienced an unprecedented legislative revolution which led an American historian to declare: 'New Zealand is the birthplace of the Twentieth Century.'

The Liberals who ruled New Zealand from 1890 to 1912 were un-doctrinaire, experimental 'state socialists'. They accepted the role of the state as the guarantor of the welfare of the individual. Government railways, telegraphs and life insurance were well-known in New Zealand; now government coal mines, fire insurance and mortgages were added. But the chief innovations of the Liberal programme were their land, labour and social reforms.

New land laws were designed to reduce large, under-used holdings and to increase the number of small farms. General graduated land and income taxes were imposed; a tax was placed on unimproved land;

and the government set aside money to pay for the buying of large estates. Factory laws were imposed and stringently enforced by inspectors. Most significant of all, the labour law provided for compulsory arbitration of labour disputes. Local arbitration boards were created, from which appeals might go to a Court of Arbitration, whose judgments could be given the force of law. An old-age pensions bill provided for the first, modest, non-contributory pension in the English-speaking world. Public health legislation led to the appointment of Health Officers, who ordered land drainage schemes, registration of diseases and the building of government sanatoria.

'New Zealand democracy is the talk of the world today', declared a famous American radical. As if to prove it, New Zealanders gave the vote to women in 1893 and in Richard John Seddon, premier from 1893 to 1906, they found their first great popular leader. Seddon was a bluff Lancashireman, who made his name as a miners' leader in Westland, South Island. As premier he inspired a warm devotion. When talking to delegates from a constituency or trade union, he was not above arranging for his secretary to come in to say that the Cabinet was waiting for him. 'Let them wait,' the premier would say, 'I'm talking with friends.' Seddon seemed to embody the young nation's equalitarian viewpoint.

Yet Seddon was also a great 'imperialist'. He hankered after British expansion in the Pacific and he even tried to resist the American annexation of Hawaii. Seddon was one of the few premiers from the empire to support ideas of imperial consolidation. New Zealand eagerly sent support to the British army during the South African war. Seddon cultivated close relations with Australia, but when it came to the question of federation he hesitated.

By the time the Australian colonies joined together in the Commonwealth of Australia in 1901 New Zealand had achieved a sense of national identity, combined with cordial relations with the mother country. Seddon's view was that they should wait and see how federation turned out before deciding whether to enter. But, as we shall see, although New Zealand delegates went to the early federal conferences, New Zealand remained a separate nation.

4

The New Nations of the Victorian Age: Australia and South Africa

THE FEDERAL MOVEMENT IN AUSTRALIA

IN THE mid-Victorian age, while Canada and New Zealand created strong central governments and Britain conceded them a wide measure of autonomy, relations with the Australia colonies were less satisfactory. A general approval for the idea of federation, first accepted in Britain in the 1840s, was reaffirmed on numerous occasions. But federation was very slow to catch on in Australia.

At the same time, the individual colonies resented interference by the mother country. Under responsible government a number of crises, of a rather technical constitutional nature, arose. Australian politicians espoused causes like commercial freedom, neutrality during British wars, even independence or republicanism. In an era when Britain found Canada and New Zealand professing a new loyalty based upon full internal self-government, many English leaders believed the Australian colonies would go the way of the United States. They could only hope that the colonies would unite before they did so. Sir Frederic Rogers, permanent under-secretary for colonial affairs, wrote in 1870, 'What I have always hoped has been that the Imperial connection could be maintained till the Australian colonies could be united, somehow, into a body politic.'

Provincialism in Australia

Why were the Australians so slow in desiring unity? The simple answer is that there was no overriding motive for unity to counteract colonial provincialism and rivalries. Arguments of convenience – about the need for a common tariff, for standard railway gauges, and for economic administration – were regarded as academic. The colonies would only work together if the need was imperative. Thus

89

their desire to modify the British policy of free trade by gaining the right to make inter-colonial reciprocity agreements led to a series of inter-colonial conferences in the years 1870–73 in order to concert their demands on the British government. But when the Secretary of State tried, instead, to persuade them to form a Customs Union, Victoria's protectionism could not be reconciled with New South Wales's free trade. The suggestion was rejected. Rivalry between Sydney and Melbourne dogged all early attempts at co-operation. When the first Federal Council was created in 1885, New South Wales remained outside, fearing dominance from Melbourne. The prime minister of New South Wales rudely dubbed the neighbouring colony a 'cabbage patch'.

A secondary reason for the delay of interest in federation may be found in the political instability which so often followed responsible government. In the absence of clearly defined political parties, politics in the Australian colonies, as in the Maritimes before Confederation, tended to be personal and petty. In the first forty years of responsible government, New South Wales had twenty-eight ministries, Victoria twenty-six, and South Australia no less than forty-two. With politicians preoccupied in the mechanics of getting and holding office, major issues of government were neglected, let alone the wider matter of inter-colonial union.

The Growth of National Feeling

In the middle of the 1880s a change became evident in Australia. Federation began to be urgently canvassed. After 1890 the argument became one about means rather than ends. How can we account for this sudden rise of federalism?

To couch the answer first in general terms, we may say that Australians were discovering a national consciousness. Sir Henry Parkes of New South Wales, one of the leading 'fathers of federation', called upon the colonies 'to rise to a higher level of national life, which would give them a larger space before the eyes of the world'. By 1890 as the population approached 4 million, 75 per cent native-born, Parkes calculated that the average *per capita* wealth of Australia was higher than in the U.S.A., Britain, France, Germany or Austria.

Australia's growing nationalism also displayed certain definite characteristics. One was a desire to exclude non-European immigrants. Ever since acts to exclude Chinese were passed at the time of the gold rush, Australian policy ran counter to British agreements with China. But the British government left immigration in the hands of the colonial parliaments, and in 1888 even negotiated a treaty with the Chinese government to discourage emigration to Australia. In a rather crude tract in 1888 entitled *Australian Nationalism*, the writer said of the Chinese: 'Their crime is that they are a cheap race – cheap to a degree that is destructive to the white race.'

In the same way the employment of Polynesians, 'kanakas' as they were called, on the sugar plantations of Queensland, which began in the 1860s, was regarded as a threat to Australian working men. In 1892 the premier of Queensland declared that their employment led to absentee farming and to the idea that labour in the tropical belt was degrading. More significantly he argued that 'the permanent existence of a large servile population amongst us, not admitted to the franchise, is not compatible with the continuance of our free political institutions'. The origins of the 'White Australia' policy of today lay in the fears of late Victorian colonists that their hard-won standards might be jeopardized by the presence of a potentially servile class.

A belief in the superior democratic and equalitarian nature of Australian society, therefore, formed the second ingredient of Australian nationalism. In the 1880s the colonial parliaments awoke from their political torpor and passed Australia's first great wave of social reforms. As in New Zealand, a firm belief grew up in the role of the state as guardian of the welfare of the individual. The eastern colonies passed laws to divide up the land into smaller holdings. Graduated income taxes, land taxes and death duties were imposed, and industrial arbitration, factory laws and old-age pensions introduced. In addition to the new laws, the rise of the trade unions and colonial Labour Parties led to a real demand for the redistribution of wealth. 'I am sure the growth of Socialism, true Socialism,' wrote a Labour journalist in 1892, 'will destroy tyranny and make men what men should be – *mates*. . . . Socialism is being *mates*, and you can't be made mates by legislation.'

Thus, 'mateship' rather than ideology formed a basis of Australia's equalitarian nationalism of the late Victorian age. A French observer who visited the colonies in 1900 coupled Australia with New Zealand as 'the workers' paradise'.

The Australasian worker has become a 'gentleman'. He dresses himself after his work, he is housed, and he behaves like a person of good society. . . . More and more one can observe the external difference between the worker and the bourgeois diminishing except during working hours.

Yet 'mates' displayed little solidarity with the international proletariat. They revered the Queen, went to church, supported temperance societies in great numbers and cheered Britain's imperial expansion.

Because of the widespread acceptance of, and pride in, this pragmatic, non-revolutionary doctrine of equality and political democracy the federal movement in Australia included a factor which was markedly absent in Canada: popular agitation for union. Trade unions had been holding inter-colonial congresses since 1879. A decision of the seventh Trade Union Congress in 1891 to enter politics on a national level led to the founding of the Australian Labour Party. Labour soon had definite views about the goals of a federation. The Australian Natives Association and the Federal League were organized specifically to popularize federation. With so much general interest in federation it is hardly surprising that the Australian constitutional convention was elected and that the draft constitutional bill was submitted to a referendum.

The Making of the Commonwealth of Australia

If national feeling, racial solidarity and equalitarian conviction formed the background to Australian federation, why and how did the actual constitution come to be made? Here it is possible to narrow the discussion of motive to the specific issue of defence.

Ever since the 1860s Australians had tried to proclaim a kind of 'Monroe Doctrine' for the South Pacific. France's annexation of New Caledonia in 1853 had been a warning that the region was not automatically a British sphere, and Australians and New Zealanders frequently called upon the British government to annex New Guinea, Fiji, Tonga, Samoa and other Pacific island groups. In the 1880s the sudden growth of international rivalry sparked off by the 'Scramble for Africa' made the colonies apprehensive about French and German designs in the Pacific.

In 1883 an inter-colonial conference was called, in which Fiji (annexed in 1874) and New Zealand also participated, where it was decided that an Australasian Federal Council should be formed. One problem, above all, was urgent. In fact, to forestall the Germans in New Guinea the government of Queensland went as far as annexing the eastern portion of the island to the colony. When Britain's disavowal of this act was followed by German annexation of the northern part of Papua in 1884, and by an undignified scramble on the part of Britain in the following year to secure the coast opposite Queensland, Australian resentment was understandable. Some colonial leaders claimed that if the Federal Council had existed in 1883 the Germans might have been kept out of New Guinea.

The Federal Council was created in 1885 by a British act of Parliament. The Council was supposed to meet bi-annually, in different capitals; self-governing colonies could send two representatives, Crown colonies one. In theory the Council was to make laws for certain matters of general concern such as relations between the colonies and the Pacific Islands. But the Council was a failure: New South Wales and New Zealand stayed out; Fiji was only represented at the first meeting, and South Australia did not join until 1889. By this time the defence issue had been given an entirely new complexion by the report of a British general on the Colonies' defences.

Major-General Bevan Edwards reported in 1889 that inter-colonial co-operation for defence was hampered by the difference in the militia organizations, the variety of railway gauges, and the isolation of the smaller colonies. The separation of Western Australia and Tasmania from the main centres of Australian life posed a threat to the east coast colonies. Edwards suggested federalizing the colonial military forces. His report appears to have convinced Sir Henry Parkes of New South Wales that the Federal Council was inadequate. He now called for a genuine federal Parliament. In 1890, when the first Federal Conference was held in Melbourne, Parkes spoke grandiloquently of an Australian nation taking its place in the British empire. 'Why should not the name of an Australian be equal to that of a Briton?' he asked. The Melbourne Conference decided to call a National Australasian Convention in 1891. Here, in Sydney, Parkes presented resolutions which formed the general basis of the constitution of the Commonwealth of Australia.

He proposed that the Australian federation, unlike Canadian Confederation, should bear a close affinity to the American Union. The existing colonies should retain all rights not delegated to the federal government, they should also have power to amend their constitutions. In the Federal Parliament, the upper house would follow the senate – both in name and in its continuous life (only one-third of the members retiring at each election). The House of Representatives would be elected by constituencies formed on the basis of population and would have sole power to vote money bills. The Federal Executive was, on the other hand, to follow British practice and be conducted in the name of the Governor-General by his advisers (the Cabinet) sitting in Parliament. In broad outline Parkes's project was accepted and largely embodied in the Commonwealth of Australia Act of 1900.

In view of this early agreement, why did the achievement of federation take a further ten years? First, there was disagreement about the division of revenue between central and states governments. Secondly, a decision had to be made on how the constitution would actually be drawn up. Thirdly, in view of the welling up of popular interest in the 1890s, the question arose as to how public consent should be expressed. Should the draft be submitted to the colonial parliaments, as in Canada? Sir Henry Parkes thought not. He suggested an elected Convention of delegates to draw up the constitution. This was agreed by a conference of premiers in 1895, which also decided that the constitution should be submitted to the electorate in referenda.

The elected drafting Convention met in Adelaide (March–April 1897) Sydney (September 1897) and Melbourne (January–March 1898). By now Fiji and New Zealand had definitely decided to stay out, but Western Australia (which received responsible government in 1890) was considering entry. The Convention drew up a Bill which was to be passed, like the British North America Act, by the British Parliament. A referendum was held in four colonies in 1898. But in view of the narrowness of the majority in New South Wales, a premiers' conference met in Melbourne in 1899 to consider amendments. These provided a method of dealing with deadlocks between houses in the federal Parliament; a division of customs and excise revenue which reserved at least three-quarters to the states; and a commitment to build eventually a federal capital which had to be at least 100 miles from Sydney. Referenda in all the colonies confirmed the draft bill in 1899–1900. It only remained then for delegates to take the bill to London and for Parliament to approve.

The Commonwealth of Australia and the Empire

The Commonwealth of Australia was proclaimed in Centennial Park, Sydney, on New Year's Day 1901. 'A continent for a nation and a nation for a continent': these words of Edmund Barton, the first Federal prime minister, pointed to one of the chief factors which marked off the new nation from New Zealand, the insular small nation, and Canada, the large North American state. Australia had less than 4 million people, concentrated mainly in one corner of a vast dry continent. Unlike Canada and New Zealand residual powers rested in the states; the central government received only certain specific delegated powers. But in spite of its limited powers the Commonwealth government soon followed Canada and New Zealand in laying down the direction of the nation's growth.

Some of the ablest politicians were attracted into federal politics, and the government soon espoused policies which confirmed a number of the tendencies of the previous decade. In population, the new federation would remain ethnically homogeneous. The so-called 'White Australia' policy was embodied in the Immigration Restriction Act of 1901, requiring a dictation test in a European language, and in the Pacific Islanders Protection Act of 1901 requiring that Polynesian workers should be repatriated. Thus protected racially, Australia would continue democratic and equalitarian. Manhood suffrage was adopted in 1902. Compulsory arbitration in labour disputes, on the New Zealand model, was enacted in the following year. A law of 1908 provided for modest invalid and old-age pensions for native-born subjects.

In her relations with the mother country the new Commonwealth produced her own brand of loyalty combined with nationalism. Australian contingents numbering 16,000 went to Britain's aid during the South African war. At the Imperial Conference in 1902 Barton, the premier, offered the largest colonial contribution of any dependency to Empire naval defence. To relieve the home government, the Commonwealth took over the administration of Norfolk Island and the British part of New Guinea in 1906. The territory of Papua, as the latter was called, became Australia's own colonial possession.

But Australia was by no means subservient to the British government. By agreeing to contribute £200,000 to the costs of the Royal Navy, Barton upset the advocates of a separate Australian Navy. When in 1906 Britain made arrangements for a condominium with

France in the New Hebrides islands, without consulting the Commonwealth government, Alfred Deakin, the prime minister, made a major complaint at the Imperial Conference of 1907. By doing so Australia made her first contribution to those institutions of co-operation and consultation which have remained as a major part of the life of the wider Commonwealth of Nations.

THE QUEST FOR SOUTH AFRICAN UNITY

The gradual withdrawal of imperial control over Canada, New Zealand and Australia, and the growth of the new nations of the Victorian age, may be accounted a success story. In South Africa Victorian statesmen met their greatest failures. Here they seemed incapable of withdrawing the 'imperial factor'. Gladstone was right when he referred to South Africa as the 'great unsolved, perhaps unsolvable, problem of the empire'.

The Cape and Natal were the last of the settlers' colonies to receive responsible government. Imperial troops, far from being withdrawn, frequently intervened; at the end of the century they fought the greatest of the colonial wars. Instead of handing over control of the original African inhabitants, mainly Bantu-speaking, to the colonists, as in Canada and New Zealand, Britain maintained responsibilities for three large African territories. Above all, a large proportion of the descendants of the Dutch settlers at the Cape refused to accept British rule in the same way as the French had accepted it in North America.

The Problem of South Africa

By the time responsible government was under way in the other colonies South Africa's peculiar problems had clearly emerged. Here the ingredients could not be harmonized by Lord Durham's Canadian solution. Federation, when tried, was not acceptable. Why was Britain's experience in South Africa so different from elsewhere? The answer can be found partly in the South African environment and partly in Britain's indecision.

Two features of the environment stand out. First, the original African population, numbering close on a million, far exceeded the North American Indians, the Maoris or the Aborigines. This is the cardinal fact which marked the South African colonies from their fellows. Secondly, until the discovery of diamonds (1867) and gold

(1886), settlers in South Africa found no great source of wealth. Thus the Dutch farmers – *Boers* as they were dubbed, or Afrikaners, as they preferred to be called – were accustomed to roam widely for new lands, and to spread themselves thinly over a wide area. In this way, even before Britain became involved in South Africa, Bantus and Afrikaners had begun to compete for the same soil. The clashing, intermingling and interdependence of the African inhabitants and the expanding settlers has been the central feature of most of South Africa's history.

After entering this environment Britain never made up her mind what she wished to do. For a century British governments vacillated. Four times the men in power expanded British influence and advanced. Four times they changed their minds and retired from some, or all, of the new accessions. Disunity, distrust and dissension were the legacy of Britain's indecision. When unity was finally achieved in 1910, it was too late. That modern South Africa should be the one large state to quit the Commonwealth, and by her internal policies become one of the most isolated states in the world, can in large measure be attributed to Britain's lack of consistency in the nineteenth century.

Britain and the Trek-Boers

The Cape of Good Hope was originally acquired by Britain as part of the eastern strategy during the Napoleonic wars. The backward Dutch colony of about 20,000 settlers was retained after 1815 as a base on the route to the east. Cape Town was the 'tavern for India'. But if Britain's real interest was in safeguarding a harbour and victualling station at the Cape of Good Hope, why did she progressively come to control the whole southern part of the continent? The answer to this question has to be found in the government's attitude to the Afrikaners.

The Cape Colony first became a Crown colony. The governor ruled under instructions from Whitehall. All the early governors were generals: the government clearly thought in terms of an outpost, or 'station', like Gibraltar. But, in reality, Britain had inherited a 'frontier' which was already far from Cape Town. Migrating Afrikaners had already followed the fertile coastal belt 600 miles eastwards to the region of the Great Fish River, where they had collided with the western flank of the Bantu-speaking peoples. Here they had also already demonstrated a tendency of independency towards government and aggression towards the Africans.

Although, at first, Dutch law and language were safeguarded

and Dutch colonists received office in the new Crown colony, the Afrikaners were increasingly antagonized by the British régime. The frontier farms were made subject to the Cape courts. The London Missionary Society's representatives criticized the Afrikaners' treatment of the Hottentots and other non-Europeans, such as the slaves from the East Indies. In 1828 free non-Europeans were granted civil rights, permitted to move freely without 'passes' and to buy and sell land. In 1834 slavery was made illegal, as in the rest of the empire.

Even more annoying for the Afrikaners, the government tried to prevent a headlong collision with the Bantu on the eastern frontier. First, a neutral zone from the Great Fish River to the Great Kei was created. Then in 1820 a line of English settlements was inserted around the area of Grahamstown. By the 1830s the patience of the Afrikaners was finally broken, when, under the influence of the London Missionary Society, the government also began to enter into treaty relations with, and to protect, the African chiefs on the northern frontiers. For the first time, there was a prospect that the frontiers of the Cape might be closed. This was the reason for the Great Trek.

Starting in 1835, ten thousand Afrikaners forsook their homeland in the Cape. Gathering together their lines of wagons in the foothills of Basutoland, they struck out across the Orange River. Some turned south-east over the Drakensberg Mountains towards the pasture-lands of Natal, where in 1839 they founded the first Afrikaner Republic at Pietermaritzburg. Others trekked on northwards, across the Vaal, to the high veld and to the Limpopo River. In this way Britain's incipient frontier system was breached. The Afrikaners by their epic march had smashed into the heartlands of the Bechuana, the Basuto, the Matabele and the Zulus, driving off the inhabitants where necessary, and founding their own independent communities.

What should Britain do? The dilemma was a painful one. Should the Afrikaners be left to themselves, and the Cape Colony, relieved of their presence, be strictly limited? Or should the trekkers, as colonial subjects, be pursued by government and their lands annexed in the interest of law and order? Englishmen in the nineteenth century never really made up their minds. Since self-government was usually granted elsewhere, it was difficult for liberal-minded Englishmen to deny it to the Afrikaners. But the large, and in some cases extremely warlike, Bantu populations, and the clamouring missionary influence at home, could not be ignored. Moreover, governments are not often consistent.

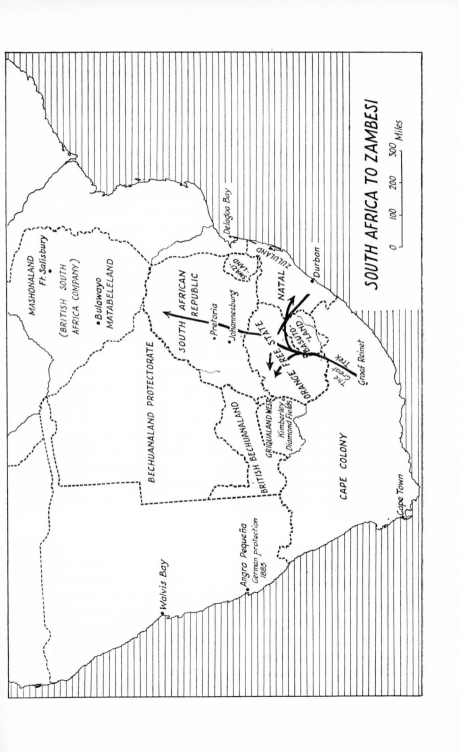

SOUTH AFRICA TO ZAMBESI

0   100   200   300   Miles

MASHONALAND
Ft. Salisbury

(BRITISH SOUTH
AFRICA COMPANY)

Bulawayo
MATABELELAND

BECHUANALAND PROTECTORATE

SOUTH
AFRICAN
REPUBLIC

Pretoria
Johannesburg

BRITISH BECHUANALAND

GRIQUALAND WEST

Kimberley
Diamond Fields

ORANGE FREE STATE

SWAZI-
LAND

NATAL

ZULULAND

Delagoa Bay

Durban

BASUTO-
LAND

The Great Trek

Graaf Reinet

CAPE COLONY

Cape Town

Angra Pequeña
German protection
1885

Walvis Bay

Britain's response to the Great Trek was governed by changing events rather than by principles.

The first reaction to the trek was the passing of an Act to apply Cape laws to British subjects up to the line of 25° S. (which is north of present-day Pretoria). Then, in cases where the trekkers disrupted the life of the Bantu, British authority was extended. The trekkers who went to Natal, moreover, not only clashed with the militarily formidable Zulus, but found a small British settlement at Durban. After several years of doubt, Britain annexed Natal in 1843. At the same time, treaty relations were entered with the Griquas and the Basuto on the northern frontiers of the Cape. Three years later, when repercussions of the trek endangered the eastern frontier of the Cape, the territory up to the Great Kei River was annexed as British Kaffraria. Finally, when trekkers returning from Natal came into conflict with the Basutos in 1848, the territory between the Orange and the Vaal rivers was annexed by Governor Sir Harry Smith. By the middle of the century, Cape Colony appeared to be growing into a British dominion to be compared with Canada and Australia.

But empire building of this sort was a thankless task. Although the 1850s were comparatively prosperous days for the Cape, and a reasonable wool and wine export developed, South Africa never attracted immigrants, nor produced great wealth, on the scale of Canada and Australia. Protecting the colonies and keeping order among the Bantu and Afrikaners was becoming a costly business. South Africa became a drain on the British exchequer. The call of the purse overcame the voice of conscience. As responsible government was granted elsewhere, Britain found ways of reducing her commitments in South Africa.

The Cause of Disunity

During the Colonial Secretaryship of the third Earl Grey (1846–52) there was a chance that the South African colonies might follow those in Canada and Australasia. The colonial reformers believed that a grant of responsible government for the Cape would be a convenient way of getting rid of expensive frontier problems. Grey, who toyed with federal schemes for Australia, thought that the Cape might be divided into two colonies and should co-operate with Kaffraria, Natal and the Orange River Sovereignty to form a closely-linked group of colonies. He even gave thought to the possibility of intervening across the Vaal. In 1847, the Governor of the Cape Colony was also made

High Commissioner to supervise trans-frontier policy. But Grey's dreams were halted by the government. Britain reduced her responsibilities and disunity was the result.

In 1852 the Cape Colony was allowed to enact a representative constitution. The Governor had received a small advisory council in 1824, and ten years later a legislative council was added, which included from five to seven nominated non-official members. The Constitution of 1852 provided for an elective legislative council of fifteen members presided over by the Chief Justice, and an assembly of forty-six members to be elected by all males aged twenty-one, irrespective of race, who occupied premises valued at £75 a year or received wages of £50 a year. This was the celebrated Cape franchise, which knew no colour bar, and remained until abolished by the Nationalist government in 1951. Natal also received representative institutions. Although there were only 7,000 settlers, they received a legislative council of sixteen (twelve elected) in 1856.

Outside the two colonies, Britain decided to recognize the self-government of the trekkers. By the Sand River Convention of 1852 Britain renounced any intention of interfering beyond the Vaal River, and disclaimed any treaties with Africans in the region. 'We agreed', wrote Sir William Molesworth, 'that the Boers should establish their own system of self-defence . . . and we agreed that a limit be put to the extent of British dominion in South Africa.' Two years later, in 1854, the Bloemfontein Convention was signed, by which Britain abandoned the Orange River Sovereignty. The trekkers were left to found two independent Republics, the Orange Free State and the South African Republic (the Transvaal). The trek and its aftermath left South Africa divided into four settler governments, which stood astride the Bantu kingdoms.

Reluctant Expansion

The four main political divisions in South Africa were not united until the twentieth century but long before then British statesmen came to regret the conventions of 1852 and 1854. Those who understood the importance of relations with the African inhabitants realized that a united approach to this problem was essential. Those concerned with Britain's strategy and prestige, especially after the 'Scramble for Africa' in the 1880s, evolved the doctrine that Britain was 'paramount power' in South Africa. The mining companies who invested in

H

diamonds and gold had their own reasons for South African unity. But although a desire for unity grew in a number of quarters, and British expansion, for all its vacillation, was fairly continuous, no consistent policy was ever evolved. Intermittent attempts to reduce commitments usually backfired.

Sir George Grey (High Commissioner 1854–59) realized that the Cape and Natal, and the Orange Free State and the Transvaal all shared the same problem of relations with Bantus on the frontiers. 'I believe', he wrote in 1857, 'that it is by a federal union alone these S. African Colonies can be made strong, and so united in policy and action that they can support themselves . . .' But, just as Galt's federal scheme for North America was rejected in 1858, so Grey's South African proposal was refused. A big opportunity for reducing British responsibilities had been lost.

In the 1860s a new mode of disengagement was tried. The British government tried to persuade the Cape Colony to advance to responsible government and to take responsibility for frontier expansion. In 1865, for example, British Kaffraria was placed under the Cape. But unfortunately this policy soon misfired. When Moshesh, ruler of the Basuto, requested annexation as a protection against the Orange Free State, the British government, after many refusals, decided that Basutoland might be annexed to the Cape. But the Cape refused to accept responsibility, and in 1868 the High Commissioner annexed Basutoland to the Crown. Similarly, after the discovery of diamonds in Griqualand West and the rapid growth of an unruly boom-town at Kimberley, the question of the annexation of the diamond fields arose. In 1871 the government, fearful that the Republics might step in, authorized the addition of Griqualand West to the Cape. But once again the Cape refused, and the territory was annexed as a new Crown colony. Finally, it was not surprising that the Cape was reluctant to accept the burdens of responsible government and self-defence. In 1869 Lord Granville, the colonial secretary, after threatening that if the colonists did not accept full responsibility, it might be necessary to reduce them to a Crown colony, insisted that 'if the colonists will not allow themselves to be governed, it follows that they must adopt the responsibility of governing'. In 1872 the Cape finally accepted responsible government. The Colonial Office declared itself quite prepared to consider a federation, as in Canada, provided it was based upon responsible government and self-defence.

The changes of the 1860s and 1870s only increased South African disunity. The existence, now, of four British territories (Cape Colony, Natal, Basutoland, Griqualand West) and two republics (Orange Free State and Transvaal) led to new problems. The Republics resented Britain's annexation of the diamond fields. An unfortunate incident in Natal, which led to the break-up of a whole tribe, revealed to the British government the disparity of African policies in the colonies. In the Cape, Africans were subject to the colonial laws and, when they qualified, could exercise the vote, but in Natal, Africans remained under their own laws in tribal areas and looked only to the Governor as 'Paramount Chief'. There were also fears that a general, united, African uprising was possible.

Carnarvon's Confederation Project

Why should not the Canadian solution be applied in South Africa? Lord Carnarvon, who returned to the Colonial Office in 1874, had been responsible for shepherding the British North America Act through Parliament. He was impressed by the way in which the Dominion of Canada permitted British disengagement from North America, and he was fearful of the growing disunity in South Africa. One of the few Victorian statesmen who was prepared to think ahead and try to forestall problems rather than wait until a crisis occurred, he decided that the best way of avoiding future troubles with the Republics and of solving the problem of relations with the African inhabitants, would be to revive the idea of federation in South Africa. In 1875 he suggested that a conference of delegates from the Republics and the colonies should meet to co-ordinate their relations with the Bantu.

Carnarvon's project, although well-meaning, was disastrous. To start with, two of the provinces were not under British sovereignty. Moreover, Canadian confederation succeeded because the initiative came from the Canadians and because such pressure as was exerted by Britain was desired by the Canadians. In South Africa the initiative was entirely British and the methods were most unfortunate. Natal was reduced to the status of a Crown colony. The Cape was antagonized by Carnarvon's disallowance of an act of the Cape Parliament and by the appointment, as his personal envoy, of the historian, James Froude, who stirred up feeling behind the back of the Cape ministry. Eventually, although the Republics were extremely lukewarm,

Carnarvon went ahead with the scheme. He presented a permissive Bill to Parliament. Finally, in a desperate gamble, he sent an agent in 1877 to annex the Transvaal, which was admittedly very weak, nearly bankrupt and badly compromised in a frontier war with a Zulu tribe. Carnarvon seemed to be making sure that all the European portions of South Africa (except the Orange Free State) came under British control. He still hoped that unity would then be achieved by consent. But his hopes were soon to be dashed.

The annexation of the Transvaal destroyed the confederation scheme. Britain found herself faced with two dangerous new problems: she inherited a Transvaal border dispute with the Zulus, and she alienated those Transvaal Afrikaners, led by Paul Kruger, who cherished their independence. The result was a series of military disasters. An attempt to occupy Zululand led to the slaughter of the South Wales Borderers at Isandhlwana in 1879. An uprising of the Transvaal Afrikaners led to further disasters, at Bronkhorst Spruit (1880) and Majuba Hill (1881). By trying to force confederation against the wishes of the Europeans in South Africa (especially the Transvaalers) Britain incurred hostility, severely damaged her prestige and destroyed the chance of unity. Her leaders found that the time had come for another great retreat.

After his victory in the Midlothian election of 1880, Gladstone returned to power and decided to restore the Transvaal's freedom. By the Pretoria Convention of 1881, 'complete self-government' was conceded subject to the 'suzerainty' of the British Crown. Britain remained responsible for the conduct of the Transvaal's foreign affairs. A Resident, representing the High Commissioner, was to remain in the Transvaal and exercise a veto over the Republic's laws relating to African affairs. Thus the Transvaal received a status not unlike Canada and New Zealand, with the difference that she was a republic within the empire and limited in her internal policies where they affected Africans. But the Afrikaners were not satisfied. In 1883, Kruger was elected President and went to England to negotiate the London Convention of 1884. In it the provision about 'suzerainty' was omitted, although the Transvaal still undertook to make no treaty with another nation (apart from the Orange Free State) or an African tribe, without the approval of the British government. The title 'South African Republic' was recognized and Britain's representative became a Consul, not a Resident. The colonial secretary told the House of

Lords that the 'substance' of suzerainty remained. But the Republic's precise international status was most ambiguous and was soon the subject of dispute. Kruger clearly wanted to gain genuine 'independence'. What is clear is that the whole confederation project left a legacy of bitterness, with South Africa more disunited than before.

The Background of the South African War

Only fifteen years after recognizing the Republic, Britain was at war. Over half a century of indecision culminated with Britain determining to obliterate Afrikaner claims of independence. How do we account for this further remarkable reversal? We need, first, to understand the effects of two entirely new developments of the 1880s, which bemused British statesmen: the 'Scramble for Africa' and the discovery of gold in the Transvaal. They both provided a spur to the ambitions of Cecil Rhodes, the Cape's greatest 'imperialist', and to Paul Kruger, the Transvaal leader.

The reasons for the 'Scramble for Africa' will be discussed in Chapter 10. Its effect on South Africa was far-reaching. Germany annexed South-West Africa in 1884 and raised the possibility that the Transvaal might extend westwards to link up with the Germans and cut off the long-established British missionary route to the north. In 1885 Britain stepped in to annex the territory between the Transvaal and German South-West Africa and to create the Bechuanaland protectorate. Similar fears of German or Transvaal extension in the south-east, led to the annexation of St Lucia Bay in 1884, and the declaration of British protectorates in Pondoland (1884) and Zululand (1887).

The discovery of gold in the Transvaal changed the entire balance in South Africa. The Transvaal was a poor, backward, pastoral state, where the supply of land was running out: already Afrikaner sons were migrating elsewhere. But after 1886 the Transvaal became the great magnet of South Africa. In only a year Johannesburg became a town of 6,000; in subsequent years thousands more immigrants were attracted and British and colonial capitalists moved in. Soon the Cape and Natal railways were competing for the Republic's traffic.

Both the international scramble and the rise of the Transvaal gold-fields challenged the ambitions of Cecil Rhodes, the English parson's son, who had made his fortune in the diamond fields in the 1870s. By 1887, Rhodes's Consolidated Gold Fields had become one of the major mining firms on the Rand. But in his mind Rhodes had been building larger empires. He not only revived the idea of a unified South Africa under British control, but he went on to dream of a belt of British territory stretching northwards to the Nile.

The emergence of a wealthy Transvaal and the news that, in 1887, the Transvaalers were opening relations with Lobengula, King of the Matabele to the north, led Rhodes to desperate measures. First, he persuaded the High Commissioner at the Cape to send an emissary to ask Lobengula not to part with any territory without consulting the British. Then, after getting the concession of mineral rights in Lobengula's realms in return for the promise of £100 a month, a thousand rifles and a steamboat for the Zambesi, Rhodes persuaded the British government to approve a chartered company. In 1889 the British South Africa Company was authorized to open up the territory north of the Limpopo River for prospecting and colonization. Unfortunately when they approved the charter the British government did not know that Lobengula had already had second thoughts. Thus when Dr Jameson was sent from the Cape to start prospecting he first had to 'reinstate' the concession.

But Dr Jameson was a gay and canny adventurer, who left some notorious marks on South African history. Partly by treating Lobengula's gout and partly by threats of force, he received permission to prospect in Mashonaland, to the east, and to make a road up from the Cape through Matabeleland. This was the signal for advance. Lobengula had 'sanctioned our occupation of Mashonaland', telegraphed Rhodes to the High Commissioner, with a certain poetic licence. In 1890 the British South Africa Company's 'Pioneer column' marched north from the Cape, through Bechuanaland, and into Lobengula's lands. In the next few years both the Matabele and the Mashona were crushed by force and treaties were made with the Barotse, north of the Zambezi. Lobengula died, a sick, defeated, demoralized monarch. In a few bold strokes, Rhodes had laid the foundations of the new colony of Rhodesia, foreign powers had been excluded from a large part of central Africa, and the Transvaal had been cut off from the north. Britain was, clearly, now acting on the assumption that she was 'paramount power' in South Africa.

But international rivalry and gold also acted as a spur to President Paul Kruger of the Transvaal. The wealth of the mines and the possibility of finding allies among Britain's foreign rivals gave him the chance to challenge British paramountcy and assert full independence. As a first step, the opening of a railway from the Transvaal to Lourenço Marques, in Mozambique, gave him a British-free outlet to the sea. There was, however, a major flaw in Kruger's scheme for self-determination.

The Afrikaners were a patriarchal, Bible-fearing, and farming people. The gold mines were, in a very literal sense, an alien intrusion in their land. Most of the companies, the miners and the labourers were foreigners – 'uitlanders', as the Afrikaners called them – and most of them were of British origin. By 1896 there were about 44,000 uitlanders on the Rand, along with 42,000 Africans and about 8,000 other non-Europeans. Although not constituting the bulk of the population of the Republic (as some Englishmen claimed), the uitlanders made up a majority of European males. They received no political rights. Kruger realized that if the new population of the gold-fields was granted the vote, and some seats in the Volksraad, he could eventually expect that normal democratic processes would end Afrikaner control and probably end the Transvaal's hope of independence. Here, then, was the situation which led to war: Britain claiming paramountcy, the uitlanders claiming political rights, and the Transvaal claiming full independence.

Anglo-Transvaal Negotiations

It is impossible in the space of a few paragraphs to convey the complexity and growing passion of Anglo-Transvaal relations in the 1890s. There were genuine grievances and real attempts at compromise on both sides.

It would be hard to deny that the unenfranchised uitlanders, who had to pay their taxes and were sometimes pressed into Republican military service, had grievances, or that Kruger's Old Testament régime was blinded by prejudice against them. But when, in 1894, the High Commissioner, Lord Loch, suggested that the uitlanders might revolt against the Transvaal government and receive support from a force of British police from Bechuanaland, the Colonial Office rightly rejected the plan. 'Every nerve should be strained to prevent such a disgrace as another S. African War', wrote the permanent head of the office. Yet a plot of this kind was undoubtedly hatched, and led to the ignominy of the Jameson Raid.

In 1895 Cecil Rhodes, who had capped his control of the diamond fields and his large stake in the gold-fields and the British South Africa Company with the premiership of the Cape, planned to support a rising of uitlanders which was to take place in Johannesburg at the end of December. The plan was well-known in high circles both in South Africa and London. Joseph Chamberlain, the colonial secretary, undoubtedly had foreknowledge and later admitted frankly: 'I knew all about the revolution.' But he could not have expected what actually took place. For although the Johannesburg uprising was postponed at the last minute, Dr Jameson, the B.S.A. Company's administrator in Rhodesia, who was Rhodes's commander of the support force, decided to ride into the Transvaal on 29 December 1895. Technically he was 'invading' Republican territory; two days later he surrendered to Kruger's troops.

After the Raid an atmosphere of tension attended South African affairs at all levels. Rhodes resigned as prime minister of the Cape, and both he and Chamberlain appeared before the notorious Commission of Inquiry into the complicity of the Colonial Office. Jameson, at the same time, became something of a hero in Britain. Afrikaners, both in the Republics and in the colonies, were embittered. Jan Smuts, a brilliant young, Cambridge-educated, Cape lawyer, renounced his British citizenship and moved to the Transvaal. The Kaiser lent moral support to President Kruger. The latter refused to discuss the question of uitlander grievances and proposed using the Raid as a pretext for ending the London Convention of 1884 and gaining complete independence.

It was most unfortunate that Joseph Chamberlain sent Sir Alfred Milner into this highly charged atmosphere in 1897 as High Commissioner. Milner was a brilliant Oxford scholar, who had made a great reputation as a civil servant in Egypt and England. But Milner's brand of race-conscious patriotism was as blindly prejudiced and unswerving as Kruger's Afrikaner nationalism. Milner believed that his own doctrine of 'imperialism' had 'all the depth and comprehensiveness of a religious faith'. He intended to use the uitlander grievances and the question of the Africans in the Transvaal to assert British control over the Republic. He sensed that the whole future of the British empire and Britain's position as a power was under test in South Africa. He was convinced (and in the long run he was proved right) that if the Afrikaners succeeded in maintaining their régime in the Transvaal, they would eventually prevail in the Cape, as they already did in the Orange Free State. South Africa would eventually be lost to Britain and become an Afrikaner republic. Milner was also very anxious about relations with South Africa's majority African population. 'That the white man must rule is clear – but *how*?' he asked.

Chamberlain was much less pessimistic than Milner. He believed that a 'Lord Durham solution' was possible and that large-scale British immigration would enable Britain to dominate in South Africa. But in 1897 Chamberlain reasserted British 'suzerainty' over the Transvaal. Kruger took it as a challenge to the status of the Republic. For a further twenty months the two sides negotiated. Ostensibly the debate was about political rights for the uitlanders. In reality, it concerned Britain's claim to suzerainty in South Africa and Kruger's claim of Transvaal independence. As Chamberlain admitted, 'there is a greater issue than the franchise or the grievances of the Uitlanders at stake . . . our supremacy in S. Africa and our existence as a great Power in the world is involved.'

The quarrel was an unedifying one, and yet there were earnest attempts on both sides to keep the peace. Sir William Butler, the British commander-in-chief, who acted as High Commissioner when Milner was on leave in 1898, did his best to quieten the atmosphere. Cape and Orange Free State leaders tried to mediate. The younger members of Kruger's government, notably the 28-year-old States Attorney, Jan Smuts, persuaded Kruger to make notable concessions and to grant the vote to uitlanders. In the British Cabinet Arthur Balfour realized the Transvaal's predicament and admitted that if he were a Boer he would want to resist a constitution which would turn his country into an English-dominated one. The drama of the negotiations has recently been summed up in the words: 'The peace party was strong in the Transvaal, in the Cape and in Britain. There were moments when a successful settlement seemed within reach, yet in the end Milner's obstruction and Kruger's suspicions wrecked all hope of avoiding war.'*

A conference between Milner and Kruger at Bloemfontein in May 1899 failed to resolve the issue. Chamberlain was prepared for a compromise. Kruger offered votes to the uitlanders who had lived in the Transvaal for seven years, but he requested that the 1884 Convention, which was still the basis of the Transvaal's international status, should

* J. A. S. Grenville, *Lord Salisbury and Foreign Policy*, London, 1964, p. 240.

be considered by impartial arbitrators. Milner refused. He was tired and irritated and he simply did not trust the Transvaalers. Kruger was left crying: 'It is our country that you want.'

Yet even after the break-up of the Bloemfontein conference hope of a settlement was not lost. In July 1899 the Volksraad went ahead and granted the vote to uitlanders who had resided in the country for seven years. Chamberlain was delighted at the news, but Milner called it a 'sham concession'. Thus, instead of accepting Kruger's offer, Britain reopened the idea of a tribunal to arbitrate on the question of suzerainty. Now the boot was on the other foot. Kruger was rightly annoyed. But in August 1899 Smuts made a final attempt at settlement by proposing a vote for uitlanders with five years' residence.

Milner continued to mistrust the Transvaal, however, and when Kruger added, as a condition of the five-year franchise, the ending of British suzerainty, the High Commissioner's stand seemed vindicated. The now unhappy Joseph Chamberlain came to accept Milner's viewpoint. On 24 August he wrote: 'We cannot go on negotiating for ever and must try to bring the matter to a head. . . . I dread above all the continual whittling away of differences until we have no *casus belli* left. . . .' Salisbury, the prime minister, believed that war was now inevitable and the Cabinet turned to military preparations. On 8 September 1899 it ordered reinforcements to South Africa. A month later Kruger declared war. The Transvaal already had a military alliance with the Orange Free State. Afrikaners took up their arms once more to fight for their independence.

The Aftermath of the South African War

Three bitter years of war followed. Sixty thousand Afrikaners, fighting for their freedom, challenged the power of the British empire. Eventually, 400,000 troops were needed to win the war, and they included detachments from Canada, Australia, New Zealand and India. To permit the armies to lay waste the Republican farms, over 100,000 civilians were gathered into camps. Thousands of women and children died. By 1902 the Republican armies were exhausted and the generals decided that 'the bitter end has come'. Kruger went into exile. General Smuts and General Hertzog negotiated with Lord Kitchener, the British commander, the generous Peace of Vereeniging on 31 May 1902. Afrikaners who took an oath to the Crown were to be released, the Afrikaner language was to be safeguarded, civil government was to be restored when practical, and self-government granted. The question of granting the vote to Bantu inhabitants was postponed till after self-government.

Thus, finally, in the greatest of her colonial wars, Britain gained supremacy in South Africa. Milner believed that the way to ensure a stable future was to apply Lord Durham's remedy for French-Canadian nationalism of the 1830s. He envisaged a line of self-governing settler communities eventually stretching from the Cape to the Zambezi, living amid justly treated African inhabitants, the whole leavened by a large injection of British immigration.

As a first step the Orange Free State and the Transvaal were annexed. Milner and a brilliant team of young civil servants from Britain worked energetically to rehabilitate the Republics. British and colonial governments spent £14 million in grants for war compensation and resettlement. A £35 million loan, guaranteed by the British government, was made to the Free State and Transvaal governments, mainly for railway reconstruction. Special attention was paid to the gold mines, South Africa's single greatest source of wealth. But Milner was not eager to grant the ex-Republics self-government. They became Crown colonies. All members of the executive and legislative councils were officials until 1903 when the Transvaal Legislative Council received a minority of nominated non-official representatives. The High Commissioner was anxious that the firm hand of Britain should consolidate Britain's dearly won supremacy.

Milner did not get his way. Yet in one sense his dream of a British South African dominion was fulfilled. In 1910, by unanimous consent of British colonial and Afrikaner leaders, the Union of South Africa was created. What had happened, in so short a time, to wipe out much of the bitterness of the war, and enable a fourth 'new nation' to take its place among the self-governing states of the empire?

The Union of South Africa

A new era of co-operation began, in the first place, because of the great Liberal election victory in 1906. The Liberals wished to preserve British supremacy in South Africa, but sought to do so by winning over the Afrikaners. Henry Campbell-Bannerman, the prime minister, pledged himself to grant responsible government to the ex-Republics. In 1907 the Transvaal and Orange Free State received their new Constitutions. The Parliament of the Transvaal was to consist of a nominated legislative council, and an assembly elected by all white males aged twenty-one. English and Dutch languages could both be used in Parliament. After the first general election in 1907, *Het Volk*, the Afrikaner party, formed a government led by ex-General Louis Botha, with Smuts as colonial secretary. The Free State Parliament followed the same pattern. The Afrikaner party, *Orangia Unie*, won the first election and Abraham Fischer became prime minister, with ex-General Hertzog as attorney-general and minister of education.

As if to emphasize the return of the Afrikaners to power, the South African Party won the Cape Colony general election in 1907 and John X. Merriman, of English origin, formed a largely Afrikaner ministry. Only five years after the war, then, three of the self-governing colonies were ruled by Afrikaner parties. As Botha said in his first speech as premier of the Transvaal, 'Was it possible for the Boers ever to forget such generosity?' When he attended the Imperial Conference in London in 1917, the former enemy general symbolized what he hoped would be a new era of conciliation by presenting the world's largest diamond to be added to the Crown.

But for all the new atmosphere of co-operation, and the fact of British sovereignty, South Africa was still divided. Four self-governing colonies (Cape, Natal, Free State and Transvaal), three African protectorates (Basutoland, Bechuanaland and Swaziland) and the B.S.A. Company's territory in Rhodesia, were far from constituting a nation. Certain problems were little changed from before the war. The most contentious problem was the dependence of the coastal colonies, for railway and customs revenues, on trade with the former Republics. Kruger's railway to Lourenço Marques still carried more traffic than the routes to Durban and Cape Town.

Conferences were held in 1905 and 1906 to consider joint railway management and a customs union. But they failed to resolve the basic economic conflicts. The Transvaal gave preference to the Portuguese route because they recruited African labourers from Mozambique. The coastal colonies' need of high tariffs clashed with the low tariff needs of the Transvaal. Above all, the Transvaal with its gold was likely to dominate. As customs union and railway agreements failed, the only way for all the colonies to share the Transvaal's prosperity was to join a Union.

The idea of federal union was already being considered by British and Afrikaner leaders. Smuts, who was impressed by the rise of a federal Labour Party in Australia, wrote to Merriman in 1904:

> Don't you think that as the liberals get into power we ought to make a move in the direction of federation? . . . You know with the Boers United S.A. has always been a deeply-felt political aspiration.

Two years later some of the English civil servants broached the idea to Lord Selborne, the High Commissioner. In 1907, Selborne published a memorandum outlining three alternatives for South Africa: a makeshift unity under the High Commissioner's co-ordination; jarring separation as in South America; or noble union like the United States. Afrikaner leaders were not unduly impressed by Selborne's initiative. But after the Imperial Conference of 1907 Smuts and ex-President Steyn, of the Free State, began to realize that Canada and Australia had made their unity a stepping stone for a nearly complete autonomy.

Once their minds were made up, the South African leaders evolved a surprisingly rapid time-table for Union – much faster than the achievement of federation in Canada and Australia. At an inter-colonial conference in May 1908 Smuts proposed that delegates chosen by the colonial parliaments should gather in a Constitutional Convention before the parliamentary sessions of 1909. After ratification by each colony, the draft would then be submitted to the British government to be authorized by an Act of Parliament.

The National Convention sat in Durban, in October–November 1908, and reconvened in Cape Town, where its work was completed by the beginning of February 1909. Many of its secret debates were hard-fought and numerous behind-the-scenes compromises had to be made. Yet in the end, thirty-three delegates (most of whom had been wartime enemies) unanimously added their signatures.

The chief work of drawing up a project for Union was done by Smuts. Federation was abandoned in favour of a unitary constitution. This left the way open for a British-style unlimited power of parliament, as opposed to the limited American or Australian model. Parliament was to have a Senate, of which eight members were to be elected by the Provinces and eight were to be nominated by the Governor-General. The House of Assembly would be elected according to the electoral laws of the Provinces. Cape delegates put up a fight for the extension of the Cape franchise, without colour bar, but the ex-Republics refused to accept. Careful provisions were made, on the insistence of Hertzog, of the Free State, for the absolute equality of Afrikaans and English as official languages. Provincial government would be by an Administrator (appointed by the Governor-General in council) and elected Provincial Councils, who would have delegated responsibility for lands, mining, roads, administration of justice, hospitals and public works. The Supreme Court of the Union would consist of a new Appeal Court and existing provincial and district courts. After acrimonious debates over the future capital city, which nearly broke up the Convention, it was decided to divide the capital: parliament at Cape Town, government at Pretoria, and the Appeal Court at Bloemfontein. Representatives of the British South Africa Company and Southern Rhodesia attended the Convention, and provision was made for the future admission of Southern Rhodesia and the African protectorates, but they were not to be founding provinces of the Union. After the draft constitution was published in 1909, the colonial parliaments considered it in March. The Convention met at Bloemfontein in May to consider proposed amendments.

Africans in all the territories were bitterly disappointed by the colour bar on the franchise outside Cape Colony. A number of protest meetings were called and some of the notable Cape leaders tried hard to get an amendment to the draft. But they failed. In June 1909 the parliaments of the Transvaal, Free State and Cape approved the constitution; in Natal consent was given in a referendum. 'Seldom, if ever, has the adoption of a democratically drafted Constitution so clearly represented the will of an electorate', is the verdict of a recent constitutional authority.* It should, however, be remembered that the electorate represented less than $1\frac{1}{2}$ million whites, and excluded the vast majority of the 4 million Africans, whose few articulate leaders opposed the voting system.

On behalf of the latter a last effort was made by William Schreiner (a former premier of the Cape) who went to Britain in 1910, unofficially, while the Union Bill was before Parliament. A few interested Englishmen took up the cause of the African vote. Some letters appeared in *The Times*. During the parliamentary debates Sir Charles Dilke warned: 'I do not think it can be said that we are strengthening the Imperial fabric in an Empire where there are 360 millions of coloured

* L. M. Thompson, *The Unification of South Africa 1902–1910*, Oxford, 1960. p. 397.

people under our rule.' Keir Hardie, and other Labour members, tried hard to move a franchise amendment.

But Britain's political leaders wanted to allow the Union to determine its own affairs. Arthur Balfour, the leader of the opposition, spoke for the majority of his Edwardian fellow-countrymen when he said:

> All men are, from some points of view, equal; but to suppose that the races of Africa are in any sense equals to men of European descent, so far as government, or society, or the higher interests of civilization are concerned, is really, I think, an absurdity.

The prime minister, Herbert Asquith, rather more charitably, deeply regretted the voting colour-bar, and earnestly appealed to the South Africans 'that they, in the exercise of their undoubted and unfettered freedom, should find it possible to modify the provisions'. The Bill passed without amendment. The Union of South Africa was proclaimed on 31 May 1910, the eighth anniversary of the Peace of Vereeniging. Botha became the first prime minister, and in the general election of 1910 led the new Nationalist Party to victory.

In many respects the Union represented Britain's last great retreat in South Africa. As in Canada, New Zealand and Australia, a new state had been born. But Milner's dream remained unfulfilled. The flood of British immigrants did not materialize. The Union lacked the sense of 'British nationality' which accompanied the growth of the other new nations. The Union was, instead, the fulfilment of Afrikaner unity after seventy-five years of division. It is true that under Smuts's guidance the Union was to make a notable contribution to the Commonwealth, but when the men who were infected by the conciliatory spirit of the post-war years and the wave of optimism which gave birth to the Union passed away after the Second World War, Afrikaner nationalism was to take a more virulent, protective form. The success of the rising force of Asian and African nationalism in changing the nature of the Commonwealth in the 1950s, would then lead the Afrikaners to revert to Republican status and finally to leave the Commonwealth.

The New Nations

In the half-century which followed the grants of responsible government, a series of new nations grew up within the British empire.

Responsible government, which was a specifically political device, had been granted with so many loose ends untied that it proved to be a transitory phase. By various forms of union, confederation or federation, viable states were created. Colonial provincialism gave way to regional nationalism. The mother country was quietly, and on the whole willingly, obliged to concede a wider measure of autonomy. Yet in spite of all the assertions of freedom from Whitehall and aspirations to nationhood, when British authority was challenged in South Africa in 1899, Canada, New Zealand and Australia (although not entirely unanimous) revealed deep seams of imperial loyalty.

But certain fundamental questions remained. How could a very wide measure of autonomy be reconciled with legal subordination to Britain in many fields? What international status was to be accorded to the new nations? In his speech introducing the South Africa Bill in 1910 Lord Crewe referred to the 'very difficult problem of co-operation all over the Empire in the policy of the Empire'. There were many statesmen, both at home and in the colonies, who firmly believed that 'nationhood' should be made compatible with imperial 'consolidation'. By the twentieth century, as Britain began to feel herself vulnerable before the growing power of Germany, Russia and the United States, and made an alliance with Japan, the rising power of Asia, the new nations began to have their own views on foreign policy. Thus the question became urgent.

It was, in fact, only a twentieth-century version of the old question: what should be the relationship of the mother country to her communities overseas now grown to maturity? The answer, as we shall see, was the idea of the Commonwealth.

2 Edward Gibbon
Wakefield

3 Sir Frederic
Rogers

1 Lord Durham

4 The Third Earl Grey

5 Edward Cardwell

6 Dominion of Canada: Parliament Hill, Ottawa

7 Sir John A. Macdonald

8 Sir Wilfred Laurier

9 Canadian Pacific Railway: first transcontinental train, 1886

10 S.S. *Dunedin*: first ship to carry New Zealand frozen meat to Britain, 1882

11 Dominion of New Zealand: old Government House and Parliament House, Wellington

12 Sir Julius Vogel

13 Richard Seddon

14 Commonwealth of Australia: Parliament Building, Canberra

15 Sir Henry Parkes

16 Sir Robert Menzies

17 Colonial Premiers at Colonial House, May 1907

18 The Imperial War Cabinet, 1917

19 Anzacs at Gallipoli, 1915

20 General Currie, commanding Canadian Corps on the Western Front, 1917

21 Keith Holyoake

22 Leopold Amery

23 Jan Smúts

24 Mackenzie King

25 A New Zealand light anti-aircraft post, Alamein

26 The Commonwealth Division, Korea, 1951

27 The Mahatma Mohandas Karamchand Gandhi

28 The Secretariat: New Delhi

29 Dadabhai Naoroji

30 Jawaharlal Nehru

31 Pakistan: New capital at Islamabad

32 Mohammed Ali Jinnah

33 Mohammed Ayub Khan

34 Don Stephen Senanayake

35 Tungku Abdul Rahman

36 Lee Kuan Yew

38 Kwame Nkrumah

37 J. B. Danquah

39 Sir Abubakar Tafawa Balewa

40 Nnamdi Azikiwe

41 Sir Milton Margai

42 Julius Nyerere

43 Jomo Kenyatta

44 Hastings Banda

45 Milton Obote

46 Kenneth Kaunda

47 Sir Alexander Bustamante

48 Eric Williams

49 The State Opening of Parliament in Jamaica

50 Harold Macmillan delivering the "wind of change" speech beneath the Union Convention Painting, Cape Town, 3rd February 1960

51 Hugh Gaitskell attacking the Common Market policy at the Labour Party Conference, Brighton, October 1962

52 The Commonwealth Conference, 1965.
Harold Wilson entertains Commonwealth leaders in No. 10 Downing Street

53 Arnold Smith:
first Secretary-General, 1965

54 The main conference room at Marlborough House

5

Dominion Status

THE MOST striking fact about the development of the Commonwealth is that its evolution has always been gradual and not marked by rigid constitutional formulas. It is true that there are very definite historical steps in its evolution, and that once important decisions were made for one colony they have tended to be applied fairly soon elsewhere. But since Britain herself has no written constitution, her relationship with the 'new nations' was never finally or definitively set out. If you ask a Canadian, Australian or New Zealander when his country became independent, he finds it difficult to answer.

Shortly after Canadian Confederation Lord Granville actually used the phrase 'the growth of their independence', but the first specific 'Independence Act' was the Indian Independence Act of 1947. If countries became 'independent' without ever having their 'independence' formally decided, it is obvious that the key to the evolution of the Commonwealth should not be sought in terms of precise and definitive labels. An excellent example of this is to be found in the story of 'Dominion status'.

By the end of Queen Victoria's reign the status of the new nations gave rise to some confusion. No one denied their nationhood, but they still accepted a unity under the British monarchy. Even such a great imperialist as Milner could describe the empire in 1901 as

> a group of sister nations spread throughout the world, united and not divided by the ocean, each independent in its own concerns, all indissolubly allied for a common purpose, all free and willing subjects of the most ancient and august Monarchy in the world.

In 1907 the label 'Dominion' was adopted as a way of distinguishing the self-governing colonies from the Crown colonies and India. During the 1914–18 war, in which Dominion armies fought valiantly for the home country, the question as to what 'Dominion status' really meant was earnestly debated. The Imperial Conference of 1917 agreed that 'the re-adjustment of the constitutional relations of the component parts of the Empire' would have to be discussed by a special conference after the war.

In 1920 an Australian, Duncan Hall, argued in a study for the Fabians, that the main problem was one of reconciling 'the absolute equality of nationhood with the formal unity of the Empire'. Leopold Amery, one of the most ardent imperialists of the inter-war years, believed that the 'peculiar characteristic' of the British empire was the way it combined 'complete independence of its parts' with 'unity revealed by the Crown'. In 1926, after a great deal of discussion in no less than four imperial conferences, the celebrated Balfour declaration provided the clearest definition that has ever been given of the relationship between Britain and the self-governing Dominions.

> They are autonomous Communities within the British Empire, equal in status, in no way subordinate one to another in any aspect of their domestic or external affairs, though united by a common allegiance to the Crown, and freely associated as members of the British Commonwealth of Nations.

This was not the 'constitution' for the Commonwealth which many desired, nor was it an 'act' which provided for something new, as some believed. It is of the utmost importance for an understanding of the Commonwealth to realize that the 1926 declaration was a description (and a very brilliant and succinct one) of what had *already happened*. Moreover, it had not simply happened during the debates following the 1914–18 war. The evolution of Dominion status, as described in 1926, can be traced back to Canadian Confederation and beyond, to the problems of responsible government. It can be followed through the late Victorian debate between those who wanted always to loosen, and those who wished to consolidate, imperial ties. It may be seen in the rise of the word 'Commonwealth' itself, first popularized by the 'consolidators', and finally adopted as the title of a purely voluntary inter-national association.

TWO VIEWS OF EMPIRE

After the creation of the Dominion of Canada two very different views about the future of the empire prevailed in Britain. One school of thought believed in 'freedom and voluntaryism' and held that the colonies should receive the maximum of self-government and remain associated with the mother country only by ties of interest and sentiment. The opposing school of thought wanted to 'reconstruct' and 'consolidate' imperial ties, to create a Britannic union or imperial federation, to make the empire, in short, a super-state. Adherence to these two schools cut across political party ties, although the Liberals and Tories of late Victorian England tended to become associated in the popular mind with one or the other.

The conflict between the two schools first became pronounced after Granville had referred to the growing 'independence' of Canada and had insisted on withdrawing the garrisons from New Zealand in 1869. A somewhat illogical fear suddenly grew in England and in the colonies that Gladstone's government (1868–74) wanted to dismember the empire. In 1870 Lord Carnarvon rose in the House of Lords to charge, rather melodramatically, that there were 'whispers abroad that there is a policy on foot to dismember this Empire. . . . If there is such a policy in God's name let us know it; if there is not, let it be disavowed.' The government were able to answer the charge. In fact, the Liberals numbered several notable imperialists in their ranks, and during Gladstone's later ministries (1880–85, 1886, 1892–94) large portions of the map were painted red. Nevertheless, the Liberals came to be known as the anti-imperialist party, and broadly speaking, this was accurate.

Voluntary Ties of Sentiment and Advantage

The Liberals were the early exponents of the 'voluntary tie' school of thought. They looked to a logical extension of responsible government. Gladstone (when colonial secretary) had written to Canada in 1846:

It is to the free and loyal attachment of the Canadians at large that Her Majesty will ever look for the maintenance of the connection between the Province and this country.

It is not her desire that it should subsist upon a narrower basis than that of cordial good will and reciprocal advantage. The connection of this country with its transmarine possessions cannot be maintained through coercion or through any vexatious thwarting of the social tendencies of the communities by which they are inhabited: nor ought it to be so maintained even if it were possible.

In 1871, Gladstone's colonial spokesman in the House of Commons clearly re-stated the same view: 'The Government wished to retain the Colonies: but they wished to retain them bound to this country by ties of kindred and affection.' Gladstone believed in the moral virtue of self-government and self-defence. He wished to apply it as widely as possible and, indeed, devoted the later part of his political career to trying to secure it for Ireland. He defined the doctrine of the loose tie as early as 1855 with the exhortation: 'Govern them upon a principle of freedom – let them not feel any yoke upon their necks – let them understand that the relation between you and them are relations of affection.'

This 'voluntary' view of empire was taken up in the twentieth century by notable colonial leaders like Sir Wilfrid Laurier, the Canadian Liberal prime minister, who referred to the empire in 1902 as 'a galaxy of independent nations', and by Andrew Fisher, Australia's Labour premier, who declared in 1911: 'We are now a family of nations.' Britain's Liberal prime minister, Sir Henry Campbell-Bannerman, also adhered to this tradition. He gave responsible government to the Orange Free State and the Transvaal in 1906. General Smuts enthused: 'They gave us back our country in everything but name. After four years. Has such a miracle of trust and magnanimity ever happened before? Only people like the English could do it', and henceforth Smuts became Britain's firm friend. Exponents of the 'loose tie' did not want to *abolish* the empire, but they believed that the fullest self-government was the only possible salvation for empire. Colonies should not be held against their will, their ties with Britain could be based only upon consent, not force. 'The colonial ideal is an alliance', wrote Richard Jebb in his *Studies in Colonial Nationalism* in 1905. 'Alliance recognizes separate national aspirations.'

Imperial Federation

The opposite view was a compound of idealism and political opportunism, of strategic concern and economic anxiety. During the early 1870s calls for empire unity and consolidation came from many different quarters. James Anthony Froude, the historian and editor of *Fraser's Magazine*, summed up in 1870 many of the arguments in favour of unity. He believed the empire had to be retained as a place of emigration and capital investment, so that it could help to solve Britain's social and economic problems. He drew a contrast between an empire of 'inexhaustible resources' and a small country where the multitude were sacrificed to the luxuries of the few. He believed in a large empire which would help to abolish war over wider portions of the globe. He laid stress on the 'prestige' Britain gained from the empire, and her need of 'largeness' in face of the growing power of the United States, Russia and Germany. He wanted to respond to the loyalty recently expressed by Canada and New Zealand, and he recognized the power of the sentiment of patriotism. He appealed to Disraeli, the leader of the opposition, to take up the cause of empire unity.

To Disraeli many of these ideas were familiar. Since the original grants of responsible government he had been uneasy about the 'loose tie' view of empire. But in the 1850s he failed to persuade his party to evolve a policy of empire 'reconstruction'. By the 1870s he decided that the time was ripe. He was among the first European statesmen to recognize the importance of developments outside Europe: the rise of the United States, the potential of Japan, the westernization of China and Britain's position in India were questions which deeply interested him. 'The day is coming . . . when the question of the balance of power cannot be confined to Europe alone', he foretold in 1859. In 1866 he insisted that 'England is no longer a mere European power; she is a metropolis of a great maritime Empire extending to the boundaries of the farthest ocean.' After all the criticism of Liberal policy during 1869–70 Disraeli realized he could use his ideas to gain political advantage. In a speech at Manchester on 3 April 1872 he suggested that the colonies would 'in due time exercise their influence over the distribution of power'. In the famous Crystal Palace speech of 24 June 1872 he castigated the way in which responsible government had been given without clear definition as to who was responsible for defence. Self-government, he argued, should have been conceded 'as part of a great policy of Imperial consolidation. . . . It ought, further, to have been accompanied by the institution of some representative council in the metropolis, which would have brought the Colonies into constant and continuing relations with the Home Government.'

Disraeli thus associated the Conservatives with the cause of empire union or imperial federation. In the early 1870s a number of schemes were mooted, ranging from the Duke of Manchester's idea of making the colonies an integral part of the United Kingdom, to James Spedding's plan for a Federal Union, and stark alternatives posed by the Canadian, Edward Jenkins: 'federation or disintegration'. Several writers (including Disraeli) were impressed by the system of the United States whereby the western territories were eventually admitted to Congress as states on an equality with the rest of the Union. Various projects were devised for admitting colonial members into Parliament at Westminster, or creating a special Colonial Council or even a colonial committee of the Privy Council.

When Disraeli became prime minister (1874–80) he did very little in practice to fulfil these ideas, just as Gladstone in the 1880s found himself presiding over policies which ran counter to *his* ideals. But the possibility of imperial 'consolidation', which Disraeli had urged, continued to fascinate the later Victorians. Economic depression in the years 1876–79, 1883–86 and 1893–94, the growth of high protective tariffs in Germany and the United States, the 'Scramble for Africa', the spread of international rivalry for territory in Asia and the Pacific, and the challenge of Germany as a naval power, all fostered the growth in Britain of what, after the 1870s, came to be called 'imperialism'. In 1883 Sir John Seeley, the Cambridge historian, argued that Russia and the United States were great powers because of their bigness, and that Britain should unite with the 'Greater Britain' beyond the seas to form a third world power.

In 1884 this trend took a more practical form in the foundation of the Imperial Federation League, a pressure group to popularize federation. Although the League disbanded after nine years, there was undoubtedly a remarkable growth of popular 'imperial' sentiment in the 1880s and 1890s. The first colonial conference was held in 1887 in an attempt to inaugurate closer co-operation with the self-governing colonies in providing for defence. The second conference, in 1897, coincided with the diamond jubilee of Queen Victoria's accession, which was made into a great imperial pageant.

By this time, moreover, the imperialists had made their greatest convert in Joseph Chamberlain. Chamberlain was a rather puzzling, changeable man, with somewhat unstable enthusiasms, who after leaving school at sixteen established himself as a wealthy and successful businessman in a firm of Birmingham screw manufacturers. Attracted to politics by the Radicalism of John Bright, he became a reforming Mayor of Birmingham at the age of thirty-seven, and was elected to Parliament three years later after bitterly attacking Disraeli, then prime minister. He joined Gladstone's Cabinet in 1880 at the age of forty-four and was expected by many people to succeed Gladstone as the Liberal leader. By the end of the century he was the most magnetic political personality in Britain. Some people regard him as the greatest 'might-have-been prime minister'.

In what sense was Chamberlain an 'imperialist'? He certainly did not support Disraeli in the 1870s. In fact when Disraeli challenged Russia in the Eastern Question (1876–78) Chamberlain denounced imperialism if it meant 'jingoism'. But in the 1880s Chamberlain became interested in colonial affairs. He was not entirely convinced of the wisdom of giving up the Transvaal in 1881. He began to have doubts about Britain's rigid adherence to free trade in a world where high-tariff industrial nations were beginning to compete with her. He was antagonized when the French, Russians or Germans appeared to 'steal a march' on Britain in Africa, Asia or the Pacific. He visited Egypt after the British occupation in 1882, and although he had disliked the original intervention, he was impressed by the sight of British administration. These incidents began his conversion. His split with the Liberal Party in 1886 over Gladstone's policy of home rule for Ireland, gave him, for a time, an independent position. In 1887 he visited North America.

From this period onwards two ideas combined in Chamberlain's mind to produce a new brand of the ideal of empire consolidation. The first was the need for social reform at home. The second was an enthusiasm for Anglo-Saxon solidarity abroad. The two together produced a vision of a united empire, developing its backward portions, and contributing to Britain's ability to meet her industrial competitors and to wipe out poverty at home. He planned to do this by abandoning free trade and granting preferences to colonial goods, thus making the empire into an imperial customs union.

In 1895 Chamberlain threw in his lot with the Conservative Party and from 1895 to 1903 filled the office of colonial secretary. He certainly gave the Colonial Office a stronger voice in the Cabinet, endeavoured to quicken the pace of expansion and development in the tropics, and, of course, he played a major, and sometimes unfortunate, role in the polemics that led to the South African war. But he failed to consolidate the empire. He could not persuade the self-governing colonies to enter a Federal Council or a customs union. Thus in 1903 he resigned from office, broke with the Conservative leadership, and set out on his campaign for tariff reform.

His campaign was a crusade for social reform and imperialism. 'Tariff reform means work for all,'ran his slogan. 'My lads,' he cried to a working men's audience,

> you see those works yonder – closed and dilapidated and fallen into decay. When you were boys, £200,000 a year in wages was earned in those works. What killed them? Foreign competition. What ought you to do? Keep the foreigner out.

He appealed to employers and employees alike with the argument that trade, wages and profits 'all depend upon the maintenance of this colonial trade'. He proposed a tariff of 5 per cent on meat and dairy imports, and 10 per cent on manufactures, combined with exemption for colonial goods. Thus Britain's industries were to be protected, while colonial raw materials and food would be admitted cheaply. Tariff reform was an economic refinement of the movement for empire consolidation. Imperial federation and imperial preference were to be the means of bringing together the empire in a more tangible way than ties of sentiment and affection. The overall objective was to ensure Britain's world power in the twentieth century.

ELIMINATING THE IMPERIAL FACTOR

The question of the relationship between Britain and the self-governing colonies received more attention in the last three decades of Victoria's reign than at any time previously. As Canada, Australia and New Zealand became nations in their own right, as South Africa moved from crisis to crisis, and Britain expanded her possessions in Africa, Asia and the Pacific, empire became a major topic of political controversy, academic debate, and even popular literature. Leopold Amery, who grew up in these years, confessed that the starting-point of all his political thinking 'from school days onwards, had been the British Empire and Commonwealth conceived as a unit and as the final object of patriotic emotion and action'.

But these years have so far been discussed in terms of ideas and dreams. We now have to ask: what actually happened? And the first thing that stands out is that in an age when grand and visionary ideas were being freely bandied about, the men in Whitehall, civil servants and ministers, did not often indulge in flights of imperial fancy. They merely dealt with problems as they came up. Only rarely did they prejudge future issues by thinking ahead. Responsible government and Canadian confederation left many legal ends untied, but British statesmen resisted the temptation to settle the issues by precise constitutional formulas. In this practical, informal way, imperial ties were progressively loosened.

The Colonial Laws Validity Act

An excellent example of this approach to problems may be seen in the one piece of legislation of general constitutional application in the nineteenth century: the Colonial Laws Validity Act of 1865. This act was designed to clarify the position of colonial parliaments in relation to the theoretical supremacy of the British Parliament. It arose from peculiar circumstances.

When responsible government was originally granted certain limits to colonial legislation remained. It was assumed, in the first place, that matters of general, 'imperial', interest (such as trade and defence) would come under the British Parliament. Therefore the Crown in Parliament remained supreme in the empire. Colonial laws were also limited to the territory of the colony concerned and were subject to the traditional check first imposed on the Virginia Assembly, that they should not conflict with, or be 'repugnant' to, British law. But what was the real difference between 'imperial' and 'colonial' business, and what did 'repugnancy' amount to? These matters had not been defined. The Colonial Office had been left to determine whether acts of colonial parliaments either impinged upon the general business of the empire, or conflicted with British law. The Colonial Office fulfilled its responsibilities with great restraint, but Sir Frederic Rogers defended the retention of theoretical supremacy, in case the colonies passed 'immoral' laws.

In 1858 they received a rude shock from South Australia. Here Judge Benjamin Boothby of the colonial Supreme Court challenged the validity of the South Australian Constitutional Act, claiming that some of its provisions were not specifically authorized by the British

Parliament, and went on to declare four bills of the colonial parliament similarly invalid. That Boothby was quite correct made the matter all the more embarrassing.

The Colonial Office hastily prepared two acts of Parliament which were passed to validate the South Australian constitution and the other laws. Rogers was prompted to suggest that a 'Constitution for the responsible government colonies' should be written. But Edward Cardwell, the colonial secretary, resisted this idea and the only result was the Colonial Laws Validity Act of 1865. This unexciting piece of law upheld the disputed South Australian laws. It also enunciated two points of general application, by confirming that colonial parliaments had the right to amend their own constitutions, and by declaring that the doctrine of 'repugnancy' should apply only to colonial laws which conflicted with specific British Acts of Parliament (or Orders in Council), not with the 'general principles' of English law. Thus a considerable constitutional landmark was passed, but only in response to the acts of a pedantic judge.

Canada's Freedom of Action

In a similar, practical way, the Dominion of Canada was gradually conceded her 'independence' after Confederation. When government departments in Whitehall tried to assert their authority in matters concerning Canada, the Colonial Office stepped in to uphold the Dominion's point of view.

The Treasury tried in the 1870s to dictate the way the Canadian government utilized loans which had been guaranteed by Britain. But Lord Carnarvon, the colonial secretary, brushed technicalities aside and told the Cabinet in 1877 that it was 'highly inexpedient on political grounds' to interfere with Canada's financial affairs. Similarly, when the Board of Trade, as guardian of Britain's policy of free trade, queried Canada's adoption of protective tariffs as part of the 'National Policy', Robert Herbert, the permanent under-secretary, wrote in 1879: 'It is not the province of Her Majesty's government to comment upon – still less to interfere in – its policy.' The Colonial Office also sympathized with the Canadian case, when the Lord Chancellor objected in 1875 to a clause in the bill creating a Canadian Supreme Court, which curtailed appeals by Canadians to the judicial committee of the House of Lords. In all these cases, orthodox thinkers argued in favour of the financial, commercial or judicial 'unity' of the empire. The Colonial Office, while not denying the theory, argued that on grounds of *policy* Britain should not, in practice, meddle with Canadian affairs.

Even when it came to the cherished doctrine of the 'diplomatic unity' of the empire, by which the Foreign Office conducted foreign affairs for the empire as a whole, the Canadians gained one or two minor advances. In 1871, when an Anglo-American commission met in Washington to find ways of settling several disputes, which included the question of fisheries off the east coast of the Dominion, Sir John Macdonald, the Canadian prime minister, was one of the British envoys and he was a signatory of the Washington Treaty. After the British government had conceded to Canada and the Australian colonies the right to make their own tariff arrangements, clauses were inserted into British commercial treaties either excluding or including the colonies.

In 1880 the Dominion made a further advance by appointing the first High Commissioner in London. By so doing she pioneered one of the distinctive features of the modern Commonwealth. Many of the colonies had long maintained 'Agents' in London. After confederation Canada experimented with representation by Emigration Agents, by appointing a Canadian-born M.P. as 'General Resident Agent', by sending a notable Canadian leader as 'Financial Commissioner'. But this was not satisfactory. In 1878 Macdonald, the prime minister, inquired whether a Canadian representative might be given semi-diplomatic status in London, to be a form of 'Canadian ambassador'. But the Colonial Office preferred that the Canadian representative should have a more 'domestic' position, and be able to talk with government departments other than the Foreign Office. The High Commissioner, first appointed in 1880, combined something of the function of ambassador, with that of an informal delegate of the Canadian government.

After the appointment of a High Commissioner in London, the Canadians made further inroads into diplomatic affairs. When, for example, the Canadian government wished to negotiate with Spain over trade with Cuba in 1884, the normal procedure was followed by which the Foreign Office conducted the negotiations. But as one of its envoys it appointed Sir Charles Tupper, the Canadian High Commissioner, who conducted the negotiations. At the same time Canada demanded representation at an international conference on the question of submarine cables. The Canadian delegate to Paris in 1883 was the first independent Canadian envoy.

Thus although the Foreign Office still formally controlled the foreign policy of the empire, in the 1870s and 1880s Canadians not only were consulted when their interests were at stake, but in certain minor matters they were delegated by the Foreign Office to conduct diplomatic business. In the same way, the Federal Council in Australia was intended to give the Australian colonies a say in relations with the Pacific Islands. In these practical ways, new forms of the 'loose tie' theory of empire were evolved.

The Imperial Conference

If the Liberal view of empire was fulfilled by giving practical answers to specific questions, what became of the projects for consolidation and imperial federation? Here again, the matter was approached in an experimental manner. Federation was never accepted. Yet unexpected, and surprisingly workable, forms of co-operation and consultation emerged. By 1907 the 'Imperial Conference' had established itself as the institution of consultation between the self-governing colonies and the mother country. How, we must ask, was this system evolved?

The first colonial conference was called in 1887 for a mixture of practical, ceremonial and visionary reasons. Empire defence was the prime concern and had already been the subject of a Royal Commission in 1879. Lord Salisbury, the prime minister, took the opportunity of the golden jubilee of Victoria's accession to call a conference to see what help the self-governing colonies could give Britain towards the defence of the empire. He also fulfilled the wishes of the Imperial Federation League, who had petitioned for a Royal Commission to discuss a possible federal union.

The 1887 conference was a large gathering which consisted of more than a hundred ministers from Britain and the colonies, representatives from the Crown colonies, and interested M.P.s and ex-governors. Its sessions, however, were confidential and a report was presented to Parliament afterwards. The government gained little support for imperial defence, other than an agreement by the Australasian colonies to subsidize the naval squadron in Australasian waters. Imperial federation appeared on the agenda. But expressions of colonial nationalism came as a revelation to most of the British delegates and Federation was definitely rejected.

The same thing happened at the second colonial conference in 1897. By this time Joseph Chamberlain had taken up the cause of empire unity. As colonial secretary he forcefully advocated to the conference the creation of a 'great Council of the empire' which he envisaged as a federal Parliament. But his only support came from New Zealand and Tasmania. Most of the leaders of the self-governing colonies, led by Sir Wilfrid Laurier, the Canadian Liberal premier, were 'generally satisfied under the existing conduct of things'.

Chamberlain returned to the subject of federation at the third colonial conference in 1902, at the time of Edward VII's coronation. After the success of Australian federation and the support of Canada, New Zealand and Australia in the South African war, Chamberlain now approached the colonial leaders with 'great anticipation'. He repeated his call for federation and for a Council of the empire. He also put forward a War Office proposal for creating an imperial reserve. But once more Laurier stood out in favour of the 'loose tie'. The imperial reserve was rejected. Imperial federation was not even discussed. The only constructive result of Chamberlain's last attempt at imperial consolidation was agreement to hold the colonial conferences regularly at four-yearly intervals.

By the early years of the twentieth century, it was quite clear that in view of the growth of colonial nationalism, the relationship between the self-governing colonies and the mother country needed re-definition. Imperial federation was clearly not the answer, yet new words were needed to describe the relationship, possibly new constitutional forms were needed to embody it. In 1900 George Bernard Shaw wrote that 'the words Empire, Imperial, Imperialist, and so forth are pure claptraps, used by educated people merely to avoid dictionary quibbles'. A Canadian writer in 1904 said: 'We are a colony . . . but we do not like the word. We feel it carries with it a flavour of inferiority.' Richard Jebb forcefully rejected the 'official imperialism' of the Chamberlain type and advocated a new 'constructive imperialism' which would place the new nations in an independent position. 'Do what you will with the word "Empire",' wrote a New Zealander in 1911, 'you will not rid it of an ungrateful harshness.'

A few people began in these years to substitute the word 'Commonwealth' for 'empire'. As far back as 1868 Lord Carnarvon had declared in the House of Lords that they belonged to an 'Imperial Commonwealth'. Lord Rosebery, after noticing the rise of Australian nationalism, remarked to an Adelaide audience in 1884: 'There is no need for any nation, however great, leaving the Empire, because the Empire is a Commonwealth of nations.' Bernard Shaw insisted that in 1900 the empire was no longer an old-fashioned, autocratic empire but a 'democratic Commonwealth'. In the same year Sir Henry Campbell-Bannerman told the Australian federation delegates that he approved of the 'homely, native phrase, the British Commonwealth' and felt it a pity that Australia had appropriated it. Thus, in the new atmosphere of colonial nationalism, 'Commonwealth' came informally into use. But it is very important to remember that it was used at this stage merely as a more friendly-sounding substitute for 'Empire', or for what Edmund Barton of Australia called the 'brotherhood of nations'.

Because of this new atmosphere, the colonial conference which met in 1907 was of the greatest significance. In preparation for the conference Lord Lyttelton, the colonial secretary, made yet another bid for imperial consolidation. He circulated a proposal that the conference should become an 'Imperial Council' and that a permanent 'Commission' should be created to provide continuity between meetings. Now a clear division appeared between the Australians and New Zealanders, who on the whole favoured the idea, and the Canadians, who stood by the existing arrangements. Laurier wanted to keep Canada out of the 'vortex' of European militarism and he stood out against the idea of an imperial Council or Parliament. The conferences had become meetings on a 'cabinet to cabinet' basis: Canada wished to preserve this. The 1907 conference decided, therefore, to compromise. A resolution was adopted which, in a sense, set out a 'constitution' for the conference. The real significance of the 1907 resolution lay in the important new phrases which it used to describe imperial ties.

The first was the title 'Imperial Conference'. It would, in future, be held every four years under the presidency of the British prime minister, and the premiers of the self-governing colonies, along with the secretary of state for colonies, would be *ex officio* members. A second significant change was the use of the title 'Dominions'. Laurier had expressed dissatisfaction with the phrase 'Dominions beyond the Seas' as it equated Canada with Crown colonies like Trinidad. The New Zealand prime minister therefore suggested 'self-governing colonies', but Laurier wanted something which would 'strike the imagination more'. After various technically correct (but very inelegant) phrases had been considered, such as 'self-governing communities of the Empire', 'British Dominions possessing responsible government' and 'self-governing Dominions', Laurier fell finally for the simple word 'Dominion'.

The third new word was 'consultation'. It was agreed that if important issues arose within the four-yearly intervals which required 'consultation between two or more governments', subsidiary conferences should be called, and it was suggested that a permanent secretarial staff should be created to handle the colonial secretary's correspondence about the conference. In other words, the Imperial Conference became, after 1907, an established 'institution' – with a fixed membership, regular meetings and procedures for reaching agreement by a system of 'one government, one vote'.

In this rather unexpected way the movements to 'loosen' and to 'consolidate' imperial ties, in a sense, coalesced. The extremes of independence or federation were avoided. Colonial nationalism received full expression, yet a satisfactory institution of consultation was created where matters of common concern could be aired. But would the Imperial Conference solve permanently the question of Britain's relations with the new nations? The test of the new system came in the 1914–18 war.

THE DOMINIONS AND THE 1914-18 WAR

During the first world war co-operation between Britain and the Dominions reached its highest and closest level, through the development of the Imperial War Cabinet in 1917–18. This rekindled the hopes of the supporters of imperial federation. But, in fact, the war only confirmed the strength of nationalism, which had also now welled up in India. Notable contributions by Dominion armies and navies in the war confirmed a trend towards 'separate' armed forces which was pronounced just before the war. The negotiations for a peace settlement after the war gave the Dominions greater international recognition, which culminated in separate foreign offices, diplomatic representation and negotiation of treaties.

Imperial Defence

Defence had been one of the anomalies of the era of responsible government. Even after the withdrawal of the garrisons in 1869, it was still assumed that the defence of the self-governing colonies from external attack and the maintenance of sea-power were British responsibilities. However, no very precise arrangements were made. Ever since the first colonial conference in 1887 the British government had sought some colonial contribution to empire defence. Canadian boatmen and New South Wales volunteers who served in the Gordon Relief Expedition to the Sudan in 1885 were useful tokens of goodwill. But as international territorial rivalry intensified after the 1880s and Germany began to compete in naval power in the 1890s, the defence issue became urgent.

The first support came from Australasia. After considerable discussion in the early 1880s the Australasian colonies decided that a powerful naval squadron was needed in Australian waters to ward off potential raiders, and prevent disruption of shipping lanes or a threat via the Pacific Islands. At the 1887 colonial conference the Australasians agreed to pay an annual subsidy of £126,000 for ten years towards the cost of the Australasian squadron. To this was added, after the 1897 conference, £30,000 from the Cape and £12,000 from Natal. These were really, in the widest sense, only token payments.

During the South African war more tangible aid came in the shape of 16,000 Australian, 8,000 Canadian and 6,000 New Zealand troops, sent and financed by the Dominion governments. But after the war the dream of a truly 'Imperial Navy' or 'Imperial Reserve' proved as false as the hope of imperial federation. It is true that considerable effort was made to co-ordinate the administration of defence. The creation of the Army Council in 1904 was followed by the Canadian Militia Council and the Australian and New Zealand Defence Councils. A special imperial defence conference was held in London in 1909. Dominion officers attended the Staff College, and Dominion Staff Colleges were also founded. Slightly increased naval subsidies were forthcoming from Australia, the Cape and Natal, also from New Zealand and Newfoundland. In 1912 the Canadian High Commissioner in London joined the Committee for Imperial Defence. But when it came to actual armed forces, Canada and Australia, after considerable controversy, favoured separate Dominion services. By 1914 the first ships were delivered.

New Zealand was the one Dominion to hold out for imperial forces. She supported the idea of an imperial reserve in 1902. She stood by the principle of 'one sea, one empire, one navy' when Canada and Australia planned their national navies. In 1909 New Zealand offered to pay for two first-class battleships for the Royal Navy and in 1911 Sir Joseph Ward, the prime minister, made a last effort at getting unified defence by proposing to the Imperial Conference an 'Imperial Parliament of Defence'. But after his failure, even New Zealand ordered a cruiser in 1913 for a 'New Zealand Division' of the Royal Navy, to be under New Zealand control in time of peace. By the time war broke out in 1914, the Dominions had certainly given considerable thought to defence questions. Many matters of administration had been co-ordinated with Britain, but the principle of 'separate' forces had been accepted.

The Dominions' War Effort

The trends of the previous decade were confirmed by the experiences of war. Close imperial co-operation continued along with the growth of well-proven national armies. 'Whatever happens, Australia is part of the Empire. When the Empire is at war, Australia is at war': the sentiments of the Australian prime minister on the eve of war were echoed widely in the Dominions. When Britain declared war on 4 August 1914, the empire was committed as a whole. Australia had already offered 20,000 men, New Zealand 8,000 and soon Canada offered a Division, although there was later great soul-searching about the war. Only in South Africa was there serious talk of staying out of the war. Some of the more extreme Afrikaner nationalists, led by Colonel Maritz, who held a commission in the German colonial forces, revolted against the government. Thus the Union's war effort began with a campaign against the rebels. By the end of the war, more than a million Dominion troops had served alongside 5 million from the United Kingdom and $1\frac{1}{2}$ million from India. Nearly 150,000 Dominion soldiers and sailors lost their lives in the war.

Full justice to the exploits of the Dominion armies in the 1914–18 war cannot be done in a few paragraphs. They bore the brunt of the campaigns to capture the German colonies in 1914–15. The Australians captured New Guinea; the New Zealanders, Samoa. The South Africans took German South-West Africa and contributed to the campaign in German East Africa. A celebrated Australian and New

K

Zealand Army Corps fought against the Turks by defending the Suez Canal in 1915 and also in the ill-fated Gallipoli campaign, where nearly 10,000 of their number gallantly laid down their lives. 'Anzac Day' (25 April, the anniversary of the landings) is still celebrated as a day of remembrance in the Antipodes. The Australians and New Zealanders, along with a South African brigade, also served in the western desert and in Palestine.

The greatest Dominion contribution was made on the western front in France. Here, by 1918, there was a Canadian Corps under the Canadian, General Currie, and an Australian Corps under the Australian, Sir John Monash, a New Zealand Division, and a South African Battery, a Newfoundland Battalion and a small detachment from Rhodesia. Twelve thousand Canadians flew in the Royal Flying Corps and Australia founded an Air Squadron of its own. A rough comparison of military contributions may be given as: Great Britain, 700,000 lost out of 6 million serving; Canada, 156,000 lost out of 450,000 sent overseas; Australia, 59,000 lost out of 330,000 sent overseas; New Zealand, 17,000 lost out of 112,000 sent overseas; and South Africa 7,000 lost out of 76,000 serving out of the Union. If these exploits gave to the ordinary soldiers and sailors of the Dominions, and their relatives at home, a sense of national pride, what attitude did the political leaders take to the war?

The Dominions and Foreign Policy

The most significant effect of the war for imperial relations was the insistence of the Dominions for a voice in the making of foreign policy. Although slight concessions had been made in the Victorian age by admitting Canadians into certain negotiations which concerned the Dominion, the Canadians had felt betrayed in 1903 when Britain gave way over the Alaska boundary to the United States in the interest of Anglo-American relations. Laurier bitterly told his Parliament: 'So long as Canada remains a dependency of the British Crown, the present powers we have are not sufficient for the maintenance of our rights.' Similarly, Australia and New Zealand protested when the Anglo-French Condominium in the New Hebrides was arranged in 1906 without consultation with them. Such incidents stressed the desire of the new nations for a new status and for regular consultation, which led to the changes of the 1907 conference. Yet the 'diplomatic unity' of the empire proved to be the hardest feature of British control to break. This was well illustrated at the Imperial Conference of 1911.

The 1911 conference was the first to be held under the 1907 'constitution' and was graced by the presence of the British prime minister in the chair. It was held in the Foreign Office rather than the Colonial Office and Sir Edward Grey, foreign secretary, came to outline British foreign policy. But this was hardly 'consultation', in the full sense of the word; the Dominions were being 'told'. In fact, the whole point of the New Zealand premier's abortive project for a Parliament of Defence was to give the Dominions 'some voice – proportioned it may be, to their size, and contributions, in such vital questions of peace and war'. Sir Robert Borden, who succeeded Laurier in 1911, had the same end in mind, when he told the Canadian Parliament in 1912: 'When Great Britain no longer assumes sole responsibility for defence upon the high seas, she can no longer undertake to assume sole responsibility for, and sole control of, foreign policy.' The Imperial Conference obviously did not meet Dominion views on foreign policy. The declaration of war in 1914 was a British decision, and for three years the Dominions, while giving willing and generous aid, were not consulted on strategic planning.

Thus it became evident in the early years of the war that the Dominions needed wider recognition of their nationhood than the 'Dominion status' they had been accorded in 1907. Sir Clifford Sifton (Canadian Defence Minister) declared in 1915 that 'it will no longer do for Canada to play the part of a minor'. She had forces greater than the combined might of Napoleon and Wellington at Waterloo and had just dispatched to Europe the greatest army ever to cross the Atlantic. He believed the rest of the world would henceforth say to Canada: 'You can attend to your own business.' Yet the Foreign Office still spoke for the empire. The strength of Dominion feeling about this final anomaly was illustrated vividly when Andrew Fisher arrived in London as High Commissioner for Australia and remarked:

> If I had stayed in Scotland, I should have been able to heckle my member on questions of Imperial policy, and to vote for or against him on that ground. I went to Australia. I have been Prime Minister. But all the time I have had no say whatever about Imperial policy – no say whatever. Now that can't go on. There must be some change.

How would Britain, with the Anzacs being slaughtered at Gallipoli and Canadians suffocating from poison gas at Ypres, meet the

Dominion demand for a voice in the high councils of the empire?

The answer was the Imperial War Cabinet. First of all, Dominion premiers were merely invited to attend the Cabinet if they happened to be in London. In 1915 Borden, of Canada, and in 1916 Hughes, of Australia, briefly joined their British colleagues in this way. But after Lloyd George's accession to the Prime Ministership in 1916 a dramatic change was made. He called all the Dominion premiers and representatives of India to London in 1917, not only for a session of the Imperial Conference (which was overdue), but also to attend an entirely new body, the Imperial War Cabinet. It consisted of the five members of the British War Cabinet, the Dominion premiers (although the Australian prime minister was detained by a general election at home), two Indians, a Newfoundlander, the colonial secretary and the secretary of state for India.

The Imperial War Cabinet met in the years 1917–18 to discuss war aims and the post-war settlement, and became the high-water mark of close co-operation with the Dominions. It was the nearest approach to an 'Imperial Council' such as the federation school had dreamed of. But, like so many recent developments in imperial relations, it was really only a practical way of meeting an immediate crisis, not a model for the future. Sir Robert Borden, the Canadian, described it best as 'a Cabinet of Governments':

> Every Prime Minister who sits around that board is responsible to his own Parliament and to his own people; the conclusions of the War Cabinet can only be carried out by the Parliaments of the different nations of our Imperial Commonwealth. Thus, each Dominion, each nation, retains its perfect autonomy.

Although it excited the exponents of federation to make their last attempts to create an organic unity, the War Cabinet, as Borden indicated, had the opposite effect.

Federation finally failed because the Dominions were forced to consider their international status at the time of the peace settlement. They were not consulted over the Armistice in 1918 and it was originally proposed that they should be represented at the Paris peace conference only as part of a British empire delegation, which was to be equal to that of France, Italy, Japan and the United States. But this was not acceptable to Dominion leaders, especially the Canadians and Australians. They demanded at least equal treatment with small states like Belgium. In part they got their way. Britain, as one of the great powers, was finally given five delegates to the conference (which could include Dominion representatives). Canada, Australia and South Africa received two delegates each, and New Zealand, one. India, which (as we shall see in Chapter 7) had just been promised responsible government in the future, was granted two delegates. Thus, if the Dominions did worse than Brazil, Belgium and Serbia, which each had three, they had the unique advantage of 'double' representation through their own delegates and the British delegation.

How did membership of the peace conference affect the international status of the Dominions? No clear answer was ever given to this question. 'Double representation' certainly gave them a big influence. General Smuts (who went as a member of the British delegation) was one of the major figures at Paris. But the precise status of the Dominions was left curiously ambiguous. They became eligible for membership of the League of Nations Assembly, but the Council of the League was to consist of the five great powers and four other 'states'. Were the Dominions 'states'? Even this was not settled. A resolution was merely agreed making the 'self-governing Dominions' eligible for membership, and Canada was in fact elected to the Council in 1927.

The ambiguity of the Dominions' status continued when it came to the signing of the Treaty of Versailles. Borden proposed that under the general heading, 'The British Empire', separate signatures should be added beside the United Kingdom, the Dominion of Canada, and so on, to emphasize their equality. But on the rather more ceremonial document itself the British representatives signed in the name of the Crown and the Dominions followed under sub-headings: 'for Canada', etc. Even the printing of an alphabetical list of signatories of the League of Nations Covenant, with the names of the four Dominions and India indented after 'British Empire', did nothing to resolve the precise international status of the Dominions. This became an immediate problem for the post-war Imperial Conferences.

Full Equality

Much thought was devoted to the meaning of 'Dominion Status' in the post-war years. One reason for this was a resolution passed by the Imperial Conference which met in 1917 (at the same time as the War Cabinet) that a special constitutional conference should meet after the war to consider the 'constitutional relations' of the component parts of the empire. But the main reason was that the war and the peace conference had both proved that Dominion status, as determined in 1907, was unsatisfactory. General Smuts warned in 1921: 'Unless Dominion status is settled soon in a way which will satisfy the legitimate aspirations of these young nations, we must look for separatist movements in the Commonwealth.' Would a genuine 'constitution' for the empire have at last to be written?

A few dreamers still hankered after imperial federal union. In fact, during the war Lionel Curtis, an Oxford historian, published two books *The Problem of the Commonwealth* and *The Commonwealth of Nations* (both in 1916) which did a great deal to popularize the word 'Commonwealth', which, as we have seen, had come into use informally before the war. But Curtis's 'Commonwealth' was to be an organic union. His books were the result of the work of *Round Table* study groups, which had started in 1910, and one of the questions they studied was 'how a British citizen in the Dominions can acquire the same control of foreign policy as one domiciled in the British Isles'. He was at pains to refute the arguments of those who said federation was impossible. He suggested that an 'Imperial Convention' should be called after the war to draft a constitution, just as the Anglo-Scottish Union and the Canadian, Australian and South African unions had been made.

General Smuts, on the other hand, wanted to keep to a loosely knit Commonwealth. Early in 1921 he drafted a statement on the 'Constitution of the British Commonwealth' in which he emphasized the continuing ambiguity of the Dominions' position in foreign affairs. Other nations, he insisted, could not understand the unwritten British constitution or 'how, without a change of law, a British Colony became in constitutional fact an independent state'. He also supported the idea that a declaration of constitutional rights should be published which would indicate that the British Parliament had no power over the Dominions and that in foreign policy the Crown in the Dominions had the same position as it did in Britain.

Smuts also wanted to find a peacetime version of the close co-operation of the war years. To do this he wanted to supersede the Imperial Conference by a three-tier system of consultation: a wider four-yearly 'Commonwealth Congress' (an embryonic Commonwealth Parliamentary Association), a two-yearly prime ministers' meeting, and a smaller 'Dominions Committee' of premiers or deputies, served by a Commonwealth 'Secretariat' to give continuity in between. Finally, Smuts stated his preference for the name 'Commonwealth of Nations'.

The first post-war Imperial Conference met in 1921, but rejected the idea of a constitutional conference. The Canadians were as satisfied as ever with the loose tie, and Hughes (of Australia) declared himself 'strongly opposed to any attempt to reduce the Commonwealth to writing'. The delegates decided that 'continuous consultation' would require great improvements in communications to be effective. In view of 'the constitutional changes since 1917' they agreed there was no need for a constitutional conference.

What were these 'constitutional changes since 1917'? Were the Dominions really satisfied? They had seen the Imperial War Cabinet, received separate representation at the peace conference, and they were members of the League of Nations. In 1920 a further step was made by Canada, who gained the right to appoint a minister in Washington. Dominion status also received, perhaps, slightly greater international significance when the Irish Free State was given the same constitutional status as Canada in the Anglo-Irish 'Treaty' of 1921. The Dominions were represented, on Smuts's insistence, as part of the British Empire delegation to the Washington conference of 1921–22 and they signed the naval limitation and Pacific treaties. If these continuing 'informal' steps were possible, why did the 1926 declaration become necessary? The answer may be found in a series of events which made Canada and South Africa press for a new definition.

The first breach in the diplomatic unity of the empire occurred in 1922 over the Chanak incident. Britain, occupying a neutral zone between Greece and Turkey, was threatened by the Turks. There was a chance of war. Lloyd George, the prime minister, cabled for help from the Dominions. While Australia and New Zealand gave somewhat doubtful consent, Canada and South Africa refused. Fortunately, there was no war, but the incident revealed that rapid consultation and genuine 'joint control' over foreign policy was difficult. It also showed, for the first time, that the Dominions were no longer willing to follow Britain automatically. Moreover, when a settlement was reached with the Turks in the Lausanne Treaty of 1923, Canada was most reluctant to ratify it, since she was not a signatory.

Another landmark was passed in 1923. Canada negotiated the

Halibut Fishery Treaty with the United States without the Foreign Office. The negotiations took place to regulate halibut fishing off the Pacific coasts of North America, and they concerned the U.S.A. and Canada alone. The British Ambassador in Washington refused to allow the Canadian envoy to sign on his own, but when the Canadian government insisted, Britain gave way. At the Imperial Conference of 1923 a recommended method of treaty-making by the Dominions was drawn up. Britain was one of the first to adopt the new arrangements. When in 1925 she signed the Locarno Treaty guaranteeing the territorial boundaries of the 1919 peace, India and the Dominions were exempted from its provisions.

Finally, two political changes in the Dominions further hastened the need for a declaration. The first was the election victory of General Hertzog, the Nationalist Party leader, in South Africa in 1924. Hertzog was pledged to secure the Union's 'independent' status before the world. But after studying Smuts's draft 'constitution' of 1921, he came to the conclusion that South Africa had already secured 'a complete, international, independent status equal to any other Dominion'. He told the South African Parliament that the Union was 'as free and independent as England itself'. He wanted a formal declaration of this position. Hertzog defined a Dominion, most aptly, as 'a free, independent State with the right of international recognition by foreign powers, but with a common bond between it and Great Britain, residing in the sovereign'. He went to the Imperial Conference of 1926 to secure a formal adoption of this view.

Mr Mackenzie King of Canada came to the conference fresh from a dramatic constitutional crisis in the Dominion. A general election in 1925 had left the parties precariously balanced in the Canadian Parliament. Mackenzie King's government had to rely on independents for a majority; and so when faced with a motion of censure in 1926, the prime minister asked the Governor-General, Lord Byng, to dissolve Parliament and call an election. To his surprise Byng refused, as he believed Mr Meighen, the opposition leader, could form a government. Thus Mackenzie King resigned. But Meighen could not maintain a majority; he too had to ask for a dissolution, and in the election Mackenzie King was returned to power. He went to the Imperial Conference determined to get a ruling about the powers of a Governor-General.

Much of the controversy of the early 1920s might seem now to have been technical quibbling. But it was obvious that the tides of nationalism were running high in the Dominions and that insistence on the old forms would prejudice Dominion co-operation – and might even lead South Africa to secede. The 1926 Imperial Conference set up a committee on inter-imperial relations with the Earl of Balfour as chairman. After listening to a moderate statement of Hertzog's views and discussing the problem for several days, they presented their celebrated report.

They rejected the idea of a 'Constitution' for the empire and provided instead the Balfour declaration. The four basic characteristics of the Dominions were finally settled: their 'equality' of status; their 'autonomy' in internal and external affairs; their 'common allegiance' to the Crown; and their 'free association' in the Commonwealth. On the subject of the power of governors-general the committee decided that a governor-general represented the Crown, not the British government. The report concluded with a recommendation that the legal relationship of the Crown to Acts of Dominion Parliaments and the problem of technical limitations still remaining on Dominion laws, as laid down in the Colonial Laws Validity Act, should be considered by experts. This formed the subject of a special conference in 1929 and further discussion at the Imperial Conference of 1930. The movement towards full equality reached its culmination in the passage of the Statute of Westminster in 1931.

The Statute of Westminster

After the simplicity and clarity of the Balfour definition of 1926 the Statute of Westminster was enough to dampen anyone's ardour. There were plenty of people in the Dominions and in Britain who did not really wish to press the matter of Dominion status further. Mr Scullin, of Australia, expressed these misgivings vividly to the 1930 conference:

> We hold it is quite possible to reconcile complete and effective autonomy of the Dominions with the unity of the British Common-wealth as a whole – but not if we dot every 'i' and cross every 't'. We are a free association of peoples – to my mind there is nothing to be gained and perhaps a great deal to be lost, by attempting to crystallize our relations too closely within the confines of any formal document.

Similar fears were expressed in the House of Commons by Winston

Churchill who, while affirming his support for the 1926 declaration, called the new statute 'pedantic', 'painful', even 'repellent'.

For all its seeming technicality the Statute of Westminster was, however, a great landmark. Three centuries after the meeting in Virginia of the first colonial assembly, the supremacy of the British Parliament was breached. The Act recited in its preamble the part of the Balfour declaration about the Crown as symbol of the free association of the members of the Commonwealth, but the main provisions of the Act affirmed the supremacy of the Acts of Dominion Parliaments.

Limitations on Dominion laws laid down in the Colonial Laws Validity Act were repealed. The doctrine of the 'repugnancy' to British law, as a limit to Dominion law, was ended; Dominion parliaments were permitted to make laws which could apply outside their territory; British law would not extend to the Dominions unless the Dominion parliaments consented. Then, having swept aside the long-cherished principle of British Parliamentary supremacy, which in the eighteenth century had led to the loss of the American colonies, the Act provided certain qualifications. Some laws of general colonial importance were retained as they affected the rest of the empire. The Canadian, Australian and New Zealand constitutional Acts were exempt, by request of the Dominions. The Australian states were protected from extensions of the Australian federal government's powers. Finally, the application of the Act was left to the Dominions themselves. The Act amounted therefore to a renunciation by Great Britain of any rights over the Dominions and a confirmation of Dominion parliamentary sovereignty.

It was perfectly in keeping with the practical, rather than the theoretical, development of the new Commonwealth relationship that it took the Dominions some time to act upon the 1926 declaration and the Statute of Westminster. The main provisions of the Statute were not adopted by Australia until 1942 and New Zealand until 1947. Dominion sovereignty was demonstrated in the 1930s in the more tangible form of full Dominion control of their foreign affairs.

Even here the pace was uneven. The Irish Free State was the first to appoint a Minister to Washington in 1924, although Canada had been conceded the right three years earlier. Britain adapted herself to the new relationship quickly by creating in 1925 a separate Dominions Office, which received a separate secretary of state in 1930. Now that the Governor-General could no longer represent the British government, a High Commissioner was sent to Ottawa (1928), followed by appointments to Pretoria (1930), Canberra (1936) and Wellington (1939).

Canada had had a small department of External Affairs attached to the prime minister's office since 1912 and did not create a separate ministry until 1943. Her first Ministers went to Washington in 1927, Paris in 1938 and Tokyo in 1929. By 1938 she had High Commissioners in the other Dominion capitals. South Africa was quick to found a department of External Affairs in 1927 and soon sent legations to six European states and the U.S.A. But Australia did not send her own ambassadors abroad until 1940, when they went to Washington and Tokyo. Her department of External Affairs waited until 1943. New Zealand was slowest of all the Dominions to enter into the diplomatic field. She contented herself with a High Commissioner in London until 1943. A department of External Affairs was added to the prime minister's office in 1944. Thus, if diplomatic equality was the last right to be gained, the Dominions were obviously not eager to shoulder many burdens of diplomacy.

Commonwealth and Empire

By the 1930s the answer had finally been given to the question first raised on the eve of the American revolution, as to what the relationship should be between the colonies and the mother country. It was not such a readily understood answer as that given by the Americans in the Declaration of Independence. Indeed, it was an answer which some folk find difficult to grasp even today. The American tourist in the 1950s who said of the scarlet-coated, bearskin-helmeted soldiers 'changing the guard' at the Citadel in Quebec, 'That's the English garrison', obviously did not notice the name of the regiment. It was a French-speaking parachute battalion of the Canadian Army. Behind the trappings of symbolic and ceremonial British usages like the 'Crown', 'Parliament', 'Prime Minister', the 'King's Highway', the Honours List and, in Canada, even scarlet tunics, Dominion independence was real.

The Liberal view of empire had triumphed. By progressively relaxing the ties between colonies and mother country Britain had permitted new nations to grow, which became completely independent in internal and external policy, but which voluntarily maintained a close association under the Crown. The Dominions forced the mother country to evolve the Commonwealth of Nations.

But the Dominions, which were the basis of the Commonwealth, represented only one portion of the British empire. They were the true British *colonies* – in the sense of communities of British settlers who went to North America, South Africa and the Antipodes to build a new life and create what Gladstone called 'so many happy Englands'. They had, to a degree, come to terms with the existing French-Canadian and Afrikaner colonies. Parliamentary government in the Dominions could be interpreted as an extension of the rights which their citizens would have received if they had stayed at home.

But what of the rest of the empire – the old West Indian colonies, the Crown colonies, the new protectorates in Africa and Asia, the Indian empire? Here, by the 1930s, nationalism was also stirring. Would responsible government and Dominion status, the experience of the century from 1839 to 1939, provide a guide for British policy in Asia, Africa and the Caribbean. For British India it had been accepted in 1917. But elsewhere in the 1930s the answers to these questions were by no means clear.

6

The Doctrine of Trusteeship

DOMINION STATUS was evolved because the four new nations wished to be distinguished from the rest of the empire. But the conventional label 'dependent empire' hardly does justice to all those British possessions which had not yet received self-government. Some of the West Indian colonies retained their seventeenth-century legislatures; large parts of Africa and Asia were ruled by their own monarchs, under British protection; the Indian empire was always kept as a separate entity, with its own organs of control in London; some of the Crown colonies were simply seaports or strategic bases. If responsible government became a standard device of self-government in some areas, diversity seemed to be the order of the day in the rest of the empire.

But one basic historical distinction can be made between the Dominions and the rest of the empire. The new nations in Canada, New Zealand, Australia and South Africa were formed by settlers from Europe, mainly British (along with some French and Dutch), who went to make a new home in comparatively temperate and sparsely populated lands. We must not forget that the original inhabitants, were they Australian Aborigines, Indians of the Canadian west, Maoris or Bantu, all at various times put up a stout fight for their lands. But the colonists, because of their superior power and (apart from South Africa) their greater numbers, became supreme. Thus the new nations were European political societies, planted in America, Africa or the Antipodes, which, in common with the United States, developed their own characteristic brands of nationalism and democracy in the nineteenth century.

The remaining portions of the British empire were not 'colonies' in this sense. It is true that some of the planters in the West Indies made permanent homes there, and some European planter and merchant communities remained in places such as Mauritius, Ceylon and Singapore. In the twentieth century, of course, a new generation of settlers made colonies in the highlands of Kenya and in Rhodesia. But by and large, the British possessions outside the four Dominions were not 'colonies of settlement'. They were a legacy of Britain's trade and strategy.

In many cases the climate in these regions was tropical. In some cases, particularly in West Africa, mortality from diseases like malaria and yellow fever was a deterrent to Europeans until the development of preventive medicine. Moreover, these regions did not on the whole present 'wide open spaces' like the Canadian prairies, the Australian outback, and the South African veld. Large populations already existed, particularly in India, Ceylon and the Niger Delta. The Europeans came first on sufferance as timid visitors and often found well-developed societies: in some cases great and ancient civilizations. That these societies disintegrated to an extent which left Britain (and other European states) in control of a large part of Asia and Africa in the nineteenth century, can partly be attributed to existing power-struggles within Africa and Asia, but mainly to the effects of European commerce, power, technology and ideas.

In 1869 Sir Charles Adderley, the colonial reformer, defined the difference between the two sorts of empire as the 'Grecian' and 'Roman' aspects of empire. He saw the one consisting of kinsmen who formed new nations as partners. The other consisted of regions where trade and strategy were the main interest and he believed that territory gained temporarily in pursuit of these interests had to be ruled autocratically from home.

Britain's Motives in the Tropics

Why did Britain become involved in these regions? The simple answer is that Englishmen went to trade. They went to find raw materials and to sell manufactures. It is also remarkable that most of the empire in Africa, Asia and the Caribbean stemmed from two branches of Britain's overseas trade: the West India trade and the East India trade.

Trade with the West Indies was a major part of the so-called 'triangular trades' of the Atlantic. Slaves from West Africa were shipped to the West Indies; sugar and molasses from the West Indies were carried to New England and to England; New England rum was taken to England, the West Indies and West Africa, and English manufactures to America, West Africa and the West Indies. The 'geometry' of trade was, in fact, complex. These trades became so valuable in the seventeenth and eighteenth centuries that intense international competition developed and during the great wars from 1756 to 1815 Britain endeavoured to oust her rivals. The legacy, by the early nineteenth century, was the empire in the Caribbean and the small West African settlements.

The East India Company's trade led to rivalry with Portugal, France and Holland, and eventually to some form of British control throughout India, Burma and Malaya. Profit from the India trade came to depend on the tea trade from China, and the defence of the trade routes to India and China led eventually to the control of the Cape, Mauritius, Ceylon, the Malay Peninsula and Hong Kong. Control at the Cape led, as we have already seen, to the idea of 'paramountcy' in South Africa. When international rivalry resumed in the later nineteenth century, the maintenance of supremacy in South Africa, the Indian Ocean and the Suez Canal route led on to British control in Egypt and East Africa. Thus, over three centuries, the repercussions of two branches of Britain's trade seemed to be boundless.

But why did trade lead to 'control', and why was control exercised autocratically from London? Many statesmen who were involved in the expansion of the British empire would have found it difficult to answer that question. They were genuinely puzzled by what seemed an endless growth of irksome responsibilities. Adderley, who gave considerable thought to the problem in the mid-Victorian age, believed that it was 'always impossible for a great power like England to push itself in such neighbourhoods [Africa and Asia] without extending or being implicated'. He once declared to Disraeli: 'It looks just now as if the English were destined to open up Africa, but it's an awful destiny.'

There was, however, one theme which constantly reappeared on the lips of statesmen who considered these growing entanglements. It was that power brought responsibility. Edmund Burke declared, during a debate on the East India Company's charter, that political power over any men, or privileges granted to the exclusion of others, 'ought to be in some way or other exercised ultimately for their benefit'. Power and privilege was 'in the strictest sense a *trust*; and it is of the very essence of every trust to be rendered *accountable*'. Thus, while Britain progressively relaxed her ties with the self-governing colonies, she tended to increase her powers over British possessions in Asia, Africa and the Caribbean. She evolved what came to be called in the twentieth century the doctrine of 'trusteeship'.

How did this doctrine originate and in what specific ways did it affect the empire? It stemmed originally from a mixture of humanitarian, political and commercial motives. In the nineteenth century these motives had a profound impact upon the West Indies, West Africa and India. The first practical manifestation of this spirit was the campaign of evangelical Christians against the slave trade.

Humanitarians and the Slave Trade

During the three and a half centuries of the trans-Atlantic slave trade no less than 10–15 million Africans were carried off to the New World, where they were the progenitors of the modern Negro populations of the U.S.A., the West Indies and Latin America. By the beginning of the nineteenth century British traders had captured the lion's share of this trade. Fortunes made out of the slave trade and slave-operated plantations in the West Indies were used to found landed families in England, to build up the port of Liverpool and to provide some of the capital which enabled Britain to become the pioneer industrial nation. But at the same time as the British slave trade reached its peak in the eighteenth century, the great spiritual stirring known as the evangelical revival led a number of men to campaign against the trade.

In practice it took many years to end slavery. Although the Quakers of Pennsylvania began to urge their brethren to release slaves at the end of the seventeenth century, it was not until 1864 that the Royal Navy captured its last slaver off West Africa. The U.S.A. did not abolish slavery until 1865 and it continued in Cuba and Brazil until the 1880s. But by the middle of the eighteenth century the influence of Quaker pamphlets, the evangelical movement and the growth of humanitarian feelings had created a small but significant body of opinion hostile to slavery. West Indian planters who brought their slaves back to England (where, it is said, there were 15,000 in 1770) provided an immediate target. Granville Sharp, a lawyer and civil servant, studied the legal position of slaves. By forcing the celebrated

Somerset case in 1772 he secured Lord Mansfield's judgement making slavery illegal in Britain.

Slavery and the slave trade still remained in the British empire. But the loss of the American colonies in the War of Independence somewhat narrowed the target. Moreover by the 1780s the anti-slavery movement had gained momentum. William Wilberforce, the M.P. for Hull and a friend of Pitt, the prime mininster, became one of its most noted campaigners. An abolition society was formed which soon found a notable focus in the 'Clapham Sect', the influential followers of the Rev. John Venn, rector of Clapham. By 1791 the first of a series of abolition resolutions had been attempted in the House of Commons. Further organized support came from the newly founded overseas missionary societies. The Baptists led the way in 1792, followed in 1795 by the Independents, who formed the London Missionary Society, and in 1799 by the Anglican Church Missionary Society. Finally in 1807 (three years after Denmark pioneered the way) Parliament decreed that slave trading by British subjects was illegal. By the time of the Congress of Vienna in 1815 most of the major European powers, except Spain and Portugal, had legislated against the slave trade. Some states granted Britain the right to intercept suspected slave smugglers.

The abolition laws could not end the slave trade overnight and plantation slavery, of course, remained quite legally in the West Indies and in new possessions like the Cape, Mauritius and Ceylon. Some of the Clapham sect were too conservative to go on and demand the emancipation of the slaves. But reports of slave smuggling from West Africa and cruelty in the colonies kept alive humanitarian pressure.

Government action continued with the stationing in 1810 of a special squadron of the Royal Navy to cruise off the West African coast and intercept slaving ships. In the next 50 years, some 70,000 'recaptives', or 'Liberated Africans' as they were called, were freed and settled in Sierra Leone. In order to check illegal importing of slaves to the West Indies a system of slave registration began in Trinidad in 1812. Slavery was forbidden in the Albany settlement in South Africa in 1820.

Gradually a new generation of philanthropists, led by Thomas Fowell Buxton, a wealthy brewer and member of parliament, set out to banish slavery from the British empire. In 1823 a 'Society for the mitigation and gradual abolition of slavery throughout the British

Dominions' was founded. Its first success was the adoption of a policy of 'amelioration', under which slaves were given religious instruction, were permitted to make lawful marriages and could give evidence in court. After a slave revolt in Jamaica in 1831 led to the death or execution of 500 slaves, public attention was focused on the issue. The emancipation act was passed in 1833. From the next year all slave children were to be freed; adults would become 'apprentices', working three-quarters of their time for their former masters for wages in order to purchase their freedom. Compensation, to the total of £20 million, was also paid to owners by the British government.

The West Indies after Emancipation

What effect did the ending of slavery have on the British empire in the Caribbean? The answer depends upon the direction from which the question is viewed. In one respect, emancipation gave the final blow to the one-time brightest jewels of the empire. In the middle of the eighteenth century the West Indies were still a great source of wealth. Government House, Jamaica, was a sought-after seat. But by the beginning of the nineteenth century the original British islands, the Leewards, Barbados and Jamaica, were suffering from competition with new possessions captured in the wars between 1756 and 1815, such as the Windwards, Trinidad, Tobago, and British Guiana. Even more important, they suffered from competition from sugar produced more cheaply in the French islands, Guadeloupe and Martinique, and from Santo Domingo, Cuba and Brazil. Indeed, Dr Eric Williams, the historian, who in 1962 became the first prime minister of Trinidad and Tobago, has suggested that this situation provided an economic motive for abolishing the slave trade. British leaders, he argues, realized that British West Indies sugar could not compete, so that the islands and the slave trade had both become a liability. They therefore sponsored an international crusade to abolish slavery in order to ruin the French and Spanish sugar producers and leave the way open for British East Indian sugar to capture the European market.

Whatever truth there is in this interpretation – and there is no doubt that some East India merchants gave their vote to abolition for selfish reasons – it cannot detract from the genuine humanitarian revulsion against the slave trade at this time. What is certain is that there were plenty of indications before emancipation that the British West Indies were in decline. Two-thirds of the planters were 'absentees' living in

Britain. This not only encouraged lax and inefficient operations on the estates, but drained the islands of capital and leadership. Trade was upset by the wars between 1756 and 1815, which interrupted shipping and led to repeated conquests and restorations for some islands. After the Latin American republics gained their independence in the 1820s and Britain opened direct trade with the former Spanish and Portuguese lands, the West Indies lost their value as entrepôts. With the rapid growth of British manufactured exports to the U.S.A., the West Indies also lost their attraction as a market.

Finally, the emancipation of the slaves in 1834 was followed by the reduction of preferences on West Indian sugar, and, in 1854, by free trade in sugar. The plantations then rapidly declined. Sugar production fell by 50 per cent in ten years and by 1865 half the estates had closed. The spoilt children of the old empire had become the proud and awkward pensioners of the Victorians.

But, if the West Indies after emancipation are looked at from a different angle, we may recognize that a new concept of empire was evolving. In Jamaica, for example, a new economy emerged in the wake of the plantations. Former slaves began to cultivate new lands in the interior or to 'squat' on decayed estates. They made their living by growing provisions to sell in the towns. Thus, although by 1860 there were only twenty-nine large estates left in Jamaica, 50,000 small properties had appeared. After a steamer line was opened to New York in the 1860s a potential outlet for tropical fruit was evident. By the 1870s Jamaica found a new source of income in bananas. So although the traditional export economy had declined, a new indigenous way of life slowly emerged and new cash crops were possible.

A similar transformation took place in the government of the West Indies. Although the Windward Islands, which had been captured in 1763, had been granted representative assemblies on the old American and West Indian pattern, we saw (in Chapter 1) how during the Napoleonic wars the new Crown colony system was adopted in places like Trinidad and British Guiana. In the mid-Victorian age nearly all the rest of the West Indian islands were 'reduced' to Crown colony status.

The island assemblies fought bitterly against slave emancipation, and when it was forced upon them by the British government, these assemblies continued to represent a narrow, now resentful, propertied class. Emancipation did not give political rights to the bulk of the island populations. With the assemblies at odds with the British government, a situation developed which may in a sense be compared with that in upper Canada before responsible government. Indeed, after the inauguration of responsible government in Nova Scotia and Canada, Earl Grey proposed that responsible government was the only way to bring government and assembly into harmony in the West Indies. He suggested that they should be granted constitutions on the Canadian model.

For a short period in the mid-Victorian age the West Indies received a modified form of responsible government. In 1854 the Jamaican constitution was altered after the assembly refused to vote supplies as a protest against free trade in sugar. Under the new arrangements the legislative council consisted of four officials and thirteen nominated non-official members. The assembly, which remained elected by a narrow class of 2,000 voters, lost its right to initiate financial legislation. The 'executive' was to consist of the Governor, advised by a Privy Council made up of his chief officers, the Chief Justice and the Bishop and an entirely new body called the 'Executive Committee'. This committee, which was designed to associate the legislature with the Governor, consisted of four nominated non-officials – one from the legislative council and three from the elected members of the assembly. The Executive Committee thus bore a very slight resemblance to the ministries in Canada before the inauguration of full responsible government. But its position remained anomalous, since it was not fully responsible either to the Crown or to the legislature. Similar arrangements were made in the 1850s in Tobago, St Kitts, Nevis and Antigua.

The Colonial Office soon realized, however, that the West Indies were quite unsuited for self-government. How could assemblies so blatantly unrepresentative of the bulk of the population be granted responsibility, asked the veteran civil servant, Sir Henry Taylor? As the islands were fast becoming financial liabilities, the old representative constitutions became a bar to good government. The new free populations could never be 'represented' under existing conditions. Thus the idea took root that the West Indies should be persuaded to reconsider their constitutions and become Crown colonies.

In 1865 an uprising in Jamaica, followed by rash and ruthless reprisals by the governor, caused Cardwell, the colonial secretary, to suspend the constitution. By an Order in Council of 1866 Jamaica was reduced to a Crown colony. A single-chamber legislative council remained, which was entirely nominated and was made up of six officials and five non-officials. During the following decade constitutional negotiations were begun with all the islands. By 1875 all the Caribbean colonies except Barbados (to which might be added the Bahamas and Bermuda) agreed to give up their old constitutions and became Crown colonies. In 1868 the colonial secretary announced that the new legislative councils would all have a basic feature: 'that the power of the Crown in the Legislature, if pressed to its extreme limit, would avail to overcome every resistance that could be made at it.' In other words, the British government had stepped into the West Indies to protect the population from the power of the former slave-owning class.

The West African Settlements

The aftermath of the slave trade left Britain with three small footholds in West Africa. Merchants trading to Africa and slave traders had operated first in the River Gambia and then moved eastwards to

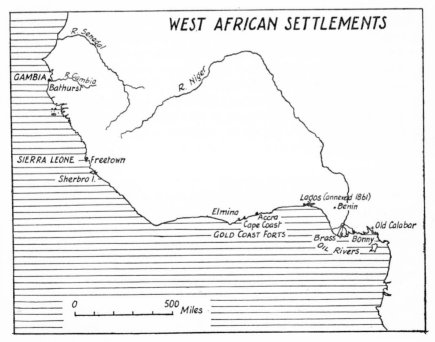

WEST AFRICAN SETTLEMENTS

the Gold Coast and the Niger Delta. To conduct their trade they built forts at the mouth of the Gambia and along the Gold Coast. In the Niger Delta they operated from hulks anchored in the main inlets. Their position was at all times precarious. Britain was not a colonial power in West Africa in the era of the slave trade.

The Gambia and Gold Coast forts were run, from 1750 to 1821, by a Company of Merchants and they frequently changed hands during European wars. The land on which the forts stood was not British-owned, but was rented from local African rulers. An interesting experiment between 1765 and 1783, known as the Province of Sene-gambia, with a constitution modelled, as far as possible, on the American colonies, came to grief in the War of Independence. Britain's first real possession in West Africa was the tiny settlement on the Sierra Leone peninsula, founded in 1787 by a philanthropic company. A colony of free slaves from England, Nova Scotia and Jamaica began at Freetown, which was intended to be the beginning of 'the foundation of happiness in Africa'.

By the beginning of the nineteenth century these small private enterprises in West Africa were in difficulties. The company could not manage Sierra Leone. And just as the law against the slave trade was about to remove the function of the Gold Coast forts, the African rulers in their vicinity were, in 1806, overrun by the powerful inland Ashanti state. Would Britain wash her hands of West Africa to expunge the guilt of the slave trade?

She did not. For more than half a century, it is true, West Africa was a bane to Whitehall and numerous attempts were made to get rid of the settlements. But a few small footholds were retained. They were the scene of some notable experiments in the Victorian age. They became the basis, eventually, of the independent nations of Ghana, Nigeria, Sierra Leone and Gambia.

Why did Britain stay in West Africa? One basic theme provides a clue to all her early nineteenth-century activities: the extirpation of the slave trade. Sierra Leone was taken over by the Crown in 1808. St Mary's Island in the mouth of the Gambia was annexed in 1816 and the town of Bathurst laid out. The Company of Merchants, which had administered the Gold Coast forts, was abolished in 1821 and the forts were taken over by the government. There was even a brief attempt in the 1820s to open diplomatic relations with Ashanti. But it was cut short and in 1826 Britain had to help the Fante states on the Gold

Coast to defeat the Ashanti army. After this Britain stopped paying rent for her forts on the Gold Coast and claimed the sites as British territory. In addition to these three territorial footholds in the Gambia, Sierra Leone and Gold Coast, a squadron of the Royal Navy patrolled the coast to intercept slaving ships. From such unpromising beginnings, and in spite of considerable official reluctance, Britain evolved some interesting experiments in new forms of tropical empire.

Sierra Leone came to have an influence out of all proportion to its size because of the unique nature of its society. In addition to the original 400 settlers from England (mainly freed slaves with some white women), the thousand or so loyalist Negroes from Nova Scotia and 500 rebel 'Maroons' from Jamaica, the population was steadily increased by migrants from the neighbouring regions, such as the Temne, and the recaptive slaves released by the Royal Navy.

These 'Liberated Africans' were usually enslaved as a result of warfare in the region of present-day Dahomey and Nigeria. They were purchased by slave dealers, often Portuguese or Brazilian, who tried to ship them to South America. If the British squadron managed to intercept the slavers the recaptives were taken to Sierra Leone, where in a generation, a most remarkable community grew.

Adults were supported by government for six months, given tools to build homes and encouraged to settle new farms and villages. Children were apprenticed to the settlers and were sometimes adopted by them. A large number were educated in mission schools run by Anglicans, Wesleyans and the Countess of Huntingdon's Connexion. Many were baptized and given European names. Some of them were recruited into the West India Regiment, which garrisoned the settlements. Later the War Office, worried about mortality among European officers, selected a few Sierra Leonians for training as army doctors. Others built up their own business houses and prospered in trade along the coast. The missions found valuable recruits for teaching and the ministry. By the middle of the nineteenth century some of the Sierra Leonians had made a notable career.

William Fergusson, a medical graduate of Edinburgh, Afro-West Indian by origin, was appointed governor of Sierra Leone in 1844. John Ezzidio, a Nupe ex-slave, who became a wealthy trader and a pillar of the Wesleyan Church, was elected a member of the legislative council under a new constitution in 1863, which provided for representation of the mercantile community. Most famous of all was

Samuel Ajayi Crowther, a Yoruba, enslaved at the age of fifteen in 1821. After landing in Sierra Leone, he was taken by missionaries to England, where he went to school for a time. Returning to the colony, he was the first student at Fourah Bay College, was ordained into the Anglican ministry, and took part in the official British expeditions to the Niger in 1841, 1854 and 1857. After founding the Anglican Niger Mission on the latter trip, he was consecrated as first bishop of the Niger in Canterbury Cathedral in 1864.

Crowther was only the most notable of several thousand Liberated Africans who returned to their homeland in the old Yoruba kingdom of Oyo, now part of Western Nigeria. Here they were responsible for inviting the Christian missionaries to follow them and they became the spearhead in the introduction of new influences.

On the Gold Coast, Britain's main influence was political, rather than social and religious. Here there was no philanthropic settlement like Sierra Leone, and the British government wanted to abandon the old slave traders' forts. In 1829 they were handed over to a committee of London merchants. The committee sent as its representative a remarkable young Scots soldier, Captain George Maclean, who turned out to be the unofficial 'empire builder' of the Gold Coast.

Maclean found trade on the coast unsettled by continuing rivalry between the small states of the seaboard and the strong Ashantis inland. In 1831 he negotiated a three-sided agreement. Ashanti renounced claims to rent from European forts or tribute from the seaboard states. The latter undertook not to molest Ashanti travellers to the coast. Maclean undertook to guarantee the agreement. Over the next ten years Maclean became a sort of 'arbitrator' for the Gold Coast. His sole legal power was that of a J.P. of the Sierra Leone courts with jurisdiction over British subjects within the forts. But African rulers sought his advice in their disputes. Soon he came to exercise a wide informal jurisdiction by consent.

In the 1840s the British government decided that Maclean's system was so beneficial that it should be made official. Thus in 1843 the government took over the forts, as an outpost of Sierra Leone. In the following years a number of Gold Coast rulers (not all) signed a 'Bond' by which they consented to Maclean's continuing officially as Judicial Assessor, 'moulding the customs of the country to the general principles of British law'. By these unexpected ways the so-called 'Gold Coast protectorate' was born. The third Earl Grey was so impressed by the experiment that in 1850 the Gold Coast forts became a separate Crown colony. When an Assembly of chiefs agreed to a poll tax to provide revenue, he later saw it as the beginnings of a 'rude Negro Parliament'. Grey believed that it should be Britain's aim

> to train the inhabitants of this part of Africa in the arts of civilization, until they grow into a nation capable of protecting themselves and managing their own affairs.

Although this proved a vain dream in the nineteenth century, Grey was one of the first to hint that self-government, which was becoming the basis for policy in the 'colonies', might also be applied in 'dependencies'.

The Niger Region

While new patterns of empire were evolving in Sierra Leone and the Gold Coast, various events conspired to focus attention on the Niger Delta region, where there was no British territory. In 1832 the Lander brothers discovered the mouth of the Niger and soon Macgregor Laird, the Liverpool shipbuilder, planned to use the Niger as a highway for trade into the interior. The Royal Navy squadron found that interception at sea was insufficient to check the export of slaves. Naval officers decided to tackle the slave trade at source. They intervened in local wars in the Niger Delta and in 1836 King Pepple of Bonny was the first Delta ruler to sign a treaty pledging himself against the slave trade. But by far the greatest influence in directing attention to the Niger was Thomas Fowell Buxton.

Philanthropists were shocked to find that even after the emancipation of slaves in the British colonies, the slave trade to South America continued unabated. In memoranda to the government, and finally in his book *The African Slave Trade and its Remedy*, published in 1840, Buxton demanded a new policy in West Africa. Britain should step ashore in Africa. The coast would have to be studded with trading stations, African rulers made to sign anti-slavery treaties, and while Britain kept the peace, new industries and agriculture should be promoted. A new economy was needed in West Africa to supplant the slave trade. Africa must be saved by 'calling forth her own resources'.

Official attempts to follow Buxton's lead soon came to grief. The Admiralty's Niger expedition in 1841 was turned back by malaria, and was soon ridiculed by Dickens as so much 'Borrioboola-Gha'. Early efforts to trade up river were disappointing. But when the Sierra Leonians began to re-emigrate back to their homeland in the 1840s a surprising new ground for Buxton's theory appeared.

Many of the Christian Sierra Leonians were Egba by origin and returned to the new Egba town of Abeokuta. Here they called for the missionaries to follow them: Wesleyans, Anglicans and later American Baptists. Soon cotton gins were supplied by English philanthropists. and Abeokuta was hailed as the 'Sunrise in the Tropics'. Finally in 1849 Lord Palmerston, who took a particular interest in the crusade against slavery, appointed a consul to watch over these growing interests. By the 1850s John Beecroft, consul in the Bights of Benin and Biafra had become, like Maclean of the Gold Coast, the un-official arbitrator of the Yoruba country and the Niger Delta.

By the middle of the nineteenth century, then, as imperial responsibility began to be asserted in the West Indies, Britain awoke to some sense of responsibility for the effects of the slave trade in West Africa. In Sierra Leone, the Gold Coast and the Niger Delta region imaginative ideas were born. In the short run, they all came to very little. Sierra Leone stagnated, the Gold Coast protectorate became involved in wars with Ashanti, and in the Niger region Britain became entangled in Yoruba wars and inter-city wars in the Delta.

But if Britain did little to fulfil the ideals of visionaries like Buxton and Grey, her presence in West Africa sowed new ideas among some of the coastal inhabitants. Celebrated Africans from the settlements like Bishop Crowther of the Niger, Sir Samuel Lewis, the Sierra Leonian lawyer and Legislative Councillor, and Dr James A. Horton, who served in various officials posts and wrote a book in 1868 urging the creation of new independent nations on the Gold Coast, were the progenitors of a new *élite*, whose twentieth-century successors would resent the extension of colonial rule caused by the 'Scramble for Africa'.

The Select Committee on Aborigines

The aftermath of the slave trade and slavery saw new ideas of trusteeship evolved in the West Indies and West Africa. But what of the original inhabitants in the self-governing colonies? We have seen how the Maoris in New Zealand, the Bantu in South Africa and the *métis* in Canada received short shrift from the colonists. This problem was not neglected by British philanthropists. But, as in the Caribbean and West Africa, they found it difficult to fulfil their ideals.

Shortly after the passing of the slave emancipation act, a group of philanthropists in Parliament, largely influenced by missionaries in the Cape, turned their attention to the whole problem of 'aboriginal populations'. In 1835 a Select Committee of Parliament was formed under the chairmanship of Fowell Buxton. After sitting for no less than three parliamentary sessions the Aborigines Committee produced its celebrated report in June 1837.

The slave trade and slavery had been abolished, but the committee found that another great evil remained: the oppression of the original inhabitants in the colonies of settlement. The Committee declared that no national interest was served by encroaching on 'the rights of aboriginal inhabitants'. Britain's wealth and power had been 'given for some higher purpose than commercial prosperity and military renown'. Indeed, the God who had bestowed his gifts on Britain would ask how her wider influence had been employed. The country needed to decide upon the principles which should 'guide and govern our intercourse with these vast multitudes of uncivilized men'.

The committee, fully realizing that they were considering diverse peoples whose customs and institutions could not really be compared, enunciated three principles. The protection of 'aborigines' should be a duty of imperial government – it was not a 'trust' which could be left to local parliaments. On the whole, the committee opposed British territorial expansion and favoured 'protecting' aborigines. Thus labour contracts should be limited, lands not taken, British subjects outside the colonies be made amenable to British law, and the law tempered for aborigines within the colonies. Treaties, which in these circumstances could only be between unequal partners, were to be discouraged. Finally, Christian missionaries were to be encouraged in their work, but not only as pious and zealous men who brought moral and religious instruction. Missions should also bring 'well-matured schemes for advancing the social and political improvement of the tribes'. This report, it should be remembered, was published before the *Durham Report*. How far were its principles successful?

A number of experiments were made in the 1840s to fulfil the committee's ideals. Perhaps the most notable efforts were the schemes of Sir George Grey, as governor of South Australia (1841–45), New Zealand (1845–53) and governor of the Cape and High Commissioner in South Africa (1854–61). In each of these governorships Grey arrived at a time of trouble and fighting with the original inhabitants.

In each case he tried to follow the same principles in his policy.

Grey believed that the 'aborigines' should be 'civilized'. He wanted traditional authority systems and social customs to be superseded gradually by a new 'mixed' society. First, government would restore law and order. The police would protect the original inhabitants and a mixed constabulary would be formed. Resident Magistrates would administer the law, along with 'Assessors' so that British law could be tempered by customary usages. Missionaries were to spread Christianity and the government would assist mission schools. Government would also offer regular employment on road building and new agricultural developments; it would also create boarding schools, hospitals and savings banks. Thus Grey sought to turn his Australian Aborigines, Maoris and Bantus into law-abiding citizens, part of a European economy and society.

In some measure Grey inaugurated his programme in Australia, New Zealand and the Cape. The Resident Magistrates began work, hospitals and schools were created, and public works made a start. But the scale was all too small, in face of the size of the populations. And behind Grey's ideas was an oversimplified, even patronizing, attitude to traditional society. On the whole, the Aborigines Committee failed to save the peoples it considered from hardship. The Aborigines Protectorates of the Australian colonies failed to check a decline in population. Grey's successors in New Zealand allowed the colonists to take over Maori policy. In South Africa the Great Trek and the overcrowding of Bantu into some areas led to a series of conflicts. In Canada, the Indians and part-Indian *métis* found their interests neglected and feared the loss of their land. Yet, if the Aborigines committee achieved little in practice, particularly in the self-governing colonies, it publicized principles which were never completely forgotten. As British expansion in Asia, Africa and the Pacific reached its climax early in the twentieth century, the principles of trusteeship came to have a wider field of application.

What the example of Governor Grey vividly illustrates is the basic dilemma which the doctrine of trusteeship implied. Should Britain fulfil her 'trust' by policies of 'protection' or 'assimilation'? On this issue the Aborigines Committee report was somewhat ambiguous. It deprecated expansion and advocated limiting British contacts with non-European peoples. Yet it encouraged missionary work, and not only evangelism but also social and political improvement. Many times in Asia and Africa the 'protectors' and 'westernizers' would be joined in a debate which continued well into the twentieth century. In some parts of the remnants of empire, such as the Fiji Islands, the dilemma has yet to be resolved.

The East India Company in India

Nowhere was the dilemma of trusteeship so critical as in India. In a sub-continent which had been the seat of ancient, wealthy and powerful empires and was peopled by more than 100 million, differing in race, language and religion, Britain encountered the greatest of all her imperial problems. Here, on the one hand, the instruments of the Old Colonial System lingered on, in the shape of the East India Company, until 1857. Yet on the other hand, the Company was gradually transformed into an enlightened despotism. The government stepped in, as in the West Indies and West Africa, to regulate Britain's relations with the peoples of India. The scale of the task was altogether greater in India. But the basic dilemma was the same: should Britain fulfil her responsibility by keeping order and preserving the old India, or by creating a new Europeanized state?

Why did Britain embark upon the colossal task of ruling a population fifteen times bigger than her own? Put in the simplest terms, the answer is that the break-up of the Mughal Empire of India in the eighteenth century, combined with rivalry from the French, led the East India Company to become a great military power in India. When its wealth and power threatened to upset political stability at home, Parliament demanded the regulation of the Company. Thus the original idea of 'trusteeship' in India, as enunciated by Edmund Burke at the time of the American revolution, stemmed from domestic and political, rather than humanitarian, motives. Trusteeship first meant making the Company responsible to the Crown. Only at a later date did the Company servants begin to intervene in the role of the modernizers of India. In order to sketch this development we must turn back briefly to the Company's position in the eighteenth century.

The Company becomes a State

The turning-point in the East India Company's position in India occurred in 1765 when it was granted by the Emperor the *diwani*, or authority to collect the revenues, of Bengal, Bihar and Orissa. From that moment the scrutiny of Parliament at home, and the practical

problems encountered in India, led to progressive government intervention in the affairs of the Company. How, then, did the Company
reach such a position?

Until the eighteenth century it concentrated upon trade. When it
was excluded from the East Indies by the Dutch, it found India
relatively prosperous and stable under the Mughal Emperors at Delhi.
The Company created three main trading bases in its Presidencies –
trading stations under the charge of a President – at Bombay, Madras
and Calcutta. Around these centres prosperous trading towns
developed.

But after the death of the Emperor Aurangzeb in 1707 the decline of
the Mughal Empire threatened India's peace. The sub-continent
became divided into virtually independent principalities as many of the
provincial governors of the Mughals carved out their own kingdoms.
Wars became frequent. By the 1760s a new and precarious situation
confronted the Company. In the south, the powerful Muslim-ruled
kingdoms of Mysore and Hyderabad emerged. Central India was
dominated by the warlike Hindu Maratha chiefs. Afghan invaders fell
upon Delhi itself. Farther north, Sind, and Punjab to the west, and
Oudh, Bihar, Bengal and Orissa in the east, fell away. Although the
Marathas saved the Emperor from the Afghans in 1761, they soon fell
to quarrelling among themselves. As the titular Emperors of Hindustan
lost their domain, a dangerous power vacuum remained.

Mughal decline and subsequent power rivalries in India led the East
India Company, and its French rival, to seek Indian allies in order to
protect their property and trade. Thus, when Britain went to war with
France in Europe and the New World, fighting also extended to India.
After the end of the Seven Years War in 1763 the French were excluded
from India, except as traders. During the American War of Inde-
pendence and the Napoleonic wars, France gave aid to Britain's
Indian enemies, in the hope of recovering her power in India. Not until
Napoleon's defeat was the East India Company finally secure from
France in India.

By fighting the French the East India Company made Indian
enemies. Thus in the century from the 1740s to the 1840s the Company
engaged in a long series of wars, which it fought to maintain its position,
and by which it eventually emerged supreme in India. The main stages
in its expansion may be noted briefly. In 1757 the ruler of Bengal was
defeated, and the Company soon gained a free hand in Bengal, Bihar

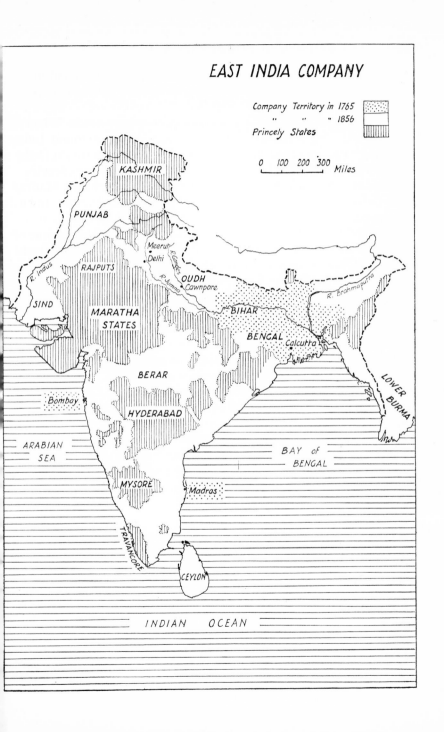

EAST INDIA COMPANY

Company Territory in 1765
"   "   " 1856
Princely States

0   100 200 300 Miles

KASHMIR

PUNJAB

R. Indus

RAJPUTS

SIND

MARATHA
STATES

Meerut
Delhi

R. Ganges

R. Jumna

OUDH
Cawnpore

BIHAR

R. Brahmaputra

BENGAL
Calcutta

LOWER
BURMA

BERAR

Bombay

HYDERABAD

ARABIAN
SEA

BAY of
BENGAL

MYSORE

Madras

TRAVANCORE

CEYLON

INDIAN   OCEAN

and Orissa. In 1799 Mysore, the biggest opponent in the south, was defeated. In 1801 the Company took over the Carnatic. By 1818 the Marathas had been reduced and British control asserted up to the River Sutlej. Later, to secure the frontiers, Sind was annexed in 1843, followed by the Punjab in 1849. By 1852 the Company had also taken Lower Burma. After this great era of war the East India Company, by its domination, imposed peace in India.

But the Company did not unify India. The political fragmentation which followed the Mughal decline and the European wars remained under the Company's régime. The dilemmas posed by the Company's new-found power are vividly illustrated by the distinction which was maintained (and so continued until 1948) between the territories annexed to the Company's Presidencies of Bombay, Madras and Bengal and the Indian 'Princely States'. The latter numbered more than 500 and were governed by their own monarchs, subject to Company advice and control of foreign policy. They varied from the large Kingdom of Hyderabad (nearly as big in area as Ireland) to hundreds of very small principalities. India's political patchwork was the legacy of a trading company which was gradually converted into a great power. By the time its conquests were complete, with the formal annexation of Oudh in 1856, the Company had ceased to trade at all. A relic of the old empire had been transformed, as we shall see, into a surprisingly modern Asian state.

Regulating the Company

Why was the Company brought under government control? The answer is not simple, because motives were very mixed. They were much more connected with British politics than with ideas of justice for India. The East India Company was one of the great institutions of the English state. Most of the directors were Members of Parliament, it sometimes lent money to the government; its stocks were virtually a 'gilt-edged security'. But the success in Bengal in the 1760s led many men-on-the-spot to neglect the Company's trade, while they amassed great fortunes themselves. General Clive, the Company's hero, extorted no less than £234,000 from the Nawab of Bengal. Many lesser men also made fortunes and returned to join the 'nabobs' who combined to foster their interests in the Company's meetings and in Parliament. But a faction in the Company, led by Lawrence Sulivan, were anxious about the Company's finances and feared that abuse of its new power might bring about a challenge to its charter. Thus in 1758 a series of contests for the control of the Company began which came to have a significance in London akin to great Parliamentary contests.

Further opposition came from outside the Company. Parliament had approved aid to the Company from British military and naval forces during the French wars. Now that the Company was permitted to collect the revenues of Bengal it was felt that the government should have a share. As the defeat of the French in America had saddled Britain with a large debt and new responsibilities, the Bengal revenues were regarded by some politicians as a 'heaven-sent' opportunity for balancing the budget.

Thus considerations of domestic politics led to parliamentary inquiries into the affairs of the Company. In 1767 the Company agreed to pay £400,000 into the Treasury for two years. In 1773, with the promise of a loan from the government and help in disposing of a tea surplus (which led to the Boston Tea Party) the Company submitted to the first attempt of the government to regulate its affairs. Lord North's Regulating Act provided that the Company should be supervised at home by the Court of Directors elected every four years. In India, the Governor-General of Bengal was given the oversight of Madras and Bombay and the Company's outstations in the East Indies. He was to consult a Council of four members. A new Supreme Court was to be created under an English Chief Justice. Governor-General, Councillors and Chief Justice would not engage in trade. North's Act introduced one element of a 'colonial' constitution into the Company's rule, in that the governor was subject to the check of a council, where he could, in theory, be outvoted. This provision led to endless bickering, which distracted Warren Hastings as he faced dangerous external threats during the American War of Independence.

After the American war, Pitt's India Act of 1784 produced a more satisfactory system. The Directors of the Company were now divested of their political responsibilities. They were left to carry on trade and retained the right to appoint Company servants. Political supervision at home was to be exercised by a new body, known as the Board of Control, consisting of six Privy Councillors, under a President, who would also be a member of the Cabinet. At the same time, the governor-general became, like the colonial governors, a Crown appointment. The Governor-General-in-Council became the Supreme Government of all the Company's possessions. This basic framework continued until 1858, but it was only one step in the controlling of the Company. Periodical reviews of the Company's charter by Parliament led to a progressive transformation of its government.

In 1813 the Company lost its monopoly of the India trade. Its territories were opened for free trade, and at the same time, freedom was given for missionary activity. In 1833 the Company lost its remaining monopoly of the trade to China. It was then left with the single great task of administering the British possessions in India. The Directors were still permitted to nominate candidates for the Company's civil service. Its servants ruled British India under the aegis of the Royal Governor.

By the early Victorian age the Company's government in India began to resemble, at the centre, the system which had been applied in the Crown colonies. The Governor-General's Council was extended to include a Law Member and official representatives of Bengal, Madras, Bombay and Agra. The Governor-General, along with the Law Member and three other councillors, were empowered to act as a legislature for British India. In 1853 the Governor-General was relieved of the provincial government of Bengal, and a lieutenant-governor was appointed there. He was now provided with a legislative council of twelve members. Thus, as the Old Colonial System was swept away in the colonial empire by the advent of free trade and responsible government, so, in India, free trade and official, conciliar government was evolved. As yet, there was no representative government. But during the debates on the Reform Act in Britain in 1832, when East India Company interests in Parliament opposed the Bill, Joseph Hume, whose son would one day found India's great national party, put forward a remarkable suggestion. In place of the 'nabobs' in Parliament, he said, there should be members for Calcutta, Bombay, Madras and Ceylon.

The Company's Impact in India

The Company came under government control and lost its monopolies largely because of political and economic developments at home. What did it do in India ? Its servants were slow to interfere with Indian life. They tackled first the task of assessing and collecting the revenue, which soon involved them in matters of police and justice. But to start with they experimented with a form of 'indirect rule' in Bengal.

The Company decided to receive the revenue and look after defence, but to rely on the Nawab of Bengal to continue his rule and to do the actual revenue-collecting for it. Under Warren Hastings, however, the Company determined to 'stand forth as diwan', and to attend to administration and revenue itself. Taxation and judicial aspects of government, which were traditionally combined in Bengal, were separated. Supreme Courts of civil and criminal jurisdiction were created. Revenue 'Collectors' were given the responsibility of receiving fixed sums (which they did not have to assess) from the Bengal landholders, or *zemindars*. In 1793 Lord Cornwallis, the Governor-General, built upon this system in his Permanent Settlement for Bengal.

In Bengal, and indeed all the subsequent annexations, revenue from land taxes became the first great concern of government. In a largely subsistence economy the produce of the soil was the one great source of taxable wealth. In concentrating on the revenue in this way the Company followed the Mughal emperors. But who was to pay? This question engaged the energies of a whole generation of officials. In Bengal, Cornwallis adopted what was called the *zemindari* system. The government determined on a fixed assessment to be paid by the great landlords. The collectors received the revenue; magistrates and district judges looked after law and order and the settlement of disputes.

But in Madras Presidency there were no great landlords to assess. Here, in a largely peasant region, Sir Thomas Munro insisted that there should be no Indian intermediary between government and the *ryots*. Thus the *ryotwari* system of collection was evolved. Judicial and revenue functions were reunited in a single local official, who made changeable land revenue settlements with the peasants. When Central India and the Punjab were annexed, yet another revenue system was necessary. Here, neither great landlords nor individual peasants were the basis of assessment. The village community, through headmen and council, became the unit for assessment. The *mahalwari* revenue system was evolved.

Outside Bengal, then, the Company's officers themselves performed all the main functions of the officials. They were little emperors in their districts.

> Our dominion in India is by conquest [wrote Sir Charles Metcalfe]; it is naturally disgusting to the inhabitants and can only be maintained by military force. It is our positive duty to render them justice, to

respect and protect their rights, and to study their happiness. By the performance of this duty, we may allay and keep dormant their innate disaffection; but the expectation of purchasing their cordial attachment by gratuitous alienation of public revenue would be a vain delusion.

The early nineteenth century saw an able, energetic, generation of Company officials brought up to Metcalfe's stern doctrine. They felt a mission to bring order, and a simple, rough justice to the people of India. But this did not mean destroying Indian society. Metcalfe deprecated meddling in the Protected States. The whole tenor of the first generation of administrators was paternal and preservationist.

Indian policy, however, could not be isolated from the intellectual currents which transformed English society, and which, as we have seen, profoundly affected the empire. Free-traders, humanitarians, utilitarians, evangelicals all argued in favour of 'assimilation' rather than 'protection' in India. Merchants, manufacturers and missionaries combined to transform Indian society. In the reform Parliament of 1833 Thomas Babington Macaulay, who is usually remembered as a historian, but who was then secretary to the Board of Control (and was shortly to go to India as Law Member of the council), enunciated a new concept of trusteeship in India:

> It is difficult to form any conjecture as to the fate reserved for a state which resembles no other in history, and which forms by itself a separate class of political phenomenon. The laws which regulate its growth and its decay are still unknown to us. It may be that the public mind in India may expand under our system till it has outgrown that system; that by good government we may educate our subjects into a capacity for better government; that, having become instructed in European knowledge, they may in some future age demand European institutions. Whether such a day will ever come I know not. But never will I attempt to arrest or to retard it. Whenever it comes, it may be the proudest day in English history.

During the Governor-Generalship of Lord William Bentinck (1828–35) the new concept of trusteeship began to imply direct intervention in Indian customs. When slavery was abolished in the colonies, the Company was instructed to end it as soon as possible in India. In 1843 the courts refused to hear claims for slaves; seven years later slavery became an offence. Bentinck tackled two cruel religious customs. *Suttee*, the Hindu custom of burning widows on the funeral pyres of their husbands, was made illegal in 1830. Until then up to 500 cases were being reported annually; now the Company began to stamp it out. A further cruel practice was the sacrificial kidnapping, robbery and murder of travellers by bands of *thugs*. Legislation to suppress the evil was passed in 1836. Judicial reforms were also made by Bentinck. The English language was adopted for the courts. Two classes of Indian judges were created and work was started on the codification of legal procedure and the penal system. The principle of equality before the courts was established.

Most notable for the future of India, however, were the changes in education. Indian education was, for Mountstuart Elphinstone, 'our high road back to Europe'. In 1835, in his celebrated and notorious Minute on Education, Macaulay pleaded that the English language should be adopted for all higher education in India, as it was already becoming the language of the government, commerce and the courts. We have to admit today that Macaulay's Minute was couched in language which displayed an arrogant contempt for Indian learning and culture. But Macaulay believed that under the inspiration of western ideas, learnt through the medium of the English language, there would develop 'a class of persons, Indian in blood and colour, but English in taste, opinion, in morals and intellect'. This view exactly parallels Sir George Grey's hopes about the Aborigines, Maoris and Bantu.

Indian society could not be transformed overnight. All British officials in India were not as convinced as Bentinck and Macaulay. In the new annexations in the North-West in the 1840s Sir John Lawrence continued the traditions of the paternal, 'protectionist' school. Thus trusteeship under the Company in India was not uniform. Some of the worst customs were abolished, new ideas were introduced by the use of English and by the legal codes. But in the countryside, where the vast mass of the *ryots* lived, the Company's impact was made through its stern administration of order and justice.

The Mutiny and the Queen's Proclamation of British Rule

On 10 May 1857 the Company received the blow which brought its end. A sepoy regiment rose against its officers. Two days later Delhi fell as the mutineers sought leadership from the descendant of the Great Mughals. On 4 June the Mutiny spread to Cawnpore. For eighty-seven days the garrison at Lucknow was besieged. Control over

Oudh and the North-West Provinces was lost. From Patna to Delhi the Bengal army turned against its officers. Delhi was not re-taken until 20 September 1857, Lucknow was not relieved until 17 November, nor were the last remnants of the mutiny quelled for a further year.

This was the greatest crisis in the period of British rule in India. It was not a national uprising. Confined as it was to the western half of Bengal, it hardly affected the other Presidency armies. It was a soldiers' mutiny, not a people's revolt. But its effects on Britain's attitude to India were of immense significance. Why did it happen, and what results followed?

The Mutiny occurred partly because of the tensions engendered by the changes in India which we have already considered. The Company seemed now to be imposing an alien civilization, by its new land assessments and its social and language reforms. Many of its servants, moreover, particularly some of the army officers, were enthusiastic Christian evangelicals. The Company's régime also brought economic changes. A new, largely Hindu, class of financiers was rising in the Company's state, who welcomed western technical and commercial ideas. Old land-owners were sometimes alienated by annexations and land assessments. Among the sepoys of the army themselves there was unrest. The Company's armies were reduced, now that the main conquests were over. Discipline in peacetime relaxed. But a new duty to serve overseas, as in Burma in 1850, offended Hindu caste rules. In such an atmosphere, rumours that cow and pig grease on the cartridges for new Enfield rifles was a conspiracy against the Hindu and Muslim religions could not be checked. Even the withdrawal of the cartridges, and a government announcement that sepoys could make their own grease, failed to check them. Unreasoning fear, in an unhappy atmosphere, led to a spontaneous explosion, which a few dispossessed rulers then tried to use for their own ends. It was, in fact, the last protest of the old India.

On both sides there were atrocities. Fear engendered passion among the mutineers and the British. Thus, after Nana Sahib's massacre of 200 English women and children at Cawnpore General James Neill's reaction was harsh.

> Who could be merciful to one concerned? . . . every stain of that innocent blood shall be cleared up and wiped out, previous to their execution, by such miscreants as may be hereafter apprehended, who took an active part in the mutiny. . . . Each miscreant, after sentence of

death is pronounced upon him, will be taken down to the house in question under a guard and will be forced into clearing up a small portion of the bloodstains; the task will be as revolting to his feelings as possible and the Provost-Marshall will use the lash in forcing anyone objecting to complete his task. After properly clearing up his portion the culprit is to be immediately hanged.

The British troops, in their disappointment at the defection of their often much loved sepoys, and their anger at the treatment of women and children, fought grimly and recovered. Henceforth British regiments were to equal sepoy regiments in the Bengal Army.

The chief effect of the Mutiny was the abolition of the East India Company and the assertion of royal sovereignty in its territories. On 1 November 1858 a royal proclamation to India was issued by the Viceroy. It was, in effect, a formal affirmation of the concept of trusteeship. The Queen bound herself to the inhabitants of the Indian empire 'by the same obligations of duty which bind us to all our other subjects, and those obligations, by the blessing of Almighty God, we shall faithfully and conscientiously fulfil'. Above all, the proclamation stressed the intended impartiality of the British Raj.

We declare it to be our royal will and pleasure that none be any wise favoured, none molested or disquieted, by reason of their religious faith or observances, but that all shall alike enjoy equal and impartial protection of the law; and we do strictly charge and enjoin all those who may be in authority under us that they abstain from all interference with the religious belief and worship of any one of our subjects, on pain of our highest displeasure.

And it is our further will that, so far as may be, our subjects, of whatever race or creed, be freely and impartially admitted to offices in our service, the duties of which they may be qualified by their education, ability, and integrity duly to discharge.

The Queen's proclamation, which Indians of a later generation could recite by heart, was a manifesto of general intent, not an outline of policy. How far it was implemented in practice will be discussed in the next chapter.

But two points may be noted about the concept of trusteeship after the mutiny. First, there was to be no interference with religious belief and practice. In a land where Hindu and Muslim customs and philosophy so deeply pervaded all aspects of life, this implied a return to a more 'protective' brand of trusteeship. In the Protected States this doctrine remained unchanged. Yet, at the same time, all the inhabitants of British India were, in theory, now able to enter the government service where they were qualified. This implied an expectation that Macaulay's breed of Anglicized Indians would appear. In other words, the basic dilemma of British trusteeship in India remained unresolved. At the outset of the ninety-year *Raj*, Britain had no clearly defined goals in India.

Ceylon – the Model Dependency in the Tropics

In the great island of Ceylon the *Pax Britannica* took a rather different form than it did in India. Although the ports and coastal regions of Ceylon were captured from the Dutch in 1796 for strategic reasons, because of the French threat to India, and the island was at first administered as part of the Madras Presidency, the East India Company's administrative methods caused disruption and unrest. In 1802 Ceylon was detached from the jurisdiction of the East India Company and placed under the control of the secretary of state for war and colonies. Britain thus created her first Crown colony in Asia, which would one day be regarded as the model tropical dependency.

The first steps of the government, as in India, involved re-organization of the administration, the courts and the revenue, and the conquest of opponents. After a disastrous attempt to subjugate the Kingdom of Kandy, in the hills of central Ceylon, failed in 1803, the government courted disaffected Kandyan nobles. By 1815 the King of Kandy had been captured and, although some chiefs revolted a few years later, by 1818 Kandy was brought under British administration.

By the 1830s the same intellectual forces which led to Bentinck's reforms in India began to affect Ceylon. A Commission of Inquiry under Major William Colebrooke and Charles Cameron visited Ceylon in 1829 to report for Parliament. Although their names are largely forgotten today, Colebrooke and Cameron deserve a high place among empire idealists. They proposed limiting the powers of the governor by creating executive and legislative councils and by making a separate judiciary, to which Cameron wanted to appoint Ceylonese judges. They also advocated abolishing feudal labour services, recognizing equality before the law, admitting Ceylonese to the higher civil service and opening up educational opportunities.

Although not all the Colebrooke-Cameron ideas were immediately

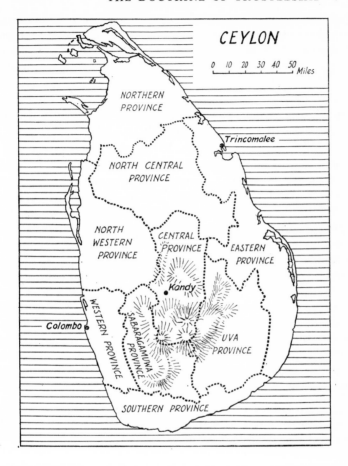

adopted, their main constitutional proposals were quickly carried out by Sir Robert Wilmot-Horton, a former energetic under-secretary of state for war and colonies, who became governor of Ceylon in 1832. The 1833 Constitution remained substantially unchanged until the twentieth century. As in all the Crown colonies, the governor's executive council was made up of officials. But in his legislative council, in addition to nine officials, the governor nominated three Ceylonese (a Burgher, a Tamil and a Sinhalese) and three Europeans as un-official representatives. Cameron, who wanted to promote Ceylonese in the civil service and the judiciary, believed that:

The peculiar circumstances of Ceylon, both physical and moral, seem to point it out to the British Government as the fittest spot in our eastern dominions in which to plant the germs of European civilization, where we may not unreasonably hope that it will hereafter spread over the whole of these vast territories.

How was this fine idea to be realized?

The answer seemed to lie in centralized administration, the unification of the island into provinces each under an Agent, strategic roads (later railways), and above all, the plantation economy. Coffee has been singled out as the chief agent of change in Ceylon. As free trade removed West Indian preferences, Ceylonese coffee enjoyed a boom in the 1840s. By mid-century exports has risen to 278,000 cwt a year. When coffee was affected by blight in the 1860s, the planters began to lay out the tea estates which still cover the hills of Ceylon.

The plantation system transformed the landscape, economy and society of Ceylon, just as British rule and English education transformed administration and the law. A new class of comfortably off, English-educated Ceylonese grew, as in India. After a brief outbreak of revolt in Kandy in 1848, British rule gave peace and prosperity to the island. Although several thousand British settlers, who were attracted to Ceylon, demanded something like the self-government of the other colonies, the governors resisted demands from such a tiny minority in the interests of the Sinhalese and Tamil masses. Sir George Anderson declared:

> The Crown must for many years hold the balance between European and native interests, if it wishes to see order maintained and legislation impartially conducted.

In the years up to the 1914–18 war Ceylon's prosperity and good order, Ceylonese representation in the legislature, and the slow growth of the nationalist movement, as compared with India, gave the first Crown colony in Asia a notable, and now often forgotten, significance for the doctrine of trusteeship. In fact a historian writing in 1911 – the year after Ceylonese-elected members were added to the legislative council – suggested that Ceylon could claim to be the 'political laboratory for the non-European races of the Empire'.

The Ambiguity of Britain's Trusteeship

The 'Roman' portions of Adderley's empire were notable for their great diversity. If trade and strategy, followed by humanitarianism and later a sense of mission, provided Britain's basic motives, the results in Asia, Africa and the Caribbean were very different. The doctrine of trusteeship should not be over-simplified. Britain was never actuated by a single-minded purpose.

Thus, in their empire in the tropics the Victorians were curiously uncertain as to their ultimate goals. Even Macaulay, the confident historical analyst, could not guess the outcome of Britain's presence in India. Above all, the Victorians were not united in their methods. The evangelical fervour of the 1830s, which led to the abolition of slavery, Bentinck's reforms in India, the Ceylon constitution and Grey's experiments in Australia, South Africa and New Zealand, was not sustained. For those who wanted to transform all men into multi-coloured Englishmen, there were those who wanted to shield and protect Asian and African societies from the influences and culture of Europe. There was no agreement about the time-scale of Britain's involvement in the non-colonial regions. While many Company servants expected Britain to retire from India and while politicians and humanitarians hoped to leave Africa to traders and missionaries, there was a growing body of opinion which began to envisage something of a permanent British presence in India and Ceylon and increasing expansion and paramountcy in Africa. Only a few visionaries as yet suggested that parliamentary institutions, which were being extended to the colonies of settlement, could be adopted in Asia, Africa and the Caribbean.

7

The Indian Empire

INDIA was Britain's greatest possession. Many Englishmen agreed with Lord Curzon that India was 'the only part of the British Empire which is an empire'. In the twentieth century India was responsible for the greatest single landmark in the development of the Commonwealth. If Canada pioneered the way for the Dominions, India was the first member of the 'New Commonwealth'.

In the nineteenth century there were really two British empires: Adderley's 'Grecian' and 'Roman' branches of empire. In the colonies of settlement responsible government became the orthodox policy, and the result was Dominion status for Canada, Australia, New Zealand and South Africa. In the 'dependencies' Britain pursued her somewhat ambiguous policy of trusteeship. Here the ultimate goals were not clear. Britain was drawn into Africa and Asia but was not sure where she was going. India's great contribution to the Commonwealth was her uniting of the two great streams of British policy. When the 'Grecian' and 'Roman' aspects of empire finally coalesced, the empire itself passed away.

Shortly before he died in 1911 Sir Alfred Lyall, a former Lieutenant-Governor of the North-West Provinces, suggested: 'It is not impossible that the twentieth century may see the complete withdrawal of Europe from Asia.' Few of his countrymen believed him. When, during the second half of the nineteenth century Indian nationalists proposed that the Canadian solution should be applied to India, most responsible Englishmen scoffed. Lord Kimberley in 1890 called it 'one of the wildest imaginings that ever entered the minds of men'. Few could see the end of British supremacy in India. Yet, as in the Dominions, nationalist pressure mounted. During the 1914–18 war important converts to the idea of Dominion status for India were won in Britain. In the 1920s a few English-educated Indian Liberals began to talk of the Commonwealth, with India as an equal partner, as something 'unique amongst the political constitutions of the world'. It would stand, they felt, for 'the reconciliation of the East and the West'.

Unfortunately, the British government was slow to concede the goal of self-government for India. Moreover, the delaying tactics of imperialist 'die-hards' held up every step in India's political progress. For a quarter of a century after 1919 there was growing estrangement and bitterness on both sides. But when in 1950 India became a Republic and remained within the Commonwealth, the Commonwealth itself had obviously changed. The 'New Commonwealth' became, as an Indian had predicted in 1923, a 'bridge' between East and West. India proved to Britain that responsible government was 'suitable for all races and kindreds and peoples and tongues'. By doing so she pioneered the way for the rest of the new Asian, African and Caribbean members of the Commonwealth.

British Rule in India

After the Mutiny the shape of British rule in India remained largely unchanged. 'British India', the former Company territories, was divided into provinces centralized under the Viceroy. The 'Princely States', 562 in all, continued as protected states, where British Residents acted as advisers. But in British India a significant change occurred in the spirit of the British Raj.

Macaulay had been uncertain as to Britain's goals in India. But he, and a number of other early-nineteenth-century Company servants, believed that Britain's rule would be temporary, that they would call forth a new India and retire. Hastings predicted in 1818:

A time not very remote will arrive when England will, on sound principles of policy, wish to relinquish the domination which she has gradually and unintentionally assumed over this country.

'The moral', declared Mountstuart Elphinstone, 'is that we must not dream of perpetual possession.'

But this is precisely the moral which later Victorian administrators forgot. India appeared now as a vast inscrutable, possibly incorrigible, problem. Britain's evangelical fervour of the 1830s was lost, and while ever-increasing efforts were made to foster material progress, much of India's traditional life was left untouched. Above all, a sense of the permanency of British rule set in. It was accompanied by a growing feeling of racial superiority. Thus, when it was proposed in 1883 to give Indian judges the same authority to try Europeans as their English colleagues possessed, there was an outcry. A former civil servant spoke up for

> the cherished conviction which was shared by every Englishman in India, from the highest to the lowest, by the planter's assistant in his lowly bungalow and by the editor in the full light of the Presidency town – from those to the Chief Commissioner in charge of an important province and to the Viceroy on his throne – the conviction in every man that he belongs to a race whom God has destined to govern and subdue.

This illustrates the most striking thing about the late Victorian administrator: his conviction that he was born to rule.

In material terms he and his fellows achieved some great things for India. Public works were pressed forward with vigour. The 200-odd miles of railway which existed at the time of the Mutiny grew to 25,000 by 1900. Railways stimulated in India, as they did in Europe and America, the coal and steel industries and the growth of social mobility. Improved communications and new agriculture stimulated by irrigation enabled government to respond rapidly to threats of starvation. The Famine Code laid down regular procedures for tackling one of India's traditional problems, and deaths from famine became rare. New export crops were introduced, particularly tea. India, in fact, began to develop a modern economy.

Government remained firmly in the hands of the bureaucracy. Although since 1853 the Indian civil service was open to competition and the Queen's Proclamation of 1858 forbade any racial or colour bar, the examinations were held in London. A handful of educated Indians were able to travel to London and satisfy the examiners from the 1860s onwards. But the proportion remained small until after 1922, when examinations were also held in India. In the period when parliamentary government was leading rapidly towards full internal autonomy in the Dominions, the executive dominated in India, where the legislatures were still composed of officials.

Yet two modest advances were made in the legislative framework in the nineteenth century. First, a measure of representation was permitted. Since 1853 four provinces had sent official representatives to the Governor-General's Council. By the Indian Councils Act of 1861 non-official representatives were added. The central legislative council was enlarged to include six to twelve members nominated by the Governor-General. Half of the new members were not officials and most of those appointed were Indians. Provincial councils were also created, although the central legislative council remained supreme. By the same act the Governor-General's executive council was enlarged to include five members, who were given departmental responsibility; thus there emerged an embryo official 'cabinet'.

An even greater step was the introduction of the elective principle in India. Gladstone, as we have seen, believed in the moral virtue of self-government. To him it was a calamity that 'we have not been able to give to India the blessings of free institutions'. Lord Ripon, whom he appointed Viceroy, proposed in 1881 that elected members should be added to the legislative councils. It took more than ten years for Ripon's proposals to be accepted. A long controversy ensued about the right sort of electorates. Finally in the Indian Councils Act of 1892 a system of 'corporate' election was adopted. In the central legislative council five of the non-official representatives were to be elected – four by the non-official members of the Madras, Bombay, Bengal and Agra provincial councils and one by the Calcutta chamber of commerce. Election to the provincial legislative councils was even more indirect. Corporate bodies, such as universities, chambers of commerce and municipalities, were to suggest candidates, who would then be nominated to the council in the traditional way. Thus, by the end of the nineteenth century a slight political advance had been made in India. Representative and elective principles were established to a very limited extent in central and provincial legislatures. How far did this satisfy Indians?

The New Elite

Macaulay dreamed of 'a class of persons, Indian in blood and colour, but English in taste, opinion, in morals and intellect'. Western education, modern government and economic development soon produced a new *élite* in India. But it was very different from Macaulay's ideal. One of the chief reasons for this can be found in the influence of Ram Mohan Roy, the first great Indian scholar to urge Indians to come to terms with western thought without abandoning their ancient heritage.

Roy was a one-time East India Company servant, a wise Bengali, founder of the Hindu College of Calcutta and an accomplished linguist. In 1828 he founded a 'Divine Society' which continued after his death in 1833. His teaching, in essence, was that Hindus should re-establish their basic precepts, abandoning all that was irrelevant and antediluvian, and accept from Christianity its great ethical precepts and its concept of human dignity. Roy was a scholar and lacked mass appeal. But his ideas had considerable impact upon the Indian intelligentsia of the mid-Victorian era. His followers eagerly absorbed western political, economic and ethical ideas, but remained loyal to Hindu society and ideals. In other words, Macaulay's doctrine of 'assimilation' operated in the opposite direction. A class of Indians grew, proud to be Hindu in feeling and thought, but nevertheless absorbing selected western ideas into their field of vision.

If western ideas influenced their thought, the British Raj determined their role. While many of the old ruling classes of British India had been defeated in war, made landless by annexation or impoverished by land reform, a large new class emerged who made their living by serving the new régime. Indians had flocked to the Presidency towns in the days of the Company. Some became wealthy as agents or merchants. In the nineteenth century this class rapidly widened. Indian capitalists founded banks, businesses and industries. Indian professional men proliferated – lawyers, journalists, teachers and doctors. Large numbers from the new class served as subordinate government officials. Some rose to judgeships, later to the High Courts of India. A few qualified to be mandarins in the Indian Civil Service.

Against the background of the Indian masses, who by the twentieth century numbered nearly 300 million, the Victorian intelligentsia was small. But the new men had certain significant features in common. They were educated in the English language and English liberal traditions, they performed functions in the modern Indian state and they possessed western professional skills. Like their Victorian contemporaries in Britain they organized for reform. Their efforts led to Indian's political awakening.

The Rise of Nationalism

Indian middle-class organizations began on a humble scale, but they evolved a remarkable consistency of aim. They took note of the growth of responsible government in the colonies and they demanded the same for India. In 1851 the Bengal Landholders Society amalgamated with the Bengal British India Society to form the British Indian Association. In the following year it petitioned for a legislature similar to those in the colonies. Three years later Dadabhai Naoroji, one of the Bombay Association's leading figures, went to London to join an Indian business house.

Naoroji was profoundly influenced by what he saw in London. He was impressed by liberal political ideas, parliamentary government and the gradual growth of democracy. He was convinced that India could achieve the same and that the British could be made to agree. He would say to Englishmen:

> We Indian people believe that although John Bull is a little thick-headed, once we can penetrate through his head into his brain that a certain thing is right and proper to be done, you may be quite sure that it will be done.

With the help of W. C. Bonnerjee he formed the London India Society and the East India Association to promote interest in India's aspirations. Bonnerjee pleaded before the latter body in 1867 for 'Representative and Responsible Government for India'. Naoroji returned to India in 1869 to preach the goal of a Parliament for India. He became the first great nationalist and is known as the 'Grand Old Man of India'. He was even elected in 1892 as M.P. for Finsbury. The first Indian to sit in Parliament, he entered the headlines after Lord Salisbury's haughty doubt that 'a British constituency would elect a black man'. He was later President of the Indian National Congress.

From the 1860s onwards conservative, educated, comfortably-off Indians like Naoroji, who were loyal, even affectionate, towards the British Raj, looked to the attainment of responsible government in India as in the new colonies. An Indian editorial in 1874 found it odd that India should be denied the elected legislature that Barbados took for granted. 'Canada governs itself. Australia governs itself', declared Surendranath Banerjea in 1880, '. . . surely it is anomalous that the greatest dependency of England should continue to be governed upon wholly different principles.' Such expressions of opinion were put forward as general expectations rather than specific policies. As yet Indian organizations were small and diffuse; they were not political parties. But at the end of the 1870s a new mood became evident in India.

N

It is highly ironical that while Disraeli's Bill granting Queen Victoria the title of Empress of India was designed to impress and attract Indian opinion, the acts of his government had the opposite effect. The Royal Titles Act was unpopular in Britain. The acts of Lord Lytton's viceroyalty (1876–80) antagonized educated Indians. An attempt was made to regulate the Indian-language newspapers. A reduction in entry age for the Indian Civil Service examinations in London made it harder for Indians to qualify. At the same time Indian troops were used in the service of two controversial incidents in Disraeli's forceful diplomacy – in the Afghan war and the Balkan crisis. Discrimination in favour of Indian textiles and in favour of Englishmen in Indian courts soon followed.

The result of this growing estrangement was the founding of the Indian National Congress in 1885. From modest, conservative beginnings the Congress grew to become one of the greatest mass political organizations in the world. Today it remains the ruling party of India. One of its leading founders, and secretary-general for its first twenty years, was an Englishman. Allan Octavian Hume, son of the radical M.P., Joseph Hume, retired in 1882 from the Indian Civil Service, where he had been a progressive-minded district officer before the Mutiny. In 1883 he appealed in a circular to Calcutta graduates for fifty volunteers to found a new national movement:

> If you, the picked men, the most highly educated of the nation ,cannot, scorning personal ease and selfish objects, make a resolute struggle to secure greater freedom for yourself and your country, a more impartial administration, a larger share in the management of your own affairs, then we your friends are wrong . . . let us hear no more factious, peevish complaints that you are kept in leading strings, and treated like children, for you will have proved yourselves such. *Men* know how to act.

Two years later seventy Indian graduates, mainly lawyers, teachers and journalists, formed the Indian National Congress in Bombay.

For twenty years the Congress remained a small, middle-class annual conference, dedicated to passing resolutions in favour of three main demands: enlarged legislative councils, civil service examinations in India and a duty on cotton imports. The tone of its meetings was loyalist and moderate and intellectual. Several Viceroys regarded it as a valuable 'safety valve' for Indian opinion. No less than four Englishmen were elected President. Influenced as they were by English education and liberal ideas, the early Congressmen assumed from the start that India might eventually have a national Parliament. But this was, as yet, no political programme. Hume probably expressed the correct mood in 1888:

> So far as I know, no leading member of the National Congress thinks that for the next twenty years at any rate the country will require or be fit for anything more than mixed Councils that have been advocated at Congresses. But we, one and all, look forward to a time, say 50, say 70 years hence, when the Government of India will be precisely similar to that of the Dominion of Canada.

Another idea, mooted somewhat academically, was for a United States of India. Thus in terms of ideas and general aspirations the Victorian Indian *élite* looked to the Dominions, but made more modest practical demands.

By the first decade of the twentieth century the Congress's approach was challenged. How do we account for the rise of radical nationalism in India? The explanation may be found partly in developments in India, but also in significant events in the world outside.

Within India there was an awakening of communal rivalry. Muslims came to realize that most of the new educated *élite* were Hindus. Sir Sayyid Ahmad Khan, the first of the great Muslim westernizers, who wanted to do for Islam what Roy had done for Hindus, warned his fellow Muslims that responsible government in India would be a return to Hindu dominance. At the same time Bal Gangadhar Tilak, a noted Sanskrit scholar at Fergusson College, Poona, gloried in the Maratha past. In 1890 he embarked on a career as a journalist and nationalist agitator and part of his appeal was to anti-Muslim feeling. At this moment, when a radical generation came to the fore, who also drew strength from appeals to India's ancient past, opinions were inflamed by the actions of Lord Curzon as Viceroy (1899–1905).

Curzon was one of the most active Viceroys in pressing India's material progress. He was of Milner's generation of passionate imperialists. He believed Britain's relationship with India was 'so mysterious as to have in it something of the divine'. Unfortunately, like Milner in South Africa, he was a poor politician. He believed Congress was 'tottering to its fall' and his ambition was 'to assist it to a peaceful demise'. His scheme for partitioning Bengal, on the grounds of efficiency, had quite the reverse effect. Bengal had a population of

78 million. Curzon created two parts by dividing the Bengali-speaking peoples into Eastern (mainly Muslim) and Western (mainly Hindu) provinces. The move led to massive protests by educated Hindu Bengalis. When the Congress took up the issue it became India's first nation-wide campaign of resistance.

The annual meetings of the Indian National Congress now took on a new more urgent note. A radical wing, labelled 'extremists' by the older Congressmen, emerged to press for clearer political goals. While the moderates like Naoroji continued to demand a form of government similar to the self-governing colonies, Tilak raised the slogan: '*swaraj*', 'self-rule'.

One of the radicals wrote: 'The Congress has contented itself with demanding self-government as it exists in the Colonies. We of the new school would not pitch our ideal one inch lower than absolute *swaraj* – self-government as it exists in the United Kingdom.' To stop Tilak's election as President of the Congress in 1906 the moderates had to call Naoroji from England as their candidate. The veteran leader carefully glossed over the split in Congress by proclaiming the beautifully ambiguous goal of 'self-government or *swaraj* like that of the United Kingdom or the Colonies'. But while the moderates held their own in the Congress, terrorism broke out in Bengal and a spate of murders followed. It was obvious that there was a growing impatience in India.

At the same time Indian radicals were aware of significant events outside. Britain's relative decline in power was illustrated by her un-popularity at the time of the South African war; her search for allies such as France and Japan; her diplomatic retreats before the United States in the new world. Japan's dramatic victory over Russia in 1904 symbolized Asia's mastery of western methods. The nationalist move-ment in China led to a boycott of American goods in 1905. The United States, having herself recently become an Asian colonial power, proclaimed the objective of self-government in the Philippines. Among Muslims, the Pan-Islamic reform movement attracted eyes towards Egypt. In fact, by the early years of the twentieth century, European hegemony was challenged and India took note. What of the British government? How did it respond to Indian nationalist demands?

Reluctant Concessions of Political Advance

Growing unrest among the Indian intelligentsia, the rapid spread of 'extremism', and the more serious outburst of terrorism, forced the

British government to introduce measures of political advance in India. In 1909, 1919 and 1935 major Acts of the British Parliament set India along the path towards responsible government. But each step was made reluctantly. Ultimate goals were not set out clearly. Thus, Indians were dissatisfied. The nationalist movement eventually became a bitter struggle.

After the great Liberal election victory in Britain in 1906 the portents were at first promising. In the summer of that year Gopal Krishna Gokhale, an ardent but moderate nationalist, who was a member of the central legislative council and was Congress President in 1905, called upon Lord Morley, the secretary of state for India. He expressed the hope that India might become like 'a self-governing colony'. Morley was doubtful, but realized that some changes would have to be made. As tension mounted in India, an address from the Emperor, Edward VII, in 1908, to mark the fiftieth anniversary of the 1858 proclamation, indicated that the princes and peoples of India were to have 'a greater share in legislation and government'. The Liberal government's intentions were set out in the Government of India Act of 1909.

The 'Morley–Minto reforms', as they were called after Morley, the secretary of state, and the Viceroy, Lord Minto, led to some important political changes. But Britain failed to make the most of them. Indians were certainly given a further voice in the government of India. Two Indians were to sit on the secretary of state's council in London and one on the Viceroy's executive council. Sir Satyendra Prasanno Sinha became Law Member in 1909. Indians were also added to the pro-vincial executive councils.

In the legislatures membership of the central legislative council was increased to sixty, twenty-seven of whom were to be elected by in-direct means. Six seats were reserved for Muslim representatives. Officials and nominated members together retained a majority, but the officials were for the first time in a minority. The scope of debates in the council was widened by permitting the submission of supple-mentary questions. Similar changes were made in the provincial legislative councils, where elective majorities were admitted. These reforms were followed by the important announcement that a new capital for India would be built at Delhi, seat of the Mughal Empire. In 1911 George V and Queen Mary went to Delhi to attend a grandiose durbar. Lord Hardinge, who went to implement the reforms, was personally popular in India. Yet the 1909 reforms can hardly be accounted a success. Why, we must ask, were they so short-lived?

The Morley–Minto reforms had, in the first place, one basic weakness: they avoided a clear statement of ultimate goals. They were regarded as ambiguous. The reason for this is that both the secretary of state for India and the Viceroy did not believe India was suitable for the parliamentary system. Morley told the House of Lords that he hoped the 1909 Act would persuade Indians to abandon their dream of responsible government like the colonies. In the same year Minto bluntly wrote: 'As far as we can look ahead the existence of India must depend upon British supremacy.' Only a few radicals in Britain believed, as yet, that the logical development for India would be responsible government. Most British statesmen could not see the end of British rule in India. There was no notion that there should be a 'time-table' for self-government.

Yet this is precisely what was necessary. In 1911 an Indian journalist in fact demanded such a time-table: 'a solemn and authoritative declaration that within a fixed period, say twenty or twenty-five years, self-government would be granted in India.' In the same year the Viceroy informed the British government that provincial autonomy should be the goal in India. When this caused a stir in Britain, Edwin Montagu, the under-secretary of state, declared: 'we cannot drift on for ever without stating a policy.' Before the government produced a policy, the 1914–18 war broke out and Indian affairs gained an entirely new complexion.

India and the 1914-18 War

The role of the Dominions in the 1914–18 war has already been discussed. The feats of their armies, membership of the Imperial War Cabinet and separate representation at the peace conference, all enhanced their status as nations. In a somewhat similar manner the war brought major advances to India.

On the declaration of war in 1914, India went to war along with the rest of the empire. As in the Dominions, there were immediate professions of loyalty and unity. The central legislative council, the Indian National Congress, the princes, all rallied to the imperial war effort. The Indian army expanded and eventually over a million men took part in the war. An Indian corps fought in France, and Indian forces played an important part in Mesopotamia, Palestine, Macedonia and

German East Africa. Over £100 million were voted from the revenues of India; some of the princes also contributed men and money.

But the first wave of enthusiasm for the war was not sustained. The war brought inflation to India. Muslims were unhappy about fighting against their Islamic brothers, the Turks. When the war excited the imperial federationists in Britain, Indians began to fear that their own political advance would be forgotten in a welter of grander imperial schemes. Thus there were renewed demands that Britain should declare her ultimate goals in India. In 1915, Sinha, the only Indian on the Viceroy's executive council, gave warning in a speech to the Congress that unless a clear statement of the goal of self-government within the empire was published, the Indian moderates in the Indian National Congress would not hold their own.

Sinha's warning did not go unheeded. Lord Chelmsford, who became Viceroy in 1916, agreed that a declaration of policy was necessary. He drafted a possible statement for the secretary of state. A committee of the India Office mulled it over for five months before reporting in March 1917. There was general agreement in the office that a policy statement was needed. On its contents, however, they were less sure.

Chelmsford soon found unofficial, but influential, allies in the 'Round Table' group, who, as we have seen, publicized the name 'Commonwealth' through Lionel Curtis's books in 1916. They dreamed of accomplishing imperial federation after the war, but India, as an empire in its own right and apart from the colonies, had always presented difficulties for their schemes. After the 1909 reforms their difficulties were gradually resolved. Unlike the majority of British leaders, the Round Table group quickly grasped the long-term significance of the 1909 Act. One of the members told Lionel Curtis that 'self-government . . . however far distant, was the only intelligible goal of British policy in India'.* Curtis, who had previously thought that self-government was only applicable to the settlement colonies, now saw that India might follow the Dominions, and thus enter an imperial federation and send its members to the new Imperial Parliament. A study group set about devising a practical method of introducing responsible government into India. The system they suggested

* I am indebted for this important new material on the role of Curtis and the Round Table group to S. R. Mehrotra, *India and the Commonwealth 1885–1929*, London, 1965, pp. 79–86.

was to transfer, first of all, responsibility for certain items of business, while retaining others in official hands. In various ways the Round Table group had a great influence behind the scenes. Chelmsford studied their reports. Curtis toured India in 1916. One of the group's members, Philip Kerr, was private secretary to Lloyd George as Prime Minister.

The year 1917 produced great hopes in India. Lloyd George insisted, against Canadian and Australian advice, that Indians should be represented in the Imperial War Cabinet. It was, in many ways, a remarkable move. Three representatives of autocratically governed India sat with the Dominion premiers. There was an English official from the Viceroy's executive council and two Indians, Lord Sinha and the Maharaja of Bikaner. An even more astonishing step, in many Englishmen's eyes, was the appointment as secretary of state for India in 1917 of Edwin Montagu, a known critic of the Indian Civil Service, who had long been convinced of the need to define Britain's aims.

Chelmsford, the Viceroy, now had a superior after his own heart. The Cabinet gave serious thought to India. On 20 August 1917 Montagu announced to the House of Commons that British policy looked to

the increasing association of Indians in every branch of the administration, and the gradual development of self-governing institutions, with a view to the progressive realization of Responsible Government in India as an integral part of the British Empire.

A good deal of quibbling followed as to the precise implications of Montagu's announcement. Curzon (who had, in fact, largely drafted it) told the House of Lords that it was not a programme, only a 'broad general declaration of principle'. But as an earnest of his goodwill Montagu toured India in the winter of 1917–18. It was difficult to deny that the true implication of the Montagu–Chelmsford report of 1918 was eventual Dominion status for India. Representation at the War Cabinet and later at the peace conference underlined this point. Britain now had a policy for India. What did it mean in practice, and how did it work?

The 'Montagu–Chelmsford reforms' were embodied in the Government of India Act of 1919, which took effect two years later. The central government remained responsible to London, not to the legislature, but the Viceroy's executive council was enlarged to include six members, three of whom were Indians. Big changes were made to the legislatures. Indeed, the new central legislature appeared very much like a bi-cameral colonial Parliament. An upper house, or Council of State, was added consisting of sixty-one members elected for five years by a small select electorate of 17,000. In the Legislative Assembly the majority – 106 out of 146 members – were now to be elected. The vote, by property qualification, was extended to 5 million, including women. Constituencies were to be partly general, but some were reserved for Muslim members. Provision was also made for a Chamber of Princes. The central legislature received many of the powers of a Parliament, but the government of India was not made responsible to it.

In the provinces, however, a measure of responsible government was granted. The provincial legislative councils were enlarged and well over half the members were non-official. But the significant change was the introduction of the system known as 'dyarchy'. Government business was divided into two categories, one of which was 'reserved' for officials, the other being 'transferred' to fully responsible Indian ministries. The reserved departments concerned finances, law and order, and were still filled from the Indian Civil Service. Power was transferred in matters which directly affected the welfare of the populace – such as education, local government, health and economic development. Thus half the provincial government was a ministry of Indian politicians responsible to the legislative council, as in the Dominions, and the other half was responsible to the governor. Able governors did their best to work the system without friction and to keep the two 'halves' of the government operating together. 'Dyarchy' looked untidy and the Indian National Congress refused to support it. But through this system, which was inaugurated in 1921, Indians first held office in the provinces. In Madras the Justice Party and in the Punjab the Unionist Party were the first to follow the path pioneered in Canada. One distinguished authority on India, Dr Percival Spear, has asserted that without the Montagu–Chelmsford reforms Indian political development would have been 'belated, erratic, and probably revolutionary'.

Gandhi and the Demand for Full Equality

Dyarchy was an important step forward, but, like the 1909 reforms, it failed to satisfy Indian aspirations. Britain had now stated her aims and began to implement them. The Indian National Congress was, at first, disposed to welcome the reforms. Why, then, did a mass movement of protest emerge in the 1920s which led to the demand for nothing short of full equality? The answer may be found by considering the Amritsar massacre, the attitude of the British 'die-hards', and the extraordinary impact of Mohandas Gandhi. All three factors were closely linked.

During the 1914–18 war Gandhi supported the war effort and encouraged recruiting for the army. Indeed, as he happened to be in England in 1914, he intended to serve himself in an ambulance unit, and was only prevented by a serious illness. He returned to India in 1915. Although he did not emerge as a leader for several years his basic views were already formed. He had already come to believe in the doctrine of passive resistance and had evolved his tactics of civil disobedience. In the 1920s he emerged in India as one of the greatest popular leaders the world has ever seen.

In 1888, at the age of eighteen, Gandhi had defied his family and the rules of his caste in sailing to England to qualify for the Bar. He also studied Christian ethics and became attracted to Tolstoy's doctrine of non-violence. In 1893 as a young barrister he was called from India to Durban in South Africa as legal adviser to an Indian company. There, within a few days of his arrival, he was asked, while travelling by train, to vacate a first-class compartment for which he had a ticket. He refused, and was removed from the train by a policeman. In this way Gandhi began to learn how his countrymen were treated in South Africa. He soon led their movement of protest.

When the Natal government sought to disfranchise Indians in the colony, Gandhi organized the Natal Indian Congress and appealed to Indian leaders like Naoroji. Assuming the leadership of the Indian community in Natal, he organized his first passive resistance campaign and underwent his first spell in jail. Although during the South African war he supported the government and organized Indian ambulance units, after the war he found himself again at odds with the government. In 1907 the Transvaal government ordered all 'Asiatics' to register their finger-prints. Gandhi led a boycott of registration and, when fined by the magistrates, declared: 'I elect to go to jail.' His courageous stand was eagerly followed in India and the influence of the Viceroy and the secretary of state for India was exerted on the South African government to secure his release. But Indian lives had been lost during the anti-discrimination campaign. Thus Gandhi made a threefold vow of suffering: he would wear only a loin cloth and dhoti, walk barefoot and take only one meal a day. His disciplined persistent campaign led to a 'pact' with General Smuts in 1914.

At the age of forty-six, Gandhi left South Africa. After a visit to England he returned to India in 1915, where he agreed not to make political speeches for a year. Then his first excursions into politics were modest. He advocated the use of home-made products. He called for confidence and respect between government and people. 'I want to purge India of this atmosphere of suspicion on either side,' he said in 1915. 'If we are to reach our goals we shall have an empire which is to be based upon mutual love and mutual trust.' He supported the war effort: 'May God grant us, Home Rulers, the wisdom to see this simple truth. . . . The gateway to our freedom is situated on French soil.' In 1918 he rejected Tilak's invitation to attend the Indian National Congress.

Gandhi's approach to politics was always puzzling to friends and foes, but he was actuated by certain basic principles. They were a compound of Hindu custom, the Sermon on the Mount and Tolstoyan political tactics. First, although of a high caste, he identified himself with the people, dressed simply, spun at a wheel, even cleaned latrines with untouchables. He made the Congress a mass national movement. Secondly, he believed in non-violence, and he was to plead courageously for brotherly love between Hindus and Muslims during the final days of his life. Thirdly, he was a moralist and a man of religion. He preached service to one's neighbours and practised it in his life. Political crises were faced by Gandhi with prayer and fasting. Dr Percival Spear suggests that 'the gadfly of the British imperialists' was 'in reality their greatest friend' and that Gandhi, more than any other, prevented violent revolution in India.

Gandhi began to stand forth as a leader after dramatic, and tragic, events in 1919. Even before the Government of India Act had passed the British Parliament events occurred in India which inflamed opinion and prejudiced the success of the Act. A committee under Justice Rowlatt recommended trial by three judges, without jury, in political cases. Against the opposition of all the Indians in the legislative council the Rowlatt Acts was passed in March central 1919.

Gandhi now stood forth in protest. Adopting his South African tactics, he called for a *hartal*, a traditional Indian day of protest by stopping trade. He set off to lead a campaign of civil disobedience in the Punjab, but he was arrested. When riots and murder followed, which Gandhi loathed, he called off his campaign in a penitential fast. But more serious events soon occurred at Amritsar in the Punjab.

Rising unrest was accompanied by the murder of Europeans and the looting of property, and the governor called in the army. Brigadier Dyer, the local commander, proclaimed all meetings of more than four persons illegal. On 13 April 1919 Congress nevertheless called a mass protest meeting in the *Jallianwala Bagh*, a walled area in the centre of Amritsar. A crowd of more than 5,000 (some say 20,000) assembled. General Dyer brought up a company of soldiers. After the order was given to disperse, the troops opened fire and went on till their ammunition gave out. Three hundred and seventy-nine were killed and 1,200 wounded. Not content with the slaughter, the commander gave an order that all Indians who passed a certain street, where an elderly woman missionary teacher had been beaten, were to crawl on hands and knees.

Amritsar became the symbol of Indian humiliation. Its effect on the 30-year-old Jawaharlal Nehru, a Brahmin with an impeccable education at Harrow, Cambridge and the Inner Temple, was rather like the effect of the Jameson Raid on Smuts. It shook his faith in British justice. Gandhi, on the other hand, did not allow his shock at the tragedy to close his mind to the merits of the Montagu–Chelmsford reforms. But the British reaction to Amritsar did.

Although the home government and the government of India condemned Dyer, who was dismissed from the army, a large body of British opinion sympathized with him. A court of inquiry under Lord Hunter reported in 1920 and did not condemn Dyer in the fullest terms. During the debates in Parliament a number of M.P.s and a majority in the House of Lords upheld Dyer's actions. Finally, the *Morning Post* organized a public subscription to compensate the general for his dismissal.

At this point Gandhi's feelings could no longer be restrained. He declared that 'co-operation in any shape or form with this satanic government is sinful'. In the summer of 1920 he called for a movement of non-violent passive resistance. He urged his countrymen to surrender offices and titles, to boycott public functions and the courts, to take their children from the schools, to refuse enlistment in the army or election to the legislatures and to consume home-made products. At the Nagpur meetings of the Indian National Congress at the end of 1920 Gandhi announced his goal as *swaraj* 'by all legitimate and peaceful means'. He went on to say: 'If the British connection is for the advancement of India, we do not want to destroy it. But if it is inconsistent with our national self-respect, then it is our bounden duty to destroy it.' After 1920 the Congress sought complete equality, within the Commonwealth if possible, outside if not.

In many ways the 1920s opened with the British régime and the Indian nationalists tragically estranged, when they might have co-operated. Britain had declared the goal of responsible government, and the Montagu–Chelmsford reforms provided a practical starting-point. But they took *two* whole years to implement, during which time Amritsar and the attitude of the British 'die-hards' prejudiced their success. Yet Gandhi was, above all, a peace-lover and he respected the English. He once said that an Englishman

> never respects you until you stand up to him. Then he begins to like you. He is afraid of nothing physical; but he is very mortally afraid of his own conscience if ever you appeal to it and show him to be in the wrong.

His passive resistance campaigns were, in a sense, directed at Britain's conscience. When, indeed, in 1921 terrorists burned down a police station in the United Provinces, where twenty policemen were burnt alive, Gandhi was so ashamed that he once more called off the passive resistance campaign. He went to jail for three years as a result of the disorders, but the judge who sentenced him did so with the words: 'Even those who differ from you in politics look upon you as a man of high ideals and of noble and even saintly life.' In other words the general goals of both sides were the same and there was still room for mutual respect. How, then, can we account for the ever-increasing bitterness?

Disunity over India's Future

The main reason for the unhappy state of India in the 1920s was disunity both among the Indians and the British. We have already seen how in the 1890s Muslims began to fear that Hindus were using the nationalist movement to achieve domination and that extremists like Tilak gloried in appeals to the Hindu past. In Britain, at the same time, all attempts to reform the Indian governments were hindered by the Conservative die-hards who did not believe that India was suited to self-government. Such tension on both sides had made Amritsar possible. In 1924 Hindu–Muslim antagonism grew worse. The basic fear of the Muslims was always that self-government would mean Hindu rule. Although numerically predominant in East Bengal, the Punjab, Kashmir and Sind, Muslims equalled only a quarter of the total Hindu population. Sir Ahmad Khan, the first great Muslim leader, believed that India was not suited to self-government and he urged his followers to keep out of the Indian National Congress. In 1906 the All-India Muslim League was founded to foster loyalty to the government and protection of Muslim rights.

Yet for a short period Muslims and Hindus were drawn together in the nationalist movement. The rise of the Pan-Islamic movement in the early years of the twentieth century and the growth of western-style nationalism in Egypt, Turkey and Persia, led a number of English-educated Muslims to enter the Congress. Mohammed Ali Jinnah (later the founder of Pakistan) was secretary to Dadabhai Naoroji. During the 1914–18 war Britain's campaign against Turkey, whose Sultan was Caliph, shocked many devout Muslims. In 1916 the Lucknow Pact was made by which the Muslim League and the Indian National Congress agreed to co-operate in the struggle for *swaraj*. But Muslims remained concerned about their own interests. In 1924 the Muslim League declared the conditions upon which *swaraj* should be based. Freedom of religion was essential. They also demanded a federal constitution, with a weak central government and autonomous provinces, in some of which Muslims could predominate. Elsewhere separate constituencies must be reserved for Muslim voters. In this demand Muslims highlighted the basic problem of democracy in India.

Ever since the British had conceded the elective principle in the nineteenth century, they had been aware of a fundamental question: what was a representative Indian electorate? 'One man, one vote' was thought hardly feasible for illiterate millions. If it was applied without regard to religious divisions it could lead only to the tyranny of the majority. For this reason responsible government in India was not to be achieved by a process of gradual franchise concession as in Britain. The 1892 Act had provided for 'corporate' electorates. The 1909 Act reserved some seats for Muslim constituencies. By the 1919 Act 'communal constituencies' had become entrenched. Alongside a majority of 'general' constituencies, special provisions were made for Muslims, Sikhs, and (in Madras) Christians. Muslims now made communal representation a basic condition of future co-operation. The Muslim League challenged the Congress's claim to be India's only national party. Communal feeling flared up in renewed rioting in 1924, particularly in Kohat, North-West Frontier Province, where 4,000 Hindus had to be evacuated.

Yet Hindu–Muslim rivalry was not the only form of Indian division. It became obvious that there were renewed strains between the radicals and the moderates in the Indian National Congress. Congress had refused to co-operate in the Montagu–Chelmsford reforms, so that dyarchy began without the support of most of India's most notable politicians. In many ways the situation was frustrating: the nationalists seemed to be cheating themselves of the fruits of their victory. Therefore a group of the Congress, led by C. R. Das and Motilal Nehru (father of the later prime minister) formed a party known as the 'Swarajists', who fought in the 1923 elections.

In the central legislative assembly they obtained forty-five seats and gained a majority in two provinces. By allying with Independents in the central legislative assembly they could outvote the government. Thus, by 1924 what might be called a 'Parliamentary Congress Party' had emerged. Gandhi, who was released from jail, disapproved and retired to the country to preach self-help. But many Congressmen began to doubt the wisdom of the boycott. By the mid-1920s the nationalist opposition seemed to lose coherence.

Indian disunity had an unfortunate effect upon the British government. Dyarchy had been launched as a genuine experiment to be reviewed after ten years. The bitterness of the early 1920s gave it a poor start. Now Hindu–Muslim rivalry and the Indian National Congress split gave an excuse for further stalling. When the Swarajists in the central legislative assembly moved in 1924 for 'full self-governing Dominion Status', the official members of the council stressed the dangers of communal divisions and raised the questions of the status of the princes and the problems of defence and economic development. Indians even began to fear that the British government would go back on the promises of 1917. Lord Birkenhead, secretary of state for India, had always been unhappy about the Montagu–Chelmsford reforms and he did not believe that India was suited for Dominion status. Die-hards in Britain were delighted that Gandhi appeared to have lost his influence. How could India, in this atmosphere, be prevented from drifting?

Responsible Government in the Provinces and the Call for Independence

At the end of the 1920s the British government made a significant attempt to improve relations with India. Eventually after eight years the Government of India Act of 1935 inaugurated another great political advance. Unfortunately, however, the genuine good will displayed by some leaders on both sides was marred by renewed extremism, and British relations with India continued to be stormy.

In 1926 Stanley Baldwin, the Conservative prime minister, decided to send as Viceroy an able, young and idealistic member of his Cabinet. The forty-year-old Lord Irwin was a deeply religious and humane man, who had recently seen something of the seamier side of imperial affairs, when he was sent to report on the West Indies. Appalled by India's suffering and strife, he determined to improve conditions. He suggested that Britain should immediately review the workings of the 1919 Act instead of waiting for the full ten-year trial period to elapse. As a result of his proposal a commission led by Sir John Simon was sent to India in 1927. One of its members was Mr Clement Attlee, who would later grant India her independence.

The Simon Report, published in 1930, might be called the *Durham Report* of India. Its proposals can be compared with the remedies outlined for Canada ninety years earlier. The chief immediate proposal was for full responsible government in the provinces. For the future, federation was to be the goal, with provision for entry by the princely states. In the meantime, a strong central government would have to be maintained, which would, of course, retain control of defence and external affairs. The Simon Report was regarded at home as a masterly document. In India the commission led to an uproar, renewed resistance campaigns and the re-emergence of Gandhi as a leader.

How can we explain the reception of the Simon Commission? It is best seen in relation to India's demands: *swaraj*, self-government, and full-equality, Dominion status. Indians expected nothing less than Canada and Australia. Yet all the members of the Simon Commission were Englishmen. The Canadian, Australian and South African federal constitutions had all been drafted by national conventions. Indians expected to determine their future in the same way. Therefore, at its annual meeting in 1927 the Indian National Congress decided to boycott the Simon Commission. The radicals, led by Jawaharlal Nehru, succeeded in persuading the Congress to re-define its goals as 'Complete National Independence'. In the following year a committee of the Congress, under Nehru's father, drafted its own proposals for a constitution as a substitute for Simon's. At the annual meeting in December 1928, Congress demanded Dominion status by the end of 1929 or threatened a massive campaign of civil disobedience. Thus, even before the Simon Report was published, there seemed little chance of its success.

Lord Irwin refused to give up and tried to salvage something from the rising flames of revolt. He returned to Britain in 1929 to consult Ramsay MacDonald, leader of the newly elected Labour government. On his return to India he announced publicly on 31 October 1929 that the government had authorized him to state clearly

> that in their judgement it is implicit in the declaration of 1917 that the natural issue of India's constitutional progress, as they anticipate, is the attainment of Dominion status.

But the Viceroy failed to satisfy Congress. In their 1929 meeting they decided to go ahead with the civil disobedience campaign. In 1930 Gandhi ceremonially led the illegal manufacture of salt from sea-water and was once more sent to jail. As the campaign spread, violent elements took over. India experienced another frightening wave of riots and terrorism.

Lord Irwin still refused to abandon hope. He permitted negotiations with Gandhi and Nehru, who were in jail. He suggested that the Simon proposals should be enlarged to include an element of responsible government in the central government. He persuaded Indian liberals as well as Muslim leaders and representatives of the princes to attend a Round Table Conference in London. He even made a truce with Gandhi, who was released from jail and agreed to represent the Congress at a second Round Table Conference.

In the summer of 1931, Gandhi, a slight, bespectacled figure, clad in his loin cloth and dhoti, arrived in the imperial capital. Although only recently dubbed a 'half-naked fakir' by Winston Churchill, leader of the die-hards in Parliament, his methods of agitation had many admirers. He first had frank private talks with Viscount Templewood, the secretary of state for India, who earnestly confessed to a desire to grant responsible government. But he pleaded that Dominion status

o

could not be given immediately in view of the attitude of the die-hards at home and the Hindu–Muslim divisions in India. At the conference Gandhi made one basic assertion supported by three conditions. India was a nation and sought equal partnership with Britain. His conditions, which many Indians outside Congress manifestly did not support, were that the Indian National Congress was the only party truly representative of India, that 'untouchables' should not be separated from the rest of Hindus, and that Muslims and Hindus could live together without communal constituencies. As to the label attached to India's self-governing state, Gandhi was disarmingly open-minded. 'Dominion status? complete independence?' he asked. 'Call it what you like, a rose will smell as sweet by another name, but it must be the rose of liberty that I want and not the artificial product.' But the Round Table conference could not resolve India's disunity with a sweep of the hand. Gandhi returned to India without a firm offer of full responsible government.

Civil disobedience and violence had resumed during the period of the Round Table conference. As Gandhi refused to repudiate the acts of Congress during his absence he was again sent to jail. The British government went ahead with the Simon and Irwin proposals. On the question of representation, the prime minister, Ramsay MacDonald, decided in 1932 to stick to communal constituencies, including some for untouchables. Gandhi's response was an announcement that he would 'fast unto death'. The effect of his act was remarkable. A wave of sympathy swept the country. Men of all religious groups called for compromise to save the life of the Mahatma, or 'Holy Man'. By the 'Poona Pact' untouchable leaders agreed to remain within the Hindu representation in order to save Gandhi's life. In 1933 the new constitutional proposals were published as a white paper.

Finally, in 1935 the Government of India Act was passed by the British Parliament after mammoth debates. The basic principle of the Act was that India should receive a federal form of constitution. Full autonomy was to be granted to the provinces and the princely states were to be gradually integrated with British India. To this end representatives of the princes were admitted to both chambers of the central legislature. For the time being British control would remain at the centre, although it was intended to introduce the principle of 'dyarchy' by appointing responsible ministers in certain departments. The Act also severed Burma from India and so laid the foundation of a separate state. The most notable part of the Act, however, concerned the provinces. Here dyarchy was abolished and full responsible government conceded. The electorate was also enlarged to over 30 million.

The 1935 Act did not meet Congress's demands for complete self-government. But the party agreed to contest the 1937 elections. In the Hindu regions their success was overwhelming. In a 54 per cent poll, the Indian National Congress won 711 out of 1,585 seats in the provincial legislative assemblies. In seven provinces they formed fully responsible ministries, which were co-ordinated by a party 'high command'. In Bengal, Punjab and Sind, Muslim-dominated governments were formed. Thus, in 1937 the Indian provinces reached the constitutional position of the Canadian and Australasian colonies in the 1850s. British members of the Indian Civil Service, the police and the army now worked in the provinces under the orders of Indian ministers, fully responsible to the legislative assemblies. The agitators were now the masters. The period 1937–39 was a vital phase in the political experience of India.

Unfortunately the 1935 Act had little chance of a fair trial. More than ten years had elapsed since Irwin's first gesture to win Indian confidence. The all-English Simon Commission, the great delays before the passing of the Act, bitter words by the die-hards in Britain and the radicals in India, had poisoned the atmosphere. As the British seemed to lose the will to rule, violence was all too common. The 1935 Act left the integration of the states to voluntary action and little was done after 1937. Finally, in 1939 came the second world war.

On the outbreak of war the Viceroy declared India to be at war with Germany. Many Indians were humiliated that India was allowed no say in the decision, although technically under the 1935 constitution the Viceroy retained control over foreign policy. The Indian National Congress demanded a statement of Britain's war aims, a promise of independence after the war and responsible government for the central government. It was hardly the best time for constitutional debates. The Congress governments in the provinces were called upon to resign. After only two and a half years the experiment of responsible government in the Indian provinces came to an end.

The Effect of the 1939-45 War

Although the war caused a set-back to Indian self-government and eventually saw the outlawing of the Congress, it proved to be a vital phase in the national movement. Dramatic military events outside India had a notable effect on British and Indian opinion. At first, India was quiet. The Indian National Congress had no relish for the Nazis and the Indian Army was not immediately in demand overseas. But the German offensive of the summer of 1940, the retreat from Dunkirk and the Battle of Britain found the heart of the empire itself in peril. Would India rally to the cause as in 1914?

'We do not seek our Independence out of Britain's ruin', declared Gandhi. Nehru agreed; but he added that 'India cannot suspend the fight for freedom'. Gandhi's attitude to the war was that of a pacifist. Nehru was prepared to support the war effort, but he made conditions. If Britain declared full independence and called a provisional government of the main political leaders, India would give its 'full weight' to the war effort.

Nehru's words were given fair consideration by L. S. Amery, secretary of state for India. Of all British politicians in the inter-war years Amery was one of the most notable erstwhile imperialists – turned Commonwealth exponent. As colonial secretary in the 1920s he had presided over the formation of the Dominions Office and had had a hand in the 1926 definition of the Commonwealth. It was his fond ambition to preside over India's advance to Dominion status. He announced that the issue of self-government must be a decision by Indians. He urged the Viceroy to summon Indians to his executive council and to try and restore the provincial governments laid down in the 1935 constitution. Here was the origin of the 'August Offer' of 1940. By its terms the Viceroy proposed adding representatives of the major Indian political parties to the executive council, thus forming a War Advisory Council, and he further promised a Constituent Assembly to draft a new constitution at the end of the war. The offer failed. It was followed by a short-lived, limited civil disobedience campaign.

In 1942 the clouds of war began to darken India itself. Japan had struck at Pearl Harbor and South-East Asia. By February 1942 Britain's 'impregnable fortress' of Singapore had fallen and on 8 March the port of Rangoon followed. The enemy was now on India's doorstep and co-operation became vital. Mr Churchill, the prime minister, therefore sent Sir Stafford Cripps, a Labour member of the wartime coalition, to seek Indian aid by promises of self-government. Cripps was already known to Nehru, who shared his socialist ideals, and he was respected by Gandhi as a devout and upright man of religion. The proposal he brought represented a major concession by the British government: it was, in fact, the full acceptance of the demands of Congress *after* the war. Immediately hostilities should come to an end, an Indian Union would be formed possessing Dominion status. A Constituent Assembly would be summoned to draft the constitution, which would include a right of secession from the Commonwealth. In the meantime, while no constitutional changes were to be made during the war, the chief party leaders might be invited to sit on the Viceroy's executive council, which would, in practice, develop into a responsible cabinet, where possible. A form of 'National Government' was envisaged, with the Viceroy retaining control of military affairs and the war effort. Nehru was at first disposed to accept the offer. Gandhi dubbed it a 'post-dated cheque on a failing bank'. The Congress insisted on immediate Cabinet government at the centre, and Cripps returned home empty-handed.

Gandhi, to the bewilderment of many Indians who feared Japanese invasion, maintained the position of an adamant pacifist. He advocated passive resistance to the Japanese as he believed that India was not Japan's enemy. This led logically to his insistence that Britain should 'Quit India':

> I feel convinced that the British presence is the incentive for the Japanese attack. If the British wisely decided to withdraw and leave India to manage her own affairs in the best way she could, the Japanese would be bound to reconsider their plans.

'Leave India to God', he declared. 'If that is too much, then leave her to anarchy.' Many of Gandhi's friends were perplexed by his stand, which also included the suggestion that Britain herself should offer passive resistance to Hitler to avoid further bloodshed. He later admitted that he did not want Japan to win the war and said that if Britain agreed to withdraw she could use India as a base, and even occupy the ports. Unpractical though his ideas appeared, Gandhi on 7 August 1942 persuaded Congress to adopt the 'Quit India' policy. Two days later he was arrested. The Congress was declared an illegal body and its leaders went to jail. Riots and violence followed and in the later months of 1942 there were a thousand deaths. But the government of India, in the interest of wartime security, relentlessly repressed opposition and by 1943 was firmly in command.

Apart from the political set-back the war had an important impact on India. It became the supply base and military headquarters for many operations in the middle east and later in South-East Asia and Burma. The Indian Army was expanded, industry was called upon on a large scale and the transport services were greatly taxed. On the credit side, this gave many Indians new skills and responsibilities and a new mutual respect grew between English and Indian soldiers who worked side by side. On the debit side, the demands of the military brought inflation and food shortages, which, coupled with the loss of rice imports from Japanese-occupied South-East Asia, led to the first serious famine in Bengal for forty years. Troops had to be called in to organize relief. By the end of the war, India was shaken but outwardly calm after the period of reversion to autocratic rule.

Independence and Partition

The chief result of the war from the Indian nationalist viewpoint was Britain's categorical offer of Dominion status and a Constituent Assembly when the war was over. In the short run, it brought failure and, for thousands, a spell of prison. But when Germany surrendered in May 1945 Indian independence was obviously near. The goal was now clear. But the method of winning it was still obscure. Why was the final achievement of self-government so prolonged and confused? The answer is simple: the British government wished to hand over power, but did not know how. Hindu–Muslim divisions dogged its efforts at every turn.

Already in 1944 Field-Marshal Wavell, the Viceroy, had urged conciliation and called for unity in India. As soon as Germany surrendered, the government authorized him to reopen negotiations with Indian leaders and on 4 June 1945 he convened a conference at Simla. Here he renewed the offer of 1942: Dominion status and a Constituent Assembly to draw up a constitution. The future government was clearly to be an Indian creation. In the meantime, however, he proposed to recall the Viceroy's executive council in the form of a coalition government. Tribute has been paid to Wavell for tackling the problem of the future of India without delay. But the Muslim League and the Indian National Congress could not agree as to who should choose the Muslim component of the executive council. Wavell's offer came to nothing.

Events moved rapidly in 1945. In July, the triumphant Labour Party achieved its immense majority in Parliament and Clement Attlee, former member of the Simon Commission, became prime minister. The dropping of atomic bombs hastened Japan's surrender on 14 August. The war in the east was now over and a friendly government in Britain could turn to India's problems. But what did India want? This was now the crucial question.

Attlee's first act was to call for elections in India in 1946 to test local opinion. The result could have been foreseen: a clear division on communal lines. The Muslim League won all the Muslim seats. Congress secured a majority in the central assembly. In the provinces, where the 1935 constitution was restored, Congress formed eight ministries, the Muslim League two (in Bengal and Sind) and a United Government was formed in the Punjab. The final step was still awaited: the creation of an interim central government, by appointments to the Viceroy's executive council and the convening of the Constituent Assembly.

Once more the Hindu–Muslim conflict dogged the government. A Cabinet mission headed by Lord Pethick-Lawrence visited India in 1946. Their chief concern was to preserve Indian unity, but provide safeguards for the Muslims. They tried to evolve a system whereby autonomous Muslim states, or groups of states, could remain within the Indian Union. But the Cabinet mission faced the same deadlock as the Simla conference. The Muslim League and the Congress could not agree.

The Viceroy, meanwhile, tried to form an interim government. He proposed appointing fourteen Indian politicians to his executive council: six Congressmen, five Muslims, and one each of the Sikhs, Parsees and Christians. He promised Nehru and Mohammed Ali Jinnah, the Muslim League leader, that the new council would be treated as a responsible Cabinet. Jinnah and Nehru met in Bombay on 15 August 1946 in a final attempt to reach agreement. But they failed. Jinnah then called for 'Direct Action' to achieve a separate Pakistan. Nehru went ahead without the Muslims. Taking office as Vice-President of the Viceroy's executive council, he became in effect India's first 'prime minister' as the final deadlock between Congress and the Muslim League appeared to have been reached.

Tragedy soon burst forth. In August 1946 Muslim demonstrators started communal riots, which snowballed into uncontrolled savagery. In four days in Calcutta 4,000 lives were lost. The army had to restore order as violence spread elsewhere. 'We are not as yet in the midst of a civil war,' declared Gandhi, 'but we are nearing it.' The riots were the worst in the experience of the British Raj – a shock to Indian and British opinion alike. In this explosive atmosphere, which has been dubbed the 'War of Succession', how could power be finally transferred?

For a brief period the Muslim League agreed to enter the government. But Jinnah made no bones about his motives: 'we are going into the interim government to get a foothold to fight for our cherished goal of Pakistan.' The bitter communal controversy now entered the highest realms of government. Uncertainty about the future began to undermine the efficiency of the civil service. Therefore at the end of 1946 Mr Attlee called the main Indian leaders to London in order to attempt a settlement. They failed to make progress. But the government made the significant announcement that it had no intention of forcing a Constitution upon 'any unwilling parts of the country'.

The prime minister now decided to delay no longer. He declared publicly on 20 February 1947 that Britain would leave India before June 1948 and that Lord Louis Mountbatten would be appointed Viceroy to effect the transfer of power. In many ways it was a splendid choice. At forty-seven, Mountbatten was comparatively young. As a member of the Royal Family he was well fitted to terminate the long line of Viceroys and he came with the prestige of victory as Supreme Allied Commander in South-East Asia. He reached India on 22 March 1947 and acted quickly. He met the main Indian leaders and achieved a close accord with Nehru. He was soon convinced that Jinnah and the Muslim League would never compromise, and he accepted the need for a partition. All turned now on procedure, and this was accepted on 3 June 1947.

India was to become the successor-state of British India. Pakistan would be a new state formed by the secession of certain provinces. Decisions to enter Pakistan would have to come from the provincial assemblies and in Bengal and the Punjab the assemblies would divide into two parts, representing the Muslim and non-Muslim majority regions. In the North-West Frontier Province a referendum was to be held. India and Pakistan would both become Dominions in the British Commonwealth. Their future constitutions and relations with the Commonwealth were to be determined by constituent assemblies. This

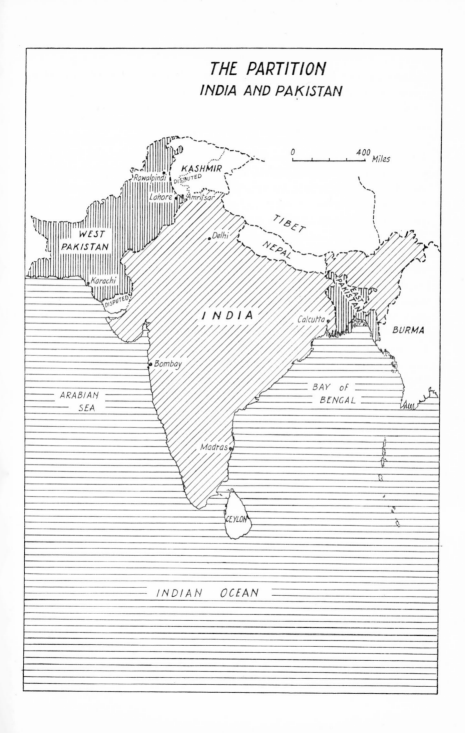

THE PARTITION
INDIA AND PAKISTAN

0   400 Miles

KASHMIR
DISPUTED

Rawalpindi
Lahore · Amritsar

WEST
PAKISTAN

Karachi

DISPUTED

TIBET

NEPAL

· Delhi

INDIA

Calcutta

PAKISTAN

BURMA

· Bombay

ARABIAN
SEA

BAY of
BENGAL

Madras·

CEYLON

INDIAN OCEAN

was the basis of the 'Mountbatten Plan' which had, in the main, been drafted by V. P. Menon, his Indian constitutional adviser.

Once the decision to partition the Indian empire had been made, the conclusion was reached swiftly. Bengal and the Punjab agreed to be divided. Sind, Baluchistan, the Muslim part of Assam and the North-West Frontier chose Pakistan. Thus the new Muslim state was to consist of two separate parts. Jinnah briefly tried to gain a territorial corridor linking the two, but did not press it. The Indian Independence Act received the royal assent on 18 July 1947 and on 15 August the British Raj came to an end.

A few irreconcilables remained. Winston Churchill, leader of the die-hards of the 1930s, had not relented and he asserted that Britain was about to hand over to 'men of straw of whom in a few years no trace will remain'. Gandhi did not disguise his deep disappointment that Indians had failed to unite. 'The British Government is not responsible for partition', he declared. 'The Viceroy has no hand in it. In fact he is as opposed to division as Congress itself. But if both of us, Hindu and Muslim, cannot agree on anything else, the Viceroy is left with no choice.' Amid the ceremonies of the transfer of power in India and Pakistan, grandiose and magnanimous words were spoken on all sides. But at the swearing-in of Lord Mountbatten, the ex-Viceroy, as the first Governor-General of India, Dr Rajendra Prasad, who was shortly to become the first President of the Republic of India, made a modest and just appraisal:

> While our achievement is in no small measure due to our sufferings and sacrifices, it is also the result of world forces and events, and last, though not least, it is the consummation and fulfilment of the historic traditions and democratic ideals of the British. . . .

India and the 'New Commonwealth'

Indian independence, for all its subsequent tragedies, was the great landmark in the evolution of the modern Commonwealth. If we look at the black side first, we must admit that the manner of its achievement left many grounds for regret. On the very day which followed the inauguration of the Dominions of India and Pakistan, communal violence broke out in the Punjab. In less than a year possibly a million lives were lost and over 5 million refugees crossed the border of Pakistan and India in the west. On top of this, Gandhi's assassination by a Hindu extremist in January 1948 cast a shadow over the birth of the new states. Gandhi was bitterly disappointed by partition and lost his life because he continued to preach brotherly love between Hindus and Muslims. Further intractable problems seemed to attend the integration of two of the largest princely states. Hyderabad was eventually occupied by Indian troops, and Kashmir became the great bone of contention between India and Pakistan. After 1948 it remained one of the Commonwealth's largest unsolved issues and in 1965 it led to the Indo-Pakistan war.

Yet for all the problems which followed Britain's withdrawal, there were great achievements. The Indian Constituent Assembly produced the promised federal constitution of 1950. With the adoption of universal adult suffrage India became the world's largest democracy. The state of Kerala even elected, and then rejected, a Communist government. In Pakistan, the failure of the Constituent Assembly was followed by martial law and General Ayub Khan's 'Basic Democracies' in 1959. A new constitution in 1962, providing for indirect elections through an Electoral College and a form of separation of powers between the President and the Assembly, led to a régime possibly more in tune with the authoritarian ethos of Islam and the martial spirit of the North-West.

From the point of view of the Commonwealth, the great change occurred in 1949 when Mr Nehru informed the prime ministers' meeting of that year of India's intention to become a sovereign independent republic, but requested continued membership of the Commonwealth. To some it appeared that common allegiance to the Crown, the last bond of unity, was about to be broken. But the premiers, with the consent of King George VI, approved the formula that the Indian Republic should remain a full member and accept the King 'as the symbol of the free association of its independent member nations, and as such the Head of the Commonwealth'. India's membership as a Republic shortly became the model for the majority of the Asian–African–Caribbean members.

Thus in the period from 1919 to 1949 India was the great pioneer of Commonwealth development because she persuaded Britain to adapt the Canadian solutions of the period 1840–1870 to the non-European empire. Lionel Curtis had recognized the significance of India's role, when he wrote in 1929:

In solving the problem of responsible government this vast and complex Oriental community will find she has solved it for the whole of

Asia, and, in the fullness of time, for Africa as well. . . . Three continents are now living in the rays of a candle lighted by England centuries ago. India now has a candle which once kindled will never be put out till all the nations of Asia and Africa walk by its light.*

* Mehrotra, pp. 246–7.

8

The New Commonwealth: Origins

The Pace of Independence – An Introductory Survey

THE INDIAN national movement pioneered the way for the Asian, African and Caribbean members of the Commonwealth. But although a few far-sighted men like Lionel Curtis realized that Britain's decision on the future of India in 1917 pointed the way for eventual self-government in the remaining parts of the empire, few Englishmen expected to see this in their lifetime. Generalized pronouncements about the goal of self-government within the Commonwealth of Nations were occasionally made after the 1914–18 war. Sir Reginald Coupland, professor of colonial history at Oxford, even suggested in 1933: 'A Dominion in Nigeria. . . . Why not?' But colonial administrators did not take him seriously.

In spite of the new era presaged in 1917 by the doctrine of 'self-determination' embodied in Woodrow Wilson's Fourteen Points and the success of the Bolshevik revolution in Russia, British policy-makers during the inter-war years were vague and unhurried. They now adhered religiously to their doctrine of trusteeship in Asia, Africa and the Caribbean, but they were convinced that they had endless years to fulfil their task. They were not even very sure about the best forms of trusteeship. To such men, the end was far out of sight; there was no 'time-table' for self-government, so there were few active preparations for its achievement.

But just as the 1914–18 war saw the Indian nationalists make great strides, so there were important stirrings elsewhere. In 1915, riots in central Ceylon led an alarmist governor to proclaim martial law and to imprison many notable Sinhalese. They included Don Stephen Senanayake (later the first prime minister), who never quite forgave the British. In 1918 the Ceylon National Congress was formed following the Indian precedent. In the same year as the Ceylon riots an abortive rising in Nyasaland, led by the Rev. John Chilembwe, demonstrated the growing passion of African nationalism. A few months later a young man, Hastings Banda, left the tense atmosphere of the colony to study in the United States. He was one of the earliest of a notable stream of future African leaders who went to live and study abroad. When he eventually returned to his homeland in 1958, he was soon to become a detained political leader, and later first prime minister of Malawi.

In West Africa the Indian nationalists had eager admirers. When India was invited to the War Cabinet in 1917 they cried: 'Why not West Africa as well?' As India and the Dominions were invited to the peace conference in 1919, Dr Nanka-Bruce of the Gold Coast sent resolutions to the western powers so that 'the voice of West Africa' could also be heard at Versailles. The first Pan-African Congress met in Paris in 1919. In the following year a National Congress of British West Africa convened in Accra and President Wilson's doctrine of 'self-determination' was taken up by the organizers. They so impressed the 25-year-old Joseph Danquah that he soon began his search for a new name for a free Gold Coast, which led him to introduce the idea of the now familiar 'Ghana'.

At the same time in Kenya the Kikuyu began to organize political associations. Lives were lost in Nairobi riots in 1922. By the late 1920s Jomo Kenyatta, general secretary of the Kikuyu Central Association, was editing the first Kikuyu-language, anti-government newspaper. Similarly, a few political movements were growing in the West Indies, such as the 'Representative Government Association' of Grenada, founded in 1914, and Captain Cipriani's 'Trinidad Workingmen's Association' which flourished at the end of the war. Marcus Garvey of Jamaica founded the Negro nationalist 'Universal Negro Improvement Association', which had brief international fame at the end of the war. Returning to Jamaica in 1927, he founded the 'People's Political Party'. Thus the period after 1917 saw a good deal of small-scale, though significant, development of Asian–African–Caribbean nationalism.

The depression of the 1930s and the 1939–45 world war caused a temporary strengthening of autocratic rule in many Crown colonies, but they forced the British government to reconsider its goals. After

1945 a new impatience shown by the populace with the pace of British policy changes led to the growth of a number of mass nationalist parties along the lines of Gandhi's Congress party. Moreover, by this time Mr Attlee's Labour government had swept into power, determined to grant independence to India. This landmark in 1947 proved to be a test-case for independence elsewhere. In 1948 Ceylon became an independent Commonwealth state after years of peaceful progress which was a marked contrast to India's violence. Burma received independence outside the Commonwealth in the same year. In 1949 a commission in the Gold Coast headed by an African judge, J. H. Coussey, drew up a constitution which provided for a transitional period of responsible government. This was followed by rapid politi cal advance and in 1957 Ghana became the first independent African member of the Commonwealth. Malaya became an independent federal monarchy in the same year, when it was agreed that Singapore should also become a Commonwealth state with internal self-government.

Ghana proved to be the test-case for West Africa. Independence followed quickly in Nigeria (1960), Sierra Leone (1961) and finally Gambia (1965). But in East and Central Africa British policy was complicated by the presence of the settler colonies in Kenya and the Rhodesias. Southern Rhodesia's settlers, although a minority of the population, had received responsible government in 1923 after the British South Africa Company gave up its rule. By the 1960s there were about 220,000 Europeans living among 3 million Africans. Kenya, on the other hand, was the first colony where a substantial body of English settlers failed to gain self-government. They numbered by the 1960s about 65,000 to over 8 million Africans and 200,000 Asians. In spite of representation in the legislative council since 1905 and adult European franchise since 1919, the Kenya settlers were never given full self-government.

But for East Africa the real test-case was the Central African Federation. This short-lived system was created by the British government in 1953 to foster economic co-operation and growth between Southern Rhodesia, Northern Rhodesia and Nyasaland and to erect a new Dominion on the basis of what was called 'partnership'. Success here would have encouraged federation farther north, for in the same year the secretary of state was also contemplating a federation of Kenya, Uganda and Tanganyika by building on the East African High Commission created in 1948.

The test came in 1959. After serious riots in Nyasaland, which led to the detention of Dr Hastings Banda, recently returned leader of the Malawi National Congress, the English judge Patrick Devlin led a commission of inquiry to report to the British government. His conclusion was quite clear: 'Always Federation was the cause of all the trouble.' Articulate African opinion in Nyasaland (and also in Northern Rhodesia) was convinced that Federation was retarding political advance and would keep the people in a position similar to their fellow countrymen in Southern Rhodesia and the Union of South Africa, with little prospect of parliamentary democracy in the future.

The Devlin Report had an immediate impact. In 1960 Mr Harold Macmillan, the Conservative prime minister, ended a tour of Africa with a speech to the Parliament of South Africa in Cape Town in which he said:

> The most striking of all the impressions I have formed since I left London a month ago is of the strength of this African national consciousness. In different places it may take different forms. But it is happening everywhere. The wind of change is blowing through this continent.
>
> Whether we like it or not, this growth of national consciousness is a political fact. We must all accept it as a fact. Our national policies must take account of it.

To the dismay of the English settlers in East Africa, Britain adapted her policies in that region remarkably quickly.

In 1960 Iain Macleod, Macmillan's secretary of state, refused to grant self-government to the settlers in Kenya. In spite of the tragic chaos which followed Belgium's withdrawal from the Congo later in 1960, and confirmed the East African settlers' worst fears, the British government firmly refused to retard the progress of African self-government. Quite the reverse. Tanganyika became independent in 1961, Uganda followed in 1962. In 1963 independence was extended to Kenya – once the 'white man's country' – under the leadership of Jomo Kenyatta, the recently detained veteran of the pre-war Kikuyu national movements. Zanzibar also became independent in the same year. In such a new atmosphere of freedom all efforts to salvage the Central African Federation failed. After only ten years of existence it was dissolved, and Malawi (formerly Nyasaland) and Zambia (Northern Rhodesia) advanced to independence in 1964. In the same year, after an armed African revolt in Zanzibar had driven out the

Arab Sultan, Tanganyika and Zanzibar united to form the Republic of Tanzania. In five years, therefore, British rule in East Africa (outside Southern Rhodesia) was dismantled and African states took their places in the Commonwealth.

Outside Asia and Africa independence was even granted to some of the small island colonies which were the legacy of Britain's past trade and strategy. In the Mediterranean, Cyprus became a republic in 1960, followed by Malta in 1964. In the Caribbean, the failure to create a lasting West Indies Federation led to the complete independence of Jamaica and Trinidad in 1962.

It is therefore obvious that since 1947 and particularly between 1957 and 1964 the British empire went through a transition even more rapid and remarkable than that which occurred between 1846 and 1855 with the original grants of responsible government in North America, Australia and New Zealand. Fourteen new states emerged from the Crown colonies in only seven years. It should also be remembered that Britain withdrew completely from certain other territories which she had ruled – Jordan (1946), Burma and Israel (1948), and the Sudan and Egypt (1956) – and that Eire and South Africa left the Commonwealth. How are we to interpret this extraordinarily rapid revolution?

The End of the Empire

In one sense the emergence of the 'New Commonwealth', with its majority of Asian–African–Caribbean members, must be set in the context of world history. Asians were, in the first place, impressed by the rise of Japan and, for a time at least, by the Chinese nationalist movement. Muslims, in India and South-East Asia, were influenced by the Pan-Islamic movement which centred on Al-Ahzar University in Cairo. Asian nationalism increased in tempo after Japan's crushing military victories over Britain, the United States and the Netherlands in South-East Asia and the Pacific in 1941–42; again after the Indonesian war of 1945–48, and finally after the Communist revolution in China in 1949.

Secondly, African nationalism must be seen partly in the context of the movement for the advancement of Negro peoples in the United States. The earliest progenitors of the Pan-African ideal and the doctrine of *négritude* were West Indians and Americans such as Edward Blyden (from the Dutch Virgin Islands), W. E. B. Du Bois (from the United States) and Marcus Garvey (from Jamaica). These men sowed significant ideas in Africa. Some of the most notable leaders of contemporary Africa, such as Dr Banda, Dr Nkrumah and Dr Azikiwe, studied in the United States and were obviously influenced by their ideals.

Finally, the spread of independence in Asia, Africa and the Caribbean is a by-product of the relative decline of the Western European colonial powers, the post-1947 tension between the United States and Soviet alliances, and the universal ideological conflict made possible by the rapid spread of education and new means of communication. In a world where knowledge knows no bounds, where subscriber truck dialling and village call boxes exist in the jungles of Malaya, where it is possible for live television broadcasts to span oceans and continents, and where it is impossible to ignore extremes of wealth and poverty, two perfectly valid roads to economic advance and social change seem to present themselves to the people. One is by violent revolution and the ruthless suppression of opposition. The other is by consent and gradual evolution.

In the 'New Commonwealth' the British government and the local *élites* co-operated to ensure that change came by consent, rather than by violence. Attempts to retard the political advance of the Asian–African–Caribbean colonies would have invited violence from within, intervention from without and the logical possibility of major wars. As Mr Macmillan frankly admitted, Britain adjusted herself to the 'wind of change'. And on the whole independence was achieved peaceably. It is true that riots, bitter destruction and even bloodshed afflicted many of these colonies for a while, as they had previously in India. But in Palestine, Cyprus, Malaya and Kenya, where there was civil war, the issue (as in India and Pakistan) was never a straightforward fight between local nationalists and the colonial power.

Will future historians view this period as the 'fall of the British empire'? Did it actually fall? Will they regard the 'New Commonwealth' as a sham designed to cushion the British people from the shock of their imperial decline? Did the buffets of the 'wind of change' prompt the Conservative government – heirs of Disraeli and Salisbury – into acts of scuttle? It is too soon to give a confident judgement.

It is, however, clear that the growth of nationalism, the rise of political parties, constitutional advance to responsible government and the achievement of independence, followed a remarkably consistent pattern in most of the Asian–African–Caribbean Commonwealth. The most crucial question-mark usually became one of pace. Once the major landmarks – India (1947), Ghana (1957), and the failure of Central African Federation (1959) – had been passed, the 'independence drill' was soon being rehearsed with precision. But what is all too easily forgotten is that, while the pace accelerated rapidly after the Indian decisions of 1947–49, the origins of the new nationalism go back a long way. The basic principles of British colonial self-government go back even further. Thus, nationalists always had a pattern to follow – that of responsible government and Dominion status. When Britain realized that the time to go had arrived she had a well-tried system to set up. Whether that system – parliamentary government and universal manhood suffrage – was appropriate to Asia, Africa and the Caribbean was left to the new states to work out.

The Cycle of Colonial Nationalism

Nationalism in Asia and Africa followed a cycle which compares very closely with the one we have observed in India. British expansion evoked certain responses from the local societies; colonial nationalists promoted various responses by Britain. If a bold generalization is not taken too literally and regional variations are later given due credit, a general cycle of Asian–African nationalism may be suggested.

British expansion brought law and order, comparatively large-scale territorial unity and a new economy. British rule gave rise to new classes, who were educated in the English language, who served the régime, acquired new skills, professions and responsibilities, and were comfortably off. Some were from the old ruling classes as in Ceylon, Uganda and Northern Nigeria; others constituted a new *élite*. A few became very rich and some also very 'British'. But the majority of the *élite*, while absorbing western knowledge and English political ideas, were reluctant to conform to Macaulay's idea of the multi-racial Englishman. Their education enabled them to see their own society and the intruding colonial régime in some perspective and led them to a deeper interest in their own country. Thus numerous small associations were formed, often with a cultural or antiquarian bias, but also in order to represent articulate local opinion to the colonial governments. These classes and their associations were the seed-bed of nationalism. Roughly by the time of the 1914–18 war and its aftermath many of the specialist associations had evolved into national congresses, dedicated to constitutional advance. During the inter-war years a few notable leaders began to emerge.

By this time government itself had become more complex – specialist departments concerned with agriculture, transport, labour, education and health were required. At the same time new classes of skilled artisans, mechanics, school teachers and small businessmen had emerged, often educated not in the English language but in the vernacular. The keynote of this era was a growing frustration. Members of the wealthy *élite* were frustrated by total refusal of (or by a very limited) admission into the legislative councils or the higher civil service. Until 1942, for example, candidates for the colonial service (as distinct from the Indian, Ceylon, Malayan and Hong Kong services) had to be of 'pure European descent'. At the same time, the much larger colonial petty bourgeoisie was frustrated by the limitations imposed on them by their lack of the English language. It is significant that in this period a number of Asians and Africans, often from this class, went abroad to reside and study for long periods. Just as Gandhi spent twenty years in South Africa before returning to lead the mass movement in India, so the great leaders of Africa like Hastings Banda, Nnamdi Azikiwe, Kwame Nkrumah and Jomo Kenyatta spent many years in Britain or the United States before returning to lead mass movements at home.

By the time of the 1939–45 world war nationalist groups were usually well established among the new *élite*, some of whom had gained political experience in the legislative councils. During the war they made little progress, although, like the Indian National Congress, a few leaders demanded a post-war time-table for self-government. Yet in other respects the war obviously proved a great watershed. On the one hand, Britain, as she fought for her own survival, made significant pledges on general post-war policy. The government sponsored Colonial Development and Welfare Acts in 1940 and 1945 which, by making available millions of pounds for social and economic development, implied an end to the brake on growth caused by the Gladstonian doctrine that colonies should be 'self-supporting' financially. The Atlantic Charter of 1941 held out the promise of freedom to colonial peoples. In 1943 the secretary of state for colonies, Oliver Stanley, rose in the House of Commons to reiterate that the government was 'pledged to guide colonial people along the road to self-government within the British Empire'.

On the other hand, many Asians and Africans served in the British armed forces, where they acquired new skills and responsibilities, and attained new standards of fitness and pay. By participating in a great international war effort – often in overseas theatres – they had a glimpse of a wider world in which Europeans fought desperately among themselves in the service of ideals such as freedom and independence. At the same time many American and British troops were stationed in the colonies. West Africa was an important staging post for the North African theatre of war, and Ceylon became the headquarters of South-East Asia Command. Thus Asian and African Crown colonies had a glimpse of westerners who were more representative than the missionaries and district officers to whom they were accustomed. British and American servicemen, from all walks of life, were suddenly injected into their midst and were seen to perform some of the menial tasks often required of the private soldier. Yet these soldiers and air-men enjoyed a standard of living and conviction of their rights quite new to many African and Asian peasants and workers. Through informal contacts with the troops the local peoples discovered the full range of human vices and virtues, aloofness and familiarity, in the fellow-countrymen of their well-established, but carefully selected, rulers.

Thus, at the end of the war, when returning ex-servicemen often found unemployment and frustration, and, above all, post-war constitutions which were much too gradual for their liking, the atmosphere was ripe for the development of mass nationalist move-ments. In some cases the old *élite* retained the loyalty of the masses, as in Ceylon and Malaya. Elsewhere (notably in Ghana and southern Nigeria) the old *élite* was swept aside by impatient nationalists who built mass parties as Gandhi had. Rioting and the detention of the leaders often followed.

The British government usually responded quickly. Once an accelerated time-table of constitutional advance was determined, educational programmes were expanded, 'localization' of the public services was hastened, and elected majorities in the legislative councils were gradually given executive responsibilities. This in turn gave radical nationalists official dignities and burdens, quietened the atmosphere and led to co-operation in achieving independence. Once independence was achieved, most of the new states followed India in emphasizing their full equality by becoming republics and sometimes announcing the future adoption of a national language.

This cycle of colonial freedom must not be allowed to distort the national histories. The time-scale obviously varied from colony to colony. It was always accelerating, and in certain possessions important stages of the cycle were short-circuited, even reversed. But as an introductory guide to the origins of the 'New Commonwealth' the cycle may serve.

9

The New Commonwealth: Asia and the Caribbean

The Eastern Colonies

THE COLONIES in Asia were all by-products of the Indian empire. Ceylon was acquired for strategic reasons during the Napoleonic wars. Burma was, until 1937, treated as an adjunct to India. The rest of the Asian colonies were by-products of the East India Company's trade to China and the Indonesian islands: they formed a line of bases on the sea route to Canton. Penang (1786), Singapore (1819), Hong Kong (1842) and Labuan (1846) were all originally conceived as strategic posts to shelter British ships, protect traders, attract island merchants, challenge the Netherlands in the East Indies, and, above all, to foster and protect the China trade.

Yet trade led to empire. Each strategic foothold became the basis for local empire-building. Ceylon, as we have seen, developed into a 'model tropical dependency'. Progressive annexations in Burma – Tenasserim, Arakan, Assam and Manipur (1826), Pegu (1852) and Upper Burma (1886) – led to the creation of a new province of India, which was detached as a separate colony in 1937. From the Straits Settlements Britain acquired influence in the states of the Malay Peninsula. In 1824 she acquired the Dutch colony of Malacca. In 1874 she began to exert political pressure on the Malay States, until, by the 1914–18 war, they were all 'protected states', ruled by their sultans under British advice. Similarly, in North Borneo, British influence was not confined to the useless island of Labuan. In 1841 James Brooke, a former East India Company officer who was in search of adventure, was appointed Raja of Sarawak by the Sultan of Brunei. In 1881 the British North Borneo Company was granted a charter to develop north-eastern Borneo (Sabah). Between them the 'white rajas' and the Chartered Company reduced the Sultanate of Brunei to its present small enclaves and in 1888 all three territories became British protectorates. Finally, the rocky, thirty-square-mile island of Hong Kong grew under British rule to become a great trading and manu-facturing city. With small territories on the mainland added, it supported by 1960 a population of more than 3 million.

From this eastern empire has come the independent state of Burma (which never joined the Commonwealth), the state (still in 1965 technically the Kingdom) of Ceylon, the Federation of Malaysia and the small states of Brunei and Singapore. Hong Kong alone remains a Crown colony.

CEYLON – THE FIRST DEMOCRACY IN ASIA

As the first Crown colony in Asia, the 'model tropical dependency' of the Victorian age, the first non-European colony to receive repre-sentative government, then the first to suspend the recruitment of Englishmen to the civil service, and finally one of the few portions of the empire to receive independence without stridently demanding it, Ceylon has a unique place in the development of the Commonwealth. In what way was she a model, and how did she develop in this in-dividual manner?

Ceylon's development owed its success to the idealism of the Cole-brooke-Cameron report of 1833, the prosperity induced by the plantation economy and the example of the Indian constitutional reforms. Under the 1833 constitution the powers of the governor in Ceylon were checked by executive and legislative councils and by an independent judiciary. Although the legislative council retained an official majority, the unofficial members were equally divided between the European and the main Ceylonese communities (a Burgher, a Tamil and a Sinhalese). All attempts by the settler minority to gain control were resisted. Thus, throughout the Victorian age the Ceylonese enjoyed a small measure of representative government. At the same time the new plantation economy, the improvement of government and transport, and the spread of education (which became a government responsibility in 1870) gave rise to new professional and commercial classes as in India. In fact the Ceylonese social system has been humorously pictured as a fourfold hierarchy: the 'somebodies', often descendants of the Sinhalese nobility, largely wealthy landowners, English-educated, often Christian, and loyal supporters of the colonial régime; the 'nobodies', who were the *nouveaux riches*, English-educated middle classes; below these *élites*, the 'anybodies', non-English-educated lower middle class; and finally the 'everybodies', the remainder, mainly peasants and labourers.

Slow Growth of Nationalism

As usual elsewhere, the English-educated *élite* began to form associations, which represented the first tentative nationalist stirrings. Early in the twentieth century specialist groups were formed, concerned with agriculture, the revival of Buddhist customs, and temperance reform. By 1908 the Ceylon National Association had emerged. One of its leaders, James Peiris, a Sinhalese who had been president of the Cambridge Union, petitioned the British government for elections to the legislative council. Soon modest constitutional changes were made. In 1909 the creation of a financial committee of the legislative council gave unofficial councillors the chance of discussing finance with the executive council. In the following year the elective principle was accepted. The government retained an official majority but the legislative council was enlarged to include six nominated non-official members and, for the first time, four elected members, one of whom was to be elected by 'educated Ceylonese'. When the first Ceylonese elected member took his seat in 1912 he was the first elected non-European councillor in the Crown colonies. The new arrangements were, however, short-lived owing to tragic events during the 1914–18 war.

In 1915 riots broke out in central Ceylon, which started when a Buddhist procession made a noise outside a Tamil mosque. The issue was purely local and communal, an outlet for pent-up frustrations. But unfortunately the governor panicked: he called out the garrison and proclaimed military law. Some rioters were shot and many prominent educated Ceylonese leaders were put into detention. These were the traumatic events which hardened Ceylon's nationalism.

Just as the Jameson Raid and Amritsar provided shocks for Smuts and Nehru respectively, so unwarranted detention shook the complacency of Don Stephen Senanayake, a wealthy, public-school-educated, cricket-playing land-owner and agriculturalist, who until then had taken no interest in politics. He now joined the politically-minded members of the new *élite* who in 1918 formed the Ceylon

National Congress. Spurred on by the Montagu–Chelmsford reforms in India, they demanded reform in Ceylon. Thus, in the 1920s Ceylon also began to advance along the road to responsible government like the Indian provinces.

Constitutional Advance

A new constitution, announced in 1920, gave Ceylon representative government not unlike the system in the Dominions in the early Victorian age. Four non-official members (not legislative councillors) were invited to join the executive council. An unofficial majority was permitted in the legislative council, including eleven members elected for territorial constituencies, six elected communally (two Europeans, one Burgher, two Kandyan Sinhalese and one Indian) and one each chosen by the Chamber of Commerce and the Low Country Producers Association. Four other non-official members were nominated by the governor to represent other minority interests. After only three years the council was further enlarged. In 1924 the officials were reduced to twelve; twenty-three members were elected (eleven communally) and three nominated by the governor. In the absence of the governor, the Vice-President (an elected member) could preside and the governor's power to limit the subjects of debate and to veto legislation was abolished (though retained by the secretary of state).

The legislative council began, in fact, to look very like the North American Assemblies in the 1830s. Indeed, the Ceylonese and early Canadian legislatures shared one basic weakness: they gained power without responsibility. The unofficial members now controlled the council, but they had no hope of forming a government. In the financial committee of the legislative council the politicians ganged up against the civil servants and brought the administration into disrepute. Within a few years the Colonial Office had to send out a commission of inquiry under the leadership of the Earl of Donoughmore, who was accompanied by two Members of Parliament and a retired colonial administrator.

The Donoughmore Commission's report in 1928 recommended a notable advance towards parliamentary government in Ceylon. They suggested universal adult suffrage and a system of partial responsible government, which might be compared with 'dyarchy' in India. In place of the legislative council, a 'State Council' of fifty members was to be elected by territorial constituencies. To ensure balanced representation of all interests three British officers-of-state and eight nominated members (half of them representing Europeans and half other minorities) were added. The council was to elect its own Speaker.

The government itself was also reformed. A 'Ministerial system' was brought into being by dividing the government departments into ten groups, each under a 'Minister'. If the language of dyarchy is applied to the Donoughmore constitution, there were three 'reserved' ministries under the British officers-of-state: the Chief Secretary (external affairs, defence, public services), the Legal Secretary (justice and elections), and the Financial Secretary. The remaining seven ministries covering development and welfare (home affairs, agriculture and lands, local administration, health, labour, industry and commerce, education, commerce and works) were 'transferred' to Ceylonese ministers. They were made responsible to the State Council by slightly indirect means. Seven executive committees of the State Council were formed to supervise these departments, each with its own elected Chairman. The three British officers-of-state and the seven Ceylonese committee chairmen together constituted the 'Board of Ministers'. Although the system was cumbersome in practice and very uneven in its effectiveness, the Agriculture and Lands Committee became the vehicle whereby D. S. Senanayake emerged as Ceylon's most effective political leader.

In one important respect, however, the Donoughmore constitution (which came into force in 1931, when the illiterate voted according to a colour symbol to distinguish the candidates) reversed two stages of the cycle of Asian national advance and in this respect harked back to the system in Australia and New Zealand in the 1850s. A measure of responsible government was achieved before the creation of coherent political parties. In the State Council elections of 1931 and 1936 members were elected as individuals and usually owed their success to family connection or local prominence. The Ceylon Indian Congress and a Tamil Congress had a purely communal appeal. A small Marxist group, which founded the Lanka Sama Samaj Party and even proposed 'independence for Ceylon', made little headway and gained only two seats.

The only member of the ruling *élite* to break new ground and attempt to build up a Sinhalese party was S. W. R. Bandaranaike, the Minister of Local Administration and Health. The son of a wealthy Sinhalese land-owning aristocrat, Bandaranaike had read classics at

Christ Church, Oxford, and had become Treasurer of the Oxford Union. Returning to Ceylon, his aristocratic birth and English education ensured his rapid political ascent. But, influenced possibly by Gandhi and Nehru, Bandaranaike consciously deviated from his class. He became fluent in Sinhalese, abandoned Christianity for Buddhism, gave up European clothes and founded the communal party, Sinhala Maha Sabha, to appeal to the non-English-speaking lower middle classes. He tried, in fact, to widen the base of Ceylonese politics. But it is significant that Solomon Bandaranaike owed his political advance not to his party but his class.

The 1939-45 War and Independence

In spite of its weaknesses the Donoughmore constitution was Ceylon's political training ground. By the 1930s the colony had become Asia's most advanced democracy. In 1938 the governor recommended ironing out the anomalies by going on to full Cabinet government on the Westminster model. Although the 1939–45 war delayed this move, it strengthened British confidence in Ceylonese capacity for self-government. The Ceylonese Ministers remained in office throughout the war and there was no boycott or violence as in India. Ceylon became a great military base and the headquarters of South-East Asia Command. In 1942 Trincomalee and Colombo harbours were bombed by the Japanese, but there was no panic. The British Commander-in-Chief did not have to exercise emergency powers as the Viceroy had had to in India. The Ceylonese Ministers co-operated in a new joint civil-military War Council, in which the Civil Defence Commissioner and Food Commissioner, Oliver Goonetilleke, Ceylon's ablest civil servant, distinguished himself.

Thus, political advance was hardly interrupted by the war. In 1942 D.S. Senanayake became Leader of the State Council. At the time of Cripps's mission to India the Ceylonese leaders demanded full Dominion status after the war. The secretary of state promised in 1943 that internal self-government and a complete re-examination of the constitution would come at the end of the war. Rather than wait for the Colonial Office to act, the political leaders decided to write their own constitution. Drafted by a distinguished constitutional lawyer, Ivor Jennings, who was then Principal of the University of Ceylon, the constitutional plan was based on the ideas of D. S. Senanayake, and was sent to Britain in 1944. By the end of the year a three-man commission under Lord Soulbury, a former British minister, was sent to Ceylon. When they reported in July 1945 the Ceylonese draft was largely accepted and they recommended the inception of full Cabinet government. Finally, in the summer of 1945 as Mr Attlee's Labour government took office, D. S. Senanayake happened to be in London and was able to discuss his own plan – for full Dominion status, implying independence – with the new government.

Thus Ceylon's achievement of independence – unlike that of India and Pakistan – was remarkably smooth. The new constitution, based on the Ceylonese 1944 draft, was published in 1946 and provided for Cabinet government on the British model. Parliament consisted of a Senate of thirty (half elected by the lower house and half appointed by the Governor-General on the advice of the prime minister) and a House of Representatives of ninety-five elected members, with six nominated members to represent minorities. The details of the transition to in-dependence were worked out in 1947 by Arthur Creech Jones, the Labour secretary of state, and Sir Oliver Goonetilleke, Ceylon's leading civil servant. For the general election of 1947 the old ruling *élite* managed to work together in the 'United National Party', which secured 42 seats – not a clear majority, but with Independent support they were able to form a government. D. S. Senanayake, the veteran leader of the Donoughmore ministries, became 'prime minister'. Finally, when Parliament was opened in 1947 it was announced that Ceylon would become independent in the following year.

When the Duke of Gloucester proclaimed independence on 4 February 1948, Ceylon reached the same status as the old Dominions. The Governor-General still represented the Crown, and the idea of republican status was not taken up urgently. In 1954 Sir Oliver Goonetilleke became the first Ceylonese Governor-General. In spite of universal suffrage and complete independence, the old *élite* of the U.N.P., nicknamed the 'Uncle-Nephew Party', retained control for eight years without a break, during which time Britain continued to use the naval base at Trincomalee and the tea companies kept their estates. In providing the venue for the first meetings which drew up the 'Colombo Plan' in 1950 Ceylon gave a name to one of the more enlightened ventures of the New Commonwealth. Ceylon, indeed, became a state and achieved the transition to Commonwealth member-ship remarkably easily and calmly. But one essential ingredient of Westminster model parliamentary democracy was lacking: a 'shadow

Cabinet', a strong opposition prepared to form an alternative government.

Democracy in Ceylon

In 1951 there were signs of a change. Solomon Bandaranaike, the one member of the pre-war *élite* who ostentatiously abandoned western ways, resigned his office as Minister of Local Government and founded the moderate socialist Sri Lanka Freedom Party. In 1956, by forming a 'Peoples United Front' with the Communist Party and the Lanka Sama Samaj Party, he swept to power in a general election which left the old government party with only eight seats in Parliament.

Bandaranaike's victory brought to power in Ceylon a leader who might, in some ways, be compared with Nehru in India. They both came from an English-educated high-caste *élite*, but their political success was based upon mass support. Nehru learned from Gandhi's example. Solomon Bandaranaike was Ceylon's first popular leader. While the ruling *élite* of the 'United National Party', being wealthy, thoroughly westernized, men of the world, tended to lose touch with the people, Bandaranaike cultivated rural constituencies, appealed to Sinhalese communal feeling, preached the mixed economy in which private enterprise would work side by side with public utilities and the welfare state, and dreamed of a foreign policy in which Ceylon would emerge as the Switzerland of Asia. For three years before his tragic assassination in 1959 by a Buddhist fanatic, he tried to fulfil his ideals. Transport and the ports were nationalized. Relations were opened with the Soviet Union and the Chinese People's Republic. Britain was requested to leave the naval and air bases in Ceylon and in the United Nations Ceylon aligned herself with the Asian-African states.

Unfortunately, however, the reign of the Sri Lanka Freedom Party, unlike that of the Congress in India, failed to fulfil its promise and uncovered dangerous tensions in Ceylon. Legislation to make Sinhalese the sole official language led the Tamils (numbering nearly 2 million) to demand a federal system, or even a separate Tamil state. Law and order declined seriously, until in 1958 there were communal riots and murders. At the same time the new economic and foreign policies antagonized the United States and frightened capitalist investors. The shock of the prime minister's assassination led to further uncertainty. A period followed when neither the Sri Lanka Freedom Party nor the United National Party could produce a stable administration. Thus the leaders of the Sri Lanka Freedom Party took the extraordinary step of requesting Bandaranaike's widow to lead their party. After some hesitation Mrs Bandaranaike agreed, and after winning seventy-five seats in a general election in 1961 she went forward to become the world's first woman prime minister.

Mrs Bandaranaike came from a high-born Kandyan family, yet for a time she received considerable support from the populace. As a woman and a widow, she excited admiration and sympathy in her election campaigns. Her political opponents in Parliament once conceded that she was the 'only man' in her cabinet. On the whole she adhered to her husband's policies of promoting the Sinhalese language, the Buddhist religion, moderate socialism, the development of national education and a neutralist foreign policy. But communal strains continued. The new foreign policies left Ceylon somewhat isolated. The government appeared to rely more and more on left-wing support. As the press began to make vicious attacks on the government, legislation to control the press was promised. Finally in 1962 an attempted *coup d'état* by the army officers was prevented, but only just in time. Ceylon was obviously divided, and many feared that the country was about to lapse into autocratic rule. When Mrs Bandaranaike decided to appeal to the electorate in 1964, they turned again to the United National Party.

Thus Ceylon – Asia's first democracy – has lived up to its title. Having elected the Commonwealth's first woman prime minister, it then rejected her by democratic process when it appeared that her government was seeking excessive powers.

MALAYA – THE FEDERAL MONARCHY

While Ceylon received manhood suffrage and the Indian Provinces received responsible government in the 1930s, Malaya – the most prosperous British possession in Asia – remained politically under-developed. While the definite goal of full self-government had been proclaimed in India, implied in Ceylon and somewhat vaguely announced for many of the African territories, no such announcement was made for Malaya. There the nationalist movement was one of the weakest in Asia. When the façade of British-controlled Malay governments collapsed before the Japanese in 1942, there was obviously no 'Malayan Nation' to resist the invaders. In fact a veteran civil servant described Malaya as 'a plural society with no corporate soul . . . a glorified commercial undertaking rather than a State'.* Malaya deviates further from our cycle of nationalism than any New Commonwealth nation. How do we account for this difference?

The Malay States

The most important thing to remember about Malaya before the 1939–45 war is that it had not been 'annexed' by Britain. Outside the Crown colony of the Straits Settlements (Singapore, Malacca and Penang) with its Chinese-majority population, British sovereignty had not been extended. The Malay States remained, in legal terms, 'protected states', and there were even variations of status within the Peninsula. Thus, though Britain certainly 'controlled' the Malay governments, and though the Malay States and the Straits Settlements together were known to the world as 'British Malaya', British rule had developed by indirect means.

As in India and Africa, British expansion in Malaya had been piecemeal. Although the East India Company created the Straits Settlements to guard the trade route to China and opened up relations with, even incurring some obligations to, individual Malay rulers in the early nineteenth century, the Company did not interfere with the states. But in 1867 the Straits Settlements were transferred from the control of the India Office to the Colonial Office. Soon the discovery that civil wars within the states adjacent to the Straits Settlements endangered the security of the colony led the government to consider some form of intervention. There were two problems in the states on the west coast of Malaya: rival parties among the Malay royal dynasties vied for control; and warlike factions among the Chinese immigrants, who engaged in tin mining, led to fighting over the mines. In some cases the Chinese sought allies among the Malays. Since the Chinese secret societies who engaged in these wars had their headquarters in the colony, disorder occasionally irrupted into British territory and involved British subjects.

In 1874 the British government decided to intervene to keep the peace in Perak, Selangor and in Sungei Ujong, one of the Negri Sembilan (or 'Nine States'). The rulers of these states agreed to accept British Residents, whose advice on government would be taken except in matters concerned with religion and Malay custom. By 1888 the

* V. Purcell, *Malaya: Communist or Free?*, London, 1954, pp. 12, 39.

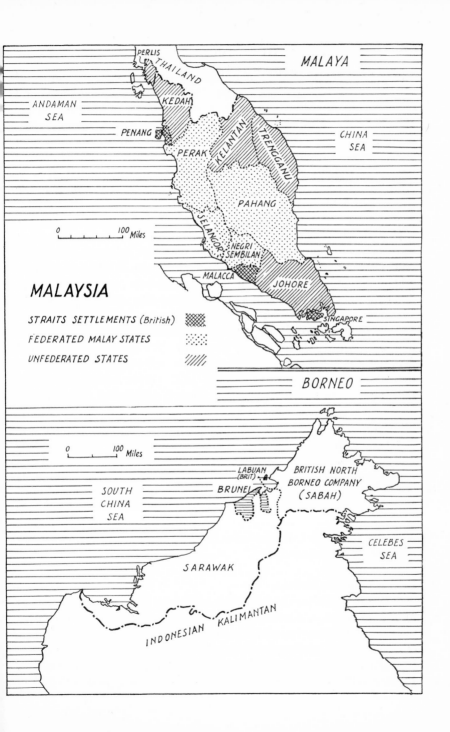

MALAYA

PERLIS
THAILAND
ANDAMAN
SEA
KEDAH
PENANG
PERAK
KELANTAN
TRENGGANU
CHINA
SEA
PAHANG
SELANGOR
NEGRI
SEMBILAN
MALACCA
JOHORE
SINGAPORE

0   100 Miles

MALAYSIA

STRAITS SETTLEMENTS (British)
FEDERATED MALAY STATES
UNFEDERATED STATES

BORNEO

0   100 Miles

LABUAN
(BRIT.)
BRUNEI
BRITISH NORTH
BORNEO COMPANY
(SABAH)
SOUTH
CHINA
SEA
CELEBES
SEA
SARAWAK
INDONESIAN KALIMANTAN

Sultan of Pahang and the remaining states of the Negri Sembilan had also accepted the 'Resident system'. Under the fiction of 'advice', and consultation in 'State Councils', British officers began to exercise effective control of the administration in four states. When highly trained specialist officers – for services like health, transport and agriculture – were required and the sort of centralization which we have observed elsewhere was thought necessary, the so-called 'Federal Agreement' was made in 1895. The result was the formation of the 'Federated Malay States', which was really an 'administrative union' with a Resident-General and secretariat at Kuala Lumpur.

Outside the Federated Malay States British influence expanded more gradually and subtly. Johore, on the shore opposite Singapore, had always had the closest relations with the British colony. Its cricket-playing ruler had been accorded the title of 'Maharaja' and had been knighted by Queen Victoria in the 1860s. But it was not until 1914 that an Adviser-General, with functions like a Resident, was appointed in Johore. In the north of the Peninsula, the Malay States had traditional relations with Thailand. But after Britain exerted pressure on Bangkok in 1909 the Thai government 'transferred' the northern states to Britain. By 1923 Perlis, Kedah, Kelantan and Trengganu had also accepted British 'Advisers'. These states, along with Johore, were referred to as the 'Unfederated Malay States'.

Thus, by the 1920s the British Malay empire comprised the Straits Settlements (to which Labuan was added in 1912), the Federated Malay States, and the Unfederated Malay States, to which might be added (as was often vainly proposed) the three Borneo protectorates, Sarawak, British North Borneo and the tiny Sultanate of Brunei. Co-ordinating British policy was the governor of the Straits Settlements, who was also High Commissioner for the Federated Malay States and the Borneo protectorates.

British Policy in Malaya

How far did Britain have a policy in Malaya? Her real interest lay in maintaining law and order and producing tin and rubber. But there were nevertheless certain noticeable political trends. By the beginning of the twentieth century the Malay Sultans resented the centralization brought about in the Federated Malay States by British civil servants. In 1903 Sultan Idris of Perak, who remembered the days before British intervention, called for a loosening of the 'federation'. There was, accordingly, a very half-hearted attempt to restore the powers of the Sultans without destroying the efficient central services. In 1909 the High Commissioner reminded the civil servants that they were 'here in a Malay country as the advisers and councillors of its Malay sovereigns'. A 'Federal Council' was created, consisting of the High Commissioner, the four Sultans and their Residents, the Resident-General (now renamed less grandly 'Chief Secretary') and four nominated unofficial members. But unfortunately the reform had an effect quite the reverse of that expected by the Sultans. Legislative powers tended to be taken out of the hands of the State Councils by the new Federal Council, where the Sultans were in a minority.

A second attempt at 'decentralization' was tried in the 1920s. In 1927 the Sultans left the Federal Council and met separately in ceremonial durbars. Annual estimates for certain state services were shown separately. Finally in the 1930s the High Commissioner made a policy statement which implied that British policy was concerned simply to preserve the individual Malay States. Sir Hugh Clifford declared that the position of the Sultans was 'sacrosanct', that any idea of granting the franchise in Malaya, as in Ceylon, would be out of the question. Granting the vote to the Chinese, Indian and English communities would be a 'betrayal' of the Malays. This meant that the Unfederated Malay States became a model for British administrators. Kedah, which had a British Adviser but a Malay civil service, was regarded as an ideal Malay State. In 1931 the Chief Secretary was further demoted by being assigned the title of 'Federal Secretary' and the States were given certain increased powers over health and public works.

The 'decentralization' issue posed a basic dilemma for the civil servants, planters and Malay aristocrats. Should their aim be the creation of a unified modern state in Malaya, or the preservation of the individual Sultanates? On this question the British government had very few ideas. In 1926 a wealthy Chinese unofficial member of the Straits Settlements legislative council, Tan Cheng Lock, suggested that the goal should be a unified, self-governing British Malaya. But Sir Cecil Clementi, the High Commissioner, tried in 1931 to restore the integrity of the individual states as preparation for the creation of a 'Malayan Union', which would then unite with the Straits Settlements and the Borneo territories. Thus, there was a wide divergence of opinion as to the goals of Malaya, and political parties were slow to develop.

Political development was retarded in Malaya because it tended to follow communal lines. The English-educated Malay aristocrats, who were nominated to the Federal Council criticized the government and urged the promotion of Malays in the civil service. Pan-Malay conferences, which were held in 1939 and 1940, had a largely cultural bias. Among the Malay-speaking intelligentsia educated in the teacher training and technical colleges there was interest in the Pan-Islamic movement centred on Cairo, in Sukarno's Indonesian National Party and the idea of a unified, free Malay world, or in the radical party known as the 'Union of Malay Youths'. The Chinese tended to join branches of the Kuomintang and to focus their interest on China. A few joined the Malayan Communist Party, which perpetrated some acts of terrorism and sabotage in the mid-1930s. In 1937 a Central Indian Association was formed, but it indulged in little political activity. Malayan political organizations, then, were modest and communal in scope. The only element of representation in government was the unofficial nominated group in the Federal Council and the Straits Settlements legislative council.

The Japanese Occupation and Malayan Union

The watershed in the growth of Malayan nationalism was the Japanese occupation. In 1941–42 British power tumbled in fifty-four days. But the Japanese never completely subjugated the Peninsula. Chinese communist guerrillas (of the Malay People's Anti-Japanese Army) and a few Malay and British groups operated in the jungles throughout the war. Moreover, the sudden surrender of Japan on 14 August 1945, precipitated by the dropping of the atomic bombs, meant that the British did not return to Malaya as a victorious liberating army. Indeed, there was a time-lag of several days before the British 're-occupation' could commence. This sudden end to the war, followed by a few days' hiatus, coupled with the fact that the Japanese had always been resisted from within the territory, meant that the Colonial Offices' carefully planned post-war policy was unacceptable to the Malay *élite*.

Pre-war policy had been based upon the doctrine of preserving the Malay Sultans and avoiding democratic government because of the complicated communal mixture of Malays, Chinese, Indians and

Europeans. During the war this policy was reversed. The Colonial Office decided that, while the Malays needed to be safeguarded, 'reforms were overdue in the system of representation' to allow the Chinese and Indians a reasonable position. Thus at the end of 1945 Sir Harold MacMichael, a former civil servant in Palestine and Sudan, toured Malaya and got the Sultans to sign documents superseding the old treaties. They agreed now, for the first time, that 'full power and jurisdiction' should be vested in the Crown. Having gained what it believed was a *carte blanche*, the British government created a 'Malayan Union', with a common Malayan citizenship. Singapore remained a separate Crown colony. It was then expected that Malaya would fall in line with other British possessions and move gradually along the path to self-government, as in India and Ceylon.

The Malay aristocracy, however, reacted immediately and effectively to the threat of Malayan Union. Almost overnight the *élite* created nationalist organizations to challenge the British move. The old Malay cultural organizations merged in 1946, under the leadership of Dato 'Onn, into the 'United Malays National Organization'. A few smaller, radical, less communal parties were formed in Singapore among the highly educated. The Malay leaders boycotted the installation of the governor of the Union. In fact they caused the British government to back down very quickly.

By 1948 Malay Union was dead and a constitution had been produced for the 'Federation of Malaya'. Taking the status of the pre-war Unfederated Malay States as a model, the government still appointed British Advisers but worked through Malay civil servants. The Federation was governed by a British High Commissioner, whose executive council consisted of seven officials and seven unofficial members (who included Malay ministers from the States). In the Federal legislative council the officials were in a minority. British civil servants sat with Malay Chief Ministers from the States, representatives from the Straits Settlements and fifty nominated unofficial members representing the main economic interests and racial groups. Acts of the government were made in the name of the Sultans jointly with the Crown. The British 'take-over' had been halted and representative government permitted.

But to the Chinese, to other minorities, and to left-wing organizations, the federation implied a return to the pre-war policy of preserving Malay feudalism. The Malayan Communist Party, fresh from its patriotic success in the jungles during the war, had emerged as a political party in 1946. But in 1948, just as Federation got under way, the Communists attempted violent revolution, probably on orders from Moscow. Five thousand terrorists began to dislocate communications, terrorize the rural communities and murder British planters and businessmen. In 1951 they killed the High Commissioner, Sir Henry Gurney. For twelve years Malaya continued under a State of Emergency. A costly civil war was waged in the jungles by Malay troops and police, with support from British, Australian, New Zealand and Fijian forces. When in 1960 the Emergency ended, the Communist bid for power by violent means had been successfully defeated. The jungle war in Malaya was one of the few successful anti-guerrilla wars of recent years.

Political Advance

One of the main reasons why the war was won against the Communist terrorists in Malaya was that the movement for self-government continued, and accelerated, throughout the emergency. As the war progressed Malay leaders insisted on responsible government and then on independence. Britain gave way. Thus the war could not be represented as a national uprising against an oppressive colonial régime.

The first advance occurred in 1951 with the creation of a 'semi-ministerial' system of government. Malay members of the Federal executive council were given charge of groups of government departments, somewhat in the manner of the pre-war Ceylonese ministers. Although each minister was individually responsible to the High Commissioner, something like an informal 'Cabinet' emerged. The next big step was the first federal election under universal adult suffrage in 1955, which led to a sweeping victory for the 'Alliance Party', led by Tengku Abdul Rahman, which won all but one of the fifty-two seats.

Tengku Abdul Rahman, who today remains one of Asia's best-loved democratic leaders, was a modest, Cambridge-educated Malay aristocrat, a former civil servant in Kedah, where his brother was Sultan. In 1951 he was elected President of the United Malays National Organization when Dato 'Onn sought to admit non-Malays to the party. But while preserving the Malay character of the U.M.N.O., the Tengku wisely realized that they should enter the elections with something wider than a communal appeal. Thus, by allying with the Malay Chinese Association to form the 'Alliance', he presented a broad national front. Campaigning on the slogan *Merdeka* ('Independence'), he made a successful bit for power.

In 1955 the Tengku took office as 'Chief Minister' and a period akin to 'dyarchy' ensued. The executive council still retained official members but the Tengku also selected five Malays, two Chinese and one Indian. A meeting was held with the Communist leaders which failed to end the terrorist campaign. The war went on. But the Alliance leaders still pressed Britain for independence. The Tengku travelled to London in January 1956 and found the secretary of state prepared to grant independence in the following year.

On 31 August 1957, in the stadium at Kuala Lumpur, the Federation of Malaya, after less than a decade of existence, celebrated its independence. Constitutionally its position in the Commonwealth was unique. The rulers of the States elected one of their number to be the federal monarch, the 'Yang di-Pertuan Agong', for a term of five years. As in Britain, the 'Agong' rules on the advice of the prime minister, who is responsible to the Federal Parliament. The State governments were retained with reserve powers and the State Sultans rule on the advice of Chief Ministers, selected from the majority parties in the elected State Councils. Penang and Malacca were detached from the Straits Settlements and incorporated in the Federation. What, then, became of Singapore when it was left on its own?

Singapore and Malaysia

The case of Singapore illustrates one of the major problems of Britain's 'decolonization'. What was to become of all those islands which were originally acquired in the cause of British imperial strategy: Malta, Cyprus and Gibraltar in the Mediterranean; Aden, Mauritius, the Maldives and Seychelles in the Indian Ocean; Singapore, Hong Kong and Labuan on the old trade route to China? Could they remain Crown colonies in the age of emancipation, or could they become member states of the Commonwealth on a par (as it might seem) with Canada, India and Nigeria? In the case of Malta, where a population of 300,000 Europeans is grossly overcrowded, it was thought in 1956 that a suitable solution had been found in the idea of incorporation in the United Kingdom. But this experiment came to nothing.

Singapore, meanwhile, had begun the normal advance to responsible government. As the Malayan Federation was created in the Peninsula an elected element was added to the Singapore legislative council. In the pre-war Straits Settlements there had been nominated unofficial members on the executive and legislative councils, but the only measure of election had been through the Chambers of Commerce. In 1948 six seats on the legislative council of twenty-two were opened to a largely middle-class electorate. Three years later three more elected seats were added. But outbreaks of serious rioting in the 1950s convinced the British government that Singapore's working class, largely Chinese and unrepresented and unenfranchised, would have to be given some political expression.

A commission under Sir George Rendel suggested a new constitution in 1953. There would be an elected majority in the legislative council and a form of 'dyarchy' in government. From a legislative council of twenty-five elected, four nominated unofficial and three official members, the leader of the majority party selected six members to serve in a 'Council of Ministers'. The three British officials retained control of 'reserved' departments (defence and internal security, finance and external affairs) and the other departments were 'transferred'. Under this system elections were held in 1955. As the Tengku's Alliance Party took office in Malaya, David Marshall, an impetuous Eurasian Jew, who led the 'Labour Front', took office in Singapore and soon demanded 'full self-government'.

Singapore now provided an acutely embarrassing problem for Britain. As her chief naval and military base in South-East Asia and the leading trading and manufacturing centre of the old 'Malaya', Singapore seemed hardly the place for constitutional experiment. Yet with its large, youthful, volatile, and potentially Communist, Chinese population, it could not be permanently ruled by force and it stood as a test of Britain's good intentions. Thus in 1956 a curious compromise was worked out. Singapore became a self-governing State in the Commonwealth. Instead of a Governor-General the Crown was represented by a Malay, the 'Yang di-Pertuan Negara', and a High Commissioner was appointed to represent the British government as in the Dominion capitals. The British base was retained and internal security in the island was to be controlled by a joint committee representing the Singapore, Malayan and British governments. In 1959 the brilliant, Cambridge-educated and wealthy Singapore barrister,

Lee Kuan Yew, led the 'People's Action Party' to a sweeping electoral victory by managing to gain Communist support without permitting Communist domination.

The rule of Lee Kuan Yew and the P.A.P. has been Asia's greatest political tight-rope act. By attacking the former colonial powers and the United States for neo-colonialism he has established his nationalist credentials. But by providing facilities for capitalists from all over the world he has attracted new industries which will give desperately needed employment to his urban masses and generate the revenue to service his housing and social welfare policies. Vast schemes for public housing have already been accomplished. To combat Singapore's isolation the People's Action Party took up the cause of 'merger' with Malaya.

Even when the Malays were fearful that Singapore's Chinese masses would upset the Federation's delicate communal balance, Singapore was prepared for the North Borneo territories to join a more racially balanced 'Malaysia' in 1963. But the Federation of Malaysia proved short-lived. Mounting tension among the Malay and Chinese ex- tremists on both sides led Singapore to leave the federation after only two years. Thus, once again, Singapore presents the anomaly of a separate island city-state within the Commonwealth, which relies for defence, and for a third of its employment, on the British base, and on Malaya for much of its trade. It remains one of the formidable legacies of imperialism which the Commonwealth, as a whole, might well feel obliged to assist.

THE CARIBBEAN LEGACY – A SEARCH FOR NATION- HOOD

During the fifteen years between the end of the 1939–45 war and the opening of the 1960s when the Asian states of the Commonwealth became well established and African states prepared rapidly for in- dependence, Britain's legacy in the Caribbean – the oldest remnants of the British empire – developed on somewhat different lines. It is true that many elements of the cycle of Asian-African nationalism were present: the gradual rise of the elected members of the legislative council, the grant of universal suffrage and the growth of mass political parties, the idea of federation and self-government within the

Commonwealth. What was lacking for many years was a clear focus for nationalism and an economic base for nationhood.

The British West Indian colonies were largely multi-racial, immigrant societies, in which nationalism could not be harnessed to the preservation or restoration of ancient kingdoms as in Ghana, Buganda or the Malay States. Culturally the British West Indies were in many ways extremely 'British'. It was natural, therefore, that the educated intelligentsia should expect some form of self-government. But the outstanding fact about the Caribbean islands was overpopulation and mass poverty, which made the basis for nationhood uncertain. Where a large proportion of the population are engaged in agriculture, notably sugar production, which itself accounts for a declining proportion of the island incomes, problems of economic survival have loomed large. Although bauxite from Jamaica (the world's largest exporter) and oil from Trinidad accounted for half of the total value of British West Indian exports by the end of the 1950s, they still gave employment only to 5,000 out of Jamaica's $1\frac{1}{2}$ million, and to less than 20,000 out of Trinidad and Tobago's 820,000.

Nationhood in the West Indies presupposed an attempt to solve the social and economic problems of the islands. And for many years the usual British panacea was federation. Thus the nationalist movement had an uncertain goal. Some of the educated *élite* began, under the impact of modern communications, especially air travel, to feel a 'West Indian nationality' and to look forward to federation as a method of self-government. Others found it difficult to consider anything outside their own immediate pressing problems of island development. Federation, when tried in 1958, was largely political rather than economic in scope, and by its neglect of the West Indies' most glaring needs it was doomed to failure. How, then, do we account for Britain's unfortunate failure in this, the oldest and most 'British' portion of the tropical empire?

The chief reason for the backwardness of the West Indian colonies was that during the great age of imperialism in Asia and Africa the Caribbean was neglected. While British strategy and international rivalry focused attention on Asia and Africa, Britain willingly conceded supremacy in the New World to the United States. In fact, after backing down from a stake in the future Panama Canal in 1901, Britain formally recognized the United States as the paramount power in the Caribbean. British policy in the West Indies in the twentieth century has largely been concerned with devising a constitutional framework which would govern the islands economically. In spite of Joseph Chamberlain's fine talk in 1895 about 'Imperial slum clearance' and developing 'neglected estates', a solution to the basic economic problem proved elusive. Political development, therefore, was also slow.

Politics in the West Indies

The representative institutions of the Old Colonial System survived in Barbados alone.* In the rest of the West Indies and in British Honduras and British Guiana, Crown colony government became the rule from the mid-Victorian age. Until the aftermath of the 1914–18 war, adjustments to this system were modest. In 1871 most of the Leeward Islands (Antigua, St Kitts, Nevis, Montserrat and Anguilla) were federated, but an attempt to federate Barbados, Tobago and the Windward Islands (St Lucia, St Vincent and Grenada) in 1876 failed, because of Barbadian jealousy for its representative system. Trinidad and Tobago were amalgamated in 1888. British Honduras was ruled by a Lieutenant-Governor under the governorship of Jamaica from 1862 to 1884. The Cayman Islands and Turks and Caicos Islands have also been ruled as adjuncts to the governorship of Jamaica. All Victorian suggestions of wider amalgamations or federations came to nothing.

Political developments were similarly meagre. An elective element was restored to the Jamaica legislative council in 1884 and a Reform Committee in Trinidad and Tobago petitioned in the 1890s for similar privileges. But during the period of the 1914–18 war the type of political stirring which we have seen in the Asian and African colonies was evident in some of the West Indian islands among the middle classes. In Grenada, T. A. Marryshow formed the 'Representative Government Association' in 1914 and petitioned for elected members in the Windwards legislative councils. Captain Arthur Cipriani, a middle-class Trinidadian of Corsican descent, who served overseas as an officer in the West Indian Regiment, returned to take up the leadership of the 'Trinidad Workingmen's Association'. In Jamaica Marcus Garvey tried to found his Negro nationalist movement during the 1914–18 war but, finding little support in Jamaica, set up his

* It also survives in Bermuda and the Bahamas, which are not usually considered part of the 'West Indies'.

headquarters in New York. Banished from the United States in 1927, he returned to Jamaica to form the 'People's Political Party'.

None of these early parties could be regarded as successful mass political movements. Consequently political advance in the islands was not seen as urgent. When in 1922 the parliamentary under-secretary for the colonies, Major Edward Wood (later the reforming Viceroy, Lord Irwin), went out to report on the West Indies, he could not recommend federation, but suggested an extension of the elective principle for a proportion of the legislative council members. Thus in 1924 Trinidad and Tobago received a constitution providing for a legislative council of twelve officials and thirteen unofficial members, of which seven were elected. After the first elections in 1925, when 6 per cent of the population received the franchise, Captain Cipriani was elected and began to build up the 'Trinidad Labour Party'. Unofficial members, usually from among the elected councillors, were also invited on to the executive council. In the same year elected members were also added to the legislative councils of Grenada, Dominica, St Lucia and St Vincent.

The true political awakening of the British West Indies did not take place until the 1930s. The impact of the depression on island economies, still largely dependent after three hundred years on sugar production, was immense. From the early 1930s up till 1939, unemployment, strikes, violent disorder and arrests created a near-revolutionary spiral, which awakened West Indians to the need for political organiz-ation and the British government to the plight of the islands.

Jamaica, the largest island, produced the most notable political leaders in the British West Indies. During strikes in the sugar industry during 1938 the tough, colourful, figure of Alexander Bustamante emerged as a Labour leader. He was then forty-six, Jamaican-born (of Irish and part-Indian parentage) and had led a varied, but obscure, career in the Caribbean, South America, the United States, Canada, England and Spain. As a result of his agitations in 1938 he was sent to jail, and this was followed by a complete stoppage in the Kingston docks. Peace was not restored among the Jamaican workers until Bustamante's cousin, Norman Manley, a wealthy lawyer, persuaded the government to release him, and together they negotiated between strikers and employers. Although they soon became rivals, the two cousins were thenceforth Jamaica's great political leaders.

Norman Manley presented a remarkable contrast to the bluff

Bustamante. A brilliant leader of the new *élite* in Jamaica, Manley had been a Rhodes scholar at Oxford and a champion athlete. He became a K.C. and Jamaica's most successful lawyer. He was attracted to socialism and in 1938 he accepted the leadership of the 'People's National Party', dedicated to founding an independent, socialist, Jamaican nation. Thus Manley became leader of the middle-class, political wing of the Jamaican nationalist movement, while Busta-mante, who formed the Bustamante Industrial Trade Union in the same year, led the Labour wing. For a time there was a somewhat stormy co-operation between the two, but by 1943 Bustamante had called upon his union to end its support for Manley's People's National Party and he formed his own 'Jamaican Labour Party'.

A somewhat similar division occurred in Trinidad and Tobago. While Cipriani, the Labour Party leader, gained a place in the legislative council, Uriah Butler, the leader of the oil-field workers, was expelled from the party in 1936 and founded his own 'Workers and Citizens Home Rule Party'. An attempt to arrest him while addressing the oil-field workers in 1937 led to the outbreak of violence in Trinidad. When a price was put upon his head, Butler became a national hero. But although he was the first great popular leader in Trinidad and Tobago, he failed to organize an effective party and he later addressed appeals to his comrades, styling himself absurdly as 'Commander in Chief of Trinidad's Great Army of Liberation'.

In Barbados during labour riots in 1937 a leader emerged who was in many ways not unlike Manley. Grantley Adams, a barrister who had been elected to the House of Assembly in 1934, stood out as defender of Clement Payne, the workers' leader. Like Manley, Adams was soon called upon to lead the newly founded 'Progressive League', later the Barbados Labour Party.

Extension of the Franchise

The strikes, riots and political disturbances in the West Indies during the 1930s awoke the British government to the unhappy *malaise* of the Caribbean empire. A Royal Commission, which reported on the islands in 1938–39, noted the mass unemployment and poverty of the West Indies and recommended that trade unions should be recognized and a development fund be created to find new employment. It re-cognized too that political changes were necessary. The Crown colony system condemned elected legislative councillors to permanent opposition. Just as in Canada in the 1820s and 1830s, and in Ceylon in the 1920s, elected members had no prospect of forming an alternative government. The Royal Commission recommended that unofficial elected members should be invited to join the executive councils and that the franchise should be extended with a view to the eventual achievement of self-government.

The 1939–45 war delayed these reforms and led to a period of war-time autocratic rule, as in India. But the principle of political reform was soon accepted. In 1943 the secretary of state decided to permit universal suffrage in Jamaica, which began under a new constitution in 1944. Universal adult suffrage was extended to Trinidad and Tobago in the following year. Although the economic problems of the islands were not solved, democracy was extended, and over the next decade the sort of changes we have observed in Asia also paved the way for self-government in the West Indies.

The 1944 constitution of Jamaica provided for a Privy Council, to advise the governor on the exercise of the prerogative, consisting of four officials and two nominated unofficial members. The legislature comprised two chambers, the Legislative Council (of three officials and ten nominated members) and the House of Representatives made up of thirty democratically elected members. In the executive council there were three officials, two nominated legislative councillors and five elected members from the House. The latter became 'quasi-ministers', as elsewhere, who did not as yet supervise their departments but became their spokesmen in the House. In the first general election Bustamante's Labour Party won twenty-three of the thirty-two seats and Bustamante agreed to work this frankly transitional constitutional scheme. After adjustments in 1953 by the liberal-minded governor, Sir Hugh Foot, who increased the elected members to eight and made them true 'Ministers' in control of departments, Bustamante became the first 'chief minister' in 1954. In the following year Bustamante took up the cause of complete self-government, but he lost the general election. Manley, who succeeded him as Chief Minister, pressed the Governor to concede internal self-government in 1957, when the officials withdrew completely from the Council of Ministers and Manley became the first 'Prime Minister'.

In Trinidad and Tobago universal suffrage did not make the im-mediate impact it made in Jamaica, because the political parties were less developed. Uriah Butler, the pre-war Labour leader, failed to gain a seat in the first elections in 1946 and Dr David Pitt's new socialist 'West Indies Nationalist Party' gained few seats. But in spite of its comparative lack of success one of this party's members, Dr Patrick Solomon, proposed in 1948 that responsible government was needed in Trinidad and Tobago. Solomon lost his seat in the 1950 election, but a new constitution was inaugurated which gave an elected majority to the legislative council. There were eighteen elected members to five nominated members and three officials. In the executive council, three officials and one nominated member served with five members chosen from the elected legislative councillors, who became 'quasi-ministers', as in Jamaica, and advised the governor on policy. The leader of the unofficial executive council members was Albert Gomes, a former trade unionist of Portuguese descent, who now led the middle-class political groups. Thus Trinidad and Tobago approached responsible government without a clear political party system. This deficiency was remedied in 1956 by the founding of a truly national party.

The 'People's National Movement' was founded by Dr Eric Williams, an Oxford-educated historian of international renown, who had lectured for nine years at the George Washington University and since 1948 had been deputy chairman of the Research Council of the Caribbean Commission. Dr Williams contributed his wide knowledge of British and American democracy and he selected outstanding lieutenants. Dr Solomon, the first proponent of responsible government, became deputy leader and Leary Constantine, whose name, as that of the most famous cricketer of the West Indies, was a household word, was the party chairman. The People's National Movement campaigned in favour of popular political awareness, nationhood and honest government. Dr Williams began his campaign as a crusade in political education. In Port of Spain he organized the 'University of Woodford Square' – a series of lectures, pamphlets and meetings about democracy and self-government movements, with particular emphasis on the anti-colonialist crusades of India and Ghana. In the general election of 1956 the People's National Movement won thirteen out of twenty-four seats.

Now the ministerial group in the legislative council came from a single political party and Dr Williams took office as 'chief minister'. Indeed, to strengthen his administration, the governor used the nominated seats to increase the party's majority. Crown colony rule soon ended, following the P.N.M.'s success. By the constitution of

1959 Dr Williams became premier with a Cabinet of nine ministers, the legislative council elected its own Speaker and the official element was reduced to two. After constitutional talks in London in 1959 and 1960 full internal self-government was granted in 1961. The legislature consisted of a nominated Senate of twenty-one members and an elected House of Representatives of thirty. Dr Williams, the prime minister, established himself as an effective popular leader and his government vigorously tackled the problems of economic development in Trinidad and Tobago.

Meanwhile in Barbados, which still retained the old representative system, a 'quasi-ministerial' system was adopted in 1946, and in 1954 the governor agreed to ask the leader of the majority party in the House of Assembly to be premier. Sir Grantley Adams became the first premier on 1 February 1954.

The Short-lived West Indies Federation

While the larger colonies in the Caribbean made progress towards self-government, the idea of federation was discussed and had particular attractions for the smaller colonies. Several proposals had been made in the 1930s for federating the Leeward and Windward Islands. The Royal Commission had detected a 'West Indian' nationalism among the educated *élite*. A number of common services had developed during the war. In 1945 the secretary of state urged the governments of all the islands to consider federation. Thus in 1947 all the islands (except the Bahamas) were represented at a conference in Montego Bay, Jamaica, presided over by the secretary of state, Arthur Creech Jones, who for a number of years had been one of the Fabian Society's colonial experts.

The 1947 conference was followed by ten years of study and negotiation. A 'Standing Closer Association Committee' was set up to study the question. By 1953 a constitutional conference met in London which produced a draft constitution and a British commitment to continue financial aid after federation. In 1956 the British Parliament passed a permissive act for a 'British Caribbean Federation' and the constitution was published in 1957. The 'West Indies Federation', as it was called, began in January 1958. Early in March Sir Grantley Adams, of the West Indies Federal Labour Party, took office as prime minister, leading a Council of State of ten ministers, which became styled the 'Cabinet' in 1960. The federal legislature consisted of the

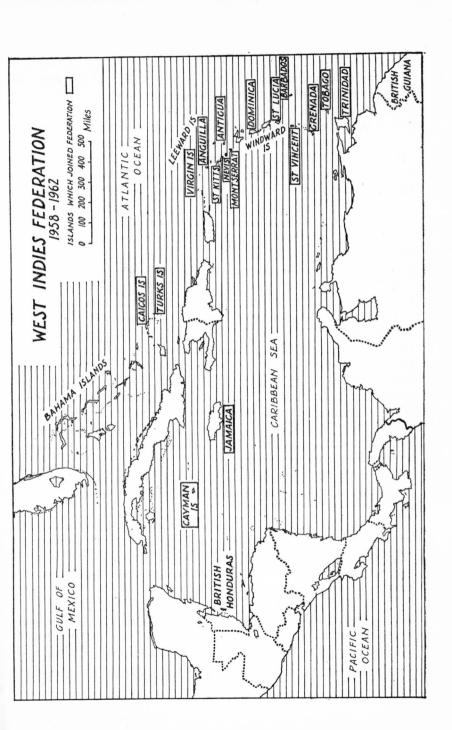

WEST INDIES FEDERATION
1958 - 1962

ISLANDS WHICH JOINED FEDERATION ☐

0 100 200 300 400 500 Miles

ATLANTIC OCEAN

GULF OF MEXICO

BAHAMA ISLANDS

CAICOS IS

TURKS IS

CAYMAN IS

JAMAICA

BRITISH HONDURAS

CARIBBEAN SEA

PACIFIC OCEAN

LEEWARD IS

VIRGIN IS

ANGUILLA

ST KITTS

NEVIS

MONTSERRAT

ANTIGUA

DOMINICA

ST LUCIA

BARBADOS

WINDWARD IS

ST VINCENT

GRENADA

TOBAGO

TRINIDAD

BRITISH GUIANA

Senate of nineteen and the House of Representatives of forty-five. By 1960 federation had been adopted successfully in India, Nigeria and Malaya – why did it fail in the West Indies?

The West Indies Federation failed for three reasons. First, it was, as one writer put it, 'one of the weakest federal systems ever to come into existence'.* Its main powers concerned external affairs, migration, trade and inter-island communications. Residual powers rested with the individual islands. The federal budget was much smaller than those of the large islands, and a third of it was spent on the University College of the West Indies in Jamaica. The second reason for failure was that the federation did not solve, or even appear to tackle, the basic economic needs of the West Indies. There was no customs union, no federal economic development plan. Finally, Jamaica and Trinidad and Tobago, the largest territories, were under-represented in the federal legislature and remained sceptical about the whole project.

Jamaica received at first only 38 per cent of the seats when she might have expected 52 per cent. In the first federal government Jamaica (with more than half the population) received only two posts while the smaller islands (representing less than a quarter of the population) had eight posts. At the same time Jamaica, with its Industrial Development Corporation, and Trinidad with its oil, had their own development programmes in train. While Trinidad and Tobago was prepared for a genuine strong federation, Jamaica stood out for states rights. British Honduras and British Guiana, the mainland colonies, remained outside the federation altogether.

In September 1961 a referendum was held in Jamaica on the future of federation and, much to the shock of the educated *élite*, the electorate decided in favour of leaving the federation and seeking Jamaican independence. Thus the West Indies Federation was quickly dismantled. During a constitutional conference in London in February 1962 arrangements were made for Jamaica's independent nationhood. On 6 August 1962, after 307 years of British rule, the Union Jack was hauled down in Jamaica.

It was hoped that an 'East Caribbean Federation' might survive, but the People's National Movement of Trinidad and Tobago preferred to follow Jamaica's lead. A constitutional conference was held in London in May–June 1962, and on 31 August 1962 Trinidad and

* D. G. Anglin, in *The West Indies Federation* (ed. D. Lowenthal), New York, 1961, p. 54.

Tobago became the second Caribbean member of the Commonwealth. Dr Williams, the prime minister, who marked independence by publishing a most readable and highly opinionated *History of the Peoples of Trinidad and Tobago*, approached the future with modesty, by declaring: 'a country will be free, a miniature state will be established, but a society and a nation will not have been formed.' The future was now in the hands of the inhabitants.

Whether the remaining islands, the 'Little Seven' of the Leewards and Windwards, would enter a new federation, or a Caribbean common market, or receive self-government in 'free association' with Britain had still to be decided. In March and April 1966 the British government agreed, after conferring with island delegates in London, that full internal self-government should be granted and that independence could be conferred by Order in Council if, and when, it was requested. In their future relations with Britain these islands would accept a new status of 'associated state'.

Guyana

While the political development of the Caribbean islands was, on the whole, slow but steady, that of British Guiana, which never joined the federation, was marked by violent internal dissension, which led to major constitutional set-backs. Internal self-government, when first granted in 1953, was suspended after a few months. Independence, when it was finally agreed upon in November 1965, was regarded by *The Times* as 'a calculated gamble'. How do we account for Guiana's chequered development? The answer may be found largely in the mutual suspicions of the two main immigrant communities: those of Indian and African descent. An international commission of jurists which visited the colony in 1965 discovered that, while over the previous twenty years the 'African' population had increased from 143,000 to 200,000, the 'East Indians' had grown more rapidly from 163,000 to 320,000. This faster-growing community, largely living in rural areas which were short of schools, sought a greater role in the civil service and the police. Ever since mass political parties emerged and universal suffrage was granted in 1953, the division of the races had been politically explosive.

Before the extension of the franchise Guiana's political development was similar to that of the other islands which had representative institutions. Its peculiarities were inherited from the era of Dutch occupation. For most of the nineteenth century the governor's council was called the 'Court of Policy' and consisted of four officials and four unofficial representatives selected by a planter's electoral college. When finance was discussed six 'Financial Representatives' were added to form a 'Combined Court'. In 1891 the more orthodox executive council (of five officials and three non-official members) was created, and three nominated officials and three elected members were added to the 'Court of Policy'.

After the 1914–18 war the same stirrings we have observed in the islands spread to British Guiana. A Tobagan, A. R. F. Webber, founder of the 'Popular Party', was influenced by the ideas of Marryshow and Cipriani. After a Colonial Office inquiry, a new constitution was inaugurated in 1928, providing for a conventional legislative council of ten officials, five nominated unofficials and fourteen elected members. The colony then appeared to progress along the normal lines for a Crown colony. By 1943 there was an unofficial majority on the executive council and an elected majority in the legislative council. A series of 'advisory committees' (not unlike the executive committees in Ceylon) enabled legislative councillors to discuss affairs with government department heads. In 1950 a Royal Commission under Sir John Waddington recommended that it was time to introduce adult suffrage and an interim scheme of responsible government.

The 'Waddington Constitution' of 1953 implied a form of 'dyarchy'. A two-chamber legislature was created, some responsible ministers were appointed, but officials retained control of the 'reserved' departments of security, the civil service and external affairs. A House of Assembly included three officials and twenty-four members elected by universal suffrage. The nine-member State Council included six councillors nominated by the governor, two by the ministers and one by the opposition. In the new executive council the governor sat with three officials, one state councillor and six 'Ministers', who were assemblymen, one of whom became 'Leader of the House'. Here was a perfectly orthodox constitution. But it was suspended after six months. Why did British Guiana suffer such a set-back?

The chief answer, at this juncture, lay in the personality and methods of Dr Cheddi Jagan, the leader of the 'Peoples Progressive Party', which won eighteen out of the twenty-four elected seats in the 1953 election. The son of an Indian sugar estate worker, Jagan trained as a dentist in the United States, where he also married an American.

Returning to Guiana in 1943 the Jagans began to build a popular movement by borrowing from the techniques of communist agitation. By 1953 Dr Jagan was declaring himself a Marxist and arguing that socialism should evolve itself into 'the higher Communist state of society'. Although, as leader of the majority party in the Assembly, he became Leader of the House and took office as Minister of Agriculture, Forests, Lands and Mines, he and his ministerial colleagues continued to behave as an 'opposition'. They met before executive council meetings as a 'Council of People's Ministers'; they filled the public galleries of the Assembly with supporters; they staged walk-outs from debates, and addressed rowdy mobs outside. In such an atmosphere, peaceful progress towards internal self-government was unlikely.

Thus in October 1953 the constitution was suspended, British troops were sent to keep order, and for four years the colony reverted to the older representative system. In 1955 the P.P.P. leaders, who served a spell in jail, split between those of African and Indian descent. After a period when there were two rival P.P.P.s, Forbes Burnham, a large Negro, London-trained barrister, and former President of the Waterfront Union and Mayor of Georgetown, formed the 'Peoples National Congress'. Constitutional advance resumed when the 'Renison Constitution', announced in 1956, provided for an executive council of three official, two nominated and five elected members, and a legislative council of three official, eleven nominated and fourteen elected members. Elections were held in 1957 and a marked racial division was evident: Negroes supporting Burnham, and Indians Dr Jagan, who secured a majority. Thus Jagan was called upon to form a Cabinet and he took office again as Minister of Trade and Industry. A constitutional conference was held in London in 1960, when Iain Macleod, the colonial secretary, agreed that Guiana should receive full internal self-government in 1961. The legislature was to consist of an elected Assembly of thirty-five members and a nominated Senate of thirteen. A 'Council of Ministers' would be responsible to it. In the election of August 1961 Dr Jagan again received a majority and became British Guiana's first prime minister. He immediately demanded independence in 1962, but it was delayed until 1966. How do we account for this further set-back?

The answer now lay in two related problems which led to two years of bloodshed and strife: the growth of violent racial clashes, and the refusal of the political parties either to form a coalition or to agree upon a constitution for independence. From 1962 to 1964 George-town, the capital, was the scene of intermittent riots, British troops and marines had to be called in, and numerous lives were lost. Two constitutional conferences in 1962 failed to find a basis for independence. Offers of mediation by Dr Eric Williams, the respected premier of Trinidad and Tobago, were rejected. Thus in October 1963 the British government decided to attempt an election by proportional representation. In 1964 the party leaders were appealing for the end of racial violence and Dr Jagan warned that the 'alternative is national extinction'. But, when the new voting system (which was observed by a team from six Commonwealth nations) prevented him from gaining an absolute majority in December 1964, he declared the election fraudulent and tried to cling to office.

After earnest appeals from the secretary of state, Burnham, who formed a coalition with the 'United Force' party, was able to form a Cabinet and take office. Guiana now had a responsible government headed by someone other than the controversial Dr Jagan. Arrangements for independence were finally planned in London in September 1965. Although Jagan and the P.P.P. boycotted the constitutional conference, the British government agreed that the new state of Guyana should receive full sovereignty on 26 May 1966.

*   *   *

Apart from the case of Guyana, the transformation from colonies into Commonwealth was comparatively smooth in the major Asian and Caribbean countries. Ceylon followed India and Pakistan closely because of her long tradition of representative government. In the West Indies and Malaya Britain had lacked a clear sense of direction before the 1939–45 war. But the impact of the depression in the West Indies and the Japanese occupation and its aftermath in Malaya provided the stimulus for a political awakening. When we turn to Africa, however, we shall find that the development of the Commonwealth was more uncertain. From the 1930s, successive British governments were forced to pay attention to tropical Africa, but their policies were often contradictory.

10

The New Commonwealth: Africa

BOTH THE British empire and the Commonwealth got lost in Africa. The great continent turned out to be a maze into which adventurers and idealists, private enterprise and government, white supremacists and Pan-Negrists entered, mingled and lost their direction. Thus in Africa the empire and the Commonwealth met their greatest crises and produced their most puzzling paradoxes. For the past century British policy-makers have been continually overtaken by the pace of change in Africa. While millions of Africans continued to live by primitive methods of subsistence farming which have existed for centuries, the political map of Africa underwent dramatic changes of colouring.

We have already seen how in South Africa British colonial policy met its greatest reverses. Throughout the nineteenth century Britain marched forwards and backwards. In the twentieth century the Union of South Africa was launched amid loud protestations of harmony. But in less than forty years Afrikaner Nationalists were entrenched in power. In 1961 they left the Commonwealth. In tropical Africa the pace of change has been equally kaleidoscopic.

In 1856 Dr David Livingstone, fresh from accomplishing the first transcontinental journey across Africa, begged a Cambridge audience to direct its attention to Africa. If his hearers went home to consult their maps they would have found much of the internal geography of the continent unknown and European interests and annexations confined to the coasts. Yet fifty years later the 'scramble for Africa' was about to reach its culmination in the race for the upper Nile. European control had enveloped the whole continent except for Ethiopia and Liberia. Later, Ethiopia briefly fell prey to the Italians.

In the two world wars major campaigns were fought in Africa and the political map changed again, notably by the elimination of the German possessions in 1915–18 and of the Italians in 1940–41. But apart from these wartime changes the political map remained, until 1957, very similar to the one nearing completion fifty years before. Then, in less than a decade, British, French and Belgian rule was dismantled with extraordinary speed. By 1965 European rule in Africa was confined to the Portuguese colonies, the Republic of South Africa (with South-West Africa) and Southern Rhodesia – all of which were police states – and the Spanish provinces of Sahara, Ifini and Equatorial Guinea, French Somaliland, and the British High Commission Territories, two of which were approaching independence.

In less than a century formal European control arrived and departed. In many inland regions close European administration hardly got under way at all. How do we account for these rapid changes? What caused the 'scramble for Africa'? And what did the Europeans do when the race was over and the boundaries were drawn? Where and when can we find the origins of African nationalism, which appeared to take the initiative so rapidly in the 1950s?

The Scramble for Africa

One of the most important things to remember about the colonial period in Africa is that nationalism and imperialism often grew together. In some cases, in fact, imperialism was a response to nationalism, rather than the other way round. The man who first proposed an independent republic, for example, in what is now Ghana, was not President Nkrumah, who achieved it, nor even Dr J. B. Danquah, who laid the foundations, but Dr James Africanus Horton, who wrote in the 1860s and participated in an abortive nationalist movement in the 1870s – long before British sovereignty was extended widely in the Gold Coast.

It is also important to remember, as we saw in Chapter 6, that the great imperialists were often not fully aware of what they were doing in the tropics. Lord Salisbury, who was responsible for adding more red colouring to the map of Africa than anyone, told the House of Lords in 1890: 'We have had a fierce conflict over the possession of a lake whose name I am afraid I cannot pronounce correctly. . . . There are indeed grave doubts as to whether it is a lake at all or only a bed of rushes.' He admitted to a Glasgow audience that when he left the

Foreign Office in 1880 'nobody thought about Africa', yet returning five years later he found the European nations quarrelling over what portions they should take. But, he went on, 'I do not exactly know the cause of this sudden revolution. But there it is.' If the statesmen were unusually frank in their admissions that they were lost in Africa, the empire-builders themselves usually resorted to official clichés about advancing 'Commerce, Christianity and Civilization'. How have historians explained these events?

The first general explanation of the 'scramble for Africa' was given by the English economic writer, John Hobson. After reporting the background of the South African War for the *Manchester Guardian* he decided, from his observations, that the war was really being fought for a small group of German and Russian Jewish capitalists in the Transvaal gold-fields. He then constructed a theory that a form of capitalist conspiracy lay behind the 'scramble for Africa' (and Asia and the Pacific). In his influential book, *Imperialism*, published in 1902, he argued that the motive for 'scrambling' was not simply trade, since trade with the tropics (as compared with trade with industrial nations such as the United States) was very small. But the new acquisitions in Africa did benefit certain groups of traders and investors such as those in shipping and armaments. He believed that this quite small group of capitalists played on patriotic feelings and inveigled the country into the scramble for Africa and Asia. Here was a simple comprehensive explanation. And since it was borrowed, and added to, by Lenin in his little pamphlet, *Imperialism: the Highest Stage of Capitalism* in 1917, and further refined by Nkrumah in *Neo-colonialism: the Last Stage of Imperialism* in 1965, it has become one of the most potent theories of the modern age.

How far was Hobson right about Africa? Certainly as he looked at the map of the 1890s he saw a large body of evidence which seemed to support his view. By far the largest portions of tropical Africa had been first appropriated by European private companies, chartered by their governments. The Congo Free State, which became the Belgian Congo in 1908, began as the private sphere of Léopold II's 'Congo International Association', which was recognized by the major powers in 1884. German East Africa (later Tanganyika) began as the private venture of Carl Peters's 'Society for German Colonization' in 1884; the German government did not take over until 1891. The northern part of Nigeria was opened up by Sir George Goldie's Royal

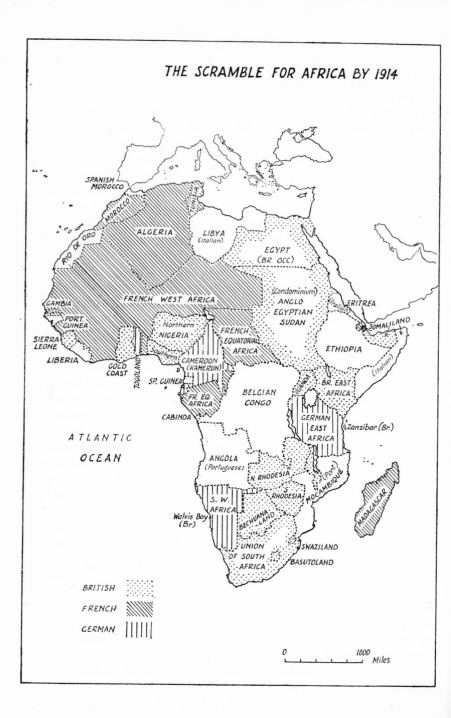

THE SCRAMBLE FOR AFRICA BY 1914

SPANISH
MOROCCO

MOROCCO

RIO DE ORO

ALGERIA

LIBYA
(Italian)

TUNISIA

EGYPT
(BR. OCC)

GAMBIA

PORT.
GUINEA

SIERRA
LEONE

LIBERIA

FRENCH WEST AFRICA

(Condominium)
ANGLO
EGYPTIAN
SUDAN

ERITREA

Italian

SOMALILAND

Northern

NIGERIA

FRENCH
EQUATORIAL
AFRICA

ETHIOPIA

(Italian)

GOLD
COAST

Southern

TOGOLAND

CAMEROON
(KAMERUN)

SP. GUINEA

FR. EQ.
AFRICA

BELGIAN
CONGO

UGANDA

BR. EAST
AFRICA

CABINDA

GERMAN
EAST
AFRICA

Zanzibar (Br.)

ATLANTIC

OCEAN

ANGOLA
(Portuguese)

N. RHODESIA

(Port.)

MOCAMBIQUE

MADAGASCAR

S. W.
AFRICA

S.
RHODESIA

Walvis Bay
(Br)

BECHUANA-
LAND

UNION
OF SOUTH
AFRICA

SWAZILAND

BASUTOLAND

BRITISH

FRENCH

GERMAN

0   1000
├──┴──┴──┴──┤ Miles

Niger Company, chartered in 1886. The government did not create the protectorate of Northern Nigeria until 1900. The regions of East Africa which later became Uganda and part of Kenya were first the territory of Sir William Mackinnon's Imperial British East Africa Company, chartered in 1888; the government did not step in until 1894, when the company began to fail. Best known of all the companies (and still in existence as a trading concern) was Cecil Rhodes's British South Africa Company, chartered in 1889 and the original ruler of Southern Rhodesia and the western part of Northern Rhodesia. Hobson did not suggest that Africa could avoid contact with the industrial nations in the nineteenth century. But he deprecated the idea that the relationship between the two should be based on what he called 'private commercialism'. Africa, he declared, had been left 'helpless prey to the offscourings of the civilized nations'.

The fact of the great chartered companies is undeniable. But what really was their motive? Why, if, as Hobson argued, the African trade represented such a small proportion of the British economy, should the government have bothered to grant the charters? Here Hobson's idea of the capitalist conspiracy is less helpful. More light was thrown on this question by diplomatic historians between the two world wars, when European powers started publishing documents, going back to the 1870s, in an attempt to show up their enemies' sins prior to 1914. They now proposed that Africa had become a sort of safe 'tournament ground' for European power rivalries. The so-called 'German irruption' into Africa in 1884–85 represented the most dramatic case.

German explorers, missionaries and traders were active in Africa from the earliest days of European contact. But during the first decade of the German Empire, founded in 1871, trade to West Africa grew by more than 500 per cent. Bismarck therefore had to consider how best to support these ventures. In 1882 a company trading to the south-west coast of Africa proposed buying land to develop some plantations, and asked the German government to accord official support. This usually meant placing the trading post under the jurisdiction of the nearest German consul (in this case at Cape Town) and ensuring that the post received periodical visits from German gunboats. But, as Bismarck well knew that Britain was established in South Africa, he instructed his embassy in London, in February 1883, to find out the limits of British territory, to assure the government that Germany had no wish to interfere, and to request that Britain might protect the

German merchants. Later in 1883 he asked more specifically whether Angra Pequena (modern Lüderitz) was under British sovereignty.

Unfortunately, it took Whitehall rather a long time to find the answer. The Foreign Office did not know. They consulted the Colonial Office, who rightly said they would have to consult the Cape Colony, which had responsible government. But reference to Cape Town produced the somewhat complicated answer that the only territory actually claimed by Britain was at Walvis Bay and the Angra Pequena Islands, although claims by other powers in this area would infringe the rights of the colony. In view of the doctrine of paramountcy in South Africa, discussed in Chapter 4, this answer was to be expected. To the Germans it sounded like the doctrine of the 'dog in the manger'. Bismarck was most dissatisfied. When he again failed to get a straight answer to a specific inquiry as to what protection Britain would give to the German firm, he decided in the spring of 1884 to overstep the normal limits of German consular oversight. He announced that Angra Pequena would be under the 'protection' of the German Empire. This immediately caused the Cape government to insist that Britain annex the territory from the Orange River northwards to Angola. But in June 1884 there was such reluctance in London to anger Bismarck that the government gave way to the Germans, and contented itself with annexing Bechuanaland so as to prevent the Transvaal from linking up with German territory. As to why Bismarck allowed a quarrel to develop over South-West Africa, there are conflicting views. The most plausible suggestion is that partly he was courting the votes of the pro-colonial interests in Germany in view of a forthcoming election, and partly he was desirous of forcing Britain to wake up to the fact of German power, since Britain needed German support elsewhere in the world.

Neither reason, we must notice, was a specifically 'African' one. But they resulted in Germany becoming a major factor in Africa. Togoland and the Cameroons were acquired in West Africa shortly after. Bismarck took the initiative in calling an international conference in Berlin at the end of 1884, where it was agreed that, if territory in West Africa was to be taken by European powers, they should notify one another of their actions and provide sufficient administration to protect trade and navigation. As this conference was drawing to a close, in February 1885, Bismarck went on to announce the charter of Peters's Colonization Society for its venture in the region of Dar-es-Salaam, which was followed by German intervention at Witu, some 300 miles to the north, in the same year. Thus within two years of the 'German irruption' there had been such major territorial changes that it might seem that Bismarck 'sparked off' the 'scramble for Africa'.

There is, however, a serious flaw in this suggestion, since neither Britain nor Germany were 'scrambling', in the positive sense, for territory. Gladstone, who found himself backing down before the Germans, thought there was room for all in Africa. But what the story of the diplomatic crisis does help us to understand is *why* the British chartered companies were permitted. At the Berlin conference the major powers agreed that if claims to West Africa were to be maintained there should be signs of occupation and administration, and protection for European nationals. For government this would have been a costly business, quite unacceptable to Parliament. What better, therefore, than to turn the matter over to private enterprise? Far from being a 'capitalist conspiracy' the chartered companies were a way of fulfilling national obligations on the cheap.

Both of the explanations of the 'scramble for Africa' which we have considered put the causes *outside* Africa. It is significant that more recent explanations bring Africa squarely into the picture. Thus the much-debated 'Robinson-Gallagher thesis' suggests that the 'scramble' occurred because of 'nationalist crises in Africa itself'.* Two movements are said to provide the key. Firstly, the Egyptian nationalist movement of the 1870s, which led to the British occupation of Egypt in 1882. Here, say the proponents of the new view, the motive was protection for the Suez Canal, the main trade route to India, the Far East and the Pacific. In other words, Britain went into Africa from the north-east, not to carve out an African empire, but to protect the existing Indian empire and the Dominions in the Pacific. Secondly, the Afrikaner nationalist movement is said to have started the 'scramble' in the south. The rise of the Transvaal threatened British paramountcy in South Africa and so the old Cape route to the east.

The importance of the Transvaal for South African policy has already been stressed. For East Africa the new theory also fits well. The scramble for this region had more to do with Egypt and the Nile than

* R. Robinson and J. Gallagher, *Africa and the Victorians*, London, 1961, p. 465. See also by the same authors 'The Partition of Africa', *New Cambridge Modern History*, vol. XI.

with the profitability of the territory which became Kenya and Uganda. British interest arose originally because of the Zanzibar slave trade, but it became urgent in the 1870s because of Egypt's bankruptcy. By borrowing from European bankers, investing in the Suez canal and conquering the upper Nile as far as Bunyoro (in present Uganda) Khedive Ismail of Egypt overreached himself. Selling his Suez Canal shares to Britain did not save him. In 1876 the Europeans intervened in Egypt, first to create a Public Debt Commission to stabilize the finances, and then to depose Ismail and replace him with a more pliant ruler who received British and French advisers. These actions led to an uprising of Egyptian nationalists in 1879–80.

The Egyptian rising presented Gladstone, who returned to office in 1880, with a dilemma similar to that created by the Transvaal rising at the same time. Was it really a 'nationalist' movement, like that of the Belgians, the Greeks or the Italians, which it had long been Britain's tradition to support, or were the Egyptian nationalists a set of 'ignorant barbarians', as Evelyn Baring, the secretary of the Debt Commission, insisted? Gladstone's dilemma was painful: his instinct was always on the side of self-government. 'Egypt for the Egyptians' was a cry he understood. But, as so frequently happened, the opinion of the man on the spot prevailed. Britain and France announced their support for their puppet ruler. In 1882 Britain alone (unsupported by France) sent in Sir Garnet Wolseley, the 'modern major-general', to quell the nationalists. Gladstone sincerely believed that the occupation would be temporary. But Britain remained in Egypt until 1956.

The effects of the occupation on Africa were immense. To secure agreement from the European powers to her anomalous position in Egypt, Britain sought the support of their representatives on the Debt Commission. This was one of the main reasons why Gladstone backed down before Bismarck in South-West and East Africa. But, above all, Egypt's African interests now became Britain's. If Egypt had tried to control the Nile, Britain would soon find herself doing the same. When three developments during the middle of the 1880s constituted a threat to the Nile, the 'scramble' for East Africa was set off. First, the rise of the Mahdist State in the Sudan cut off the Equatoria Province of Egypt. Secondly, the massacre of Christian missionaries by the King of Buganda in 1885 raised the possibility of another hostile Muslim state close to the Nile. Thirdly, the intervention of the Germans at Dar-es-Salaam and Witu, and of the Italians at Massawa on the Red Sea, raised the possibility of European rivals controlling the Nile head-waters.

Thus when Lord Salisbury, the shy, genial nobleman who was Britain's first prime minister under a democratic franchise, resumed office in 1886, he faced African decisions even more difficult than Gladstone's dilemmas in the Transvaal and Egypt. What could he salvage in the region of the Nile from the confusion caused by the German irruption, Italian ambitions, the Mahdist uprising and Britain's Egyptian liability? How could British influence in the middle part of Africa, which had been first invoked by Livingstone's indict-ment of the Arab slave trade, be supported?

Salisbury first accepted the German chartered company, like his Liberal predecessors, and in 1886 he negotiated a line from Vanga to Lake Victoria (the present boundary of Tanzania and Kenya). He then turned to private enterprise and in 1888 the Imperial British East Africa Company was chartered to occupy the British sphere to the north and to open up communications with the Uganda kingdoms north of Lake Victoria.

In 1889 an even more important decision was made. Salisbury became convinced that the British occupation of Egypt could not be ended (as Gladstone had hoped) in the foreseeable future. Partly because of the situation within Egypt and the unlikelihood of being able to hand back power to a viable régime, but mainly for strategic reasons, Salisbury decided that Britain's communications to the East depended on Egypt. If Egypt was to be held, other powers would have to be kept away from the Nile. The partition of East Africa proceeded from Salisbury's commitment to Egypt.

Foreign powers were to be checked where possible. Salisbury believed that African hostility to Europeans in the vicinity of Lake Nyasa and Lake Tanganyika (the region referred to today as 'Central Africa') was connected with the Muslim uprising in the Sudan. In this he was wrong. But it reinforced his willingness to permit Rhodes's British South Africa Company to open up the regions north of the Transvaal in 1889. At the same time he also gave orders to the British Consul in Mozambique, H. H. Johnston, to sign treaties with the chiefs north of the Zambezi and between Lakes Nyasa and Tanganyika, which laid the foundations of British control in Nyasaland and north-eastern Rhodesia and checked Portuguese expansion in the region.

After this Salisbury persuaded the Germans in 1890 to give up their interest at Witu, north of the 1886 partition line, and to recognize Zanzibar as a British protectorate. When the financially embarrassed Imperial British East Africa Company announced that it would have to withdraw from Uganda, the government (in this case the Liberals) stepped in to create the Uganda protectorate in 1894, and the East African protectorate (most of later Kenya) followed in 1895. The government began to assist in the tremendous project of building a railway from Mombasa to Lake Victoria which was to be the spinal cord of the later Kenya Colony. Finally, the control of the Nile was the motive behind the decision to invade the Sudan in 1896 to put down the Mahdists. When this was challenged by the French expedition to Fashoda on the upper Nile, Salisbury risked a major dispute with France to uphold Britain's supremacy on the Nile. Between 1889 and 1899, then, in the service of his Egyptian policy, Salisbury nearly achieved the all-red route from the Cape to Cairo.

When we turn to the partition of West Africa we find that the new theory is seriously challenged. Robinson and Gallagher suggest that Britain's occupation of Egypt so offended France that they sought ways of inserting 'pin-pricks' in Britain's side and found a vulnerable spot in West Africa. But this view is disputed. An authority well versed in the records of the French government for this period, C. W. Newbury, argues that 'there is not a shred of evidence to connect West Africa with Egypt'.* French and Belgian records suggest that France did indeed desire patriotic consolation at this time, but mainly because of her humiliation by Germany in the Franco-Prussian war of 1870–71, and only partly because of Britain's occupation of Egypt. Opportunity for aggrandizement offered, however, not in terms of rivalry with Britain, but with Léopold II's venture in the Congo, which came to a head because of the work of the French explorer de Brazza in 1882.

Brazza, while leading a scientific expedition in the Congo basin, signed a vague treaty with Makoko, ruler of the area north of Stanley Pool – site of present-day Brazzaville – and returned home to Paris in 1882. Signing treaties like this or running up a national flag was an occupational weakness of lonely officers in the jungle and the European foreign offices had suitable pigeon-holes in which to stow away their treaties. Brazza rather expected that his superiors would give him the usual routine acknowledgement. He was, however, a born

* *Journal of African History*, 1962, 3(3), p. 496.

propagandist. He had influential friends, and France was eager to restore her prestige. The press took up his treaty with remarkable unanimity. Lyrical praises were sung of the supposed wealth of the Congo. The result was that the Foreign Ministry gave in. The treaty was ratified – much to the surprise of Léopold II and the British and Portuguese governments, who immediately reacted by staking out new claims in West Africa. This, in the view, of Jean Stengers and Henri Brunschwig, makes de Brazza a better candidate for setting off the 'scramble' for West Africa than either Gladstone, by his Egyptian intervention, or Bismarck, by his action at Angra Pequena.* Where a link between west and east can perhaps be found is in Salisbury's general inclination to give way to the French in West Africa, where British trade was not large, so as to ensure acquiescence in British control of the Nile. Thus the hinterlands of the British colonies of Gambia, Sierra Leone, the Gold Coast and Nigeria all fell to France. The comparatively generous boundaries of the Gold Coast and Nigeria owe their existence to Chamberlain's belated attempt to build up a West African empire after joining the Colonial Office in 1895.

Indirect Rule

Although the 'scramble for Africa' took place mainly for strategic reasons, Britain incurred immense responsibilities by undertaking to control vast tracts of territory. How did she govern them? Some form of law and order, administration of justice and rudimentary government was necessary to prevent the African millions from falling into anarchy, but to provide the full panoply of modern government in the Victorian age would have been hopelessly inappropriate and costly. Thus, in large portions of the tropical African empire Britain ruled by the sort of indirect methods which had been applied gradually elsewhere.

The chief difference in Africa was that the pace of the 'scramble' had been so rapid that the sudden need to govern large expanses literally forced the government into this course. But, at the same time, a number of administrators were now convinced that the early Victorian doctrines of assimilation were wrong, and that African traditional authorities had to be preserved before they could be modernized. Thus,

* J. Stengers, 'L'Impérialisme coloniale de la fin du XIXe siècle: Mythe ou Réalité', in *Journal of African History*, 1962, 3(3), pp. 469–91; Henri Brunschwig; *Mythes et réalités de l'imperialisme colonial français*, Paris, 1960, pp. 42–45.

S

the doctrine of Indirect Rule is peculiarly associated with Africa.

We have already noted that in India a large number of Indian rulers, great and small, had been retained and that the 'princely states' were not annexed, but remained as 'protected states'. In Malaya the Sultans had also been retained. Further experiments had been made by Sir Arthur Gordon, who ruled through the chiefs in Fiji in the 1870s, and by Sir William MacGregor, who attempted the same in Papua in the 1880s. Sir Harry Johnston's Buganda Agreement of 1900 confirmed the King of Buganda in power subject to British 'overrule'. But it is with Nigeria that the doctrine of Indirect Rule is particularly associated because of the famous instructions of Lord Lugard.

Lugard based the administration of Northern Nigeria (and later Southern Nigeria, when he became Governor-General) on the principle that the 'chiefs should govern their people, not as independent, but as dependent rulers'. British Residents, as in Malaya, were appointed to advise but Lugard instructed them not to interfere incessantly. Lugard summed up his system in these words in 1912:

> This system is clearly only adapted in its fullest application to communities under the centralized rule of a paramount Chief, with some administrative machinery at his disposal, and finds its best exposition in the Moslem communities of the North [of Nigeria]... The first step is to endeavour to find a man of influence as chief, and to group under him as many villages or districts as possible, to teach him to delegate powers, and to take an interest in his 'Native Treasury', to support his authority, and to inculcate a sense of responsibility.

The chiefs had, then, a clearly defined role in government. There were not two systems of government, one British and one Nigerian, but a single government in which the chiefs had 'an acknowledged status and equality with the British officials. Their duties should never conflict and should overlap as little as possible; they should be complementary to each other'. The doctrine of Indirect Rule, although most remembered from its application by Lugard in Nigeria, was widely adopted in West and East Africa in the twentieth century.

African nationalists often bitterly criticized the system as one which either perverted the role of Chief by making him a British government officer, or one which propped up forces of African 'feudalism'. But to its most idealistic exponents Indirect Rule was but a specialized road to self-government. Lugard, in his book *The Dual Mandate in British*

Tropical Africa, published in 1922, wrote: 'Liberty and self-government can best be secured to the native population by leaving them free to manage their own affairs through their own rulers'. He did not pretend that the sole object of the colonial powers after the scramble for Africa was to inaugurate African self-government. He realized that they hoped to gain some profit, but he believed that the benefits could 'be made reciprocal, and that it is the aim and desire of civilized administration to fulfil this dual mandate'. Sir Donald Cameron, who served in Lugard's secretariat, who then, as governor of Tanganyika after the 1914–18 war, adopted similar policies there, and later returned as governor of Nigeria, preferred to call the system 'indirect administration' rather than 'rule'. He was particularly concerned to make Africans proud to be Africans 'on the basis of a true African civilization stimulated in the first instance by our own culture and example'. Progress in Africa ought, he believed, to be evolutionary, and he summed up his policy in 1934 with the words:

> The great aims to be followed throughout are those of building on the existing organization and ideas of the people, of leaving it to the people themselves, assisted by sympathetic advice, to devise and develop their own local institutions according to the standards of modern civilization. . . .

Thus, put at its best, Indirect Rule represented a policy of 'wait and see' in Africa. Large African populations could not be suddenly ruled by alien laws and customs, and therefore in many colonies the indigenous machinery of government was retained. Yet in many ways Indirect Rule might be said to have failed: the new Africa which emerged as a result of the colonial period was built by African nationalists whose ideas came from outside Africa.

The Origins of Nationalism in British Tropical Africa

Once the 'scramble for Africa' was over, British policies in tropical Africa took different paths in West Africa and in East and Central Africa. In the first place, British contact with the West coast had existed since the slave trade of the seventeenth century, while in East Africa it stemmed largely from the attempt to check the Arab slave trade by putting pressure on the Sultan of Zanzibar from the 1850s. In East Africa the 'scramble' had been based on strategic considerations connected with Egypt and the Transvaal, while in West Africa it arose from more localized attempts to control a modest part of the hinterlands of Sierra Leone, the Gold Coast and the Niger Delta. Finally, and most important, the climate and diseases of West Africa deterred British settlers, while in the upland regions of Rhodesia and Nyasaland, Tanganyika and Kenya, settlers were attracted in considerable numbers in the twentieth century.

Of these distinguishing features between east and west, length of contact played a larger part in the origins of nationalism than did European settlement. Thus, African nationalism developed in the West African colonies earlier than in the East African. Nationalism did not spring from opposition to settlers so much as from the development on the west coast of new classes, as in India and Ceylon, who were detached, in part, from tribal society and made susceptible to European ideas by their role in the new trades which gradually supplanted the slave trade. Two movements in particular indicated West Africans' receptivity to ideas from outside, and laid the foundations of West African nationalism. These were the Fante Confederation movement on the Gold Coast in the 1870s and the Pan-African movement emanating from the New World.

The Fante Confederation was one of several abortive attempts to create African states on the west coast which would blend the traditional authority of chiefs with western notions of government. It stemmed from the decision of a Select Committee of Parliament in 1865 to abandon all the West African Settlements except Sierra Leone (which had a special role) and to rely on relations with African rulers to foster British interests. Thus a group of English-speaking Gold Coast Africans joined together with some chiefs to draw up a constitution for the 'Confederation'. They were considerably influenced by the writings of a government official, Dr James Africanus Horton, an African graduate of Edinburgh, who suggested in 1868 that the Parliamentary resolution had laid down the 'great principle of establishing independent African nationalities'. The Fante Confederation was hailed in 1872 by the *African Times*, published in London, as 'the birth of a Nation'. In this movement the Fante leaders were merely taking literally the resolutions of the Parliamentary Select Committee and they hoped that by doing so they could forestall the extension of colonial rule. Unfortunately for the participants, quite the reverse happened. The Fante were treated with contempt by British officers and by the Colonial Office. They were swept aside and in 1874 British influence (though not, as yet, sovereignty) was extended in the Gold Coast protectorate.

The second external influence which contributed to West African nationalism was the idea of the 'African personality' and 'Pan-Africanism' which spread from the United States and the West Indies. One of the earliest exponents of this idea was Edward Blyden, who was born in the West Indies in 1832, and emigrated to the United States and then to Liberia. There he had a chequered career as college professor in Monrovia, Liberian Ambassador to Britain, Foreign Secretary, and for a time in the 1870s the Sierra Leone government's Agent in the interior. He visited Britain and the United States on a number of occasions. He produced, for the governor of Sierra Leone, some interesting schemes for a West African University and for British relations with the Muslim States of West Africa, which were dismissed as preposterous in Whitehall. But if Blyden was not taken seriously in Britain, his ideas had considerable influence on the early-twentieth-century generation of West Africans.

As early as 1862 Blyden declared in New York: 'An African nationality is the great desire of my soul.' In 1874 he extolled the virtues of the pure Negro race. He expected African peoples to 'take their place in the great family of nations – a distinct but integral part of the great human body, who will be neither spurious Europeans, bastard Americans, nor savage Africans, but men developed upon the base of their own idiosyncracies.' Without attacking the spread of European rule, for which he sometimes expressed admiration, Blyden insisted on the superiority of the Negro race and sought to ensure that the African developed 'as an African'. This stress which Blyden placed on the specifically 'racial' doctrine focused interest on the movement for Negro emancipation in the United States.

Already by the end of the nineteenth century there were various connections between the American Negro and Africa through a trickle of African students – often Christian ministers – who attended American Negro colleges, and American missions which were interested in Africa. John Chilembwe, who was to become the hero-figure of Malawi nationalism, visited the United States in 1897. In the same year, the English missionary who had converted him and who took him to the United States coined the phrase, 'Africa for the Africans': the title of a pamphlet in which he attacked the European 'scramble' and urged the African, 'sympathetically led by his more experienced Afro-American brother, to develop his own country . . .'

Through the American Negroes Africans became aware of various movements for the advancement of the Negro population of the United States. Some, like James Aggrey of the Gold Coast, were attracted to the ideas of Booker T. Washington, principal of the Tuskegee Institute, Alabama, who in 1895 proposed that before they fought for equal rights, Negroes should qualify themselves, by learning skilled trades, for economic self-support. By the early years of the twentieth century, however, a greater influence was exerted by Dr W. E. B. Du Bois, the first Negro graduate of Harvard, who in 1909 was one of the founders of the National Association for the Advancement of Coloured Peoples, and who finally became a citizen of Ghana just before his death in 1963. Du Bois preached the doctrine that the *élite* of the Negro race, his so-called 'talented tenth', should develop their abilities to the highest degree in order to give leadership to their fellows.

By the time of the 1914–18 war, which seemed to spell the end of European imperialism and led to the enunciation of doctrines like 'national self-determination', American Negro reformers and African nationalists came together in a number of short-lived international movements which stressed the 'Pan-African' ideal. As early as 1900 a Pan-African conference had been organized in London by a West Indian lawyer. In 1911 a Universal Races conference was also held in London. During the 1914–18 war a series of West African student organizations were formed in London which linked up students from the four British colonies. Finally, during the Versailles Peace Conference W. E. B. Du Bois, the American, and some West African leaders called the first 'Pan-African Congress' at Paris in an attempt to influence the great powers in their decisions about Africa. Their aims were modest. The immediate object was the participation of Africans in colonial government, but the ultimate goal was clear: 'that, in time, Africa be ruled by consent of the Africans'.

Although the Pan-African movement achieved very little, it had a wide and continuing influence. The short-lived 'National Congress of British West Africa' followed in the 1920s. A series of Pan-African Congresses were held in London, Brussels and Paris (1921), London and Lisbon (1923) and in New York (1927). The 'Pan-African' ideal continued to excite the minds of many Africans. Eventually in 1945 the fifth Congress was held in Manchester, attended by W. E. B. Du

Bois, Kwame Nkrumah, Jomo Kenyatta and others, in an atmosphere where the hopes of the nationalists ran high.

While the 'Pan-African' ideal gained ground among students and the Negro *élite* during the 1914–18 war, a rather different form of Negro movement was founded by Marcus Garvey, the Jamaican. In 1914 he founded his 'Universal Negro Improvement Association'. Transferring his headquarters to New York two years later, he proceeded to turn his association into a mass movement. With his slogans 'Wake up Africa!' and 'Africa for the Africans!', Garvey attracted a certain amount of interest in the West African colonies. In 1920 he called his first international convention in New York, and was elected the 'Provisional President of Africa'.

When we come to discuss the political and constitutional progress of the African colonies after the 1914–18 war, we shall see how little these international Negro movements achieved. But their true impact lay in the exciting new horizons they opened up for thoughtful, young, ambitious Africans in the 1920s. It is most significant that in these years some of the most notable of modern African politicians left the British colonies for a prolonged period of residence and study abroad, in the United States or in Britain. When they returned after the 1939–45 war it was to lead their countries to independence.

Hastings Banda, a Nyasa, was in the Union of South Africa, the United States and Britain, where he trained and practised as a doctor, from 1915 to 1956, when he moved to Ghana for two years. He then returned to lead Malawi nationalism in 1958. Nnamdi Azikiwe, an Ibo from Nigeria, studied in the United States and lectured at Lincoln University from 1925 to 1934, when his application to teach at King's College, Lagos, was rejected. He then edited a newspaper in Accra for two years. Returning to Nigeria in 1937 to run the *West African Pilot*, he became wealthy and independent and the leader of the nationalist movement. Jomo Kenyatta of Kenya, who became general secretary of the Kikuyu Central Association, was assisted by the association to go to England to study in 1931. After working at the London School of Economics he published an anthropological study in 1938 entitled *Facing Mount Kenya*, in which he glorified the Kikuyu tribal past and criticized the influence brought from the west. He did not return to Kenya until 1946. He was associated in 1945, at the Pan-African Congress in Manchester, with Kwame Nkrumah, who had left the Gold Coast in 1935 for study in the United States and then at the

London School of Economics. Nkrumah returned to the Gold Coast in 1947 to become organizing secretary of the nationalist party.

While most of the Asian nationalist leaders whom we have discussed – the *élite* of India, Ceylon and Malaya – also studied abroad, it is significant that they were usually of high social class and were educated at Oxford, Cambridge or the Inns of Court, whereas many of the African nationalists went to American universities or to the London School of Economics.

11

The New Commonwealth: Nationalist Pioneers and Political Evolution in West Africa

Ghana

IN THE West African colonies the Gold Coast led the way in the growth of nationalism and the achievement of constitutional advance, as India did in Asia. In many ways the Ghanaian national movement closely paralleled the Indian national movement, although on a smaller, retarded, scale.

The origins of Gold Coast nationalism may be found in the abortive Confederation movement of the 1870s and in cultural associations among the new *élite*, who, in the 1880s, sought to revive interest in local customs. A few English-speaking pastors, traders, lawyers and teachers founded the 'Fante National Political Society' in 1879 to stop 'further encroachments into their nationality'. They tried to revive the dress, music, language and titles of their region. They began to study the history of their people. They questioned the use of the English language in mission schools. Their interests were chiefly cultural. But when in 1894 the colonial government of the Gold Coast, which was alarmed when speculators tried to get mineral and timber rights by doubtful means, sought to pass a Crown Lands Bill to vest control over waste lands, forests and minerals in the Crown, there was an outcry from the new *élite*. The 'Aborigines Rights Protection Society' was formed to combat the new law. A deputation was sent to London in 1898 to petition the Colonial Office and the Queen. The Bill was withdrawn. Thus the A.R.P. Society represented the first successful Gold Coast agitation against the colonial government. But the society, like the Indian National Congress in its early years, was confined to a narrow *élite* from the coastal towns and was generally loyal towards the British régime. After the 1914–18 war it went into decline.

269

By 1914, the influences from outside, which we have already discussed, began to quicken the tempo of Gold Coast political life. Already by 1914 the idea of a conference of British West African leaders had been mooted. Thus in 1915 the Governor of the Gold Coast decided to emulate the example of Ceylon and to add more non-Europeans to the legislative council, to which a few Africans had been admitted in the nineteenth century. By the 1916 constitution the council was enlarged to twenty-one, twelve of whom were officials. Of the nine non-official members, three were nominated Europeans, three chiefs, and three members of the new *élite* representing the Western Province, Cape Coast Castle and Accra.

The new constitution made a start to constitutional advance, but the African intelligentsia was not satisfied. Newspapers called for a legislative assembly modelled on the House of Commons. The West African Congress of 1920 demanded elections for the African representative members. Thus in 1925 Sir Gordon Guggisberg, a remarkably forward-looking governor, who encouraged the development of education and even drew up a plan for the 'Africanization' of the civil service, sponsored another constitutional advance. First, a series of provincial councils were created, which elected representatives from themselves to sit in a new legislative council. This council was enlarged to thirty members: sixteen official and fourteen unofficial (of which five were Europeans and nine elected Africans).

But the elections were complicated. The nine elective seats were allocated to provide a measure of representation by population. One member was elected by the Western Province, two for the Central Province and three for the Eastern Province, and one each to represent the Ga, Ewe and Akan language groups. But only three of these members were elected directly by adults over twenty-one occupying property valued at £8 a year. This occurred in the three towns of Accra, Cape Coast and Sekondi. The other six elected members were selected by the provincial councils. Thus the democratically elected element was small. Nevertheless, here was a constitution which became a focus for modern nationalist pressure by the *élite*. Self-government and Dominion status now appeared to be attainable goals. In 1929 J. W. de Graft-Johnson defined the goal of moderate nationalists:

Under the tutelage of Britain, therefore, the inhabitants hope to realize their dreams of a nation within the Commonwealth; they wish to be not only 'civilized into an orderly community' but 'welded into a Nation'.

During the depression of the 1930s, when revenue was short, little progress was made. How, then, did the Gold Coast nationalists achieve their aims?

The 1939–45 war proved, as we have seen, to be a great divide for the tropical empire. The war brought prosperity: 65,000 Gold Coast men joined the army, many served overseas and learned new skills, others experienced the outside world through the European troops stationed on the coast. At the same time the Colonial Development and Welfare Acts and the government's self-government pledge indicated a notable change in official British policy. During the war Sir Alan Burns, the governor, invited two Africans to serve on the Executive Council. But the post-war constitution published in 1946, although providing for an African majority on the legislative council, bitterly disappointed expectant African opinion.

The 'Burns constitution' increased the number of Africans in the council to eighteen, but it perpetuated the old electoral system. Only five members were elected by the urban voters, while thirteen were still chosen by the chiefs' councils. In one sense the creation of an African majority in the council fulfilled the long-standing dreams of the African *élite*. But in the post-war period it became a focus of discontent among the frustrated new lower middle class of teachers, clerks, shopkeepers, small farmers, and more particularly the demobilized ex-servicemen. In 1948 a series of veterans' demonstrations developed into serious riots in the Gold Coast. These, in turn, attracted membership to the first genuine political party to make a mass appeal.

In 1947 Dr J. B. Danquah, now a 52-year-old lawyer, who remembered the exciting dreams of the 1920s and had, indeed, already selected the name 'Ghana' for his nation, founded the 'United Gold Coast Convention'. The aim of self-government was now announced frankly. Even more important, Danquah called from Britain, as party secretary, Kwame Nkrumah, who had left his homeland twenty-two years before to study in the United States and England. After the riots in 1948 the U.G.C. Convention leaders were detained. But when a British jurist declared that the Burns constitution had been 'outmoded at birth', the government created a committee of leading Gold Coast citizens, led by Mr Justice Coussey, and asked it to recommend a new constitution.

The all-African Coussey commission represented the turning-point for the Gold Coast. Now constitutional advance was being placed in African hands. But the commission, obviously appointed under the auspices of the government, presented a dilemma for the nationalist leaders. Danquah, the leading politician of the old *élite*, agreed to sit on the commission. But Nkrumah refused to serve. He broke with the U.G.C. Convention to form his own 'Convention People's Party' with a popular rallying-cry of 'self-government now'. His campaign caused great excitement in the Gold Coast. When he demanded a campaign of 'Positive Action' leading to strikes and sabotage, Nkrumah and his lieutenants were sent to jail.

Meanwhile, the Coussey commission recommended that a new legislative assembly of seventy-five elected members should be called, from which the leaders were to be selected to receive a limited form of responsible government as a preparation for eventual full self-government. In 1951 the first elections were held and proved to be a landslide victory of the Convention People's Party, whose leaders, including Nkrumah, were still in jail. Nkrumah's party gained thirty-four seats to Danquah's three. The old *élite* had been swept aside by one of the first successful mass parties of Africa.

In a dramatic bid to win African support for the new constitution so as to provide the chance for a period of peaceful transition, Sir Charles Arden-Clarke, the governor, released Nkrumah from jail and invited him to be 'Leader of Government Business' in the Assembly. A 'Cabinet system' was inaugurated in which British civil servants co-operated with African politicians. In the following year Nkrumah was accorded the title of 'prime minister'. After a further election victory in 1954 an all-African Cabinet was created and the Assembly was left to consist of entirely elected members. By 1956 the British government had accepted the idea that the Gold Coast should be granted full independence in the Commonwealth. On 6 March 1957 – 103 years after the signing of Maclean's Bond – Ghana became independent.

But the transfer of power was provided for by a British Act of Parliament and the new constitution took the usual form of an Order in Council. Although the word was not used in the Independence Act, Ghana was in status like a Dominion, in which the legislature consisted of the Queen and the National Assembly. The constitution was a British creation negotiated with the Ghanaian leaders. It was not obviously Ghanaian. Therefore Nkrumah proposed that Ghana should become a Republic. In 1960 a Constituent Assembly convened at which Dr Nkrumah declared: 'Imperialism dies hard . . . again another Constitution was imposed upon the peoples of Ghana by an Imperial power. We had no choice in the [1956] constitution but to accept it.' He appealed to the Assembly to support a constitution which gave Ghanaians 'an indisputable right to think for themselves and to act for themselves'. The Assembly's acceptance was upheld by a plebiscite in April 1960. The Assembly then met to enact the Republican constitution. Under its terms the President received wide powers. He became, like the President of the United States, both Head of State, Head of Government and Supreme Commander of the armed forces. He was to be elected by Parliament but had the power to dissolve Parliament.

After Ghana became a Republic, President Nkrumah increasingly emerged as Ghana's 'strong man'. In the general election of 1962 he won a sweeping victory which left his opponents with only nine seats in the National Assembly. His power was considerably enhanced by his life-chairmanship of the C.P.P., by his chairmanship of the Volta River Project, and by the detention of his opponents. In February 1964 Ghana (after a referendum) became a one-party state and the President received the power to dismiss judges. But the most notable feature of Nkrumah's years of power was his upholding of the 'Pan-African' ideal first enunciated by American Negroes in the Victorian age. Ghana, as the first colony to become independent, became in the later 1950s a centre of 'anti-colonialism'. Nkrumah became a leading antagonist of what he called 'neo-colonialism', and consistent with this whole trend of policy was his breaking of diplomatic relations with Britain over the Rhodesian crisis of 1965. For a decade Nkrumah appeared to the world as the symbol of Africa's self-assertion.

But by 1965 Ghanaians and their overseas well-wishers were increasingly disenchanted with 'Nkrumaism'. The death in jail, at the age of seventy, of Dr J. B. Danquah, the veteran nationalist leader of the inter-war years, the reviver of the name 'Ghana', and the politician who, indeed, brought Nkrumah into the nationalist struggle, was a pertinent reminder that Ghana had gone far along the path to becoming a 'police state'. Immense, much publicized development projects, which excited admiration from visitors, led to a rapid depletion of Ghana's sterling reserves. Wasteful prestige projects drained foreign aid and numerous public corporations lost money. More and more Russian and Chinese advisers and technicians came into Ghana, as training centres were founded to foster Pan-Africanist agitation else-where. In fact, Nkrumah's inclination to meddle in the affairs of other African states led the African summit conference which met in Accra in October 1965 to reject his plans. Both inside and outside Ghana, Nkrumah's régime made many enemies.

Thus, in the early hours of 24 February 1966, while Nkrumah was away on a mission to Peking and Hanoi, his government was over-thrown in a military *coup*. Lieutenant-General Joseph Ankrah, a former commander of the army, who had been dismissed by Nkrumah eight months earlier, became chairman of the 'National Liberation Council'. The Convention People's Party was abolished and Nkrumah was deposed. His preventive detention laws were repealed and two thousand political prisoners released. A message from Ghana Radio announced to the people: 'The myth surrounding Kwame Nkrumah has been broken.'* Investigations by the new government soon revealed that the deposed president had amassed a considerable personal fortune.

As Nkrumah became more and more discredited, the new govern-ment turned to restore Ghana's dignity as a nation. On 5 March 1966 diplomatic relations were resumed with Britain, while a foreign policy of 'balanced neutrality' was announced. Above all, the government looked to the International Monetary Fund for credit so that Ghana's once prosperous economy could be restored.

Nigeria

Nigeria's political development closely followed Ghana's. Although the nationalist movement there (particularly in the Muslim states of the north) was much later in its growth, constitutional advance in the post-1945 period closely paralleled Ghana's. In 1960, with its population approaching 40 million, the Nigerian Federal Republic became Africa's most populous state.

* Nkrumah promised to return to Ghana but, instead, one of the oddest events in recent international politics followed. In 1958 Ghana and Guinea formed a union, which became a dead letter. After Nkrumah's deposition, President Sekou Touré invited him to become 'Head of State' of Guinea.

'Nigeria' was not really created until 1914 and it was the result of piecemeal expansion. Lagos Island was annexed in 1861. After more than thirty years of intermittent intervention, part of the Niger Delta was acquired as the Oil Rivers protectorate in 1885, supervised by the Foreign Office. Slightly extended in 1893, it was re-named the Niger Coast protectorate. Up river, the Royal Niger Company opened up certain belts of territory between 1886 and 1899. After the ending of its charter, the protectorate of Northern Nigeria was created. At the same time, the Niger Coast protectorate and part of the former Company territory up to Idah was placed under the Colonial Office as the protectorate of Southern Nigeria, to which Lagos was added in 1906. A single governor was not placed over northern and southern protectorates until 1912. The governments were finally amalgamated under a single Governor-General in 1914. Thus before the 1914–18 war, since 'Nigeria' hardly existed, there was little focus for nationalism.

During the war, however, Africans in the region began to feel the

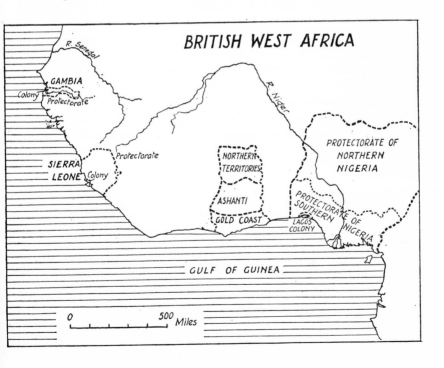

influence of Gold Coast nationalism and the international Negro movements. During the war Nigerians participated in African student organizations in London and gave some support (though much less than the Gold Coast) to the Congress of British West Africa. The *Lagos Weekly Record*, which since 1891 had been extolling African race consciousness and criticizing the British régime, drew attention to the Indian nationalist movement and urged the British government to declare its aims in Africa:

> British politicians and administrators have been shouting us almost deaf with such phrases as trusteeship for the subject races, but there does not seem to be any definite programme as to how we are to be educated to take over our trusteeship.

As in India, the British were ambiguous in their trusteeship. While Lugard sought to preserve and develop the traditional authority pattern of the Muslim states in the north, others began to realize that a role had to be found for the westernized *élite* of the coast. 'We are busy manufacturing black and brown Englishmen,' wrote Sir John Rodger in 1909, 'turning them out by the score and cursing the finished article when the operation is completed.' As in India, many Englishmen preferred the true man-of-the-soil to the accomplished, English-educated lawyer from the towns.

Yet, after the 1914–18 war, Sir Hugh Clifford, who was certainly no radical and who attacked the idea of a 'Nigerian Nation', nevertheless inaugurated the beginnings of a new policy in Nigeria. In 1920 he insisted that due attention be paid to 'the more highly educated sections of the African communities of Nigeria'.

> I maintain [he went on] that every European in this country has towards them very special obligations and responsibilities which should inspire him with a deep sympathy for them and with an eager desire to aid and befriend them.

Two years later Clifford announced a new legislative council, which included the first elected African members in a British colony. Its powers extended only to the southern part of Nigeria; the northern provinces were still governed by edict. The new legislative council retained an official majority and seven of the Africans were nominated. But the election of four African members (three representing Lagos and one Calabar) became a focus of political aspiration. The Lagos-centred 'Nigeria National Democratic Party', led by Herbert Macaulay, emerged as the chief political force throughout most of the 1920s and 1930s. Like the Indian National Congress and the Aborigines Rights Protection Society on the Gold Coast, Macaulay's party represented the *élite* and was loyalist. Its chief aim was 'government of the people by the people and for the people' as an integral part of the British Imperial Commonwealth. There was, however, little constitutional development for twenty years after 1923.

Yet, while only modest advances were made, the 1920s saw a proliferation of specialist associations interested in furthering trade, tribal and cultural activities. These became the province of a growing, literate, lower middle class. Some associations developed into literary and debating societies such as the Young Men's Literary Association organized by Azikiwe in 1923 before he left for the United States. The first African graduates to return from the United States in this period appealed to Nigerian youth to develop a national feeling. Finally, in 1937 Azikiwe returned, after ten years in the United States, to lead the 'Nigerian Youth Movement', to found his radical paper the *West African Pilot*, and to make the first attempt to build a truly national, non-tribal, mass movement.

'Zik', as he came to be called, was the son of a Nigerian soldier who left the army after being insulted by a British officer. He was brought up away from the tribal home, educated in mission schools and became a clerk in the Lagos Treasury. In 1925 he left for the United States, where he obtained his M.A. from Columbia and a Ph.D. from the University of Pennsylvania, and lectured in Political Science at Lincoln University. After such a notable academic career his rejection for a teaching post at King's College, Lagos, in 1935 was a bitter blow, and he retired to Accra for two years as a newspaper editor. After 1938 Azikiwe emerged as Nigeria's greatest nationalist leader. Through his papers, and the Nigerian Youth Movement, he appealed to the younger, educated, Nigerians. He brought into the movement students returning from abroad, such as H. O. Davis, who had lodged with Jomo Kenyatta while at the London School of Economics. In 1938 the Youth Charter proclaimed the goal of 'complete autonomy within the British Empire – a position of equal partnership with other states of the British Commonwealth – complete independence in the local management of our affairs'.

During the 1939–45 war, sensing the changed atmosphere brought about by Britain's precarious position in 1940, Azikiwe pressed his aims. In that year he called for an end to Indirect Rule, for representation for the north in the legislative council, and for wider opportunities for Africans in the civil service. As a member of a deputation of West African journalists who went to London in 1943, he drew up a remarkable document entitled 'The Atlantic Charter and British West Africa', which proposed nothing less than a time-table for West African independence. He wanted an immediate end to Crown colony status, the 'Africanization' of the civil service, a 'crash programme' of 400 scholarships a year to equip Nigerians for responsibility, and a period of ten years' representative government followed by five years' responsible government leading up to independence in 1958. As may well be imagined, Azikiwe's radical time-table (which incidentally was very nearly fulfilled) fell on deaf ears. He returned to Nigeria disillusioned.

As in the Gold Coast, British policy-makers trod very cautiously. In 1943 two Africans were invited on to the Nigerian executive council. In 1945, while one of Zik's lieutenants attended the Pan-African Congress at Manchester, Sir Arthur Richards, the governor of Nigeria, proposed a constitution, which was designed as a first step towards making a bridge from Indirect Rule to the normal system of self-government. The central legislative council was enlarged and empowered now to legislate for the north, and it received an African majority. But the four members elected for Lagos and Calabar remained the only directly elected members. The chief innovation of the new constitution was the creation of three groups of provinces, now called 'Regions' (East, West, and Northern), each with a regional House of Assembly, the members of which were selected by the traditional African authorities. This move was attended by some decentralization of finance and administration. The Houses of Assembly could discuss general legislation and also elect five members each to the central legislative council. The central executive council remained official. The constitution was designed to avoid an over-large central legislature in which the educated minority from Lagos and the coast could dominate. Yet the 'Richards Constitution' was denounced by the nationalist leaders.

In 1945 a general strike was called. When Azikiwe's newspapers were banned for their part in fomenting the strikes, Azikiwe claimed he was to be the victim of an assassination plot. He announced melodramatically that he would return to 'the Niger whence I came' and sent telegrams to newspapers all over the world and to heads of state as diverse as Stalin and the President of Liberia. The governor pointed out that the plot was a 'silly invention', but all the publicity turned Azikiwe into a major national personality among the Nigerian masses. His 'National Council for Nigeria and the Cameroons', founded in 1944, became, for a decade, the chief nationalist party. Azikiwe and his party leaders toured Nigeria. 'Zikism' became a kind of evangelical crusade, especially among the young in Nigeria, until the movement was discredited by an attempt in 1950 to assassinate Hugh Foot, the chief secretary.

The sudden quickening of the tempo of nationalism with the growth of a large political party in the post-war years forced Britain to accelerate constitutional development, as she had in the Gold Coast. In 1948 a new governor, Sir John Macpherson, announced that the 'time-table' would be reviewed. Even more important, he made it plain that Nigerians would be consulted at all levels. Village and district discussions would take place and finally a general conference would draft a new constitution which would be discussed both in the regional Houses and the central legislative council before going to the governor and the Colonial Office. As an earnest of his intentions he soon appointed five Nigerians to the central executive council.

Nigeria now had every chance of making big strides towards self-government. Macpherson announced an accelerated programme of 'Nigerianization' of the civil service; Azikiwe was one of the commissioners appointed to supervise the scheme. Soon increasing numbers of able, young, educated Nigerians found careers open to talent in the public service. The atmosphere quietened. In 1949 the Constitutional Conference started work and recommended a federal system for Nigeria. In 1951 the 'Macpherson Constitution' was inaugurated, which, although short-lived, proved to be an important landmark.

In the new constitution, the regional Houses of Assembly were retained and were still elected indirectly by 'electoral colleges'. But regional executive councils, with African majorities, were created. The central legislature was enlarged to become the 'House of Representatives'. Only six out of its 142 members remained officials, but elections were still indirect, by the regional Houses. North and South received equal representation and no concessions were made for minorities. The central executive council became a 'Council of Ministers' consisting of six officials and four Africans nominated from each regional House. Thus, rather as under 'dyarchy' in India and elsewhere, Africans were in the majority in both regional and central governments, but there was no real element of 'responsible government' as the Ministers were merely departmental 'spokesmen' in the legislatures, and at neither level were 'leaders of government business' or 'premiers' appointed. The constitution soon changed, but it had important political results.

The first elections under the 1951 constitution vividly illustrated a tendency to regional, even tribal, nationalism, which had developed in the post-war years. Azikiwe's 'National Council for Nigeria and the Cameroons' was the only truly national party, and yet even then had made most headway among the Ibo people who originated in Eastern Nigeria. In 1948 the Nigerian Youth Movement had split because of tribal feeling, and Azikiwe himself accepted the presidency of the 'Pan-Ibo Union'. In the predominantly Yoruba western Nigeria, a cultural association entitled 'Egbe Omo Oduduwa' had been formed in 1948 to foster Yoruba interests. By 1951 Chief Awolowo had founded the 'Action Group' (uniting the Yoruba middle class and the chiefs) to oppose the N.C.N.C. in the west. In the predominantly Muslim north, nationalism had been slow to take root. A few small teachers' organizations, such as the 'Bauchi General Improvement Union' (which started in 1943) and the 'Northern Teachers Association' (formed in London in 1947) were interested in pressing for gradual reforms. As Azikiwe called for a united Nigeria, northerners feared that, if independence came quickly, 'southerners will take the place of the Europeans in the north'. Thus, in 1949 the 'Northern Peoples Congress', led by the ex-headmaster Abubakar Tafawa Balewa, one of the founders of the Bauchi Union, was formed to resist the threat of southern dominance. Ahmadu Bello, the Sardauna of Sokoto, a descendant of the early-nineteenth-century conqueror of the north, lent his prestige as spiritual leader of the northern Muslims.

These regional tensions became politically 'fixed' after the elections of 1951–52. In the Eastern Region the N.C.N.C. received a large majority; in the Western Region the Action Group gained a small majority; and in the Northern Region the Northern Peoples Congress achieved a landslide victory. Azikiwe, the apostle of Nigerian unity, failed to get elected to the federal House of Representatives because he stood for the Western House of Assembly, where the Action Group majority would not elect him for the Central House. The ideal of a unified Nigeria received its final blow in 1953 when an Action Group member introduced a motion calling for self-government in 1956. The northern members believed the country was not prepared for self-government and were well aware that northern backwardness might invite southern domination. They therefore opposed the motion in the federal legislature. When their members were met by insults from the Lagos mob, they returned to the north in disgust, determined to avoid further embroilment in southern politics. This, in turn, led the Action Group, who believed that the conservatism of the north was delaying self-government, to campaign in the Northern Region. The result, in 1953, was serious tribal riots in Kano where 36 were killed and over 200 injured. Thus northern determination to get a weak federation and equality in the legislature was confirmed.

The next stage in the constitutional development of Nigeria, therefore, was a conference in 1953 to draw up a constitution which would lessen tribal tensions. Nigeria remained a federation of three regions, with a federal capital at Lagos. Full self-government was inaugurated in the regions in 1954, when regional 'premiers' were appointed. At the federal level the legislature became the 'National Assembly' of 184 members, evenly divided between the northern and two southern regions. Appointments to the Federal Executive Council were made by the leaders of the majority parties in the regional Houses. The members became full 'Ministers' responsible to the legislature, but no 'Leader of Government Business' was appointed.

The 1954 constitution really represented the culmination of the national struggle in Nigeria. Full responsible government was achieved in the regions. In the National Assembly a coalition government of the Northern Peoples Congress and the National Council of Nigeria and the Cameroons was formed. After Ghana received independence in 1957, Nigerian constitutional meetings were held in London to work out the last stages of the road to self-government. The Federal Assembly was enlarged, adult suffrage begun (except in the north, where women were excluded), and a Senate was created. Provision was made for the office of Federal 'prime minister' and Abubakar Tafawa Balewa, leader of the N.P.C., took office in 1957. After a general election in 1959 the N.P.C.–N.C.N.C coalition was revived. Tafawa Balewa (now Sir Abubakar) was retained as prime minister. Dr Azikiwe, father-figure of the nationalist movement, became President of the Senate.

Nigeria's independence was declared on 1 October 1960 and, after a short period when Sir James Robertson, the last governor, was Governor-General, Azikiwe became the first African Governor-General. Three years later, in 1963, Nigeria followed India, Ghana and Tanganyika, by becoming a Republic within the Commonwealth. Azikiwe, who had produced his time-table for independence twenty years before, became the first federal President. But the veteran nationalist leader, now approaching his sixtieth year, soon found all that he had fought for endangered. Nigeria's claim to be 'Africa's bastion of democracy' was tarnished by regional and ethnic jealousies and growing violence.

The federal government continued to be dominated by the vast Northern Region. Dissension by minorities in the predominantly Yoruba Western Region led to proposals for a separate Mid-western Region, which was created after a referendum in 1963. Chief Awolowo, the Yoruba 'Action Group' Leader of the Opposition in the Federal Parliament, who had first challenged northern conservatism in the 1950s, now espoused the cause of Pan-Africanism and African Socialism. After a split occurred, during an 'Action Group' convention in 1962, between Awolowo and Chief Akintola, the premier of the Western Region, who wanted to link up with the ruling federal coalition, fighting broke out in the Western House of Assembly, which led to the declaration of a State of Emergency. In November 1962 Awolowo and thirty of his followers were arrested for conspiring to overthrow the Nigerian government by force. After a controversial trial in 1963, and protesting his innocence, Awolowo was sentenced to ten years' imprisonment. Thus Nigeria became a Republic in 1963 amid a deceptive calm. Below the surface the regional tensions of the past decade still smouldered.

Nigerian unity was again threatened in December 1964 during the first general election since independence. The federal elections were fought between two 'alliances'. Sir Ahmadu Bello, premier of the Northern Region, led the 'Nigerian National Alliance', consisting of his own 'Northern People's Party', the Western premier Akintola's new 'Nigerian National Democratic Party' and the opposition parties in the Mid-west and Eastern regions. Dr Michael Okpara, premier of the Eastern Region, led the 'United Progressive Grand Alliance' consisting of his Ibo 'National Council of Nigerian Citizens', the 'Action Group', the 'United Middle-Belt Congress' and the opposition party in the north. The N.N.A. called for a continuance of responsible government under proven leaders, but the underlying issue of the election was tribal. Muslim northerners appealed to the Yorubas to prevent Ibo domination. The U.P.G.A. attacked northern Muslims as anti-democratic, anti-Christian, and anti-Pan-African.

In spite of broadcast appeals by President Azikiwe for national unity, the election became increasingly violent, particularly in the Western Region. Dr Okpara called for military supervision of the election, and threatened Eastern secession or a boycott of the election. In the event, only 4 million out of a 15-million electorate voted. Azikiwe tried to avoid calling a new government on the basis of the results. He contemplated resigning. But on 4 January 1965 he recalled Sir Abubakar Tafawa Balewa, and the opposition parties agreed to co-operate. Dr Okpara returned to power in the Eastern Region after supplementary elections in March 1965. A further period of deceptive calm began in Nigeria.

But in the Western Region the passions inflamed by the Akintola–Awolowo split, and the latter's imprisonment, left the future of peaceful democratic government in doubt. Premier Akintola pursued his opponents into the courts. His success in regional elections during October 1965 led to charges of election-'rigging' from the 'Action Group', and Okpara and the Federal Opposition. Rioting spread from Ibadan to the federal capital. The antagonisms which had dogged Nigerian politics since the first elections in 1951 culminated in an attempted military *coup* in 1966, which eliminated the conservative leaders and halted Nigerian parliamentary democracy.

Only three days after the Commonwealth Prime Ministers' Conference on Rhodesia, which was held in Lagos, 10–12 January 1966, on the initiative of Sir Abubakar Tafawa Balewa (and while President Azikiwe was in London for an operation), the Nigerian prime minister was kidnapped. On 15 January, Ibo junior officers of the army made a bid for power. Sir Ahmadu Bello, the Northern premier, and Chief Akintola, the Western premier, were assassinated, and a few days later it was known that Tafawa Balewa was dead. Although the *coup* failed, and the army asserted the government's authority, a remnant of the Federal Cabinet handed over power to

General Ironsi, a Nigerian who had taken over command of the army from an English general eleven months before.

Thus the aristocrats, who had dominated Nigerian politics, were swept from power and the parliamentary system was suspended. The death of Tafawa Balewa, who had emerged as a major Commonwealth statesman and was regarded as a notable moderate influence in Africa, was widely regretted. The new government was represented at the premier's funeral at Bauchi. Flags were ordered to be flown at half-mast on government buildings, by General Ironsi, the Sandhurst-educated professional soldier who now faced the task of restoring Nigeria's unity.

Sierra Leone and the Gambia

Sierra Leone and Gambia had older-established contacts with Britain than Ghana and Nigeria, but nationalism was much slower to develop. It is true that both colonies were represented at the National Congress of British West Africa in 1920, but special circumstances in each colony caused the members of the new *élite* to remain politically 'conservative'. The reason for this is clear: both possessions consisted of a small 'colony' set in the corner of a large 'protectorate' which had been created by the 'scramble for Africa'. For a long period in the nineteenth century Gambia was only an outpost of Sierra Leone, and was not finally detached until 1888.

Sierra Leone consisted of the original colony on the Freetown Peninsula, with certain additions, such as Sherbro Island, and a protectorate inland which was finally demarcated in 1895 and consisted of 27,000 square miles. The Gambia colony consisted of St Mary's Island (site of Bathurst) and a portion of Kombo on the river bank (less than thirty square miles in all) along with the protectorate (determined by an Anglo-French agreement in 1887) of 4,000 square miles consisting of 7-mile-wide strips of territory on either side of the river stretching inland for about 250 miles. In both protectorates, which made up the overwhelming bulk of the territory and population, the principles of Indirect Rule were adopted. As late as 1937 the Governor of the Gambia adopted Sir Donald Cameron's Tanganyika system for the protectorate.

Because of the great disparity between colony and protectorate in both Sierra Leone and Gambia, the sort of political advance usually demanded by the coastal *élite* would have meant the neglect of the majority of the population. It is significant that the successful popular political parties in both countries have come from the protectorates, which awoke (rather like the Muslim states in Northern Nigeria) to the threat of domination by Bathurst and Freetown.

In Sierra Leone this process was particularly marked, since, as we saw in Chapter 6, the new *élite* of the colony was the oldest on the west coast. Executive and legislative councils had been created there as early as 1863, and several notable Sierra Leonians had served on them. In 1924, in common with the Gold Coast and Nigeria, the legislative council received an elected element. The official majority remained, but beside eleven officials, seven nominated unofficial members and three elected members were added. The elected members represented the colony, but three of the nominated members were paramount chiefs from the protectorate, which thus received its first representation in the legislature. This constitution remained in force until after the 1939–45 war.

Unlike Ghana and Nigeria, however, Sierra Leone did not enter the post-war era with an impatient nationalist movement. When a new constitution was proposed in 1947 by Sir Hubert Stevenson, designed to redress the balance between the colony and the protectorate, the *élite* of the colony protested vigorously; not as in Ghana because the constitution was too conservative, but because it was too radical. Stevenson wanted the people of the whole country to be gradually granted power over their affairs. He proposed an elected majority in the legislative council with the protectorate receiving adequate representation. His proposal was bitterly opposed by the leaders of the 200,000 inhabitants of the colony, who formed the 'Sierra Leone National Council'. They maintained that it 'would be an abrogation of the democratic ideal to permit the illiterate masses of the Sierra Leone protectorate to overwhelm the advanced political element of the colony'. Thus political advance was delayed until 1951.

By then the leaders of the 2-million protectorate peoples had begun to organize. The 'Sierra Leone Organization Society', which had been formed by Dr Milton Margai, a doctor related to a chiefly family in the protectorate, merged with the 'People's Party' to form the 'Sierra Leone People's Party'. Elections were held for a new legislature with an unofficial majority. Seven officials remained in the council, but seven members were elected for the colony, twelve selected by protectorate district councils, and two were nominated by the governor and two nominated by the Protectorate Assembly. Dr Margai's party won a majority and six of its members were invited to join the executive council. After a year, a 'Ministerial system' was introduced, by which elected members were given the task of departmental spokesmen in the legislature. Dr Margai became Minister of Health. In 1954, as leader of the majority party, he was accorded the title of 'chief minister'.

A new constitution inaugurated in 1956 further increased the protectorate representation, extended the franchise to the majority of adult taxpayers, and paved the way for responsible government. The legislature now became the 'House of Representatives' with only four official and two nominated members, along with thirty-nine elected members – fourteen from the colony, twenty-five from the protectorate and twelve to represent the protectorate chiefs. In the 1957 election Dr Margai again secured a majority, and in the following year, when the officials withdrew from the executive council and the legislature, Sierra Leone received full responsible government. Sir Milton Margai (as he now became) was appointed the first 'prime minister'.

A constitutional conference held in London during the spring of 1960 made the arrangements for Sierra Leone's independence, which was declared on 27 April 1961. In the following year the S.L.P.P. consolidated its position in the first elections after independence. A Sierra Leonian, Sir Henry Lightfoot Boston, became Governor-General. On the death of Sir Milton Margai in 1964, his brother Albert, the protectorate's first barrister, succeeded to the premiership.

In the Gambia, meanwhile, similar later-starting, but then rapid, constitutional changes occurred. Here, although African representatives sat in the legislative council from 1915, a sense of nationalism or party politics did not really develop until 1960.

Before the 1939–45 war Gambian representation in the council was entirely nominated, by the business, Christian, and Muslim communities of the tiny colony and by the Bathurst Urban Council and the Commissioner for the Protectorate. In 1946 an unofficial majority was permitted. Besides six officials, there were two representatives of the colony, four from the protectorate, and one each elected for Bathurst and Kombo. A year later three unofficial members were added to the executive council. A series of small personality-dominated political parties began in the 1950s: the 'Democratic Party', the Muslim 'Congress Party' and the 'United Party'. Therefore in 1953 the governor called a meeting, rather as in Ghana and Nigeria, to consult Gambian opinion about future constitutional advance. Thirty-four ex-members of the legislative council took part. Their work bore fruit in the 1954 constitution, which provided for an elected majority in the council. Seven officials remained, but there were fourteen elected members – seven each from the colony and the protectorate. At the same time an unofficial majority was admitted in the executive council, by nomination after the governor had consulted with the elected members of the legislative council. A modified form of 'dyarchy' was then tried with three of the unofficials acting as 'Heads of Ministries'.

After this comparatively smooth development, and with self-government spreading rapidly throughout West Africa, the colonial secretary, Alan Lennox-Boyd, visited Bathurst in 1959 to discuss arrangements for self-government in the Gambia. After the first general election in 1960 a 'House of Representatives' met, with an elected majority. A 'Ministerial system' began in the Executive Council, where six unofficial members became Ministers, co-ordinated by P. S. M'Jie, leader of the United Party, as 'chief minister'. But the most important step in the Gambia's progress towards full self-government was the development of a truly popular party.

In 1960 the 'Progressive People's Party' emerged, led by David Jawara, a veterinary officer of protectorate origins. As the proportion of protectorate seats in the legislature was increased, as in Sierra Leone, so the P.P.P. increased its power. In 1960 it won eight out of twelve seats; in 1962, seventeen out of twenty-five. When responsible government was granted after the 1962 election Jawara became the Gambia's first 'prime minister'. Thereafter the independence of the last British possession in tropical Africa was simply a matter of administrative organization and timing. On 18 February 1965 the British flag was lowered from the place where Elizabethan adventurers first visited West Africa four centuries before.

12

The New Commonwealth: the Failure to Achieve Unity in East and Central Africa

VARIOUS VICTORIAN attempts to unite the governments of the West African colonies failed. The four separate nations of the present are the result. In the east, the acquisition of the former German colony of Tanganyika in 1918 gave Britain her 'all red' band of territory from the Nile to the Limpopo. But unity in what came to be called East and Central Africa proved elusive. The reason is not far to seek. British expansion in this region sprang from two entirely different motives. In the north, the desire to control the Nile led to the Zanzibar, Uganda and British East African protectorates. In the south, Rhodes's determination to encircle the Transvaal and Salisbury's pursuit of paramountcy in South Africa, led to the Bechuanaland Protectorate, the chartering of the British South Africa Company and the creation of the British Central African Protectorate (later Nyasaland). North of Tanganyika, British interests were primarily official and strategic. To the south, the driving force was the private colonizing and mineral-prospecting venture of Rhodes. The interposition of the German territory between the two groups of British possessions until 1918 prevented the achievement of the 'all red' route and underlined the separateness of the two spheres of British interest.

The acquisition of the mandate over Tanganyika, while giving a superficial link between all the British territories, in the long run served to accentuate their division. By adopting the policy of 'indirect administration' and clearly accepting the primacy of African interests, Tanganyika – the largest single territory – ensured that the settler minorities in Kenya were not able to dominate the East African possessions. Although Kenya, Uganda and Tanganyika began to share certain common services, such as railways, posts and telegraphs, all attempts to federate or unite them failed because of African fears of the Kenya settlers.

In the territories of the British South Africa Company the opposite trend nearly succeeded. Settlers from South Africa and from Britain were attracted to the upland regions of Southern Rhodesia and, to a lesser extent, to Northern Rhodesia and Nyasaland. When the charter was given up in 1923 the settlers faced the choice of responsible government or incorporation in the Union of South Africa. They chose the former. Thenceforth, settler interests, rather than African interests, prevailed in Southern Rhodesia, which even led on to the short-lived federation of the Rhodesias and Nyasaland in the 1950s. By this time, however, the forces of African nationalism in West Africa, then East Africa, had become so strong that Britain was forced to dissolve the federation. Instead of the two large 'Dominions', which had been envisaged in the 1920s, independent African states were created in Tanganyika (later Tanzania), Uganda, Kenya, Zambia, Malawi and Botswana (former Bechuanaland). Southern Rhodesia alone remained a settler-dominated region. By granting the white minority the widest measure of internal self-government in 1923 the British government applied a liberal Victorian colonial policy in a way which contradicted her twentieth-century doctrine of trusteeship practised elsewhere. Thus, Southern Rhodesia became the great anomaly in Britain's voluntary dismantling of her African empire. By failing to prevent the settler régime from declaring independence illegally in 1965, the British government faced the entire Commonwealth with the greatest crisis of its existence.

EAST AFRICA

Since Britain acquired her East African empire for 'external' reasons unconnected with the potential merits of the region, it is hardly surprising that she adopted three quite different policies there. In Uganda the Kabaka of Buganda was confirmed as direct ruler of his people under British 'protection and overrule'. In Kenya, after British settlers were introduced into the healthy highlands, a series of contradictory policy statements followed. In Tanganyika 'indirect administration' was introduced into a territory where there were no predominant African states but more than a hundred tribes. Here the inhabitants were not to be turned into 'bad imitations of Europeans' but into 'good

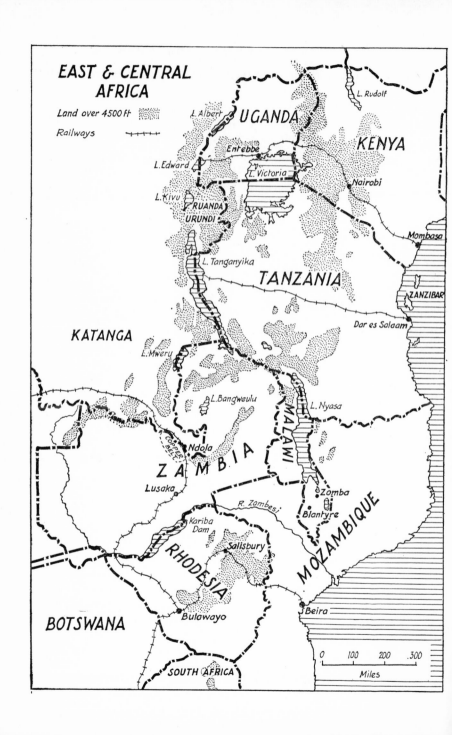

EAST & CENTRAL
AFRICA

Land over 4500 ft
Railways

Africans'. These contradictory policies reflected the piecemeal growth of British rule.

The Uganda Protectorate

In Uganda the power of the ruling aristocracy was entrenched. This reflected the government's fundamental lack of interest in the area. The Imperial British East Africa Company's sphere had been created in order to keep other powers from the upper Nile. When the Company wished to withdraw from the Kingdom of Buganda in 1891 humanitarians urged the government to step in to preserve a balance between warring Uganda kingdoms whose rivalries had become entangled with those of Protestantism, Catholicism and Islam. In 1894 the Uganda protectorate was proclaimed. Lord Salisbury's commitment to build a railway 650 miles inland from Mombasa to Lake Victoria as part of his Nile strategy gave the government an interest in the territory lying between Uganda and Zanzibar, which in 1895 became the East African protectorate. The original boundary between the two new protectorates lay along the Rift Valley, which traverses the entire region just to the west of modern Nairobi. In 1900 Sir Harry Johnston was sent to report on the future of the region.

Johnston's Uganda Agreement of 1900, signed with the King of Buganda, the Kabaka, laid the foundations of the dual system known as 'overrule'. Within Buganda, which Johnston called the 'kingdom of Uganda', the administration and jurisdiction of the Kabaka's dynasty continued, with the advice of the prime minister, the Katikiri, a Chief Justice and Treasurer, and his Council, or Lukiko, which included twenty district chiefs. In return for confirming the ruling aristocracy in power and recognizing their lands as freehold, Johnston secured Britain's right to conduct defence and external relations, he took all waste lands (half the protectorate) in the name of the Crown, and secured the right to levy taxes. Thus Buganda became an autonomous kingdom within the Uganda Protectorate. Elsewhere although the chiefs of Toro, Ankole and Bunyoro were recognized they received a less privileged position, and a protectorate administration was created under British officers. So jealous was Buganda of its rights that when a legislative council was created in 1920 Buganda refused to send representatives.

Kenya

In the East African Protectorate, Johnston, who assumed that the two protectorates would be governed together, suggested that Indian and European immigration should be encouraged. With the completion of the railway to Lake Victoria the Foreign Office decided in 1902 to add the eastern part of Uganda to the East African Protectorate so that the railways would all be under one government. Sir Charles Eliot, the first Commissioner, began to encourage settlers in order to make the railway pay its way. Soon the basic ambiguity of British policy in East Africa became evident. Eliot advertised in South Africa, Australia, New Zealand and Canada for settlers, and Lord Delamere was the first of a number of aristocratic adventurers who responded. By the time Eliot retired in 1904 he was writing of the 'paramountcy of white interests'. But the Foreign Office, shortly before handing over control to the Colonial Office in 1905, instructed Sir Donald Stewart, the second Commissioner, that the 'primary duty' of government in East Africa was the welfare of the local African peoples. Unfortunately these instructions were not published and so the East African Protectorate became known as a 'white man's country'.

This public inconsistency about East Africa continued for many years. A legislative council was created in 1906, which included some nominated unofficial members. There were then about 600 settlers, which led Winston Churchill, the parliamentary under-secretary in the Colonial Office, to remark that 'never before in Colonial experience has a Council been granted when the number of settlers is so few'. On a visit to the growing town of Nairobi on the railway, Churchill noted the problem of racial discord between settlers, Indian railway workers and the original inhabitants. He pointed out that the protectorate was not solely a white man's country, that the Indians had a role, and he reminded the settlers of the Africans, since it was '*their* Africa'. Yet in spite of such official caution by the home government, the settlers achieved complete adult franchise for legislative council elections in 1919. And General Sir Edward Northey, the governor at the end of the 1914–18 war, announced that 'this country was primarily for European development. . . . European interests must be paramount throughout the Protectorate.'

Northey's removal and the creation of the Kenya Colony in 1920 failed to remove the ambiguity of Britain's aims. On the one hand, the agitations of Harry Thuku, secretary of the Young Kikuyu Association, and M. A. Desai, an Indian newspaper editor, indicated the first political stirrings among the non-European majority. On the other hand, Delamere and the settlers petitioned for full self-government. What policy should Britain follow? The answer was never really made clear until 1960. Winston Churchill, as colonial secretary in 1922, announced that he did not anticipate preventing Kenya from becoming 'a distinctly British Colony looking forward in the full fruition of time to complete responsible self-government'. But in the following year missionary influence in Britain forced Churchill's successor, the Duke of Devonshire, to publish his celebrated White Paper declaring: 'Primarily Kenya is an African territory.' The interests of the inhabitants were to be 'paramount'. The first modest step to fulfil this aim was taken in 1924 by adding the Rev. J. W. Arthur to the legislative council to represent African interests.

Tanganyika

In Tanganyika such ambiguity was avoided. Sir Donald Cameron, who became governor in 1925, had served under Lugard in Nigeria, and he determined to introduce a form of 'indirect administration', as he called it, in Tanganyika, which would be 'more liberal' from the people's point of view than the Nigerian system. Although European settlers were encouraged to take up land where it was available and a legislative council was created in 1926, with nominated unofficial members who were all Europeans, Cameron made it clear that Britain's presence in Tanganyika was temporary. African interests were, he declared, 'dominant and should remain dominant . . . the European is the experimental factor'. He announced that the mandate in Tanganyika was not absolute. Britain would rule only until the people 'can stand by themselves'. He promulgated a series of ordinances designed to give tribal authorities in Tanganyika administrative, judicial and financial functions, and, most significant, he stressed the duty of chiefs to maintain 'peace, good order and welfare', and the tribal Treasuries. 'We must not, in fact, destroy the African atmosphere, the African mind, the whole foundation of his race,' insisted Cameron, 'and we shall certainly do this if we sweep away all his tribal foundations.'

The Closer Union Controversy

Cameron's idealistic régime in Tanganyika marked a significant divide in East Africa. For the first time serious thought was given to Britain's future policy in the region. The 1920s and 1930s saw more

U

conferences, commissions, reports, committees and White Papers on East Africa than on any other part of the empire. Most of the controversy centred on the idea of 'Closer Union' or federation in East Africa.

Johnston had originally assumed that Uganda and Kenya would be governed as one. The award of the mandate for Tanganyika quickened the discussion. Churchill mooted the idea, after the 1914–18 war, that Kenya, Uganda and Tanganyika might be united. Delamere and the Kenya settlers were anxious to create a new 'Dominion' and wanted to scotch the extension of the influence of what they called the 'west coast school', which they saw evident in Uganda and Tanganyika. The Kenya settlers, who now numbered about 9,000, assumed that 'Closer Union' would be based on 'the radiation of the civilization of Kenya' and would involve responsible government for the settlers like that granted to Southern Rhodesia. The Europeans also feared intervention by the League of Nations Mandates Commission. Their cause was taken up by Leopold Amery in 1927, rather as his son Julian was to support the Southern Rhodesians in 1965. Amery convened a series of governors' conferences to explore the possibility of union. But Cameron of Tanganyika stood firmly by the doctrine of trusteeship. He opposed giving the Kenya settlers any powers over Tanganyika.

By the end of the 1920s the 'Closer Union' project had awakened a great deal of interest in British East Africa. Lord Passfield, the secretary of state in the Labour government in 1929, at last gave a clear announcement that, while responsible government was the goal in Kenya, as elsewhere, it must be defined as 'a ministry representing an electorate in which every section of the population finds an effective and adequate voice'. Meanwhile 'ultimate decisions and final control' rested with the British government. In 1931 a joint Select Committee of Parliament brought to an end all the speculation and closed the possibility of a settler-dominated state in Kenya. Cameron reiterated the view that Tanganyika must remain separate and might go on to be a model 'mixed state'. The Kabaka of Buganda sent a memorandum insisting that if Uganda went into a 'Closer Union', Buganda would have to be excluded. The idea of an 'East African Dominion' was dead.

All that remained was technical co-operation. Tanganyika joined a customs union with Kenya and Uganda in 1933. A joint Postmaster-General was appointed, followed by a transport co-ordinator. Co-operation in economic and technical matters increased during the

1939–45 war. Finally in 1948 the 'East African High Commission' was created, with a Central Legislative Assembly consisting of ten officials and thirteen unofficial members. But the High Commission was a strictly non-political organization with authority only over the jointly operated railways, harbours, aviation services and research.

This was a far cry from the 'Closer Union' and Dominion Status dreamt of by the Kenya settlers after the 1914–18 war. Although early in the 1950s the Conservative colonial secretary, Oliver Lyttelton, made certain hints that federation might be possible in East Africa, long-standing African suspicions of 'Closer Union' prevented a British-sponsored federation. Even the federal projects of African nationalists have so far failed. The founding in 1958 of the 'Pan-African Freedom Movement for East and Central Africa' and the offer in 1960 by Julius Nyerere that he might postpone Tanganyika's independence, in order to gain it as part of an East African federation, revived the idea of unity. In 1963 the leaders of Kenya, Uganda and Tanganyika pledged themselves to 'the political federation of East Africa' but the disparity of wealth, needs and social conditions of the three territories have so far prevented its fulfilment. Independence in East Africa was, in fact, achieved by individual states.

Political Development in Tanganyika

Tanganyika was the first portion of the East African empire to receive its independence for two reasons. Firstly, Cameron's clear announcement that Britain's presence was temporary and that African interests predominated was not doubted. Tanganyika was never a conventional British colony. Secondly, as a former League of Nations mandate, Tanganyika became, in 1946, a United Nations Trust Territory. Here Britain was accountable to the U.N. for her trusteeship and she announced at the outset that the goal would be self-government or independence. Moreover, a series of U.N. missions visited the territory in 1948, 1951, 1954, 1957 and 1960, which tended to prod the British régime. The United Nations gave the nationalists of Tanganyika a useful forum. Thus from 1945, when the first four Africans were appointed to the legislative council, until the grant of responsible government in 1960, followed by independence a year later, political progress in Tanganyika was peaceful and steady.

In 1948 four unofficial members were added to the executive council (three of them Europeans, one Indian, but as yet no Africans). A

'Member system' was inaugurated whereby council members were made responsible to the governor for groups of departments. But the mission from the U.N. in the same year, although realizing that Tanganyika was not ready for independence, was critical of the British régime. At the same time the small, twenty-year-old, middle-class 'Tanganyika African Association' demanded extension of the franchise. Therefore, in 1949, Sir Edward Twining, the governor, formed a Committee on Constitutional Reform, which set going the process of constitutional change. It first bore fruit in the constitution of 1955.

Twining appealed for multi-racial partnership in Tanganyika. A system of 'balanced representation' was tried for several years. When Africans were first admitted to the executive council in 1954, the unofficial members were 'balanced' by appointing two Africans, two Europeans and two Asians. Under the 1955 constitution the legislative council was enlarged and the government and the Europeans retained a majority of one. On the government side there were twenty-five officials, and the six unofficial members of the executive council. Of the thirty unofficial members of the legislature, twenty-seven represented nine constituencies – each of which received an Asian, an African and a European member. The remaining three were general members, one from each community. At first the representative members were nominated by the governor. But the first election, with a common roll, and with each voter electing three candidates, was planned for 1958.

The period before the first election was one of rapid political preparation. As Europeans bowed to the inevitable increase of non-European representation, Asians and Africans began to organize. In 1954 the 'Asian Association' of Dar-es-Salaam looked forward to a non-racial, secular state and supported the idea of balanced representation. In the same year the formation of the 'Tanganyika African National Union' laid the foundation of Tanganyika's first mass political party. It evolved from the old Tanganyika African Association, which began in the 1920s, and, like its contemporaries elsewhere, was a small society, appealing to the educated élite of teachers and civil servants. Like the Indian National Congress it was formed by British civil servants. By the end of the 1950s its membership was about 5,000 and its organization lacked vitality.

In 1953, however, the association elected as President, Julius

Nyerere, a 32-year-old son of a chief, a Roman Catholic and a qualified teacher, who had recently returned from Edinburgh University, where he was the first Tanganyikan to graduate from a British university. Nyerere, although an ascetic looking figure, proved to be a commanding personality and a brilliant political organizer. T.A.N.U.'s aim was defined as racial equality, self-government and independence. Nyerere became a full time politician and soon built up the Union to a million members. He appealed before the United Nations for the acceleration of political advance, and while accepting the ideal of non-racialism and being prepared to work the 'balanced representation' system, he stressed that Tanganyika was an African state. While some of the European unofficials set up a rival organization, outsiders were greatly impressed by T.A.N.U.'s moderation. Attempts by Europeans and Asians to form multi-racial parties failed to gain mass support in Tanganyika. In the first election in 1958, T.A.N.U. won all the twelve contested seats. Their success was underlined when the governor opened the new legislative council by emphasizing that non-racial policies would not mean that under self-government both legislature and administration would not be 'predominantly African'.

Gradually, therefore, the machinery of responsible government, with more and more African representation, was built up. In 1957 a form of 'ministerial system' had been started in the executive council. Nine officials and seven unofficial members (including one African, a chief) became ministers responsible for departments, and six unofficials in the legislative council were appointed assistant ministers to represent departments in the council, rather like parliamentary under-secretaries. Nyerere was nominated as a member for Dar-es-Salaam in 1957, and after his party's election success in the following year became chairman of the 'Elected Members Organization'. While pressing for more rapid political advance he always appealed for communal peace. Thus by 1959 the executive council became a 'Council of Ministers' and some unofficial members received ministerial office. Full responsible government was soon announced and at the end of the year, Lord Perth, the parliamentary under-secretary, admitted that 'sooner or later we have to take the plunge with all our territories in Africa'.

After a second election in 1960 an elected majority was accepted in the Council of Ministers and T.A.N.U. won seventy out of seventy-one elected seats in the legislature. A form of responsible government was then inaugurated with Nyerere as 'chief minister', in the dual role of adviser to the governor on policy and 'leader of government business' in the council. His government took office on 3 September 1960, and soon began to make the arrangements for independence.

A constitutional conference was held in Dar-es-Salaam in March 1961 attended by Iain Macleod, the colonial secretary. Immediately afterwards independence was announced for the same year. Nyerere became the first 'prime minister' when full internal self-government was conceded in May. The Council of Ministers became the 'Cabinet' (composed of nine Africans, two Europeans and one Asian). The governor retained responsibility for external affairs and defence. This was but a short interim system. On 8 December 1961 independence was proclaimed. Tanganyika became the first Commonwealth state in East Africa and a year later became a Republic. Since independence Nyerere, like Nkrumah in West Africa, has continued to stand out in favour of the Pan-African ideal and also against racial discrimination. His article in *The Observer* on 5 March 1961, stating that Tanganyika would not remain in the Commonwealth if South Africa continued as a member, helped to precipitate the crisis which led to South Africa's withdrawal. Similarly, the Southern Rhodesian illegal declaration of independence in 1965 found President Nyerere, predictably, leading the movement for severing diplomatic relations with Britain.

Political Development in Uganda

If Tanganyika's progress to independence was comparatively smooth because of the small European population and the lack of any pre-eminent African kingdom, Uganda's development was complicated by the privileged position of the Kingdom of Buganda. Here the progress of the whole Uganda Protectorate to democratic self-government was checked for a time by the jealousy of Buganda, and to a lesser extent, of the other Uganda kingdoms. At the same time, within Buganda, the Kabaka's régime incurred opposition from those elements which resented the aristocratic privileges (particularly relating to land) which were entrenched in the 1900 Agreement. In the late 1940s these opposition forces indulged in violence. Thus, British policy in Uganda after the 1939–45 war was directed towards the dual goal of revising Buganda's relations with the Protectorate and encouraging the Kabaka to permit more democratic government within Buganda. For this reason the first big crisis in Uganda came, not from African nationalists, but from a form of 'tribal reaction'.

In 1952 Sir Andrew Cohen, from the African department of the Colonial Office, was appointed governor of Uganda. Discovering no strong nationalist movement, like those in West Africa, he feared that if the anti-colonial movement developed on tribal lines, the Uganda Protectorate would enter the era of self-government in a disrupted condition. Therefore Cohen decided to introduce on his own initiative the sort of constitutional reforms that were being demanded by nationalists elsewhere. He appointed six unofficial members to the executive council (including two Africans); he increased the proportion of representative members in the legislative council from sixteen to twenty-eight (half of them Africans); and he added ten un-officials (including six Africans) who were only expected to support the government on matters of confidence. At the same time he persuaded the Kabaka of Buganda to admit a form of responsible government in his state, by allowing a proportion of the Lukiko to be elected, by consulting it before appointing ministers, and by giving it wider responsibilities. In this way, Buganda's institutions were given a real administrative role, which Cohen hoped would enable Buganda to play an increasing part in a modernized Uganda, which could develop towards self-government as a unitary state.

Unfortunately, however, Uganda's political parties were, as yet, under-developed, and the Baganda were not anxious for reforms. Indeed, the Kabaka, Mutesa II, was in an invidious position. This 29-year-old, Cambridge-educated, monarch, was not popular. He took note of the probable fate of many traditional rulers in West Africa. Now he appeared as a tool of the British government in revising Buganda's constitution. He returned from the Coronation in 1953, resentful at receiving less diplomatic honours than the Queen of Tonga and the Sultan of Zanzibar, to find Buganda up in arms following a statement by the secretary of state that Uganda might be joined in a federation with Kenya and Tanganyika. Mutesa's patience broke. He refused to accept an assurance about federation; demanded that Buganda should be dealt with through the Foreign Office; and called for the publication of a time-table for Buganda's independence. When he refused to give an undertaking that he would accept the decisions of Her Majesty's Government and agree to Buganda's co-operation in the future development of the protectorate, he was removed from the throne and deported to London.

The Kabaka's deportation became a focus for anti-colonial

sentiment in Uganda. Even the 'Uganda National Congress' (formed in 1952), which had little success in Buganda, took up the cause of the Kabaka's recall. In many ways the Buganda crisis played a formative role in Uganda's political development. In 1954 the secretary of state appointed a committee under Sir Keith Hancock to investigate the issue, and at the same time made the first clear announcement that the goal in Uganda was self-government. Sir Andrew Cohen, the governor, made a remarkable gesture by agreeing to sit with Professor Hancock's committee to discuss the future. Here a new system was worked out by which Buganda was to receive a modified form of responsible government in which Ministers would be responsible to the Kabaka, who was recognized as a 'symbol of unity'. Buganda received assurances that it would not be pushed into an East Africa Federation. It had also forced the Colonial Office to announce that Uganda would become an African state. In return, the governor received assurances that Buganda would co-operate in the development of the Uganda Protectorate and would participate in the legislative council.

Under these terms the Kabaka was allowed to return. By implication the compromise determined that Uganda would have a federal constitution. The settlement was accompanied by constitutional advance in Uganda as a whole. In 1955 a form of 'Ministerial system' was created, and of the eleven ministers five were unofficial (three of these African, one European and one Asian). A civil servant, the Chief Secretary, still led the government in the legislative council, on which the African representative members were increased and the Europeans and Asian reduced. The government still maintained a majority through its African nominated members.

Unfortunately, political evolution in Uganda was dogged by the continuing lack of enthusiasm of Buganda and by the failure of the political parties. In 1957 the Buganda representatives withdrew from the legislative council, because they thought the election of a Speaker implied an acceleration of constitutional advance. After the first elections for the African representative seats in 1958 the 'Uganda National Congress' split up. Thus, the governor set the pace again, by slightly increasing the number of Africans in the executive council and on the government benches of the legislative council, and he appointed a Constitutional Committee headed by a civil servant, J. V. Wild, to consider plans for a general election in 1961. Buganda boycotted the committee but in 1959 it recommended that the only way to encourage genuine political development would be to call general elections on the basis of universal adult suffrage and communal electoral rolls, make the legislative council largely elective, and turn the executive council into a 'Council of Ministers', presided over by a 'chief minister', and responsible to the legislature. Only then would political parties be given an incentive for organization in order to assume 'a real share of the responsibility of government'.

The 'Wild Report' was followed by long-drawn-out negotiations between the Colonial Office and the Uganda kingdoms, which all had reservations. In Buganda a group of conservative political organizations merged to form the 'Uganda National Movement', which gained no support outside Buganda, but which attracted most political bodies in Buganda, except the Roman Catholic 'Democratic Party', founded in 1956. As the Buganda conservatives linked together, so the political parties in the rest of the protectorate merged in February 1960 to form the 'Uganda People's Congress', with Milton Obote as leader. Obote was a 35-year-old graduate of Makerere College, and had returned to Uganda three years earlier after working in Kenya, where he had come under the influence of nationalist politicians during the Mau Mau rebellion.

The first general elections were held in Uganda in March 1961 and although the Uganda People's Congress polled the largest number of votes, the Democratic Party won a majority of seats in the legislative council because it won some Buganda seats when many of the voters boycotted the elections. Thus Uganda's first 'Chief Minister' was Benedicto Kiwanuka, a barrister, who led the Democratic Party. Obote became leader of the opposition.

Now, as Uganda had the main elements of a parliamentary system (despite Buganda's non-co-operation), the round of constitutional planning for self-government and independence began. A commission under Lord Munster reported in July 1961 on the question of the relationship of the Uganda kingdoms: it recommended that Buganda's relationship should be federal, and that of the other kingdoms should be 'semi-federal'. A full constitutional conference was held in London in September 1961 which agreed that after new elections a 'prime minister' should be appointed and a 'Cabinet' (with an official as Attorney-General) be made responsible to a 'National Assembly' consisting of ninety-one elected members. Buganda's twenty-one members would be elected by the Lukiko and the Buganda government was given autonomy over courts, police, schools, hospitals and crop marketing. Bunyoro, Ankole, and Toro retained their rulers but received no administrative autonomy.

The new constitution was inaugurated on 1 March 1962, when Kiwanuka took office as the first prime minister, with a Cabinet of twelve Africans, one European and one Indian. In the general election of 1962 Obote's 'Uganda's People's Congress' won a majority by making an alliance with 'Kabaka Yekka', a Buganda party. Milton Obote became prime minister and invited four Baganda into the Cabinet in order to create national unity. Consultations were held in the Colonial Office in January 1962 to confirm the arrangements for Uganda's independence, which was proclaimed on 9 October 1962. For one year Uganda remained a sovereign state, recognizing the Crown as Head of State, but on 9 October 1963 Uganda's Head of State became the 'President of Uganda'. As if to symbolize the ending of the decade of tension the first President was Mutesa II, the Kabaka of Buganda. Thus, while Uganda politics continued to be dominated by disputes concerning the old Uganda Kingdoms Dr Obote, the prime minister, did his best to reconcile the interests of the old African aristocracy and the rising African democracy.

The political truce which accompanied independence was short-lived. After a few months Obote was accusing the opposition of 'irresponsible conduct', and he hinted that Uganda might have to become a one-party state. By the end of 1964 he had gone a long way towards achieving this goal. The Kabaka Yekka withdrew from the coalition to join the opposition in August, while in December the leader of the opposition Democratic Party and five of his main supporters crossed to join the government. In 1965, therefore, the Kabaka Yekka had emerged as the chief opposition party in Uganda. President and premier became political opponents. Tension between Buganda and the central government resumed as in the colonial era.

Thus, by the beginning of 1966, there was serious disquiet in Uganda. On 24 February Obote suspended the 1962 constitution, abolished the Presidency, and assumed full executive powers, when he feared that the Kabaka was plotting to overthrow the government with the use of foreign troops. When the Uganda Parliament was recalled in April 1966 it formally accepted an interim constitution providing for an executive President with strong powers. Milton Obote was sworn-in as President and declared: 'No federation in Uganda. It will be one people.' The historical position of Buganda thus continued to dominate Uganda politics, and secession and civil war could well follow.

Political Development in Kenya

Although Kenya was the wealthiest and most highly developed of the East African colonies and though it was there that the first nationalist movement developed, progress towards independence lagged behind that of her poorer relations. The reason is not far to seek. Kenya's wealth was based upon the agriculture of the 'white highlands', where the settler population continued to rise and to exercise an important influence on the colonial government. This made Dominion status, based on majority rule, impossible for many years.

The 1914–18 war brought the majority of Kenyans little of the hope experienced by many Asians and Africans. Instead the settlers, who numbered a few thousand, obtained laws safeguarding racial segregation in the Highlands, imposing registration of Africans, providing for elections to a 'War Council' and a promise of elections to the legislative council after the war. In 1919 all adult Europeans received the franchise and in the same year they received a governor who supported their interests and evolved what he called 'government by agreement'. The government co-operated with the elected members and Governor Northey appointed two of them to the executive council as 'members of the Government'. In spite of the announcement about the paramountcy of African interests and the future goal of an African state in 1923, the settlers were, for the immediate future, in a strong position. In their movement for 'Closer Union' they had powerful supporters in Britain. Leopold Amery spoke of sharing responsibility for trusteeship with the Europeans. Even the Hilton Young Commission in 1929, which reiterated the paramountcy of African interests, suggested that the immigrant communities (British and Asian) could justly claim 'partnership' though not control. Throughout the 1920s and 1930s, as African political organizations developed and British humanitarians upheld the paramountcy issue, politics in the Kenya legislative council was a settler concern. An Indian was nominated to the legislative council in 1909. African interests were represented by nominated missionaries from 1924.

No African was appointed to the legislative council until 1944, but from the 1920s African political organizations, like those elsewhere, began to develop at the tribal and occupational level. The commissions and debates about the future of the colony quickened African political awareness, most notably among the Kikuyu of central Kenya. In 1920 a Kikuyu Association, mainly chiefs, took up the question of preserving tribal lands. In the following year the 'Young Kikuyu Association', led by Harry Thuku, took up the cause of African labourers. When Thuku was arrested in 1922 violence broke out and over twenty Africans were shot by the police. But the organization continued as the 'Kikuyu Central Association', whose general secretary, Jomo Kenyatta, became the leading figure of Kikuyu nationalism.

Kenyatta, formerly named Kamauwa Ngengi, was born about 1893 and educated at a mission. He worked as a minor government servant for a time and then took up the fight of the Kikuyu for their lands and social customs. By the later 1920s he was editing a Kikuyu-language newspaper and had visited Britain to petition for Kikuyu schools. In 1931 he returned to Britain as a student at Selly Oak, in Birmingham, then at the London School of Oriental and African Studies and the London School of Economics. For a time he went to Moscow University. He associated with members of the international movements for Negro rights such as Paul Robeson, the American, Peter Abrahams, from South Africa, George Padmore, of the West Indies, and Nkrumah, from the Gold Coast. After attending the 1945 Pan-African Congress at Manchester he returned to Kenya in 1946 to find many Kenyans experiencing the same post-war frustrations and unemployment and lack of political expression that we have noticed in places like the Gold Coast.

Kenyatta requested nomination to the legislative council but was rebuffed by the Governor. Thus in 1947 he took over the leadership of the recently formed 'Kenya African Union' and began to exert his influence through the old Kikuyu organizations, the African pentecostal churches, and particularly through the Kikuyu schools after he took over control of Githunguri Teachers Training College. While he had been in Britain Kenyatta was regarded as a moderate. His relationship with the more violent elements of the Kikuyu was not easy to determine, but certainly he was by no means a blind demagogue. He forcefully pleaded for African self-help, honesty, efficient husbandry and co-operation with the government. What hope did the government, for its part, hold out for constructive co-operation?

As in the Gold Coast and elsewhere, the constitutional develop-ments of the post-war years were so modest that the Kenyan nationalist movement became more and more violent. By the 1950s it developed into the worst civil war of Britain's disengagement from Africa. Politics remained settler-dominated. Indeed, the association of European unofficials with the government in wartime Boards had created a precedent for the idea of unofficial 'Ministers' after the war. Thus, when Sir Philip Mitchell, who became governor in 1944, reorganized the executive council, he provided for a 'Member system' in which seven official 'Ministers' were joined by three European and one Indian unofficial members. One European 'unofficial' was actually appointed a Minister. In the legislative council the interests of the majority African population had been represented by nominated Europeans, usually missionaries. Not until 1944 did the first nominated African take a seat in the person of Eliud Mathu, a Balliol-educated Kikuyu. Two years later a Luo, J. B. Ohanga, joined him. Mitchell was also prepared for modest reforms. The governor ceased to preside over the legislative council and a Speaker was appointed. By reducing the officials in the council to fifteen and increasing the unofficial element to twenty-two he permitted an unofficial majority. But of these unofficial members, eleven were elected Europeans, five elected Indians, one elected Arab, along with four nominated Africans. The first elections held under the 'Mitchell Constitution' in 1948 still did not apply to the African majority of the country, in spite of Kenyatta's agitation and the growth of the Kenya African Union.

The visit of the inexperienced Labour colonial secretary, James Griffiths, in 1951, failed to change the general course of Kenya's politics. The 'Kenya African Union' pointed out to him the absurdity of four nominated members representing 5 million inhabitants and it asked for eight more African members to be elected according to a common electoral roll for all races. They also called for equality in the executive council, for an end to racial discrimination, including the opening of the 'white highlands', and for the expansion of education. But the sole result of the Griffiths mission was an announcement that European parity would be maintained for some years – although not permanently. One African was appointed to the executive council, and the legislative council was enlarged to provide six African seats – but the Europeans were raised to fourteen, the Asians to six, and the Arabs to two.

In view of these meagre constitutional changes and the lack of a clear goal, the rising tide of violence in Kenya in the early 1950s may be compared with the situation which had developed elsewhere. But in Kenya the violence took its own unique form. Among the Kikuyu, the taking of tribal, semi-religious oaths, and the importance of relationships within age-groups, provided a fertile soil for intimidation. Strange religious cults and attempts to revive ancient tribal practices had long been common. In 1948 news spread of the movement called 'Mau Mau' in which members were joined by oaths often of a frightening, and in some cases, of a perverted nature, and then went on to commit acts of intimidation, violence and murder. Although no regular military campaign was waged by Mau Mau, outbursts of murder and even the massacre of villages took place. Kenyatta denounced Mau Mau in a speech in 1951, but circumstantial evidence seemed to suggest that he controlled the movement: it began shortly after his return to Kenya; it was prevalent among the Kikuyu, his own people; its activities intensified in the regions he visited. Although no one really knows yet the inside story of Mau Mau, except the participants, in 1952 Kenyatta was detained under emergency regulations. Later he was sentenced for seven years.

From 1952 to 1960 there existed in Kenya a State of Emergency, which at one stage developed into a virtual civil war. Unlike the jungle war in Malaya, the Mau Mau uprising seriously damaged the movement towards self-government and a democratic party system. From 1953 to 1955 African political organizations were proscribed and then they were only permitted for a time at the local level. This break, followed by restriction, only accentuated trends in Kenyan African politics, which had existed ever since the 1920s, for organizations to be primarily tribal in character. Chronic disunity soon became one of Kenya's most serious problems.

The Emergency, in removing the main African nationalist leaders from the scene, quietened the political atmosphere. In 1954, for example, over 20,000 Africans were rounded up. But the general effect of the Mau Mau uprising was unmistakable. Although the Emergency prolonged the period of settler dominance in the legislative council, it provided a severe warning to the British government. As the Commander-in-Chief of the British security forces declared in public, Mau Mau presented more than a problem of law and order. Political solutions were needed. Thus in the 1950s a series of piecemeal constitutional changes were made, which in the eyes of African nationalists appeared as mere 'tinkering' with the existing system. No clear goal was set out. But to the settlers, all the constitutional changes were bitter pills, which culminated in the great Macleod 'betrayal' of 1960.

The preliminary stages may be summarized briefly. Under the 'Lyttelton Constitution' of 1954 a 'Ministerial system' began. The intention was a multi-racial 'Council of Ministers' consisting of six officials and six unofficials (three Europeans, two Asians and one African). Most of the African politicians boycotted the scheme, but eventually J. B. Ohanga accepted office as Minister of Community Affairs. The legislative council was changed little and stood at ten nominated members, fourteen European elected members, and six Asian and six African elected members. The majority of Africans remained aloof in their disappointment, while the Europeans split between Michael Blundell's 'United Country Party', which was ready to work with a multi-racial constitution, and Commodore Briggs's 'Federal Independence Party', which was dedicated to a policy of apartheid. This system lasted only two years, when it was reviewed by the secretary of state in 1956.

Under the 'Lennox-Boyd Constitution' a second African became a Minister, and the addition of eight African members, and the permitting of the first elections for African seats in 1957, gave Africans equality with Europeans in the Legislative Council. But the end-product of these changes was a complicated patchwork of a legislature. It now consisted of a Speaker, six civil servants, thirty-seven nominated members, twelve members 'specially elected' (that is, selected by the elected members sitting as an electoral college), fourteen elected Europeans, fourteen elected Africans, six elected Asians and two elected Arabs. Three things were lacking: a definite goal in the form of a time-table for self-government; the presence of Kenyatta, the father-figure of the largest nationalist group, since Lennox-Boyd promised that Kenyatta would not be allowed to return to the Kikuyu country after his detention; and finally, well-organized mass political parties, in place of the tribalism of so much political organization.

In 1959, however, a series of dramatic turning-points were passed. African-elected members in the legislative council demanded Kenyatta's release. Ronald Ngala, an ex-headmaster, formed the 'Kenya National Party' and demanded a time-table for independence.

The more radical 'Kenya Independence Movement' called for *Uhuru*, 'freedom'. In Britain, Iain Macleod was appointed colonial secretary by a government obviously shocked by the riots in Nyasaland during February and March 1959 and determined to adjust its policies to the 'wind of change'.

Thus in January 1960 a constitutional conference was called in London attended by the main European leaders and African delegates under the leadership of Ngala. Macleod's aim was the building of a nation enjoying responsible government with British parliamentary institutions. After a stormy conference, Macleod produced an ingenious plan which fell short of responsible government. A 'Council of Ministers' was to be appointed, consisting of four officials and eight unofficials (four of them Africans, three Europeans and one Asian). But no 'Chief Minister' was provided for. The governor selected the Ministers. In the legislative council thirty-three out of sixty-five elective seats would be filled by open elections. For the benefit of the minority populations, there would be reserved seats (ten European, eight Asian and two Arab) but elections would be according to a common roll and candidates would have to submit themselves to primaries. There were also to be twelve 'specially elected' members. The 'Macleod Constitution' should not be interpreted as yet another tinkering, complicated though it was. It represented the principle of an elected African majority in the legislature and more unofficial African Ministers than European. Its effect on the settler community was to cause a panic; capital began to flow from Kenya.

The 'Macleod Constitution' was also an incentive to African political organizations. The first elections in February 1961 indicated the pattern of Kenya's political divisions. The 'Kenya African Democratic Union', led by Ngala, gained the support of most of the smaller tribes. The 'Kenya African National Union', of which Kenyatta (still in detention) was elected President, won the support of the major tribes like the Kikuyu and Luo. Although K.A.N.U. gained eighteen seats compared with K.A.D.U.'s eleven, they refused to take office without Kenyatta. Ngala was therefore invited to become 'leader of government business' and since two Europeans were willing to take office under him, the governor used his powers of nomination to provide a majority. Both parties now insisted on Kenyatta's return to politics.

The story of Kenya's final achievement of independence is one of

Britain's belated willingness to let Kenyatta lead his people, and of Kenyatta's ability to impose his leadership on them. He finally returned home to the Kikuyu country on 15 August 1961 amid wild rejoicings. Three months later he flew to London to demand independence in the following year. Reginald Maudling, now colonial secretary, agreed that Kenyatta should be allowed to enter politics and that a full constitutional conference should be called for 1962. Thus in January 1962 Kenyatta entered the legislative council and became leader of the opposition. In February 1962 the constitutional conference met in London. Here a deadlock between K.A.N.U. and K.A.D.U., which stood out for a federal constitution, led to the 'Maudling compromise', which provided safeguards for the regions. The central government controlled foreign affairs, finance, trade and development, but six regional assemblies were to be created. The central legislature consisted of a Senate with members from forty tribal districts and one from the city of Nairobi. The House of Representatives was mainly elected from territorial constituencies. After this conference Kenya received internal self-government under a coalition ministry with the Cabinet equally divided between the two main political parties. Kenyatta became Minister of State for Constitutional Affairs and Planning. But party rivalry and internal party disputes soon threatened to wreck the 'collision' government, as it was called. At the same time the leaders of Tanganyika and Uganda criticized Britain for allowing Kenya's independence to lag, and raised the question of an East African Federation.

The British government, therefore, agreed that the question of federation should be left to an independent Kenya. After K.A.N.U.'s convincing victory in the 1963 election, Kenyatta became 'prime minister' on 1 June 1963 and immediately proceeded to London to discuss independence. As so frequently happened before in Asia and Africa, a former political detainee had emerged as the official leader of his nation. Opposition parties hastened to co-operate, and when a group of settlers called on the prime minister he asked them to let bygones be bygones and assured them that the minority immigrant communities still had a role in Kenya. Independence was proclaimed on 12 December 1963, with a British Governor-General. A year later Kenya followed her neighbours and became a Republic with Jomo Kenyatta, veteran of the pre-war nationalist movement, and now over seventy, as President.

W

CENTRAL AFRICA

Central Africa may appropriately be discussed last in our survey of the 'New Commonwealth'. Here, in Rhodesia, Britain faced her final test in Africa and was embroiled in the greatest crisis in the transformation from colonies into Commonwealth since the loss of the thirteen colonies. Central Africa was the scene of the most notable anomalies in the empire, both in the Victorian age and in the twentieth century. It was colonized by the only Victorian chartered company which remained for any time in Africa, and which planted a colony in spite of the opposition of the inhabitants of the region and of influential humanitarian opinion in Britain. Later, in 1953, Central Africa was also forced into a federation against the wishes of the majority of the inhabitants and against much intelligent opposition in Britain. This, in spite of the full knowledge that federations elsewhere, especially in southern Africa, had always required most delicate fabrication. How, then, can we account for the Central African anomalies?

Cecil Rhodes's Second Empire

The basic divisions and anomalies of Central Africa stemmed from the partial success of Cecil Rhodes's second empire. British influence in Central Africa may have begun through the explorations of the great missionary and traveller, David Livingstone, but it was consolidated chiefly because the official policies of paramountcy in South Africa and control of the Nile hinterland (discussed in previous chapters) provided a fertile ground for Rhodes's private schemes. Even in the region west of Lake Nyasa and south of Lake Tanganyika, where the real groundwork was laid by missionaries and the actual concession treaties were gained by government representatives, Rhodes contributed financially to British expansion.

His British South Africa Company, which based its claims on mineral concessions acquired from the rulers of Matabeleland and Mashonaland, was chartered in 1889 by the British government merely as an inexpensive way of encircling the Transvaal and keeping the Portuguese and Germans out of the Zambezi region. Its sphere of activity was deliberately kept vague. The charter permitted the company to work for minerals and to colonize north of Bechuanaland, north and west of the Transvaal and west of Mozambique. In 1890 the 'Pioneer Column', composed of partly British, partly Afrikaner and some overseas adventurers, struck north from the Cape to plant the Union Jack at a point in Mashonaland they called 'Fort Salisbury'.

North of the Zambezi, however, Rhodes was stalled. It is true that he bought out a concession granted in 1890 by Lewanika, King of the Barotse, and that one of his agents gained mineral concessions in the region up to the upper Kafue River (North-Western Rhodesia). He also subsidized the African Lakes Company operating around Lake Nyasa and Harry Johnston, the British consul who obtained the concession treaties in the regions of Lakes Nyasa, Tanganyika and Mweru (North-Eastern Rhodesia). But by 1891 Rhodes was paying a high price for the privilege of extending northwards. In return for a supplementary charter permitting it to operate north of the Zambezi, the British South Africa Company agreed to subsidize a police force under the control of Harry Johnston as Commissioner in the 'Territory under British influence to the North of the Zambezi'. Even more significant was Rhodes's agreement that the so-called 'Nyasaland Districts' – the chief missionary sphere – should be a separate 'British Central African Protectorate' under Foreign Office supervision. The Zambezi became, in fact, what it has always remained – a borderline dividing Southern Rhodesia, and its South African parent, from the African territories to the north. Why did this happen and what were its effects?

The answer to the first question lies in the two distinct strands of British influence in Central Africa, which were evident from the days of the charter and which always remained in conflict. The B.S.A. Company's territory – 'Rhodesia', as it was called after 1895 – became settler country on the South African model. The British Central African Protectorate became a direct responsibility of the British government, and although a few hundred planters soon arrived in addition to the missionaries, trusteeship traditions predominated. But the territory which lay between the two (the present Zambia) continued for many years to be pulled in both directions. There was plenty of pressure from the south. In North-West Rhodesia (Barotseland and the territory up to the Kafue) concessions were granted to Rhodes. In North-Eastern Rhodesia, Rhodes gained the mineral rights in return for financial help. By 1894 the Commissioner in Nyasaland was relieved of his administrative responsibilities in northern Zambesia and B.S.A. Company rule was extended. But Rhodes was never allowed a free rein north of the Zambezi.

A further reason for the continued divisions was that the Jameson Raid cast a murky shadow over the Company's name. It was not allowed to assimilate its territory north of the Zambezi to Rhodesia. The northern region – sometimes likened to a 'giant butterfly' – was divided at the Kafue into two administrations. Thus, when Rhodes died in 1902, having seen resistance from the Matabele, Mashona, Ngoni and Yao inhabitants of his second empire crushed, his hopes of a new Dominion in 'charterland' had all but faded. Britain's hold on Central Africa in the early decades of the twentieth century remained constitutionally anomalous and divided.

None of the territory had been annexed. In Matabeleland and Mashonaland the British South Africa Company had by 1900, however, created a colony of 10,000 settlers, who were governed by an Administrator, nominated by the Company and approved by the secretary of state for colonies. After the 'Southern Rhodesia Order in Council of 1898' a 'Resident Commissioner' (looking to the High Commissioner in South Africa) was added as an 'imperial watchdog' over the Company's government. A legislative council was also permitted which included four elected representatives of the settlers. But north of the Zambezi the Company's divided administration looked to two different masters. Under the 'North-West Rhodesia and Barotseland Order in Council of 1899' the Administrator of the western portion was subject to the High Commissioner in South Africa. By the 'North-East Rhodesia Order in Council of 1900' the supervision of the eastern portion was exercised by the Commissioner in Nyasaland. The Company's administration in Northern Rhodesia was not amalgamated until 1911.

Finally, the British Central African Protectorate remained a direct imperial responsibility and was transferred to Colonial Office control in 1904. Three years later, under the better-known name of 'Nyasaland Protectorate', it received a government to all intents like that of a Crown colony, with a governor, an official executive council and a nominated legislative council. But it was not annexed. Rhodes never achieved his continuous band of British territory from the Cape to Cairo. His second empire had emerged as three divided pieces. Although more than half a century of effort was later put into trying to amalgamate them, the threefold division remains today.

The End of Chartered Company Rule

Division in Central Africa was accentuated in the era following the 1914–18 war. The B.S.A. Company's charter came under review when its original twenty-five-year life expired in 1914. Although it was extended for another ten years, it was evident by the 1920s that both Rhodesian territories wished to escape from Company rule. The Company, for its part, having been informed by the Privy Council in 1918 that it could not be a landowner for commercial profit, but only as a government, was anxious to cut its administrative losses. The interesting question therefore arose as to what should succeed the B.S.A. Company.

Several amalgamation schemes were mooted. Southern and Northern Rhodesia were seen as a possible united colony. Imperialists in Britain, like Milner and Churchill, favoured uniting Rhodesia with South Africa. The Company, having found Northern Rhodesia unwieldy, suggested a threefold partition: Barotseland to be added to the Bechuanaland protectorate; the North-Eastern region to be restored to Nyasaland, and the middle belt, where the railway line from the Zambezi to Katanga was completed in 1909, to be added to Southern Rhodesia as part of the Union of South Africa. But voices were raised in protest against these schemes from very different directions.

In 1917 a missionary in Nyasaland, Alexander Hetherwick, insisted that the territory north of the Zambezi was African country. He reminded unionists that 'Nyasaland is a black man's country' and he went on to predict that the 'natural future of Nyasaland will be in association with its neighbour in the west – Northern Rhodesia'. A further refinement of this view followed in 1918 from a civil servant in Northern Rhodesia, who advocated a 'Central African Confederation' of Northern Rhodesia, Nyasaland, Tanganyika, Kenya and Uganda. But opposition to Rhodesian amalgamation schemes came not only from those who wanted to save the lands north of the Zambezi as an African preserve.

The Southern Rhodesian settlers, who by 1923 numbered 35,000, did not want to be saddled with expensive 'black protectorates'. They had managed, by their land apportionment policies, to secure 48 million acres of the best land, leaving 37 million acres for the 900,000 Matabele and Mashona inhabitants. Their system of African hut taxes (£1 a hut) successfully forced Africans to take jobs for wages, and thus provided a labour force for the new economy. Beside this, Northern Rhodesia had only 3,500 settlers and a small revenue. The full wealth of the copperbelt had yet to be revealed. Southern Rhodesians did not want northern Zambesia; nor did they want to join the Union of South Africa, as the British government wished. In a referendum in 1922 the electorate decided 8,744 to 5,989 in favour of responsible government.

Thus the mid-Victorian remedy was applied to twentieth-century tropical Africa. From 1923 until the rebellion of 1965 Southern Rhodesia held a unique constitutional position in the empire. Britain formally annexed the territory and granted a constitution not unlike New Zealand's in the 1880s. A legislative assembly of thirty elected members was created. The executive council became a Cabinet of seven ministers, led by a prime minister, who was invited to the imperial conference after 1926. The British government retained a veto over laws relating to African rights, but did not exercise it. In international usage Southern Rhodesia was styled a 'self-governing colony'. In many respects she was virtually a Dominion.

North of the Zambezi the story was, as usual, different. The Colonial Office stepped in, as it had in Nyasaland, with the eager encouragement, at first, of the settlers. They hoped for a full Crown colony administration. But Northern Rhodesia became a protectorate and began in some ways to follow Nyasaland. The governor controlled the administration, assisted by an official executive council. Although five unofficial members were elected to the legislative council, according to a high property and income qualification which excluded 'British protected persons' (the Africans), in local administration the doctrines of 'Indirect Rule' were imported from Nigeria and Tanganyika. Not until the great copperbelt discoveries after 1925 drew in more and more white workers, attracted Southern Rhodesian interest, and gave rise to the problems of an urban, industrial, African population, did Northern Rhodesia begin to look southwards. Then, as Southern Rhodesia cast covetous eyes on the copperbelt, and ideas of East African 'closer union' loomed up in Britain, serious consideration was given to the idea of ending Central Africa's divisions.

Background to Federation

The settlement which followed the end of the Company rule in Central Africa confirmed, for a while, the idea that the Zambezi was a sort of border between 'black' and 'white' Africa. In fact, in 1924 a parliamentary commission under Sir William Ormsby-Gore revived the suggestion of a confederation north of the Zambezi. But the influx of Europeans into the copperbelt in the central part of the protectorate raised the possibility, in settler eyes, that Northern Rhodesia might after all become part of the 'white south'. Sir Hilton Young, who led a royal commission on 'closer union' in 1927 supported the idea of amalgamating the Rhodesias. When his colleagues dissented, he suggested that the central railway belt should be added to Southern Rhodesia and a federal relationship be arranged between the rest. A conference of Rhodesian politicians at Victoria Falls in 1936 called for the amalgamation and complete self-government of the Rhodesias.

Thus the British government sent a further royal commission in 1938 under Lord Bledisloe, to investigate the possibility of a closer association between the Rhodesias and Nyasaland. But after noting cautiously the advantages that would follow, the commission discovered that articulate African opinion in the northern protectorates was opposed to the racial discriminations practised in Southern Rhodesia. And since Bledisloe's report came only six months before the outbreak of the war in 1939, nothing was done. The 'Central African Council' which emerged during the war was a consultative body concerned with economic and social co-operation. Once the war was over, however, Rhodesian politicians were eager to revive the amalgamation schemes of the 1930s. In 1948 an event occurred which greatly aided their cause.

The election defeat in South Africa of Field-Marshal Smuts – the Commonwealth's most respected elder statesman – by Dr Malan's Afrikaner 'Nationalist Party' was a profound shock to believers in the Commonwealth. The era of reconciliation in South Africa appeared to be coming to an end. Afrikaner nationalism was firmly in the saddle and missionary and liberal opinion watched the beginning of the policy of apartheid with dismay. A few months later an election was held in Southern Rhodesia in which Sir Godfrey Huggins, the premier, defended his tenure by offering, not a policy of apartheid (which he disliked) but a restriction of the number of African voters. After returning to power he went to London to press the project of a great 'Middle Dominion' in Africa consisting of the Rhodesias and Nyasaland, loyal to Britain in contrast to the Afrikaners to the south.

Also present in London in 1948 was the Northern Rhodesian

politician, Roy Welensky. The two Rhodesians presented a complete contrast. Huggins was a bluff, outspoken, 65-year-old English surgeon, who went to Rhodesia in 1911 and had been premier since 1933. By now he was the unrivalled leader of Southern Rhodesia's patricians. Welensky had an entirely different background. A 41-year-old, native-born Rhodesian, of poor Lithuanian-Jewish and Afrikaner origins, he was a large, tough, man, who had worked his way to prominence in Northern Rhodesia as a heavy-weight boxing champion, railway engine-drivers' leader, founder of the Labour Party and finally as war-time director of manpower. Welensky, like Huggins, was eager to amalgamate the Rhodesias. But in London they both received a shock.

The colonial secretary in the Labour government, Arthur Creech Jones, who had long been a specialist on colonial affairs, informed Welensky that no British government could consider extending to the Northern Rhodesia Protectorate the type of constitution which existed in Southern Rhodesia, or indeed permit any constitution which would place the control of several million Africans in the hands of a few thousand settlers. 'No Government,' he went on, 'irrespective of its political hue, would carry out that kind of action today. The world would not put up with it.' The Conservative opposition spokesman on colonial affairs confirmed this view. In India, Pakistan, Burma and Ceylon independence had just been conceded. In the Gold Coast and Nigeria the nationalists were active and in Kenya Jomo Kenyatta's agitation had begun. The British government saw Central Africa in this wider context. The colonists, however, were in the mood to look back to a much earlier age of empire and they began to make threats – frequently reiterated up to 1965 – that they would have to copy the 'Boston Tea Party'.

The gulf between the British viewpoint and that of the Central African settlers became public in 1949 when an unofficial conference on amalgamation was held at Victoria Falls. Southern Rhodesia, under virtually complete internal self-government since 1923, had success-fully segregated many aspects of African and settler society and ensured control by the latter. As Huggins informed the conference, for the foreseeable future Africans would have to be ruled 'by a benevolent aristocracy . . . our democratic system does not embrace mob law'. In the northern protectorates Britain retained responsibility and Creech Jones, the secretary of state, pointed out that permanent European settlement in Northern Rhodesia would have to be controlled. But

Welensky insisted that the settlers would 'not under any circumstances recognize the paramountcy of African interests'. He declared that he would never accept the idea that Northern Rhodesia would be 'an African state'.

It was significant that no Africans attended the 1949 conference. Yet there were (as we shall see) plenty of indications that the majority communities in the northern protectorates were uneasy about joining Southern Rhodesia. Thus, to avoid opposition at the next stage, Huggins arranged that a conference of civil servants should be held in London in 1951. In one important sense these officials were activated by a sense of idealism. By now the policy of apartheid was under way in South Africa; many people expected that Southern Rhodesia, where there were many Afrikaners, would follow. Yet Huggins and Welensky were proclaiming a policy of 'partnership'. Was this not a more promising alternative for Central Africa ? The idea of a federation embracing the Rhodesias and Nyasaland was seen as a way of saving Southern Rhodesia from apartheid, saving Central Africa for British influence, preventing a crude confrontation of 'black 'and 'white' blocs and ensuring rapid economic development for all three territories.

Thus a federal project was drafted under which all matters directly affecting the life of Africans would be left to the territorial governments – thus enabling the northern protectorates to maintain their trusteeship traditions. The new central government would take over foreign affairs, defence, immigration policy, economic policy, income tax, customs, and transport. The federation was to become a new Dominion like Canada, Australia and New Zealand. Although safeguards for African rights were planned, such as a Minister for African Affairs appointed by the governor with power to reserve matters for the Colonial Secretary, Huggins put the project to the Southern Rhodesian electorate with the words: 'Once the imperial government have granted this constitution, they have lost all control – don't forget that.' As for the safeguards, he dubbed them 'not worth the paper they are written on'.

The British government soon had severe misgivings. But Creech Jones, Labour's colonial expert, lost his seat in the 1950 general election. At a further conference at Victoria Falls in September 1951 the now shaky British government was represented by James Griffiths. After consulting African district councils in the northern protectorates he insisted on African representation at the conference. Huggins was furious. He felt the conference became 'a Native Benefit Society meeting led by the secretary of state'. However, the Southern Rhodesians were saved by political events in Britain. During the conference news arrived that there would be a new election in Britain. The settlers expected more from a Conservative government. And after Winston Churchill was returned to power in 1951, a full federal conference was held during the following year in secret in London. The Conservative government's plans were endorsed in March 1953, when the federal project was accepted by the House of Commons with a majority of 44 votes. In Southern Rhodesia a referendum followed, when an electorate of less than 50,000 out of the total population of over 2 million, approved the federation by a margin of 25,750 to 16,000. Northern Rhodesia and Nyasaland's decisions to join were made by their governments.

The 'Central African Federation' was launched, then, in spite of mounting opposition. In Britain, the Liberal and Labour parties opposed the form of the federation; the Churches and missionary societies spoke up for the protectorate peoples; and leading journals such as *The Times*, the *Manchester Guardian* and *The Economist* expressed their profound misgivings. What lay behind this opposition? One factor could not be ignored: federation was opposed by the African majorities in the northern protectorates. Federation was being imposed, in an era when African nationalism was on the march, upon over 6 million unenfranchised people by a community of settlers smaller than the population of Leicester. For Africans in Northern Rhodesia and Nyasaland, federation therefore became a spur to nationalist organizations and agitations like those in West and East Africa.

The Origins of African Nationalism in Central Africa

Before the 1939–45 war African organizations were not unlike the late Victorian Indian National Congress or such bodies as the Aborigines Rights Protection Society of the Gold Coast. They appealed to a small educated intelligentsia of pastors, teachers, clerks, skilled mechanics and small farmers. Possibly the most formative influences came from South Africa, and the agents of this influence were chiefly migrant Nyasas. A further indirect influence was the Negro emancipation movement of the United States, which had been so important for West Africa. African separatist Churches, which had sprung up in South Africa since the late nineteenth century, were influenced by pastors trained in American Negro colleges, such as John L. Dube, a Zulu, who in 1913 became President of the African National Congress. In the same way, John Chilembwe, who led the 1915 rising in Nyasaland, had studied in the United States and returned to found his own independent industrial mission.

Chilembwe's brief uprising in January and February 1915 was unsuccessful, but it provided a vivid illustration of the forces which would contribute to African nationalism. His aim was an African state in Nyasaland, where Europeans would be welcome as advisers. His supporters were the 'marginal men' of Nyasa society – those educated in the missions, detached from tribal life,* often skilled men or small property owners. It was men of this type who formed the 'Nyasa Native National Association' in South Africa in 1920, or the various Nyasa tribal associations, such as the 'Mombera Native Association' among the Ngoni, at the same time.

From Nyasaland this type of organization spread among migrant Nyasas into Northern Rhodesia, where the 'Mwengo Welfare Association', which existed from 1923 to 1928, numbered David Kaunda (father of the President of Zambia) among its numbers. By 1939 African Welfare Associations had spread among the literate African lower middle class all along the railway belt. One branch corresponded with Hastings Banda in America and was aware of the Garveyite movement. In the 1930s there were attempts to unite the welfare associations in Northern Rhodesia and form an African National Congress there. Opposition was voiced against the 1936 proposal for amalgamating the Rhodesias.

But it was the return of ex-servicemen from overseas during the 1939–45 war which led the African organizations in the northern protectorates to develop from welfare organizations into political parties more like those of the Gold Coast and Nigeria. Thus, in 1944, the 'Nyasaland African National Congress' was formed by uniting the welfare associations. In 1948 the 'Northern Rhodesian African Congress' grew in the same way. In that year two Africans were also appointed to the Northern Rhodesian legislative council. But, above all, the movement of the settlers in favour of federation provided a

* For a full and fascinating account of this movement see G. Shepperson and T. Price, *Independent African*, Edinburgh, 1958.

focus for African political activity and led to the emergence of major African nationalist leaders.

Dr Hastings Banda, who had left Nyasaland in 1915, was then in practice in North London, where he maintained contact with African students in Britain. In 1949 he collaborated with Harry Nkumbula, a Northern Rhodesian teacher then studying at the London School of Economics, in producing a pamphlet attacking the idea of a Southern Rhodesian dominated federation. If 'our boys', they wrote, could fight and die for the same 'right to justice, and the same empire and Commonwealth', they were entitled to the same political rights as Europeans. Federation would be acceptable only on the basis of universal suffrage in all three territories. In the following year Kenneth Kaunda (son of the first Livingstonia-trained missionary in Northern Rhodesia) persuaded his African Welfare Association at Mufilira to become an African National Congress branch. He began organizing to such effect that two years later he emerged as Secretary-General of the Congress. Even in Southern Rhodesia, where Africans were less organized, there was opposition to federation. Joshua Nkomo, a Matabele social worker with a South African degree, built up a strong African Employees Association on the railways and in 1952 attempted to create an 'All-African Peoples Convention'. Although his organizations had little effect, he continued to support the protest movement and later encouraged African nationalism in Southern Rhodesia.

Inevitably the most passionate opposition to federation came from the northern protectorates where there was still hope of appeal to the British government. Harry Nkumbula, who became President of the Northern Rhodesian Congress in 1951, publicly burnt the Government's Federation White Paper. A group of Nyasa chiefs toured Britain to state their case, and they tried to appeal to the Queen. Dr Banda, along with Julius Nyerere of Tanganyika (then a student), appeared at a World Church Rally in Edinburgh. But the protests were of no avail. The Central African Federation* came into being on 1 August 1953.

The Central African Federation

The federation lasted ten years. It ended because the British government, unlike the Southern Rhodesian government, was not prepared to ignore the wishes of the majority of the people nor to suppress

* The official style was 'The Federation of Rhodesia and Nyasaland'.

African nationalism. In material terms the federal government claimed great successes, which it felt would be thrown away by irresponsible agitators. 'Believe me,' declared Sir Roy Welensky (federal premier, 1956–63) to a Canadian journalist, 'the troubles of this country of ours are not political, they are economic.'

It is true that the European economy of Central Africa flourished in the 1950s, partly assisted by a boom in copper prices. This also led to an increase in African wages. But economists doubt whether the prosperity was specifically due to federation, and some maintain that the region's economy was distorted. A much higher proportion of resources went into industrialization, the education of settlers, and the building up of the armed services, than into the agriculture, welfare and education of the majority of the population. Above all, it became clear that Southern Rhodesia dominated the federation. The federal capital was in Salisbury. In an effort to fulfil his goal of building a 'Middle Dominion', Huggins had engaged on a remarkably successful immigration programme which more than doubled the settler population between 1946 and 1951. But the cost was high. Southern Rhodesia entered the federation £88 million in debt. The revenues of the copperbelt came to the aid of the dominant partner through federation.

Perhaps the most blatant example of Southern Rhodesia's influence, which came as a shock to many of the federation's well-wishers, was the decision to build the giant Kariba Dam on the Zambezi, with the power station on Southern Rhodesian territory. The dam cost over £100 million and its potential power output was far in excess of demand. Northern Rhodesia was dismayed to find that its own, less costly, Kafue hydro-electric project, which the federal government originally promised to continue, was abandoned. Similarly, the project for a Shire Dam in Nyasaland, to stabilize the unpredictable waters of Lake Nyasa and give proper irrigation to a large region, did not get started. Two modest projects were rejected in favour of the grandiose Kariba scheme, which appeared to be of greater benefit to Southern Rhodesia. But in the long run the failure of the federation was, in spite of Welensky's claims, political, not economic.

Federation was launched upon the pledge of 'partnership' between races for the general advance of all in Central Africa. Margery Perham, the veteran Africanist of the British academic world, pointed out quite clearly in 1953 that eventually 'power must pass into the hands of the immense African majority'. But Huggins (raised to the peerage in 1955 as Lord Malvern) interpreted this in 1956 with the words:

> We want to indicate to Africans that provision is made for them to have a place in the sun as things go along. But we have not the slightest intention of letting them control things until they have proved themselves, and perhaps not even then. That will depend on our grandchildren.

Sir Roy Welensky later added that adult suffrage was 'rubbish and completely unsuitable for Africa'. The franchise was therefore based on income and property qualifications far beyond the reach of all but a tiny minority of Africans. In Southern Rhodesia there were, in 1953, 441 Africans on the electoral rolls as compared with 50,474 settlers. In Northern Rhodesia there were only three Africans to 15,447 settlers, and in Nyasaland just over 1,000 settlers received the vote while African representatives were still selected indirectly. In the view of an Oxford scholar the franchise was 'so discriminatory as to forfeit all confidence among Africans in the sincerity of European intentions about democracy'.*

For this reason the federal era witnessed a consistent agitation in Northern Rhodesia and Nyasaland, where Britain had not yet conceded responsible government to the settlers and so retained the right to alter the government. As the 1950s wore on, all parties became aware that, in the seven-year period before the federal constitution came up for review in 1960, a desperate race was in progress. The federal government sought to eliminate all remaining imperial powers in Central Africa before the review. The African nationalists in the northern protectorates sought to obtain internal self-government so they might participate in the review and secede from the federation.

This nationalist campaign led Federal and Southern Rhodesian politicians to make increasingly crude and threatening pronouncements, which began to antagonize British public opinion. Lord Malvern announced ominously in 1956 that

> we have complete control over our Defence Forces. I would hope we shall not have to use it as the North American colonies had to use theirs, because we are dealing with a stupid government in the U.K.

* Colin Leys, 'Partnership as Democratisation' in Leys and Pratt, *A New Deal in Central Africa*, London, 1960, p. 113.

In the following year, Welensky revealed his fear that a future Labour government in Britain might 'inflict some of their half-baked ideas' on Central Africa. In Southern Rhodesia, a mildly liberal premier, Garfield Todd, who wanted to add about 8,000 Africans to the electorate, was thrown over by his own party in 1958. During a federal general election in 1958, which was boycotted by the nationalists, an extremist group of Southern Rhodesian settlers formed the 'Dominion Party' pledged to a unilateral declaration of independence if Britain imposed an unwelcome constitution on the Northern Rhodesian settlers.

The Secession Movements in the Northern Protectorates

While Southern Rhodesians closed their ranks, Nyasaland led the movement for secession. In 1955 a new constitution was agreed. Five African unofficial members were added to the Nyasaland legislative council in the following year, selected by provincial councils acting as 'electoral colleges'. They were to sit in a legislature still dominated by eleven officials and six elected members of the non-African minorities. But the concession gave some encouragement to the Nyasaland African National Congress, which gained some seats. Among the first elected members was Harry Chipembere, a prominent Congress member, who corresponded with Dr Banda (then practising in Ghana). In 1957 he urged Dr Banda, the most distinguished of the Nyasa expatriates, to return home and lead the national movement, in fact to reappear in Nyasaland as 'a kind of saviour'. Banda was reluctant to accept. But when Welensky secured the significant constitutional concession in 1957 that Britain would abandon the right to amend or repeal any federal act, Banda realized the northern protectorates were now seriously threatened. In July 1958 after an absence of forty-three years he flew back to Nyasaland amid popular enthusiasm. The government at first found him a moderate leader, but he soon demanded nothing less than an African majority in the legislative council and parity between the races in the executive council. When his demands were rebuffed by the governor, Banda's opposition became more and more determined.

Similarly, in Northern Rhodesia the nationalists gathered their strength. Here, an unofficial elected majority of settlers had been permitted in the legislature since 1945. Since 1954 the legislative council of twenty-six had been made up of ten officials, twelve European elected unofficial members and four Africans selected by African Representative Councils. Four of the elected Europeans had been granted 'ministerial' office, but responsible government had not been conceded. Britain retained control, but settler influence seemed entrenched. Thus the African National Congress formed a 'Supreme Action Council' and Kenneth Kaunda, the Secretary-General, who was impressed by his study of Gandhi's civil disobedience campaigns, organized pickets and boycotts against the colour bar in copperbelt towns. After a spell in jail in 1956 for possessing prohibited literature, Kaunda and Nkumbula, the Congress leaders, went to Britain to attend a Labour Party study group on the Commonwealth and afterwards Kaunda stayed on to study party organization. This wider experience coincided with Dr Banda's stepping up of the anti-federation campaign in Nyasaland and a willingness by Nkumbula to co-operate in a new constitution for Northern Rhodesia in 1959, by which a two-tier voting system was expected to produce a legislature of 14 Europeans and 8 Africans. Thus Kaunda and some of the radical, more educated, members of the Congress, who were dissatisfied with Nkumbula's leadership, split away to form the 'Zambia African National Congress' and to boycott the 1959 constitution.

The 1959 Emergency and the 'Wind of Change'

The turning-point in Central Africa came in 1959. After the leading nationalist leaders returned home from attending Nkrumah's 'All Peoples African Conference' in Accra at the end of 1958, tension and violence became widespread in the federation. Thus in February and March 1959 a gigantic security 'clamp down' was organized by the territorial governments, with federal aid. As riots and violence spread throughout Nyasaland, the Southern Rhodesian government declared a State of Emergency, banned the African National Congress and detained 500 nationalists. The Nyasaland government, convinced that there was a plot to massacre the Europeans, swooped down in the small hours of 3 March 1959 to arrest Dr Banda and his supporters. The Nyasaland Congress was banned. An Emergency followed in Northern Rhodesia on 11 March, when the Zambia African National Congress leaders were placed in detention.

This sudden Central African crisis in 1959, followed by the Devlin Report on Nyasaland, with its clear evidence of African antipathy to the federation and its famous phrase that Nyasaland was a 'police state', administered an immense shock to British public opinion. It may well have persuaded Harold Macmillan's Conservative government that federation could not continue. A Royal Commission under Lord Monckton was appointed to prepare the British government for the federal constitutional review which was expected at the end of 1960. The British government decided to bow before the nationalists in the northern protectorates. In the spring of 1960 Iain Macleod, a tough member of the Conservative liberal wing, was appointed colonial secretary to negotiate with the nationalists. Macmillan, the prime minister, set off on his celebrated African tour and the 'wind of change' policy was gradually revealed. At Lagos, in January 1960, he announced that Britain would not give up its responsibilities over Northern Rhodesia and Nyasaland until local opinion had been heard. When Sir Roy Welensky tried to press him on this during the premier's visit to Salisbury, Macmillan successfully evaded the issue. Macleod bluntly told Welensky that the federalist politicians in Northern Rhodesia and Nyasaland were the greatest obstacle to settlement in their Canute-like attitude to the tides of African nationalism.

The new colonial secretary first decided to win over the Nyasaland nationalists with a new constitution. A legislative council of twenty-eight was agreed upon, to be made up of twenty seats filled by voters on a 'lower roll', of quite modest income and literacy qualifications, and eight reserved for voters of high income and education, who would be largely Europeans. Five of the unofficial elected members were to be added to the executive council. Dr Banda returned from the constitutional conference in August 1960 and cried 'To Hell with Federation' to his delighted supporters.

Macleod then turned to the problem of Northern Rhodesia. In September 1960 he announced that during the federal review conference at the end of the year there would also be a Northern Rhodesian constitutional conference. He is supposed to have promised Kenneth Kaunda privately that a constitution on the new Nyasaland model would be granted. These trends were underlined in October 1960 when Lord Monckton's report noted the 'pathological' opposition to federation which existed in the protectorates and went on to recommend a wider African franchise, more African seats in the Federal Parliament, legislation to end racial discrimination and the inclusion of the secession issue in the review conference.

It is not surprising, therefore, that the review conference opened in

x

London on 5 December 1960 with Welensky and the Southern Rhodesians feeling infuriated and betrayed by the British government, while the hopes of the African nationalists ran high. Dr Banda, Kenneth Kaunda and Joshua Nkomo were invited to attend. Tension between the British and Federal governments reached such a pitch early in 1961, as the preparations for the new Nyasaland constitution went ahead and the Northern Rhodesian constitutional talks continued, that British troops were sent to Nairobi in case of trouble. On hearing of this, Welensky mobilized his Territorial Army and gave orders that British aircraft would be fired on if they tried to land troops in the federation. In such an atmosphere genuine co-operation was doomed. Although the official fabric of the federal government lingered on for two more years, the federation gradually disintegrated as the three territories prepared to go their own ways.

The Formation of Malawi

Elections were held under the new Nyasaland constitution in August 1961 and Dr Banda's 'Malawi National Congress' gained twenty-two out of twenty-eight seats. The British government decided to proceed rapidly with self-government and official rule was progressively given up. An interim 'ministerial system' was inaugurated with Dr Banda as Minister of Natural Resources and Local Government. As he led the first part-African ministry in Central Africa, Banda insisted that Nyasaland should secede from the federation. Although Welensky rushed to London in March 1961 to try to avert secession, Macmillan argued that 'It is too simple a reading of history to think that you can exercise control simply by the use of force.' Welensky went home to call a general election and seek a mandate to save the federation. But the African nationalist parties and some of the Europeans boycotted the election.

By 1962 the British government had certainly decided that federation could not continue as it was, possibly not at all. A 'Central African Office' under R. A. Butler, the First Secretary of State, was set up to co-ordinate the transition. On 19 December 1962 he announced to the House of Commons that Britain accepted Nyasaland's right to secede. On 1 February 1963 Nyasaland received full responsible government. Dr Banda became prime minister and plans began for complete independence. The State of Malawi came into existence on 4 July 1964 and Republican status followed two years later.

The Formation of Zambia

To the federal government Malawi was no material loss. Nyasaland had always been the poor relation of the federation and something of a financial drain. Only the precedent of secession hurt. But Northern Rhodesia had its rich copperbelt – the federation's greatest economic asset – and its settler population of 67,000,who had come so close to self-government themselves, and Welensky made another determined effort to save it for federation. Here he wanted to stand up to the African nationalists. In the 1959 Emergency Kaunda and his colleagues were detained. Even when Kaunda emerged from jail to take over leadership of a new 'United National Independence Party' Welensky tried to co-operate with Nkumbula and the old African National Congress and so divide the nationalists. Thus when the British government tried in June 1961 to go ahead with a constitution providing for a legislative council of forty-five consisting of 15 settler seats, 15 African seats and 15 'National' seats, Welensky professed himself reasonably satisfied. The reason was obvious. Under the proposed electoral system candidates in the 'National' seats would have to gain $12\frac{1}{2}$ per cent or 400 (whichever was less) of votes from both races. This meant that, while an African candidate might need to win 400 votes from a small European electorate of about 3,000 settlers, a European candidate in the constituency would only need to get 400 votes from the 10,000 Africans – a much lower percentage. Kaunda regarded the system as a great 'betrayal' and promised a campaign of 'non-violent positive action'. Violence soon broke out in Northern Rhodesia and the British government therefore decided to re-open the issue in spite of Welensky's cries of a 'Munich'.

The new Northern Rhodesian constitution was finally negotiated by Reginald Maudling, now colonial secretary, in 1962. The minimum vote requirement was modified. Although the U.N.I.P. rejected the constitution in principle, it agreed to fight in the election of October 1962. In fact it tried hard to woo the settler vote and convince Europeans of the party's qualifications to rule. In this it was disappointed by the results. But sufficient African members were returned in the election for the U.N.I.P. and the African National Congress to form a coalition government. It took office on 16 December 1962 with Harry Nkumbula as Minister of African Education and Kenneth Kaunda, Minister of Local Government and Social Welfare. Thus African rule was extended to Northern Rhodesia. As one political scientist wrote,

'By any standard the Territory's political metamorphosis had been phenomenal.'*

Inevitably, the first resolution presented to the new legislative council in February 1963 was a demand for secession from the federation. A delegation proceeded to London and secured the agreement of the British government in March. Welensky again rushed on to the scene to try to salvage his federation. When faced squarely with the British government's decision, he bitterly cancelled a lunch appointment with Mr Macmillan, the prime minister, because he could not 'accept the hospitality of a man who has betrayed me and my country'. Thus the Zambia nationalists administered the *coup de grâce* to the federation.

As stresses appeared in their own coalition government a new general election was called at the end of 1963, this time on the basis of universal suffrage. As a result the U.N.I.P., by now a well-organized political party, won fifty-six seats to the African National Congress's ten. Northern Rhodesia confidently prepared to receive full self-government, while on the last day of 1963 the Central Africa Federation reached its demise. On 25 January 1964 the 39-year-old Kenneth Kaunda, the most joyful looking of all the nationalist leaders, provided the Commonwealth with a leader even younger than President Kennedy. He immediately made preparations for independence and on 24 October 1964 'Zambia' became a Republic in the Commonwealth.

The Southern Rhodesian Rump

What became of Southern Rhodesia as the federation expired? 'Southern Rhodesia will have been seceded from' was the view of the prime minister, Winston Field, when the British decision on Northern Rhodesian secession was made public in 1963. After enjoying virtually complete internal self-government for forty years, Southern Rhodesia's settlers resented Malawi's and Zambia's sudden advance to complete independence. They insisted that they were entitled to the same rights. Clifford Dupont, the Minister of Justice, declared that 'Independence is our legal, logical and moral right after forty years'. He might, in a sense, have been appealing to the whole history of the Commonwealth. Yet the British Government refused. Why did it stand up to Rhodesia?

* D. C. Mulford, *The Northern Rhodesian General Election 1962*, Nairobi, 1964, p. 183.

The answer is simple, even though its implications are complex.

Autonomy, as evolved in the Dominions, had been based upon majority rule – with the controversial exception of South Africa in 1910. Independence in the 'New Commonwealth' had always been based upon majority rule and a form of parliamentary democracy – whatever happened, in some places, after the transfer of power. The Southern Rhodesian settlers were a small minority of about 220,000, ruling over 3 million Africans at various stages of educational development. The settlers always claimed that they wanted their development to be 'evolutionary' not 'revolutionary' and that as Africans became more and more educated they would get the vote. But the British government remained sceptical about these claims. What evidence did it have for its caution?

In 1964, as Malawi and Zambia prepared for independence, it was clear that Southern Rhodesia was ruled by a government which was determined to suppress African nationalism, maintain settler rule, and even to halt racial integration. Three times in seven years Rhodesian prime ministers were ousted by successors more right-wing and racialist than themselves. Although a fair number of 'liberal realists' had accepted the need to modify the long-standing system of racial segregation, co-operate with the nationalists and even accept the logic of eventual majority rule, these moderates were consistently rebuffed by the electorate.

The Right-wing Trend in Settler Politics

In 1958 Garfield Todd, a New Zealand-born former missionary, who had succeeded Huggins when the latter became federal premier, was thrown over by his own party. Todd has been called a 'paternalist liberal'; he proposed no drastic reforms. But in 1957, the year when the Southern Rhodesian African National Congress was formed, Todd proposed adding about 8,000 Africans to the electorate in order to win the co-operation of the growing educated African middle class. He pointed out that African wage levels were such that they prevented many literate and skilled people from meeting the income qualification. He therefore suggested allowing ten years of education as a qualification. But this modest move stimulated such opposition from the 'Dominion Party', which resented Rhodesia's colonial status in a largely independent Africa, that the United Federal Party jettisoned Todd, and called Sir Edgar Whitehead, the federal ambassador in

Washington, to take over. In a general election in 1958 Todd and his supporters, who formed a new party, failed to gain a seat.

Soon Whitehead showed himself to be suitably 'tough' with the nationalists. An emergency was declared during the Nyasaland riots in February 1959, when he banned the African National Congress, detained 500 members and rushed through new security laws. In 1960 he ordered the arrest of the leaders of a new party, the 'National Democratic Party' and in riots which followed twelve Africans were shot.

Yet in spite of the bloodshed and his passion for security, Whitehead was, in some respects, one of the realists. He agreed that racial discrimination should be gradually eliminated and he even came to accept the idea that the land apportionment laws should be amended. He also recognized that the franchise should be extended and agreed that the Southern Rhodesian constitution should be considered at the same time as the Federal and Northern Rhodesian reviews at the end of 1960. At the conference convened in London on 16 December 1960 he even agreed that Joshua Nkomo and the Rev. Ndabaningi Sithole of the National Democratic Party should attend.

The 'Sandys–Whitehead constitution' of February 1961 provided for an enlarged legislative assembly of 65 members and an increase in the African electorate. The franchise was a complicated system of two electoral rolls, involving 'upper' and 'lower' qualifications for the vote.* There were now to be 50 constituencies and 15 electoral districts (groups of constituencies) and each registered voter would cast two votes – one for his own constituency and the other for the electoral

* Voting qualifications under the new constitution were: a citizen, aged 21, of 2 years' residence, and
'*A*' *Roll*
an income of £720 a year and immovable property worth £1,500;
or income of £480 and property worth £1,000 and a primary education;
or income of £300 and property worth £500 and 4 years' secondary education;
or the position of headman or chief;
or a wife of someone possessing these qualifications.
'*B*' *Roll*
an income of £240 a year and immovable property worth £450;
or income of £120 and property worth £250 and 2 years of primary school;
or if over 30, income of £120 and property worth £250 and a primary education;
or if over 30, income of £180 and property worth £350;
or Kraal heads over 20 families;
or a minister of religion;
or a wife of someone possessing these qualifications.

district. In this way it was hoped that about 15 of the 65 members would be Africans, and Whitehead said he expected about 60,000 Africans to register for the vote. Although this did not represent parity with the Europeans, it would have represented about two-thirds of their total if they had been on a common roll. But Joshua Nkomo, the nationalist leader, had decided that the time for negotiation and co-operation had passed. He declared a boycott of the new constitution. Thus the 'A' roll consisted of 86,000 Europeans, 2,500 Africans and 2,000 Asians and Coloureds, while the 'B' roll reached a mere 9,814, which included some poor whites. Whitehead's appeal to Africans to help 'build a nation' failed to win over the nationalists. It also antagonized settler extremists.

Thus in an attempt to ward off attacks from the political right in 1962, Whitehead passed a series of restrictive laws, banned the new 'Zimbabwe African Peoples Party', and led a former Chief Justice of the colony to declare that Rhodesia was now a 'Police State'. While Lord Malvern, Rhodesia's apologist in the House of Lords, treated the British public to his views that the Zimbabwe nationalists were 'a devilish combination of Liberia and Haiti' and that 'all Africans are liars', Joshua Nkomo took his appeals to the United Nations, where one of Britain's delegates, Sir Hugh Foot (a former colonial governor of wide experience), resigned his post because he could no longer represent Britain's support in the U.N. for the Rhodesian régime.

Yet Whitehead's security 'clamp down' of 1962 had no more success with the electorate than Todd's dismissal five years earlier. A new 'Rhodesian Front' was formed on the right in 1962, dedicated to securing Rhodesia's independence, recognizing that European and African philosophies and ways of life were different, maintaining as sacred the basic land division enshrined in the land apportionment laws, and insisting that integration in schools was 'repugnant'. In an election in December 1962 the Rhodesian Front won 35 seats to White-head's 29. The 58-year-old Winston Field, an Englishman who had been a tobacco farmer since 1921, became premier, determined to secure Rhodesia's independence before Malawi and Zambia.

A Unilateral Declaration of Independence

Over the next year, as the federation came to an end, talk of a Rhodesian 'Declaration of Independence' became common. Field announced that 'we don't want to be members of the Commonwealth if this delays our independence'. But he drew back from the idea of a 'unilateral' declaration of independence – unless Britain interfered directly in the constitutional affairs of Rhodesia. For this reason he resigned in April 1964 in favour of his finance minister, Ian Smith. Thus a 45-year-old, South African educated tobacco farmer, who was impatient for independence, became Rhodesia's first native-born prime minister.

Smith's government soon reached an impasse in its relations with Britain. He was not invited to the Commonwealth Prime Ministers' conference of July 1964, where the premiers insisted that Britain must ensure a truly representative constitution in Rhodesia before independence. Discussions in London with Sir Alec Douglas-Home failed to take the issue further in October 1964. After Labour's narrow victory in the general election, the new premier, Harold Wilson, invited Smith to London to resume discussions, but Smith refused. Thus on 27 October 1964 Wilson warned him that independence could only be granted by an Act of the British Parliament, and that a 'U.D.I.' would be an act of rebellion, the support of which would be treasonable.

Throughout 1965 settler extremism simmered in Rhodesia, and the question of the declaration of independence seemed to resolve into one of timing. 'I cannot go on much longer leaving the people of Rhodesia, and the future of Rhodesia in suspense', Smith told a British Cabinet mission in Salisbury in September 1965. Last-minute efforts to achieve a negotiated independence were made during Smith's visit to London and the prime minister, Harold Wilson's visit to Salisbury in October 1965.

The 'Rhodesian Front' seemed determined on independence. Joshua Nkomo, the Zimbabwe leader, dubbed the Smith government a 'suicide squad', and Smith admitted to a press conference in London that he had 'a choice between taking a chance for a decent future or, by doing nothing, having no future at all'. But Wilson's government made five conditions for Rhodesian independence: a franchise giving a clear indication that majority rule would eventually come; guarantees that such a constitution would not be abrogated; an immediate improvement of the rights of the Africans of Rhodesia; an end to the discrimination laws; and assurances that the constitution was acceptable to all the people. Smith insisted, in return, that the 1961 constitution already provided for eventual majority rule. He was prepared to improve African political rights by creating a Senate of Chiefs and extending the vote to all taxpayers, but he would not increase the number of African seats in the Assembly. He agreed to modify the system of racial discrimination, but not the land apportionment laws. Some concessions were made, then, but no agreement was reached. Smith returned to Salisbury to be greeted with yells of 'U.D.I.' from his supporters.

The British government made further desperate efforts to avert a declaration. A Commonwealth Commission consisting of Sir Robert Menzies (Australia), Sir Abubakar Tafawa Belewa (Nigeria), Kenneth Kaunda (Zambia) and Sir Dudley Senanayake (Ceylon) was proposed, but rejected by Smith. Harold Wilson himself flew on an abortive mission to Salisbury, where (as he later admitted) he found among the Rhodesian Front 'a look of hatred on the faces of some' and 'some almost neurotic racialists'. Smith offered a solemn treaty to guarantee African rights after independence. Britain insisted on a Royal Commission to consult all Rhodesian opinion and to supervise the first ballots. The prime minister offered to fly to Malta to meet Smith again, but the Rhodesian leader was not deterred.

On 11 November 1965, in a parody of Jefferson's noble words of 1776, the declaration of independence was issued, and still professing loyalty to the Queen, love of the flag and of the national anthem, the Smith government rebelled against the Crown. The world watched, fearful that about 220,000 British subjects – less than the population of Stoke-on-Trent – were about to inflame the African continent. *The Times* called the action 'stupid, reckless, and bad'.

The Implications of the U.D.I.

The Rhodesian rebellion did not lead to an immediate outbreak of war in Africa – either between Britain and the rebel régime or between African states and Rhodesia. Month after month went by without dramatic change. The worst fears of the rest of the Commonwealth and the world were unfounded. But the rebellion was more than a failure in negotiation by the British government. It represented a disconcerting break in the peaceful transformation from colonies into Commonwealth, and, indeed, it presented a threat to the whole future of the Commonwealth. Not since the American revolution – which the Rhodesians had so consistently threatened to emulate – had a major community rebelled against Britain. Never in the history of the empire had a legitimate régime declared unilateral independence.

The rebellion revealed that although the disagreement between the British and Rhodesian governments on political and constitutional goals had narrowed, the emotional gulf was colossal. Britain, having successfully, if sometimes belatedly, dismantled her empire on the basis of majority rule, looked to the eventual rounding off of this policy in Rhodesia. The Rhodesian Front, in their isolation from the mainstream of Commonwealth development, their proximity to the independent Afrikaner state, and their lack of contact with governors and civil servants, even settlers and businessmen, who had founded and worked in the New Commonwealth, had permitted themselves to be by-passed by history. As a Rhodesian journalist said, 'Rhodesians are no longer capable of believing what they do not wish to believe, whether it is true or false.' A good example was Ian Smith's assertion (after half a century of African nationalism) that the nationalists of his country 'represent no one but themselves'. Many Rhodesians must have regretted their vote in 1923 to stay out of the Union of South Africa.

How was Britain to fulfil her obligations to Rhodesian citizens of all types in face of the rebellion? It could have followed the example of the government of George III and attempted to suppress rebellion by force. This was demanded by many African governments. Many humanitarians in Britain, including the Archbishop of Canterbury, believed it might become necessary. The Organization of African Unity called upon its members to break off diplomatic relations with Britain if the rebellion was not crushed by 15 December 1966. Both Tanzania and Ghana obeyed the call – the first Commonwealth members to break with Britain – although President Nyerere of Tanzania stressed the point that his state retained its Commonwealth membership.* Of Rhodesia's former federation neighbours, President Banda of Malawi urged moderation, while President Kaunda of Zambia frequently called for the use of force. At the Lagos Prime Ministers' Conference in January 1966, Sir Albert Margai, of Sierra Leone, led the exponents of force. The prime ministers' communiqué indicated that force was not precluded. But why did premier Wilson reject a resort to arms?

His chief reason was that he did not wish to divide the British people. His parliamentary majority was only four and many in Britain

* Ghana resumed relations on 5 March 1966.

remembered the passions ten years earlier at the time of the Suez war. A further, less publicized reason, was military weakness. The immense problem of assembling a force of two divisions or more to cross the Zambesi could not be solved overnight. As Mr Wilson challenged premier Margai at Lagos, 'If you were commander-in-chief, how would you do it?' Finally, the prime minister was probably actuated by genuine pacific idealism: a peaceful solution would be in keeping with the normal evolution of the Commonwealth. He did not rule out force in certain circumstances, but he rejected the idea of invading Rhodesia to unseat the Smith régime. As against the warmongers, there were certain elements in Britain and the Commonwealth who were prepared to accept the rebel government as the *de facto* government. They implied that the Rhodesia Front should be trusted to promote African development and to approach eventual majority rule at their own pace.

Wilson's government took a middle road. First they appealed to strict constitutionality, and then applied economic sanctions. The Rhodesian ministers were dismissed, the constitution suspended, and, by Order in Council, legal authority was vested in the secretary of state for commonwealth relations, represented in Salisbury by the governor. As time passed, the economic measures were drawn ever tighter. Commonwealth preferences were ended, Rhodesia was expelled from the sterling area and her reserves in London were blocked. British exports were stopped and a 95 per cent trade embargo applied. This was followed by a complete embargo, including oil. When foreign tankers attempted to break the embargo, which was supported by the United Nations, the British government secured authority in the Security Council on 9 April 1966 to use force to blockade the terminal of the pipeline to Rhodesia. All these moves were in a sense 'destructive', designed to force the Rhodesians to think again.

What positive proposals were made to secure the goal of a constitutional settlement? Three statements to Parliament by the prime minister indicated possible procedures. On 25 January 1966 he pointed out that the governor in Salisbury, Sir Humphrey Gibbs, was at all times available to receive proposals for a settlement. He reaffirmed that immediate majority rule was impossible and he envisaged a future interim government representing a wide spectrum of Rhodesian opinion – a 'representative government for reconstruction'. On 21 April 1966, when Parliament re-opened after the general election which returned his government to power with a majority of 97, Mr Wilson hinted that British officials had been available in Salisbury for discussions. 'There is a great deal which we are prepared to forgive and forget,' he said, 'but we are not prepared to legalize an act of rebellion against the Crown.' A week later, on 27 April, he broke the news to Parliament that his private secretary had been to Salisbury, made contact with the rebel government through the governor, and that informal discussions would follow 'without commitment on either side' to search for a possible basis for a constitutional settlement. On 9 May 1966 these talks began, secretly, in London.*

Uncertainties of British Policies in Eastern Africa

Why was the transformation from colonies into Commonwealth in East and Central Africa more painful than elsewhere? Why, after all the efforts to create unified 'Dominions', and to restrain African nationalism, was there a sudden change of heart, a rapid erection of five Republics, followed by the rebellion of the one colony? The answer is that British policies in this region were always ambiguous.

The East and Central African empires were founded partly for 'external' strategic reasons, partly for 'trusteeship' reasons, such as the suppression of the Arab slave trade and the following up of the interest started by the missions, and partly for reasons of private economic gain. Once the territory had been appropriated, the government supported both colonization and 'indirect rule' at the same time. As the region developed a modern economy Britain alternately followed policies of unity and diversity. But the chief reason for eastern Africa's unfortunate history at the close of the colonial era was that the two major strands of British colonial policy – responsible government and trusteeship – came into conflict.

In the Victorian age such tensions were not absent, but they were resolved by the triumph of responsible government. Maoris, Black-fellows, Bantus and North American Indians had been handed over to the mercies of the settlers. Why did this policy stop after the granting of responsible government to Southern Rhodesia in 1923? The answer to

* They were conducted by civil servants on both sides. The political leaders seemed to take irreconcilable positions. Mr Wilson said he would not recognize the illegal declaration of independence. Mr Smith insisted that he would not give up his independence.

this question must be found in India, Ceylon and West Africa. Here, where there were no 'colonies', the question of responsible government hardly cropped up in the Victorian age except in the minds of dreamers like Dr Africanus Horton or the founders of the Indian National Congress. Yet by 1917, when men like Lionel Curtis realized that responsible government might become the ultimate fulfilment of trusteeship, the two great traditions of colonial policy coalesced.

Thus the Kenya settlers were denied what their Southern Rhodesian fellow-colonists had just received. Responsible government gradually came to be equated with the paramountcy of African interests or majority rule. Although little was done in the 1920s and 1930s, largely because of the lack of educational facilities in East Africa, yet after the 1939–45 war, which proved such a revelation to many individual Africans, the British government dared not return to a policy of responsible government for settlers alone.

Why, then, it may be asked, did it take so long for responsible government and independence to be granted on the basis of majority rule in eastern Africa, in contrast to India, Ceylon, Malaya, West Africa and the West Indies? This question presents more of a puzzle and only highlights Britain's uncertainty in eastern Africa. It may be explained, in part, by the lack of a highly educated *élite* to compare with the Indian Civil Service. A major factor, which did not exist elsewhere, was the British settler community, who made the modern economy and were reluctant to give up their primacy. But the chief difference can be found in a striking parallel with the original achievement of responsible government in the Victorian age. The initiative had to come from the colonies and not from the centre. Just as responsible government in North America and Australasia in the 1840s and 1850s depended, in the last resort, upon the exertions and agitations – occasionally violent – of colonial politicians, so independence in eastern Africa in the 1960s depended on the strenuous exertions – sometimes sparking off violence – of the African nationalist leaders. In this portion of the 'New Commonwealth' Britain learnt her lessons slowly.

Conclusion

The Commonwealth Today

WHAT DOES the Commonwealth mean to the world of the 1960s? After a year like 1965, when the largest Asian members went to war with each other, two African members broke diplomatic relations with Britain, the Rhodesian rebellion appeared to threaten the whole future of the Commonwealth, and the question of Britain's own future relationship with Europe remained unsettled, it is perhaps rash to attempt an answer to this question. Certainly recent comment about the Commonwealth has been pessimistic.

'The Commonwealth has the reputation of being a bit of a bore,' ran a *Guardian* editorial in 1965. A distinguished lawyer, Professor De Smith, suggests that the legal links of the Commonwealth are reduced to 'a wisp of gossamer. . . . They are rules of convention, not of strict law – a shadowy framework of a shifting structure.' *The Economist* professed some relief after the Lagos Prime Ministers' Conference in January 1966 that 'there's still a Commonwealth'. A former diplomatist, Kenneth Younger, suggested that the Commonwealth was simply a 'lubricant' which assisted international co-operation. Can we, in face of what appears to be a growing tide of indifference, reach more positive conclusions?

A Voluntary Association

It is helpful to realize that the Commonwealth is not an organically constituted 'entity' like a state, federation, union, a defensive pact or the United Nations. It is, in the often repeated phrase of its highest organ, the Prime Ministers' Conference, a voluntary, multi-racial, association of sovereign states. Many statesmen worked in the past for a different sort of Commonwealth, but they failed.

338

The main theme of this book has been the continuous tension which existed between the opposing forces of provincialism and centralization. On many occasions voices were raised in favour of greater initiative or authority from the centre, for imperial unity or federation, for the Commonwealth to become a super-state. Their efforts failed because stronger provincial, later nationalist, pressures pulled in the opposite direction. Thus the school of thought which finally prevailed was heir to the new economists and American moderates of the eighteenth century and of the mid-Victorian liberals, who held that the only lasting relationship between the new nations which grew within the British empire could be one of trust, based upon the maximum allowance of freedom and self-government. Since the 1914–18 war, and particularly since the 1926 declaration, the advocates of the loose, voluntary, association have prevailed.

But the federalists have never been completely silenced. Leopold Amery began his memoirs in 1953 by asserting that the Commonwealth 'could form an unbreakable girdle of strength encircling the globe' and called for a British 'Declaration of Independence' from the United States. In 1965, the editor of *Time and Tide*, regretting Britain's exclusion from the race to the moon, suggested that a union of Canada, Australia, New Zealand and the United Kingdom could become so prosperous that it would no longer have to 'just watch, earthbound'. He called for a 'new exodus' of adventurers from overcrowded Britain – ten million to Canada, nine million to Australia and one million to New Zealand. Like Gibbon Wakefield, 130 years earlier, he wanted whole societies to migrate, with their due proportion of distinguished professors and milkmen. Families could visit each other by supersonic airliners; news would be broadcast by Telstar. A Canadian supporter suggested that such a 'CANZUK Union' could then approach the United States on equal terms 'and correct the division of the English-speaking people'. A youthful peer, with Australian connections, Lord Belhaven and Stenton, who took up the project, declared during a Commonwealth debate in the House of Lords on 5 May 1965:

> What glorious prospects would be opened. A great British state would emerge, lifted once more to her true position as the foremost nation of the world, possessed of the greatest extent of territory and the most energetic and civilized population. With this life-producing union, she would eventually overhaul all competitors.

Another supporter of the project suggested moving the seat of monarchy to Canberra. But these romantic schemes, based upon imperial nostalgia, represent a negation of the meaning of the modern Commonwealth. There is no evidence that Canada, Australia or New Zealand desire union with Britain or with each other.

More seriously, such dreams of union take no account of the Asian, African and Caribbean members, who now constitute the most numerous, the most vocal, the most challenging and (there is some evidence to suspect) the most influential element in the Commonwealth. To these states complete independence and sovereign dignities have become essential. So far local attempts at union or federation in the West Indies, Malaysia, East Africa and Ghana-Guinea have not proved successful. The new nations remain within the Commonwealth, accept financial, technical and, in some cases, military aid from Britain, from other Commonwealth members (and from non-Commonwealth agencies) but they will brook no interference in their affairs as they seek to find their feet in the international community and to create stability, prosperity and happiness at home.

Thus the modern Commonwealth is based upon the complete independence of its members. It is an association representing every continent and most of the world's races and cultures. If it has yet to enunciate goals as simple and clear as those of the old imperial federation school, this is hardly surprising. We forget all too often that the federalists failed to unite the Dominions, even though Dominion Status and the 1926 declaration were not formally worked out until responsible government had been tried for no less than eighty years, during which time a firm sense of nationhood could develop. The concept of a 'Commonwealth of Nations' evolved in a very leisurely fashion in the early decades of the twentieth century.

In dramatic contrast, the 'New Commonwealth' evolved in an atmosphere of frenzied haste. The final decision to withdraw from India and Pakistan, when it came, was sudden, and the tragedies of the Punjab followed. In the rest of the larger Asian, African and Caribbean colonies the decade 1956–1965 saw an extraordinary rush to provide a reasonable political framework for self-government. In East and Central Africa the turning-point was probably as late as 1959–1960. This meant that, in many cases, self-governing states emerged with their true sense of *nationhood* hardly formed, except perhaps in the minds of the educated *élite*. It is therefore hardly to be expected that the 'New Commonwealth', as opposed to the original 'Commonwealth of Nations', will have yet found a peculiar internal 'feel' or outward 'stance'.

What indications do we have, in the middle of the 1960s, of the character of the 'New Commonwealth'? A useful approach to this question is by analysis of the one truly unifying factor of the Commonwealth – that of history. The Commonwealth is not, as we have seen, a formally constituted entity; it is the legacy of the rise and decline of the British empire. In Britain's three-and-a-half centuries as a colonial power, empire meant four things, taken chronologically: trade, settlement, power and mission. By analysing the transformation of these elements, which accompanied the transition from colonies into Commonwealth, and the more recent transformation of the 'British Commonwealth of Nations' into the 'New Commonwealth', we may discover some of the leading characteristics of the Commonwealth today.

Trade and Investment

Trading links were, in all but a few cases, the oldest colonial ties, and trade remains a significant link between Britain and all Commonwealth members. But these links are always changing and must be seen in perspective.

Britain's earliest colonial policy, embodied in the trade and navigation acts, was really a policy of building up British power by an exclusive commercial system. But after American independence, Britain's industrial advance in the steam age, and, above all, after the adoption of free trade, the colonial trade was less important than trade with the United States and elsewhere. During the great scramble for territories in Africa and the Pacific in the late-Victorian era, the initial commercial value of many of the new acquisitions was very small compared with Britain's trade with highly industrial nations. Although the United States and Germany overhauled Britain in some manufactures behind their high protective tariffs, and some of the Dominions began to protect their own infant industries, Britain clung to free trade until the 1930s. Joseph Chamberlain's version of imperial unity, via high tariffs and 'imperial preference', was rejected.

But after the 1914–18 war, when Britain's industrial lag became evident, when her overseas investments were depleted and her shipping was falling behind, the ideal of imperial preference was revived. When

Y

the depression forced Britain to adopt protection, a Commonwealth Economic Conference was called in Ottawa in 1932 with the intention of working out a scheme of Commonwealth economic co-operation. The result was disappointing for imperialists. No general Commonwealth customs union was possible. A series of bi-lateral agreements were negotiated between Britain and the Dominions; the Crown colonies were obliged to give preferences to British goods. As British tariffs were raised, preferences were given to Dominion and colonial produce.

Some Commonwealth preferences survive today. But notwithstanding this legacy of the 1930s, the Commonwealth's proportion of Britain's overseas trade has been falling in recent years. At the same time, while the overseas trade of the individual members has risen, Britain's share has in many cases again been falling. Thus the Commonwealth's trade links, though significant, are gradually weakening. If Britain seeks to restore her own prosperity by joining the European Economic Community the commercial ties of the Commonwealth may receive a critical blow. Primary producing nations – New Zealand provides the most notable case – could face a severe crisis. On the other hand, special terms may be gained for their products in Europe – especially by the tropical nations. Nigeria became the first Commonwealth member to negotiate 'association' in 1966. And, if other nations which formally relied on the British market were able to develop more diverse markets in time, they would strengthen their own economies, and their contributions to the Commonwealth would be thereby enhanced.

A further economic legacy of the empire, now under review, is the 'Sterling Area'. Finance represents another link from the days of British hegemony, which must be seen in perspective. In the Victorian age, when London was the chief banking centre of the colonies, local currencies were based on the pound, the colonies borrowed in London and deposited their surpluses there. Sterling was used for payments in their external trade and London, as the banking centre, conveniently coincided with the trading, shipping and insurance centre. This position (which also came to include a number of non-colonial countries) continued until the 1914–18 war.

Since then sterling has been on the defensive. New financial centres, notably New York, have surpassed London, but have not completely superseded it. During the depression, when Britain abandoned the gold standard, what became known as the 'Sterling bloc' emerged as a defensive financial association. In order to maintain traditional and well-tried links of convenience, its members agreed to continue using sterling as their 'international currency', to keep their major reserves in sterling and to pool their scarce dollar resources, in return for free access to the London money market for borrowing. Although this had advantages for Britain, since the dollar exports of countries like Malaya and Ghana could off-set Britain's own dollar deficits, and had advantages for the area members, who could borrow freely, its usefulness is now in question.

As the immediate dollar shortage which followed the 1939–45 war eased and some members like Australia earned dollar surpluses, the rigidities of the sterling area system were challenged and in 1959 sterling was made convertible. Moreover, Britain could not afford to satisfy the sterling area's requirements for capital. Britain herself had to borrow from the United States, and other Commonwealth members also borrowed direct from the same source. Britain's cycle of balance-of-payments deficits shook confidence in sterling and led some members to profess their reluctance to keep all their reserves in sterling. And Britain has recently tried to curtail investment overseas. Thus the future of the sterling area is under review. Some truly international financial centre, possibly the International Monetary Fund, may emerge as a sort of universal reserve bank.

From the Commonwealth's point of view the sterling area is not a vital component. Canada was never a member, while some non-Commonwealth countries which bank in London were. Britain cannot now afford to supply all the capital needs of all the Commonwealth. Thus the gradual transformation, and present predicament, of sterling are both part of the gradual loosening of the economic links of the Commonwealth.

Patterns of Settlement

After trade and investment, empire meant settlement. The possibility of emigration to, say, Australia, has for over a century provided a dream of possible escape to 'El Dorado' for Englishmen. But the ties of settlement, like those of trade, must be seen in perspective. Until the twentieth century most migrants from Britain who left their homeland went to the United States. If they went to British territories they went first to Canada, then to Australia, New Zealand and southern Africa.

Thus the historic pattern of British settlement does not coincide with the modern Commonwealth, even though certain Commonwealth members still realistically conform to the Englishman's traditional dream.

The first emigrants sailed westwards to north America and the Caribbean, whence about $1\frac{1}{2}$ million had migrated by the end of the eighteenth century. The great age of British migration was from 1815 to 1914, when 20 million people left Great Britain – an average of nearly 200,000 a year. Of this massive migration, about 13 million (nearly 70 per cent) went to the United States, while only 4 million went to Canada, 2 million to Australia and New Zealand and $\frac{3}{4}$ million to South Africa. In this respect systematic colonization probably retarded the growth of the dominions. Gibbon Wakefield wanted to transplant the ordered strata of British society into the colonies, and therefore adopted the device of a high price for land. With the United States not only easier of access and developing faster, but also offering cheaper land, it was natural that it became the goal for the bulk of British immigrants.

Nevertheless, as the nineteenth century progressed the direction of the flow varied. The gold rushes in Australia and New Zealand caused a brief, exceptional attraction in the 1850s and 1860s. The pull of the United States reached a peak about the 1880s, since its economy became subject to periodic depressions. By this time the emergence of the new nations of the empire provided new attractions. By the eve of the 1914–18 war, 65 per cent of British migrants were going to the Dominions and only 27 per cent to the United States.

After the 1914–18 war the flow of migration was dramatically changed by the American immigration controls. A ceiling of 150,000 immigrants a year was imposed by 1929, of which the British and Irish quota (the largest) was fixed at 83,000. Yet, although the British and Dominion governments started assisted migration schemes in order to build up the Dominion populations, average emigration in the 1920s was only about 80,000 a year. One reason may have been that governments tended to concentrate on agricultural settlement, yet the period was one of world agricultural surpluses. Thus the depression of the 1930s severely hurt the Dominions and after 1931 a reverse flow of migration began. Before the 1939–45 war over half-a-million Dominions residents had migrated to Britain.

Since 1945, the evolution of the 'New Commonwealth' and the

spread of jet travel (which brings remote New Zealand within 36 hours of Britain) have made migration patterns more complex. A steady flow of migration to Canada, Australia, New Zealand and South Africa resumed, in proportions similar to the 1920s. An average of 70,000 emigrated to these countries each year from 1946 to 1953. From the mid-1950s the figure tended to rise and fall according to the political and economic climate in Britain. The Suez war led to a huge exodus in 1957.

At the same time, full employment, the welfare state and a shortage of labour encouraged a growing migration into Britain. From 1946 to 1962 over a million immigrants arrived: two-thirds were from Ireland; over 100,000 from Australia and New Zealand. But the largest group came from underdeveloped portions of the New Commonwealth which were overpopulated, particularly the West Indies, India and Pakistan. In the second half of the 1950s this immigration averaged about 50,000 a year. But when, in 1960, it doubled to 113,000, and in the first half of 1962 reached 94,000, a clamour for control of 'coloured' immigration followed. Thus in 1962 the Commonwealth Immigrants Act was passed, designed to reduce the flow of unskilled immigrants who, while fulfilling a vital economic role in Britain, led to housing and schooling problems and to demonstrations of racial prejudice. By 1965 the annual inflow was reduced to 8,500 immigrants. At the same time emigration continued to have its traditional attractions.

Now Australia exerted the greatest attraction and received 65,000 from Britain in 1964 alone. Canada, New Zealand and South Africa all received a steady flow. In fact, the 150,000 emigrants from Britain in 1964 and the estimated 170,000 for 1965, suggest a trend approaching the annual figures for the nineteenth century.

Settlement has become one of the contentious issues of the modern Commonwealth. All members now exercise selective immigration policies, and Britain's damming of the flow of immigrant workers brought protests from the prime minister of Jamaica, among others. At the same time emigration to Australia and Canada attracts thousands of doctors and teachers, who are expensively trained in Britain, where their skills are needed. A distinguished economist raised the question: 'Can the mother country, while suffering from an attack of anaemia, afford to go on being the blood donor of the Commonwealth?'* Part of the answer is already provided by Canada

* B. Thomas, *Migration and Economic Growth*, Cambridge, 1954, p. 218.

and Australia, whose own immigration totals now contain a declining proportion of British migrants. Like trade and investment, settlement has become a diminishing factor in Commonwealth cohesion.

Decline of Power

The third major meaning of empire during the colonial age was power. Britain's earliest colonial policy had been a defensive policy designed to foster British wealth and seapower in competition with Continental rivals. In the era of free trade 'imperial defence' became an increasing preoccupation of British policy. Later, separate Dominion armies and navies and independent foreign policies did not prevent close Commonwealth military collaboration from providing an immense boost to British power in two world wars. The huge Indian Army – the 'unparliamentary army' of the Victorian age – provided a further power reserve in the east.

In recent years, however, as British power has declined steeply beside that of the United States and the Soviet Union, and as Commonwealth members pursue their own, sometimes divergent, foreign policies, the Commonwealth has ceased to count as a major 'power'. This trend is well illustrated by changes in decision-making on such vital questions as war and peace and strategy.

In 1914 Britain's declaration of war committed the Dominions, India and the Colonies together, although there were misgivings in Canada and South Africa. Strategic planning was centralized and was later co-ordinated politically in the Imperial War Cabinet. In the inter-war years, as the Dominions were launched into the diplomatic field, military co-operation remained close through the Committee of Imperial Defence, the Imperial Defence College and the standardization of equipment. But at the outbreak of the 1939–45 war the Commonwealth did not act as one. Britain's declaration of war on Germany on 3 September 1939 took all the 'colonies' into war. The Viceroy announced that India was at war – to the chagrin of the Indian National Congress. The Australian and New Zealand governments decided separately to follow Britain without formal, independent declarations. The South African premier, Hertzog, wanted to remain neutral, but he was defeated in Parliament. Smuts was then called upon to form a government and South Africa declared war three days after Britain. Canada waited a whole week before declaring war on 10 September. Eire, the only Commonwealth member adjacent to

Britain, remained neutral throughout the war. The decision on war or peace in 1939 vividly demonstrated the end of diplomatic unity.

In the higher direction of the war there was also less Commonwealth unity. The Imperial War Cabinet was not revived. Instead, various Dominion premiers, or ministers on mission or resident in London, were invited to attend the British War Cabinet where possible. The Commonwealth's military efforts were less unified than in the 1914–18 war. The Australian government withdrew its divisions from North Africa after the Japanese offensive in 1942 threatened Australia itself. The New Zealand government left a division in North Africa and later in Italy, but its commander had a delicate task in serving his own government and his British commander-in-chief. Canada was now strong enough to contribute a complete army. The overwhelming new factor after 1942 was the massive military commitment of the United States and the consequent creation of integrated commands, which involved Commonwealth subordination to American military leadership in the chief theatres of the Pacific and North-West Europe.* But within these, now international, forces the Commonwealth's share was considerable.

The Commonwealth contribution to victory was both larger and less costly in casualties than in 1914–18. Rough comparisons show that Britain lost 400,000 out of 6½ millions mobilized: Canada lost 42,000 out of ¾ million; Australia lost 30,000 out of a million; New Zealand lost 11,000 out of 190,000; South Africa lost 8,600 out of 200,000 and Southern Rhodesia also contributed 9,000 volunteers. India incurred 180,000 casualties out of her 2½ millions mobilized. In addition to these forces half-a-million were mobilized from the Crown colonies, of whom about 7,000 were killed. Thus, as the Dominions built forces larger than ever before, thousands of men from west and east Africa also served overseas.

Since 1945 the Commonwealth's contribution to the balance of power has continued to be made through international organizations. Britain and Canada joined the North Atlantic Treaty Organization in 1949. Australia and New Zealand continued to co-operate through the 'Anzac Pact' of 1944 before they joined the United States in the ANZUS Pact (into which Britain was not invited) in 1951. During and after the Korean War, in 1951–55, a unique Commonwealth Division was formed, which has been described as 'the most perfect example so

* In Italy and South-East Asia the supreme commanders were British.

far of Commonwealth co-operation in war'.* But this contribution was, of course, small beside the might of the United States. In 1954 Britain, Australia, New Zealand and Pakistan joined the South-East Asia Treaty Organization along with the U.S.A., France, Thailand and the Philippines – while India, Ceylon and Malaya stayed out. Britain and Pakistan joined the Central Treaty Organization in 1955. Australia and New Zealand both co-operated with Britain in the Malayan Emergency, 1948–60, as they have in north Borneo since 1963. Australia and New Zealand contributed to the American military intervention in Vietnam in 1965, while Britain did not. Canada has long had close North American defensive ties with the United States. The trend, in fact, is to regional, rather than specifically Commonwealth, power blocs. The United States remains the major power in the defence reckonings of most Commonwealth members. With this there often goes standardization of military administration and of equipment purchasing.

One incident stands out as the most vivid illustration of the new diplomatic and military divergences of the Commonwealth. This was the Anglo-French Suez invasion of 1956. Already by that year India, Pakistan and Ceylon were well-established Commonwealth members, and Ghana and Malaya were about to join them. Yet, when the Egyptian government nationalized the Suez Canal in July 1956, it soon became obvious that Britain and France were preparing for the use of force. In the event, the Suez affair became the most glaring failure of Commonwealth consultation.

Only Australia and New Zealand seemed to be in step with Britain. Robert Menzies, the Australian premier, played a major role in the efforts to negotiate with Egypt. The New Zealand premier, Sidney Holland, declared that his country would stand by Britain 'through thick and thin. . . . New Zealand goes and stands where the mother-land goes and stands.' A member of the New Zealand Labour Party (then in opposition) asserted: 'It is good at times that the roar of the British lion should be heard.' But the Canadian government was dismayed by the progress of the Suez crisis and the Indian government was indignant. Canadians had no immediate concern about the canal but their government objected, from the start, to the idea of military action against Egypt. When British and French forces began to bomb and then invade Egyptian territory – without the customary prior

* C. E. Carrington, *The Liquidation of the British Empire*, London, 1961, p. 82.

consultation with Commonwealth governments – Lester Pearson, then Canadian minister of external affairs, pointed out that Canada was no longer 'a colonial chore boy running around shouting ready, aye ready'.*

Canada voted against Britain in the United Nations. But Pearson wanted peace in Egypt to mean more than a cease-fire. Severely alarmed lest the condemnations of Britain expressed forcibly by India and Pakistan, and more mutedly by Ceylon, should permanently disrupt the Commonwealth, Canada sought for a constructive solution. Pearson, in fact, took the initiative in proposing the formation of a United Nations Force to occupy the war zones. Largely through his efforts, such a U.N. military force, commanded by the Canadian, General Burns, with major Canadian and Indian contingents, entered the Port Said area in the wake of the British and French withdrawal. Menzies, of Australia, would have no truck with a force consisting of what he called 'people from Portugal and Columbia and little bits and pieces'. But New Zealand had by now had severe misgivings about her initial instinctive rallying to the mother country. She offered a detachment for the U.N. force, which was declined. Soon after the war both Australia and New Zealand began to take a closer look at their relations with Asia. After New Zealand's general election in 1957, which saw the return of Labour to power, the new premier, Walter Nash, made a prolonged tour of Asian states. South Africa, throughout the crisis, thought it wise to keep its 'head out of the beehive'.

Thus the Suez war not only illustrated the diplomatic and military looseness of the modern Commonwealth. It forced the old Dominions to reconsider their own international goals.

Mission and Politics

In the last resort empire implied, particularly for Victorians and Edwardians, a sense of mission. As Charles Dilke wrote in 1867, the possession of dependencies like India provided a 'nursery of statesmen and warriors' without which Britain would 'irresistibly fall into natural sluggishness of thought'. He felt that Britain's position in Asia and Africa imparted 'width of thought and nobility of purpose'. While this sort of conviction could degenerate into the crude racialism

* See the collection of documents by J. Eayers, *The Commonwealth and Suez*, Oxford, 1964.

and economic rapacity of Cecil Rhodes and the British South Africa Company, it also led to the high devotion to duty of the Indian Civil Service and the idea of the 'dual mandate' in tropical Africa.

For this reason Britain appeared slow at first to concede self-government. Just as the pressure which led to responsible government in the 1840s and 1850s came from colonial politicians, so the initiative in the 1940s and 1950s came from Asian, African and West Indian nationalists. Successive British governments naturally stressed their responsibility for the maintenance of good government. But good government is never preferred to self-government. Although the whole logic of British colonial policy pointed towards ultimate self-government, as Lionel Curtis and others realized before the 1914–18 war, and in principle British governments accepted this, in practice each individual decision to go ahead with independence was usually taken in some haste.

Did the passing of the empire deprive Britain and the Commonwealth partners of a sense of mission? This was surely implied by Dean Acheson's stricture in 1962 that Britain had lost an empire and had not yet found a role. The Commonwealth, as the legacy of the colonial era, has not yet enunciated clear goals. The Commonwealth, moreover, is no longer strictly British. But what many people fail to notice is that a notable transformation appears to have occurred in British politics in recent years, which could be of great significance for the Commonwealth.

For the past century the Conservative Party was traditionally regarded as the imperial party, while the Liberals, and later the Labour Party, appeared as the upholders of colonial freedom. The generalization is, of course, a crude one. Notable exceptions could be found on both sides in the Victorian age. And the modern political 'centre' in Britain has virtually achieved 'consensus' on colonial issues. But echoes of Victorian traditions were clearly evident after 1945 when a Labour government went ahead with the independence of India, Pakistan, Burma and Ceylon, with accompanying grumbles from Winston Churchill, and the Conservatives in the 1950s went to war with Egypt and dragged their feet in Central Africa, to the accompaniment of Labour and Liberal protests.

In the 1960s a dramatic transition occurred, the full details and implications of which we cannot yet know. The Conservative government, trimming suddenly to the 'wind of change', endeavoured to pull out of Africa as decorously as possible before violence and expense followed. Harold Macmillan, the prime minister, even gave hints of disenchantment with the New Commonwealth. To his obvious regret, the Asian–African–Caribbean members, led by the prime minister of Malaya and abetted by the Canadians, virtually forced South Africa to withdraw its application for republican membership in 1961. When he announced, to the Prime Ministers' Conference in 1962, Britain's intention to apply for membership of the European Economic Community, Macmillan found that all the Commonwealth premiers, except those of Trinidad, Cyprus and Sierra Leone, expressed severe misgivings about the effect of this decision on their own economies and on the Commonwealth relationship. In a broadcast on 20 September 1962, in which he tried to reassure the British electorate that they were not faced with a straight choice between Europe or the Common-wealth, he yet stressed the new looseness of the Commonwealth as compared with the unity of the old Dominions and the coming unity of Europe.

> Even at the end of the last [1939–45] war the Commonwealth con-sisted of Britain and four independent countries – all British Colonies originally, mainly of British stock, all of them subjects of the Queen. Although we differed about some things, we were a small united group with broadly the same foreign policy. We were virtually a military alliance, tested to the full in two great wars.
>
> But now it is all changed, and what used to be the British Empire has changed into a new thing – the Commonwealth. Now there are fifteen countries – in Asia, in Africa, in the West Indies, as well as the old countries of which I have spoken. Some are large, some are small, some have hundreds and millions of inhabitants, some have only a few hundred thousand. There is a great variation of policy and of tradition . . .

What did it now stand for? 'We have a kind of historic link,' said the prime minister. Was he implying that the good old days were gone?

It was left for Hugh Gaitskell, the Labour Party leader, who con-ferred with Commonwealth Labour leaders just before the Prime Ministers' Conference, to attack the Common Market policy by taking up the cause of the Commonwealth. To his annual party conference at Brighton on 3 October 1962 Gaitskell pointed out, in a memorable speech, that on Britain's recent trading form she stood to gain in markets where she sold one-fifth of her exports by entry into the E.E.C. and stood to lose in markets which took half her exports.

> It means the end of a thousand years of history. You may say, 'Let it end', but, my goodness, it is a decision that needs a little care and thought. And it does mean the end of the Commonwealth. . . . We have ties and links which run across the whole world and for me at least the Commonwealth, the modern Commonwealth, which owes its foundation to these vital historical decisions of the [1945–50] Labour government, is something I want to cherish. . . . I believe, with all my heart, that the existence of this remarkable multi-racial association of independent nations, stretching across five continents covering every race, is something that is potentially of immense value to the world. It does matter that we have these special relations with India and with Pakistan, with the African states, as well as with Canada, Australia and New Zealand, for together we can, I believe, make a great contribution to the ending of the cold war. Let nobody underestimate that.

To many Conservatives, who had set their course on 'joining Europe', Labour's enthusiasm for the Commonwealth was but another example of the 'conservatism' of the British Left.

Conservatives now insisted on a policy of realism. On 2 April 1964 a controversial anonymous feature appeared in *The Times* calling for 'Patriotism Based on Reality Not on Dreams' in which 'A Conservative' declared: 'The Commonwealth has really become a gigantic farce.' 'To participate now,' he went on, 'in the fiction of an undefined and undefinable special relationship, which separates the United Kingdom and the Commonwealth on the one hand from the rest of the world on the other' led to the imposition of 'absurdities' on British laws and had 'hagridden' British commercial policy. But the writer reserved his harshest strictures for the role of the Queen, as Head of the Commonwealth:

> It is dangerous to prostitute to the service of a transparent fiction the subtle emotions of loyalty and affection on which that heritage depends. A great and growing number of people of these islands do not like to see the sovereign whom they regard as their own by every claim of history and sentiment play an alien part as one of the characters in the Commonwealth charade.

That the Labour Party appeared to have become the 'party of the Commonwealth' only reinforced the writer's conviction. The 'apparition of Mr Harold Wilson in Lord Beaverbrook's clothing' was a firm hint to Conservatives that they should be standing somewhere else.

Yet this final taunt indicated a serious misunderstanding, on the part of the writer, of the nature of the modern Commonwealth. As Gaitskell emphasized in 1962, the New Commonwealth, with its majority of Asian, African and Caribbean members, had largely taken its shape from the historic decisions of 1947 and 1949 to grant immediate independence to India and to accept republican membership in the Commonwealth. Many Asian, African and Caribbean nationalists also had links with the Labour Party. Most of their new nations tended to advocate state action and a form of moderate socialism, which implied a 'mixed' – part nationalized, part private enterprise – economy. Above all, the Labour Party could count itself fortunate in being able to advocate a strengthening of Commonwealth ties, with a fair assurance that its efforts would not be misconstrued as an attempt to revive illusions of British power or echoes of imperial federation.

The New Commonwealth, by its very looseness, clearly demonstrates that the era of empire is past. Just as the colonial reformers, in their day, believed that the only lasting relationship could be based on a maximum grant of internal self-government, so the advocates of the New Commonwealth accept, without question, that the only lasting friendly and fruitful ties can be based upon voluntary co-operation from the standpoint of sovereign independence. Once this is accepted, it is then possible to ask: How can co-operation be made more efficient and fruitful?

Thus, after Labour's return to power in October 1964, Mr Harold Wilson, the prime minister, showed himself a warm advocate of Commonwealth 'initiatives'. Some of his plans failed; others need time before a judgement can be reached. His project for a peace mission to Vietnam in June 1965 was rejected. But the concept of an impartial multi-racial mission was welcomed in many parts of the world. Similarly his suggestion of a Commonwealth mission to Rhodesia in November 1965 was rejected by the Rhodesian Front.

The Commonwealth Secretariat

The most significant new departure was the creation of the Secretariat in 1965. Ironically, this proposal, which is reminiscent of the ideas of the imperial federalists, was proposed by President Nkrumah of Ghana, at the Prime Ministers' Conference of 1964. The context of his proposal, however, ensured that it would not be mistaken for an imperialist device, for Nkrumah propounded a set of basic principles for the New Commonwealth. They were: the recognition of the full equality and independence of members; the duty of the richer members to assist the poorer; the duty of the latter to apply their resources to industrialization; and the rejection, by all members, of the principles of 'colonialism, neo-colonialism and racialism'. Finally, having emphasized the looseness of the New Commonwealth, he went on to propose a 'properly staffed clearing-house in London which would serve all Commonwealth members equally'.

The 1964 conference agreed to instruct officials to plan a Secretariat designed to disseminate information, assist existing agencies of co-operation and to organize future conferences. Staffed by officials from member nations and serving the member nations, it was to be a 'visible symbol' of Commonwealth co-operation. The idea bore fruit at the 1965 Prime Ministers' Conference, when the 50-year-old Canadian diplomatist, Arnold Smith, was appointed Secretary-General. The Secretariat is housed in Marlborough House, London, a former Royal Palace, which was set aside as the Commonwealth Centre in 1962.

The Rhodesian rebellion overshadowed the first year of the Secretariat's life and also provided some of its early tasks. The Secretary-General was, in fact, in Kenya at the moment of the Rhodesian U.D.I. As well as consulting with the Heads of State of the East African members of the Commonwealth, he addressed large meetings of students in Nairobi and Dar-es-Salaam. Speaking with a Canadian accent and supported by his Ghanaian deputy and New Zealand special assistant, he embodied, at a historic moment, the ideal that the Commonwealth was now something wider than the British relationship. Thus, when Tanzania and Ghana felt bound to break diplomatic relations with Britain, they retained their membership of the Commonwealth. The Secretariat made the arrangements for the first Prime Ministers' Conference held outside Britain since the Ottawa conference of 1932. In January 1966 the premiers met at Lagos, on the invitation of the Nigerian Federal premier, to discuss the Rhodesian crisis. They agreed to set up a Sanctions Committee, which met regularly in London with the Secretary-General. Mr Arnold Smith has also travelled widely to visit Commonwealth Heads of State or governments in Jamaica, Trinidad, Canada, and West and East Africa. In 1966 he turned to visit the Asian members.

As well as the Secretariat, several other projects were mooted. A Commonwealth Foundation was created to co-ordinate professional interchanges. The prime minister called for a Commonwealth Trade Programme – possibly with permanent machinery. A Commonwealth Consultative Assembly, on the model of the Council of Europe, was suggested. Its members would be from all parties in the member parliaments and it would build on the foundations of the Commonwealth Parliamentary Association. There was even some discussion among lawyers, at the Commonwealth Law Conference in Sydney, about a possible Commonwealth Court of Appeal. Obviously the key to all future projects lies, in the first place, with the Secretariat, and secondly, in the Commonwealth's ability to show constructive achievements.

The Role of the Commonwealth

What tasks are suitable for the Commonwealth? Three are suggested. In the first place, the member nations should co-operate with Britain in the settling some of the still existing remnants of empire. The biggest immediate problem lies in Rhodesia. Within the Commonwealth there is an abundance of knowledge, case history, and qualified people with sound experience in the problems of education and training for self-government. But Rhodesia, by virtue of its peculiar constitutional position since 1923, largely cut itself off from this fast developing stream. When the day comes for it to resume its normal political evolution, large-scale professional assistance could be provided from Commonwealth sources.

South-East Asia and the South Pacific already provide good examples of Commonwealth co-operation. Britain's support for Malaysia was supplemented by Australia and New Zealand. Singapore in her present (possibly temporary) status of complete independence looks to British, Australian and New Zealand firms to invest in her industries. Western Samoa, a former Mandate, later a U.N. Trust territory, received independence under New Zealand tutelage and retains close ties in this direction. The future of Fiji will be of interest to India (because Indians form its major ethnic group), Australia (because of its sugar industry), and New Zealand (which supplies many public servants). In the West Indies, the failure of federation led the larger territories (Jamaica, Trinidad and Guyana) to become Commonwealth members themselves while the smaller islands were left to consider the new status of 'associate states'. Yet inter-island collaboration in such matters as the University of the West Indies and in communications could be the foundation of further regional co-operation. In Africa, as the former High Commission Territories become independent (Botswana and Lesotho in 1966 and the Kingdom of Swaziland in 1970) they will enter upon their freedom faced with the delicate task of retaining close relations with their neighbours the Republic of South Africa, the Portuguese colonies and Rhodesia, where many of their migrant workers go. At home they plan to build up small multi-racial states. In this, assistance and experience from Commonwealth members in Africa and elsewhere will be necessary.

The existence of this ever-growing store of Commonwealth expertise is also probably the brightest hope for what *The Times* has dubbed the 'debris of empire'. For small, isolated territories – often islands – which became British possessions unwittingly in the high tide of imperialism, the prospects of a lonely future are bleak. For Britain the task of providing for them is daunting. But as the New Commonwealth members build up their own stores of wealth, self-confidence and skill, Britain may well find partners better fitted than herself to administer the final tasks of empire liquidation.

The second, and related, task for the Commonwealth is to assist in the world-wide war on poverty and ignorance. In this role it is not unique or exclusive – as the Colombo Plan indicates – but its existing organizations are highly useful.

Trade and power in the age of empire brought a new prosperity, law and order, and justice to many areas. But today the spectacular economic progress of the most advanced nations and the amazing development of communications have given rise to a new concept of justice. Poverty and hunger cannot be hidden, as any visitor to one of the great cities of Asia is all too aware. Populations once isolated and docile are now confronted with two possible roads to the modern economy: one is by free discussion and consent, the other is by violent revolution. If the former is not encouraged, the latter is all too likely. The Commonwealth consists of a few prosperous industrial nations and many new, developing, nations. Numerous organizations for co-operation exist whereby the former may assist the latter.

The *Handbook of Commonwealth Organizations*, published in 1965, lists over two hundred organizations or societies which exist to foster Commonwealth co-operation, or which have branches which specialize in the Commonwealth. There are numerous societies such as the Royal Commonwealth Society, the Victoria League, the Canada Club, the Uganda–Britain Society, the Royal India, Pakistan and Ceylon Society and the New Zealand Women's Association, designed to foster friendship and understanding between ordinary citizens. A number of Commonwealth professional associations organize exchanges and seek to maintain standards in fields such as law, medicine, journalism, architecture and engineering.

Important bodies like the Commonwealth Parliamentary Association, the Association of Commonwealth Universities, the Commonwealth Economic Committee and the Commonwealth Agricultural Bureau, maintain full-time officers and arrange frequent interchanges of distinguished leaders from the member nations. Academic bodies like the Institutes of Commonwealth Studies at London and Oxford, the School of Tropical Medicine in London, the School of Tropical Agriculture in Trinidad, and the Oxford Forestry Institute have close links with the universities.

Through such specialized and often mundane organizations, thousands of students, professional men, and businessmen, as well as distinguished political and academic figures have developed a Commonwealth awareness. Annual conferences of major Commonwealth organizations and bureaux perform for these practical bodies the same task as the Prime Ministers' Conference does for heads of governments in building up close personal contacts among the member nations.

The third task for the Commonwealth is the most important and the most difficult. Even if poverty could be banished, deep crevasses of misunderstanding and intolerance remain between nations. Here the Commonwealth faces its real challenge. The educated *élites* of the Commonwealth share many ideas in common, but they also represent many different regions, races, religions and cultures. The co-operation of these governing *élites* in Commonwealth organizations gives those bodies an invaluable opportunity to understand, at first hand, how tensions grow from differences of environment, culture, religion and race. As the Secretary-General, Arnold Smith, suggested in 1966,

We cannot afford to be defeatist about humanity's prospects. We

z

must nudge mankind toward more understanding and tolerance. We have to develop quickly the habits and insights of co-operation on a global basis. The Commonwealth gives us one of the promising instruments for this purpose.

Member nations have, through the Commonwealth agencies, an intimate forum, existing on many levels, in which to explain their policies to nations from different continents. At the same time, they can learn something of the anxieties and aspirations of many diverse peoples. For this reason, as the Secretary-General has revealed, Commonwealth meetings now 'are exhilarating and significant reflections of a world, not merely a single culture'.

Peaceful Achievement

History is not generous to the achievements of peace. The New Commonwealth lacks the drama which attracted 'imperial' historians to the deeds of the great men of action. Empire-builders like Clive, Hastings, Rhodes and Goldie; proconsuls, like Curzon, Milner and Lugard, and war leaders like Chatham and Churchill, tend to be the heroes of the histories of empire. Similarly, the national spirit of the Americans, the French, the Greeks and the Irish, each of whom rebelled to achieve their self-respect, excites a more clear-cut devotion than the citizenship of Canada, Australia and New Zealand, nations which emerged only gradually from British rule, or the multi-lingual states like Nigeria, Kenya and Malaysia, whose unification is comparatively recent.

The constructive achievements of the Commonwealth are largely achievements of peace. Although the transition from colonies into Commonwealth was undoubtedly accelerated by violent outbreaks like the Canadian rebellions of 1837, terrorism in India, the Emergency in Malaya, unrest and rioting among ex-servicemen in Ghana, Nigeria, and Kenya, and the anti-federal agitation in Zambia and Malawi, full national uprisings were not necessary. Probably less bloodshed attended Britain's disengagement from empire – the 'fall of the British empire', as some will say – than that which accompanied Britain's expansion, annexations and pacification in Asia, Africa and America.

The leader who has commanded more space in this volume than any other individual is Gandhi. Combining, as he did, the thought and feeling of both 'east' and 'west', Gandhi employed a peaceful mode of agitation to bring an end to the Raj – one of the world's greatest empires. He appealed neither to the purse nor to the strong arm, but to the conscience. In so doing he probably provided the Commonwealth's most significant contribution to the politics of mankind's worst era of violence. His influence extended widely in Asia, Africa and the Caribbean. His methods have even been taken up in the industrialized democracies. If the Commonwealth can continue, in Gandhi's spirit, to pursue its goals by peaceful methods and try to reconcile peoples of differing outlook and culture, an answer may be given to the question with which this book began. An empire has indeed been ended, but the Commonwealth has a challenging role.

Suggestions for Further Reading

Place of publication is London unless otherwise stated; the most recent editions are cited where possible.

Collections of Documents

J. Simmons, *From Empire to Commonwealth. Principles of British Imperial Government*, Odhams, 1949.

G. Bennett, *The Concept of Empire, Burke to Attlee, 1774–1947*, Black, 1953.

K. N. Bell and W. P. Morrell, *Select Documents on British Colonial Policy, 1830–60*, O.U.P., 1928.

A. B. Keith, *Speeches and Documents on British Colonial Policy*, 2 vols, O.U.P., 1933.

N. Mansergh, *Documents and Speeches on British Commonwealth Affairs 1931–1952*, 2 vols, O.U.P., 1953.

N. Mansergh, *Documents and Speeches on Commonwealth Affairs, 1952–1962*, O.U.P. 1963.

J. Eayers, *The Commonwealth and Suez. A Documentary Survey*, O.U.P., 1964.

General Surveys

E. A. Walker, *The British Empire. Its Structure and Spirit. 1497–1953*, Bowes and Bowes, 1953.

J. A. Williamson, *A Short History of British Expansion*, Macmillan, 1961.

C. E. Carrington, *The British Overseas*, C.U.P., 1950.

P. Knaplund, *Britain, Commonwealth and Empire, 1900–1955*, Hamish Hamilton, 1956.

A. P. Thornton, *The Imperial Idea and its Enemies*, Macmillan, 1959.

P. Gordon Walker, *The Commonwealth*, Secker and Warburg, 1962.

D. M. Young, *The Colonial Office in the early 19th Century*, Longmans, 1961.

H. Hall, *The Colonial Office. A History*, Longmans, 1937.

Chapter 1

Cambridge History of the British Empire, vol. 1 *The Old Empire*, C.U.P., 1929.

M. Savelle, *The Foundations of American Civilization. A History of Colonial America*, New York: Holt, 1958.

C. M. Andrews, *The Colonial Period in American History*, 4 vols, New Haven: Yale U.P., 1938.

G. L. Beer, *The Origins of British Colonial Policy 1578–1660*, Macmillan, 1908.

G. L. Beer, *The Old Colonial System 1660–1754*, 2 vols, Macmillan, 1912.

G. H. Gutteridge, *The Colonial Policy of William III*, C.U.P., 1922.

L. Labaree, *Royal Government in America*, New York: Ungar, 1958.

O. M. Dickerson, *The Navigation Acts and the American Revolution*, Philadelphia: Pennsylvania U.P., 1951.

C. M. Andrews, *The Colonial Background to the American Revolution*, New Haven: Yale U.P., 1961.

L. Gipson, *The Coming of the Revolution 1763–1775*, New York: Harper and Row, 1954.

M. Jensen, *The Articles of Confederation: the social-constitutional history of the American Revolution 1774–1781*, Madison: Wisconsin U.P., 1959.

S. F. Bemis, *The Diplomacy of the American Revolution*, Bloomington: Indiana U.P., 1959.

P. Mackesy, *The War for America 1775–1783*, Longmans, 1964.

V. Harlow, *The Foundation of the Second British Empire 1763–1793*, 2 vols, Longmans, 1952 and 1964.

H. T. Manning, *British Colonial Government After the American Revolution 1782–1820*, New Haven: Yale U.P., 1933.

Chapter 2

K. E. Knorr, *British Colonial Theories, 1570–1850*, Toronto U.P., 1944.

E. G. Wakefield, *A Letter from Sydney and other writings* (1829), Dent, 1929.

E. G. Wakefield, *The Art of Colonization*, J. W. Parker, 1849.

Earl Grey, *The Colonial Policy of Lord John Russell's Administration*, 2 vols, Richard Bentley, 1853.

P. Knaplund, *James Stephen and British Colonial Policy 1813–1847*, Madison: Wisconsin U.P., 1953.

Cambridge History of the British Empire, II, *The New Empire, 1783–1870*, C.U.P., 1940.

J. S. Marais, *The Colonization of New Zealand*, Oxford, 1927.

W. P. Morrell, *Colonial Policy in the Age of Peel and Russell*, O.U.P., 1936.

R. L. Schuyler, *The Decline and Fall of the Old Colonial System*, New York: O.U.P., 1945.

H. Lucas, *The Durham Report*, 3 vols, O.U.P., 1912.

D. Creighton, *The Story of Canada*, Faber, 1959.

C. Martin, *The Foundations of Canadian Nationhood*, Toronto U.P., 1955.

A. R. M. Lower, *Canadians in the Making: a Social History of Canada*, Longmans, 1958.

J. L. Morison, *British Supremacy and Canadian Self-Government, 1839–54*, Glasgow, McLehose, 1919.

E. Dunham, *Political Unrest in Upper Canada, 1813–36*, Longmans, 1927.

H. T. Manning, *The Revolts in Lower Canada*, Macmillan, 1962.

D. Pike, *Australia, The Quiet Continent*, C.U.P., 1962.

M. Clark, *A Short History of Australia*, New York: Mentor, 1963.

A. C. V. Melbourne, *Early Constitutional Development in Australia*, Melbourne U.P., 1963.

C. M. H. Clarke, *Select Documents of Australian History 1788–1850*, Sydney: Angus and Robertson, 1950.

G. Serle, *The Golden Age. A History of the Colony of Victoria 1851–61*, Melbourne U.P., 1963.

D. Pike, *Paradise of Dissent. South Australia 1829–1857*, Longmans, 1957.

J. M. Ward, *Earl Grey and the Australian Colonies 1846–1857*, Melbourne U.P., 1958.

P. Knaplund, *Gladstone and Britain's Imperial Policy*, Allen & Unwin, 1927.

Chapter 3

P. G. Cornell, *Alignment of Political Groups in Canada 1841–67*, Toronto U.P., 1962.

P. B. Waite, *The Confederation Debates in the Province of Canada, 1865*, Toronto: McCelland and Stewart, 1963.

W. M. Whitelaw, *The Maritimes and Canada before Confederation*, Toronto: U.P., 1934.

P. B. Waite, *Life and Times of Confederation 1864–1867*, Toronto: U.P., 1964.

W. L. Morton, *The Critical Years: the Union of British North America, 1857–1873*, O.U.P., 1964.

D. Creighton, *The Road to Confederation. The Emergence of Canada 1863–1867*, Toronto: Macmillan, 1964.

G. F. G. Stanley, *The Birth of Western Canada: the Riel Rebellions*, Toronto U.P., 1963.

J. Galbraith, *The Hudson's Bay Company as an Imperial Factor 1821–1869*, Berkeley and L.A.: California U.P., 1957.

M. Ormsby, *British Columbia: A History*, Macmillan, 1958.

D. Creighton, *John A. Macdonald, the Old Chieftain*, Toronto U.P., 1955.

W. H. Oliver, *The Story of New Zealand*, Faber, 1960.

K. Sinclair, *A History of New Zealand*, Penguin, 1959.

A. H. McLintock, *Crown Colony Government in New Zealand*, Wellington: Government Printer, 1958.

G. H. Scholefield, *The New Zealand Parliamentary Record 1840–1949*, Wellington: Government Printer, 1950.

W. P. Morrell, *The Provincial System in New Zealand 1852–76*, Christchurch: Whitcomb and Tombs, 1964.

W. P. Morrell and D. O. Hall, *A History of New Zealand Life*, Christchurch, Whitcomb and Toombs, 1957.

K. Sinclair, *The Origins of the Maori Wars*, Wellington: New Zealand U.P., 1957.

A. J. Harrop, *England and the Maori Wars*, Wellington: N.Z. News, 1937.

R. L. Burdon, *Life and Times of Sir Julius Vogel*, Caxton Press, Christchurch, 1948.

R. L. Burdon, *King Dick, John Richard Seddon*, Whitcomb and Toombs, 1955.

D. K. Fieldhouse, 'Autochthonous Elements in the Evolution of Dominion Status: The Case of New Zealand', *Journal of Commonwealth Political Studies*, 1962 **1**(2).

L. Lipson, *The Politics of Equality*, Chicago U.P., 1948.

F. L. W. Wood, *New Zealand and the World*, Wellington: Dept. of Education, 1940.

K. Sinclair, *Imperial Federation. A Study of New Zealand Policy and Opinion 1880–1914*, Athlone, 1955.

Chapter 4

R. M. Crawford, *An Australian Perspective*, Madison: Wisconsin U.P., 1960.

G. Greenwood, *Australia, Political and Social History*, Sydney: Angus and Robertson, 1960.

C. M. H. Clarke, *Select Documents in Australian History 1851–1900*, Angus and Robertson, 1955.

H. Hall, *England and Australia*, Longmans, 1934.

B. R. Wise, *The Making of the Australian Commonwealth 1899–1900*, Longmans, 1913.

W. P. Reeves, *State Experiments in Australia and New Zealand*, 2 vols, Grant Richards, 1902.

A. Deakin, *The Federal Story*, Melbourne: Roberston and Mullens, 1944.

J. D. B. Miller, *Australian Government and Politics*, Duckworth, 1954.

T. Reese, *Australia in the Twentieth Century*, Pall Mall, 1964.

E. A. Walker, *A History of Southern Africa*, Longmans, 1957.

C. W. De Kiewiet, *A History of South Africa. Social and Economic*, O.U.P., 1941.

G. W. Eybers, *Select Constitutional Documents illustrating South African History*, Routledge, 1918.

W. N. Macmillan, *Bantu, Boer and Briton*, O.U.P., 1963.

E. A. Walker, *The Great Trek*, Black, 1948.

J. S. Galbraith, *Reluctant Empire. British Policy and the South African Frontier 1834–1854*, California U.P., 1963.

C. W. De Kiewiet, *British Colonial Policy and the South African Republics 1848-72*, Longmans, 1929.

C. W. De Kiewiet, *The Imperial Factor in South Africa*, C.U.P., 1937.

C. A. Uys, *In the Era of Shepstone*, Lovedale, 1933.

B. Williams, *Cecil Rhodes*, Constable, 1921.

J. G. Lockhart and C. M. Woodhouse, *Rhodes*, Hodder and Stoughton, 1963.

P. Mason, *Birth of a Dilemma. The Conquest and Settlement of Rhodesia*, O.U.P., 1958.

J. Van der Poel, *The Jameson Raid*, O.U.P., 1951.

J. S. Marais, *The Fall of Kruger's Republic*, O.U.P., 1961.

L. M. Thompson, *The Unification of South Africa 1902-1910*, O.U.P., 1960.

Chapter 5

C. W. Dilke, *Greater Britain*, 2 vols, Macmillan, 1868.

C. A. Bodelsen, *Studies in Mid-Victorian Imperialism*, Heinemann, 1960.

J. A. Froude, 'England and Her Colonies' *Fraser's Magazine*, Jan. 1870, 'The Colonies Once More', Sept. 1870.

J. Spedding, 'Our Colonial Empire', *Westminster Review*, Jan. 1870, 'The Future of the British Empire', July 1870.

E. Jenkins, 'Imperial Federalism', *Contemporary Review*, Jan. 1871, 'An Imperial Confederation', April 1871.

J. Gallagher and R. Robinson, 'The Imperialism of Free Trade', *Econ. History Rev.*, 1953, 6.

J. Galbraith, 'Myths of the Little England Era', *American Hist. Rev.* 1961, 67.

O. Macdonagh, 'The Anti-Imperialism of Free Trade', *Econ. Hist. Rev.* 1961 **14**(2).

D. K. Fieldhouse, 'Imperialism: An Historical Revision', *Econ. Hist. Rev.* 1961 **14**(2).

D. M. L. Farr, *The Colonial Office and Canada 1867-1887*, Toronto U.P., 1955.

J. E. Tyler, *The Struggle for Imperial Unity*, Longmans, 1938.

R. Jebb, *Studies in Colonial Nationalism*, Arnold, 1905.

A. B. Keith, *Responsible Government in the Dominions*, 3 vols, O.U.P., 1912.

S. R. Mehrotra, 'The Origin of the use of the Term "Commonwealth" ', *Journal of Commonwealth Political Studies* 1963, **2**(1).

L. Curtis, *The Problem of the Commonwealth* and *The Commonwealth of Nations*, Macmillan, 1916.

Cambridge History of the British Empire, vol III, *The Empire-Commonwealth*, C.U.P., 1959.

D. Hall, 'The Genesis of the Balfour Declaration of 1926', *Journal of Commonwealth Political Studies*, 1962, **1**(3).

R. M. Dawson, *The Development of Dominion Status, 1900–1936*, O.U.P., 1937.

H. J. Harvey, *Consultation and Co-operation in the Commonwealth*, O.U.P., 1952.

J. C. Beaglehope, *New Zealand and the Statute of Westminster*, Wellington: Victoria U. College, 1944.

K. C. Wheare, *The Statute of Westminster and Dominion Status*, O.U.P., 1938.

Chapter 6

G. R. Mellor, *British Imperial Trusteeship 1783–1850*, Faber, 1951.

H. Wrong, *The Government of the West Indies*, O.U.P., 1923.

E. Williams, *Capitalism and Slavery*, Chapel Hill: N. Carolina U.P., 1944.

L. G. Ragatz, *The Fall of the Planter Class in the British Caribbean 1763–1833*, New York: Octagon, 1963.

P. Curtin, *Two Jamaicas: the role of ideas in a tropical colony, 1830–65*, Harvard U.P., 1955.

P. Curtin, *The Image of Africa, British ideas and action, 1780–1850*, Wisconsin U.P., 1964.

E. C. Martin, *The British West African Settlements, 1750–1821*, Longmans, 1927.

C. Lloyd, *The Navy and the Slave Trade*, Longmans, 1949.

G. E. Metcalfe, *Maclean and the Gold Coast 1801–1847*, O.U.P., 1962.

C. Fyfe, *A History of Sierra Leone*, O.U.P., 1962.

K. O. Dike, *Trade and Politics in the Niger Delta*, O.U.P., 1956.

J. Rutherford, *Sir George Grey, 1812–1898*, Cassell, 1961.

L. S. Sutherland, *The East India Company in Eighteenth Century Politics*, O.U.P., 1952.

C. H. Philips, *The East India Company 1784–1834*, Manchester U.P., 1940.

Chapter 7

C. H. Philips, *India*, Hutchinson, 1950.

R. Masani, *Britain and India*, O.U.P., 1961.

V. A. Smith, *Oxford History of India to 1911*, O.U.P., 1919.

P. Woodruff, *The Men who Ruled India*, 2 vols, Cape, 1963.

E. D. Bearce, *British Attitudes to India 1784–1858*, O.U.P., 1961.

E. Stokes, *The Utilitarians and India*, O.U.P., 1959.

K. Ballhatchet, *Social Policy and Social Change in Western India 1817–1830*, O.U.P., 1957.

T. G. P. Spear, *India: A Modern History*, Ann Arbor: Michigan U.P., 1961.

G. Griffiths, *The British Impact on India*, Macdonald, 1952.

S. N. Sen, *Eighteen Fifty Seven*, Delhi: Ministry of Information, 1957.

S. R. Mehrotra, *India and the Commonwealth 1885–1929*, Allen and Unwin, 1965.

M. Brecher, *Nehru a Political Biography*, O.U.P., 1959.

B. R. Nanda, *Mahatma Gandhi, A Biography*, Allen and Unwin, 1959.

P. Spear, *India, Pakistan and the West*, O.U.P., 1961.

V. P. Menon, *The Transfer of Power in India*, Longmans, 1957.

H. Bolitho, *Jinnah, Creator of Pakistan*, Murray, 1956.

I. Stephens, *Pakistan*, Benn, 1963.

Chapter 9

S. D. Bailey, *Ceylon*, Hutchinson, 1952.

E. F. C. Ludowyk, *The Story of Ceylon*, Faber, 1962.

L. A. Mills, *Ceylon Under British Rule 1795–1832*.

C. Jeffries, *Ceylon, Path to Independence*, O.U.P., 1962.

B. H. Farmer, *Ceylon. A Divided Nation*, Pall Mall, 1963.

S. A. Pakeman, *Ceylon*, Benn, 1964.

R. Emerson, *Malaysia. A Study of Direct and Indirect Rule*, Kuala Lumpur: Malaya U.P., 1964.

F. Swettenham, *British Malaya*, Allen and Unwin, 1948.

J. Kennedy, *A History of Malaya 1400–1959*, Macmillan, 1961.

C. D. Cowan, *Nineteenth Century Malaya*, O.U.P., 1960.

V. Purcell, *The Chinese in Malaya*, O.U.P., 1948.

T. A. Silcock and Ungku Abdul Aziz, *Nationalism in Malaya*, New York: Institute of Pacific Research, 1950.

R. Soenarno, 'Malay Nationalism 1896–1941', *Journal of S.E. Asian Hist.* 1960, **1**(1).

W. Roff, 'Kuam Muda – Kuam Tua', *Papers on Malayan History*, Singapore, U. of Malaya, 1962.

H. Miller, *Prince and Premier. Tunku Abdul Rahman*, Harrap, 1951.

Wang Gungwu, *Malaysia – A Survey*, Pall Mall, 1964.

W. L. Burn, *The British West Indies*, Hutchinson, 1951.

W. M. Macmillan, *Warning from the West Indies*, Penguin, 1936.

M. Ayearst, *The British West Indies. The Search for Self-Government*, Allen and Unwin, 1960.

D. Lowenthal, *The West Indies Federation. Perspectives on a New Nation*, New York: Columbia U.P., 1961.

K. Norris, *Jamaica. The Search for Identity*, O.U.P., 1962.

E. Williams, *History of the People of Trinidad and Tobago*, Deutsch, 1964.

Chapter 10

J. A. Hobson, *Imperialism*, Allen and Unwin, 1902.

W. O. Aydelotte, *Bismarck and British Colonial Policy. The Problem of South West Africa 1883–1885*, Philadelphia, Pennsylvania U.P., 1937.

R. Robinson, J. Gallagher and A. Denny, *Africa and the Victorians*, Macmillan, 1961.

R. Robinson and J. Gallagher, 'The Partition of Africa', *New Cambridge Modern History*, vol. XI, C.U.P., 1962.

J. D. Hargreaves, *Prelude to the Partition of West Africa*, Macmillan, 1963.

G. N. Sanderson, *England, Europe and the Upper Nile, 1882–1899*, Edinburgh U.P., 1965.

R. Oliver, *Sir Harry Johnston and the Scramble for Africa*, Chatto and Windus, 1957.

J. E. Flint, *Sir George Goldie and the Making of Nigeria*, Longmans, 1960.

K. Robinson, *The Dilemmas of Trusteeship. British Colonial Policy Between the Wars*, O.U.P., 1965.

K. Robinson and F. Madden, *Essays in Imperial Government presented to Margery Perham*, Blackwell, 1963.

T. Hodgkin, *Nationalism in Colonial Africa*, Muller, 1956.

R. Segal, *Political Africa*, Stevens, 1961.

G. Shepperson, 'Some Notes on Negro American Influences on the emergence of African Nationalism', *Journal of African History*, 1960, **1**(2).

C. Legun, *Pan Africanism – a short political guide*, Pall Mall, 1962.

H. Kohn and W. Sokolsky, *African Nationalism in the Twentieth Century*, Van Nostrand, 1965.

Chapter 11

J. D. Fage, *Ghana – An Interpretation*, Madison: Wisconsin U.P., 1959.

W. E. F. Ward, *A History of Ghana*, Allen and Unwin, 1958.

D. Kimble, *A Political History of Ghana, The rise of Gold Coast Nationalism 1850–1928*, O.U.P., 1963.

D. Apter, *Ghana in Transition*, New York: Atheneum, 1963.

D. Austin, *Politics in Ghana 1946–60*, O.U.P., 1964.

K. Robinson, 'Constitutional Autochthony in Ghana', *Journal of Commonwealth Political Studies*, 1961, **1**(1).

M. Crowther, *The Story of Nigeria*, Faber, 1962.

J. F. Ade Ajayi, *Christian Missions and the Making of Nigeria*, Longmans, 1964.

M. Perham, *Lugard*, 2 vols, Collins, 1956 and 1960.

A. H. M. Kirk-Greene, *The Principles of Native Administration in Nigeria 1900–47*, O.U.P., 1965.

J. Coleman, *Nigeria; Background to Nationalism*, California U.P., 1959.

K. Post, *The Nigerian General Election of 1959*, O.U.P., 1963.

C. Fyfe, *A Short History of Sierra Leone*, Longmans, 1962.

J. D. Hargreaves, *Sir Samuel Lewis*, O.U.P., 1961.

H. A. Gailey, *A History of the Gambia*, Routledge and Kegan Paul, 1964.

Chapter 12

R. Oliver, *The Missionary Factor in East Africa*, Longmans, 1952.

R. Oliver and G. Mathew, *History of East Africa*, vol. I, O.U.P., 1963.

V. Harlow and E. M. Chilver, *History of East Africa*, vol. II, O.U.P., 1965.

R. Coupland, *East Africa and its Invaders to 1856*, O.U.P., 1956.

R. Coupland, *The Exploitation of East Africa 1856–1890*, Faber, 1939.

D. A. Low and C. Pratt, *Buganda and British Overrule*, O.U.P., 1960.

D. A. Low, *Political Parties in Uganda, 1949–62*, Athlone, 1962.

E. Huxley, *White Man's Country. Lord Delamere and the Making of Kenya*, Chatto and Windus, 1953.

J. Kenyatta, *Facing Mount Kenya*, Heinemann, 1961.

G. Bennett, *Kenya, a Political History: The Colonial Period*, O.U.P., 1963.

F. D. Corfield, *Historical Survey of the Origins and Growth of Mau Mau*, H.M.S.O., 1960.

J. C. Taylor, *The Political Development of Tanganyika*, Stanford U.P., 1963.

A. J. Hughes, *East Africa: The Search for Unity, Kenya, Tanganyika, Uganda and Zanzibar*, Penguin, 1963.

A. J. Hanna, *The Story of the Rhodesias and Nyasaland*, Faber, 1960.

C. Leys and C. Pratt, *A New Deal in Central Africa*, Heinemann, 1960.

P. Keatley, *The Politics of Partnership. The Federation of Rhodesia and Nyasaland*, Penguin, 1963.

R. Welensky, *Welensky's 4000 Days*, Collins, 1964.

L. Gann and P. Duigan, *White Settlers in Tropical Africa*, Penguin, 1962.

C. Leys, *European Politics in Southern Rhodesia*, O.U.P., 1959.

L. H. Gann, *The Birth of a Plural Society: The Development of Northern Rhodesia Under the British South Africa Company, 1894–1914*, Manchester U.P., 1958.

L. H. Gann, *A History of Northern Rhodesia to 1953*, Chatto and Windus, 1964.

R. Hall, *Zambia*, Pall Mall, 1965.

K. Kaunda, *Zambia Shall Be Free*, Heinemann, 1962.

D. C. Mulford, *The Northern Rhodesia General Election of 1962*, Nairobi, O.U.P., 1964.

G. Shepperson and T. Price, *Independent Africa*, Edinburgh U.P., 1958.

G. Jones, *Britain and Nyasaland*, Allen and Unwin, 1964.

Conclusion

K. C. Wheare, *The Constitutional Structure of the Commonwealth*, O.U.P., 1960.

S. A. De Smith, *The New Commonwealth and its Constitutions*, Stevens, 1964.

C. E. Carrington, *The Liquidation of the British Empire*, Harrap, 1961.

W. K. Hancock, *Survey of British Commonwealth Affairs*, 2 vols, O.U.P., 1937 and 1940.

N. Mansergh, *Survey of British Commonwealth Affairs, 1939–52*, O.U.P., 1958.

A. R. Conan, *The Rationale of the Sterling Area*, Macmillan, 1961.

P. W. Bell, *The Sterling Area in the Post-War World*, O.U.P., 1956.

A. C. L. Day, *The Future of Sterling*, O.U.P., 1954.

B. Thomas, *Migration and Economic Growth*, C.U.P., 1954.

G. F. Plant, *Oversea Migration*, O.U.P., 1951.

J. D. B. Miller, *The Commonwealth and the World*, Duckworth, 1958.

F. H. Underhill, *The British Commonwealth, an Experiment in Co-operation among the Nations*, Durham N.C.: North Carolina U.P., 1956.

N. Mansergh, et. al., *Commonwealth Perspectives*, North Carolina U.P., 1958.

V. Wiseman, *Britain and the Commonwealth*, Allen and Unwin, 1965.

J. D. B. Miller, 'South Africa's Departure', *Journal of Commonwealth Political Studies*, 1961 **1**(1).

A Handbook of Commonwealth Organisations, Methuen, 1965.

The Commonwealth Relations Office List, H.M.S.O. annually.

Index